D0931552

ENGLAND'S RISE TO GREATNESS

PUBLISHED UNDER THE AUSPICES OF THE

WILLIAM ANDREWS CLARK MEMORIAL LIBRARY

UNIVERSITY OF CALIFORNIA, LOS ANGELES

Publications from the
CLARK LIBRARY PROFESSORSHIP, UCLA

1.
England in the Restoration and Early Eighteenth
Century: Essays on Culture and Society
Edited by H. T. Swedenberg, Jr.

2.
Illustrious Evidence
Approaches to English Literature of the
Early Seventeenth Century
Edited, with an Introduction, by Earl Miner

3.
The Compleat Plattmaker
Essays on Chart, Map, and Globe Making in England
in the Seventeenth and Eighteenth Centuries
Edited by Norman J. W. Thrower

4.
English Literature in the Age of Disguise
Edited by Maximillian E. Novak

5.
Culture and Politics
From Puritanism to the Enlightenment
Edited by Perez Zagorin

6.
The Stage and the Page
London's "Whole Show" in the
Eighteenth-Century Theatre
Edited by Geo. Winchester Stone, Jr.

7.
England's Rise to Greatness, 1660-1763
Edited by Stephen B. Baxter

England's Rise to Greatness,
1660-1763

Edited by
STEPHEN B. BAXTER

Clark Library Professor, 1977-1978

UNIVERSITY OF CALIFORNIA PRESS
BERKELEY • LOS ANGELES • LONDON

University of California Press
Berkeley and Los Angeles, California

University of California Press, Ltd.
London, England

Copyright © 1983 by The Regents of the University of California

Library of Congress Cataloging in Publication Data
Main entry under title:

England's rise to greatness, 1660-1763.

(Publications from the Clark Library professorship,
UCLA ; 7)
"Published under the auspices of the William Andrews
Clark Memorial Library, University of California, Los
Angeles"—Half t.p.
1. Great Britain—Politics and government—1660-1714—
Addresses, essays, lectures.   2. Great Britain—Politics
and government—1714-1820—Addresses, essays, lectures.
I. Baxter, Stephen Bartow, 1929-   II. Series.
DA435.E53   1983   941.06   82-40095
ISBN 0-520-04572-6

Printed in the United States of America

1 2 3 4 5 6 7 8 9

841836

LIBRARY
ALMA COLLEGE
ALMA, MICHIGAN

CONTENTS

PREFACE

During the academic year 1977-1978 I had the great good fortune to be appointed Clark Library Professor at the University of California, Los Angeles. The William Andrews Clark Memorial Library in Los Angeles is a delightful place in which to work, and not merely because the building and the grounds are so handsome. Even more important is the sense of a community of learning, and the kindness of the permanent members of that community to visitors such as ourselves. It was a very special year for the entire family.

The essays in this collection are manifold and various, with differing topics, treatment, and in some cases contrasting views. But there is, I think, more of an underlying unity than may appear at first sight. Most of the authors assume that a new era began with the Restoration. A unit, which for want of a better word we may call a century, began in 1660. Whether that unit lasted precisely a hundred years or whether it came to an end in the 1780s with American independence and the beginnings of the Industrial Revolution is a matter of choice. In some ways the first twenty-odd years of the reign of George III look backward, while in others they look forward to the Age of Improvement. They form a bridge between one era and another and, like all good bridges, have one foot firmly planted on each bank of the river. Thus, while 1783 may be the most useful single date for the ending of this century, both 1760 and 1763 would have their partisans.

There might be more agreement, between readers and authors alike, about the predominant themes of this period than about its exact length. As Professor Heckscher pointed out many years ago in his great work on mercantilism, it was a century in which England had an exportable surplus of food. There was also a quite remarkable stability of currency values. On these solid foundations the more adventurous went out and built the first British empire. Scientists and philosophers and musicians at home could afford the time needed to make their own contributions, which brought the country abruptly into the very first rank in arts and letters, in the natural sciences, in music and in architecture. As is the case in every great civilization, something was owed to foreigners. The Huguenot, the Dutch, and the German contributions to English development were all substantial. But the English made many contributions of their own: for every Oldenburg there was a Newton; for every Handel, a Purcell; for every Ligonier, a Marlborough. One of the most important of the English contributions was that of a mass market for culture. Some of the culture of the century before 1642 was in a sense premature, in that the country could not really afford it. After 1660, however, there was enough money about to support a great culture in England, while that of the older Mediterranean civilizations slowly faded away.

With prosperity came new mechanisms for the diffusion of this culture. Books there had been for two centuries. Now there were more of them, so many more that writers could soon make a living from their pens. The Royal Society, the newspaper, and the post office were novelties, each of them significant in accelerating the circulation of new ideas. It was perhaps not entirely a bad thing that improvements in transportation, substantial though they were, proceeded gradually. Eventually these improvements would integrate Wales and Scotland and Ireland into the English economy. Yet these outlying regions remained far enough from the center to retain their own cultural vitality. Each made its own contribution to the common stock, one with a distinct local flavor. Beyond the seas a group of colonial cultures developed in the course of time, but the distances and also the peculiarities of local conditions were too great for these to fit entirely into the mainstream.

Wealth and the dominant culture were not the only things holding the empire together. There was also force. In 1660 there was available a large pool of veterans, men who had learned in a

harsh school the necessity of working together for common survival and prosperity. It is from the Restoration that we can date
the firm establishment of the British in India as well as in the
West Indies. Building on rather spotty earlier foundations, they
did more than merely consolidate and extend the work of their
fathers. They created a new world. Naval strength was also important for English expansion. After 1689 the navy had a major
role to play in the Atlantic and the Mediterranean as well as in
the North Sea. Even on land English military power became impressive. By 1697, certainly by 1713, English military prowess and
diplomatic skill had made her one of the great world powers, as
by 1763 she had become *the* great world power. Success on this
scale made English ideas and customs fashionable throughout
Europe. The ideas of Locke and Newton and their generation,
popularized among others by Voltaire, spread to the continent as
the Enlightenment.

Since Noah's day there have been few entirely new beginnings.
The English began the Restoration with a mixed monarchy in
which the king was under the law. That legal heritage, of which
Professor Slavin discusses one aspect in his paper, was unique in
Europe. It gave the citizen some protection for his person and
property against the state. Not enough for John Harrington, to
whose sufferings we owe the Habeas Corpus Act of 1678. Not
enough, in all likelihood, for the poor, who then as now could not
comfortably eat a civil liberty. Not enough for Jews and Quakers
and Catholics and Presbyterians. For them, at least, the empire
provided a potential refuge, one in which they could persecute
the even less fortunate Irish and Indians and blacks. Yet with all
its shortcomings the English system did give the citizen more freedom than any other, more opportunity to make and to keep a fortune. And the Poor Law, in England proper, did provide some
security for the wretched.

In 1660 England was already prosperous, already free, already
civilized, already the possessor of the makings of an empire. The
greatest political question of all, monarchy or republic as the preferred form of government, had as it happened already been
answered. England had had her Revolution and found it wanting. The Restoration restored the law, of course, and with it civil
and political liberties for the fortunate. But it also restored the
monarchy and established church. When James II abused the law

and seemed to attack the church, he was removed, as an individual, but limited Anglican monarchy most certainly did survive the Revolution of 1688: it is with us yet.

That the political battle was waged over a relatively narrow field does not deprive it of interest, and several of the papers presented here are concerned with political history. Professor Roberts quite rightly sees the power of the monarchy weakening in 1690, when Shrewsbury resigned as Restoration politicians had not done. Once the precedent had been established, the politicians were quick to develop the collective resignation as a means of forcing the crown on questions of policy. By the end of Anne's reign, if not before, they had seized much of the former royal authority in the vital fields of patronage and domestic politics. But there were some important areas in which the politicians normally took very little interest. Diplomatic and colonial matters were two things that did not often excite them. This left these fields open for continued royal activity. Professor Hatton has recently demonstrated in her splendid *George I, Elector and King* as well as in her paper here how much authority remained in the hands of that king, while my own paper discusses some of the inner workings of government a generation later. If Professor Roberts's paper does not by some chance go far enough to redress any subliminal royalist bias there may be in this collection, then surely the balance is put right by Professor Brewer's charming and delightful paper about the number 45. That gets us into constituency politics, radicalism, and the beginnings of a new age. It also gets us from the printed and manuscript sources into art, or at least into artifacts. Where a generation ago these might have been neglected, they are given careful treatment here not only by Professors Brewer and Hatton but also by Professor Schwoerer in her study of the ceremonies surrounding the accession of William and Mary. Artifacts and ceremonies alike had strong political connotations, and it is important that they are now being studied with the seriousness they deserve.

One of the distinctive features of this century is the quite exceptional extent to which England was involved with Europe. Even after 1688 England was a world power only as a member of an alliance. She relied on the Dutch for money as well as men. The other allies were paid subsidies, grudgingly and late in the day to be sure, and they were more likely to be treated as servants rather than as equals. As treaty-making time grew near, they were almost certain to be left out of the negotiations and told what was good for them by the English and French. By no means all of England's reputation as Perfidious Albion was undeserved. Of all the subsidiary allies, Savoy was one of the most successful. In the course of his long reign, Victor Amadeus II, as Geoffrey Symcox demonstrates, was able to play the English, the French, and the Austrians off against one another and to make substantial permanent gains for his house. With Savoy, as with Portugal and Hanover, the English demanded economic concessions in return for their military aid. Thanks perhaps to the skill of the prince, perhaps to the fortunate geographical location of the young state, Savoy seems to have had more value for its sacrifices than the others did. By the end of the Seven Years War, when England had become so strong that she no longer needed continental connections, the house of Savoy was able to stand on its own feet.

Although England had been manufacturing cloth for centuries, the tone as well as the nature of economic life was far more agricultural than it would be in the years after 1780. Colonial and foreign trade were considered far more important, and they were watched far more carefully, than were manufactures; and not merely because they were or could be nurseries of seamen. Some of the great lines of trade in this period, in addition to the cloth trade, were those in linen, tobacco, sugar, rice, and coal. All of these were items with an evident agricultural base. Wool and linen were of course worked up into cloth, just as sugar and tobacco and rice must be processed before they reached the consumer. Government took an interest in all this because the customs, very roughly, paid for the navy while excise, again very roughly, paid for the army. Domestic manufactures paid very little in comparison with land, which paid for the interest on the national debt through the Land Tax. Fiscally there was very little room for maneuver before the administration of the younger Pitt, and any change was feared because of its potential to increase the power of the state.

Happy Hanover had no tax changes in the period before the French Revolution, and was content. England required many changes in detail, even though the broad outlines remained much the same for almost a century after 1693, and she was very far from being content. Tax questions could make as much trouble as religious ones. In his remarkable discussion of the Excise crisis, Professor Price brings up, among many other points, one that was ominous for the future. Here was an issue important enough to bring the administration into danger, one in which the economic interests of the mother country and those of a colony were diametrically opposed. Walpole for his own reasons supported the colonial interests — which on this occasion were those of good government — and lost. The colonies could draw their own conclusions from the incident, and did so. With every year the economic, and thus the political, interests of the colonies differed more widely than before from those of the mother country. In the 1730s the colonies were not strong enough to do more than ruin Alderman Perry, but a generation later they would be able to prevent the Stamp Act from going into effect.

Dr. Price's paper raises another important issue, that of the efficiency of government. To what extent could the state do what it wished in this period? An enormous step forward had been taken in the 1640s, when — as in much of western Europe — the introduction of an excise provided funds for the establishment of a standing army. Students seem to be agreed that administrative efficiency continued to make progress, in one office or another if not in all of them at the same time, down to the end of the reign of William III. But progress was not to be a straight-line affair. Many years ago Professor Hughes noted a decline in the efficiency of the government from about 1730, and in my own research I have found there were certain things that government had been doing in the 1690s which it was no longer technically capable of doing fifty years later. In the interval, interest rates had been cut in half. But it does not help very much to have cheap money when what you need is transport vessels, at any price, and they are not to be had. Administration does seem to become more efficient during the Seven Years War, and yet more so during the second half of the reign of George III. But in the reign of George II there was not enough efficiency.

We hear much too often that there was not enough religion either. And that seems to be a serious mistake. It may be that the heroic age came to an end in about 1691, when Richard Baxter's death advertised the passing of an entire generation. Yet the passing of one eminent nonconformist divine, or even of a whole generation of them, did not mean the end of Christianity in England.

If there were a few atheists in the 1690s, there were very few of them and their conduct has received at least as much attention as it deserves. There were more Socinians and Quakers: like the atheists, their light has not been hidden under a bushel in the past two centuries and the careless tend to exaggerate both their numbers and their impact. Most educated people seem to have been Christians of the Anglican persuasion, even if they did not attend church every day like the Duke of Newcastle. Their religion may have been of the comfortable rather than the heroic variety, but it is always dangerous to underestimate the depth of someone else's religious beliefs. And certainly the record in the area of good works is impressive. Daniel Baugh discusses one aspect of this record in his paper on the attitudes of the period toward the poor. There seems to have been much more benevolence in the period before the death of George II than in the days of Jane Austen. The literate may have read Bernard Mandeville, they may have enjoyed him, but they continued to give away between 4 and 7 percent of their incomes to charity. At present the rate in the United States is about 1.6 percent, despite our much greater wealth. Doubtless there is much in the record of the eighteenth century to disgust not only the modern welfare worker but all people of good will. People could and did starve to death in the streets of London during the bad times at the end of the 1730s, as Lord Egmont noted. Such incidents were rare enough to be recorded at the time, and if we avoid anachronism we must admit that contemporaries did what they could to relieve the sufferings of the afflicted.

Of the two papers in this collection which are devoted to intellectual history, Daniel Baugh's contribution has close ties to the economic history of Jacob M. Price. Attitudes toward the poor are a function, among other things, of national prosperity. Others have noted the increasing secularity of the period, the increasing rationalism and indeed mercilessness of the attitudes of the prosperous toward those who were less fortunate. Professor Baugh does what others have been less careful to do when he ties these changes to changes in the economic terms of trade between classes and to the emergence of a cleaner, safer world in the years after 1740. This fits in very well with the long boom seen by economic historians as beginning somewhere between 1745 and 1750. One hopes that not all the rich took their ethics from *The*

Fable of the Bees, but some of them certainly did so, and it is sad that the prosperity of the eighteenth century produced such smugness.

The paper by Arthur Wilson has special personal meaning for me. When I began teaching at Dartmouth in 1954 as a Ford intern, Arthur Wilson served as bear leader for the group. He was a fine human being as well as an inspiring teacher, and his scholarship was treated with great respect by those who knew the field. Later, when the two volumes on Diderot came out, he had a wider audience; but his first monograph had established his reputation. Over the years we had kept in touch, and over those years I had continued to be bothered by the concept of the Enlightenment as it has traditionally been taught. Received opinion on the subject did not make sufficient allowance for the English experience. When this opportunity came up, I asked him to give any paper he liked but suggested, tongue in cheek, a paper demonstrating that the Enlightenment was an English phenomenon. To my surprise and delight, I found that his own thinking had been along the same lines and that he wanted to do just such a paper. Here it is, vintage Wilson, very nearly if not quite the last thing he wrote. His death was a great loss to a wide circle of friends and students, as well as to the world of letters. This book is dedicated to his memory.

CONTRIBUTORS

Arthur M. Wilson was born near Rock Island, Illinois, in 1902. He took one B.A. at Yankton College and another at Oxford where he was a Rhodes Scholar. His Ph.D. was earned at Harvard in 1933, and it used to be said that he was the only member of that class to get a job teaching in his own field. With the exception of a stint with the OSS during World War II, he spent his entire professional career at Dartmouth College, where his final appointment was as Daniel Webster Professor. In 1936 he published *French Foreign Policy During the Administration of Cardinal Fleury, 1726-1743* (Harvard). His *Diderot: The Testing Years, 1713-1759* (Oxford, 1957) was followed in 1972 by *Diderot, 1759-1784* (also Oxford). Twice winner of the Herbert Baxter Adams Prize, he was also awarded the Palmes Académique, several honorary degrees, a Joint Award from the Oxford Press and the Modern Language Association, and the National Book Award.

Arthur J. Slavin is Justus Bier Distinguished Professor of the Humanities and professor of history at the University of Louisville. He took his B.A. at Louisiana State University and his Ph.D. at the University of North Carolina. Among his many books are *Humanism, Reform, and Reformation* (Wiley, 1968); *Tudor Men and Institutions* (Louisiana State University Press, 1972); and *The Precarious Balance: Government and Society in England, 1450-1640* (Knopf, 1973).

Daniel A. Baugh is associate professor of history at Cornell University. After taking his B.A. and M.A. at the University of Pennsylvania, he earned his Ph.D. at Cambridge. His best known work is *British Naval Administration in the Age of Walpole* (Princeton, 1965). He has also written *Naval Administration 1715-1750* for the Navy Record Society (1977) and edited *Aristocratic Government and Society in 18th-Century England* (Franklin Watts, 1975).

Lois Green Schwoerer is professor of history at George Washington University. After taking her B.A. at Smith, she did her research at Bryn Mawr and won her Ph.D. in 1956. She is the author of *No Standing Armies: The Antiarmy Ideology in Seventeenth-Century England* (Johns Hopkins, 1974) and of many important articles.

Geoffrey Symcox, born at Swindon in England, took his B.A. at Oxford and his M.A. at the University of Stockholm before coming to the United States. He earned his Ph.D. at the University of California, Los Angeles, in 1967 and has been a member of that history faculty since then. He is currently associate professor of history. He has written on *The Crisis of French Sea Power, 1688-1697* (Nijhoff, 1974) and edited *War, Diplomacy, and Imperialism 1618-1763* (Harper, 1973).

Ray Clayton Roberts was born in China. Moving ever eastward, he took his B.A. and M.A. at the University of Washington and his Ph.D. at Cornell. He is now professor of history at Ohio State University. His best known book is *The Growth of Responsible Government in Stuart England* (Cambridge, 1966). With his twin brother David he has recently completed *A History of England* (Prentice-Hall, 1980).

Ragnhild M. Hatton is professor of international history at the University of London and is the author of *Charles XII of Sweden* (1968), *Europe in the Age of Louis XIV* (1969), and *Louis XIV and His World* (1972), as well as *George I, Elector and King* (Thames and Hudson, 1978).

Jacob M. Price is professor of history at the University of Michigan in Ann Arbor. After taking all his degrees at Harvard, he taught at Smith College for two years before moving west. His best-known works are *The Tobacco Adventure to Russia, 1676-1722* (1961) and *France and the Chesapeake* (University of Michigan Press, 1973).

Stephen Baxter is Kenan Professor of History at the University of North Carolina in Chapel Hill. He took his B.A. at Harvard and his Ph.D. at the University of Cambridge. He is the author of *The Development of the Treasury, 1660-1702* (Harvard, 1957) and *William III* (Longmans, 1966).

John Brewer is professor of history at Harvard University. He took his degrees at the University of Cambridge and taught at Corpus Christi College before going to Yale, where he taught for several years before moving to Massachusetts. His *Party Ideology and Popular Politics at the Accession of George III* was published by the Cambridge Press in 1976.

I

THE ENLIGHTENMENT CAME
FIRST TO ENGLAND

Arthur M. Wilson

There is something inadvertently obscure, as well as insufficiently explained by historians, regarding England's role in what we call the Enlightenment. When we speak of the Enlightenment, it is probably the France of Montesquieu, Voltaire, Diderot, and the *Encyclopédie* that first comes to mind. The Enlightenment in France, the *siècle des lumières,* represented also by Buffon and D'Alembert and Turgot and D'Holbach and Lavoisier and the Abbé Raynal and a host of others, was progressive, critical, controversial, contentious, and exciting. In its dramatic events, in its tensions between conservatives and *philosophes,* in its impact upon other European countries, the Enlightenment in France is the one best known of all.

But other countries had their Enlightenment too. There is the German Enlightenment, *die Aufklärung,* of which Lessing was the greatest luminary. This was the Germany of Christian Thomasius and Christian Wolff, of Wieland and Moses Mendelssohn and Reimarus and Schiller, the Germany in which even Frederick the Great, in his own wayward and absolutist fashion, was something of an *Aufklärer*. More submissive to political authority than the French Enlightenment, nevertheless the *Auf-*

klärung had its lights its *lumières,* too. It was Immanuel Kant who gave to the Enlightenment, everywhere, its most comprehensive and inspiring definition: "Enlightenment is man's release from his self-inflicted condition of being a minor.... *Sapere aude!* Dare to know! 'Have courage to use your own reason!' — that is the motto of enlightenment."[1]

In Italy there were Beccaria and Genovesi and Galiani and Filangieri and all the other *illuministi* studied so trenchantly and copiously in our generation by Franco Venturi. Italian *illuminismo* shared the general convictions and aspirations of the whole Age of Enlightenment, but tended to be most interested in problems of social, economic, and juristic reform. Beccaria's *Concerning Crimes and Punishment* is *illuminismo*'s most characteristic work, as well as being a monument of the whole Age of Enlightenment itself.

There was an Enlightenment in Poland, one of the most absorbing in the eighteenth century, a national revival and leap forward into contemporaneity very much like that of Czechoslovakia under Dubček and, like that, extinguished by the Russians.[2] There was even an Enlightenment in Spain, the *ilustración,* stirring faintly and perilously under the shadow of the Inquisition, and associated with the names of Feijóo and Charles III and Campomanes and Jovellanos and Pablo de Olivade.[3] There was an Austrian Enlightenment, made illustrious by the name of Josef von Sonnenfels and memorable by the overhasty reforms of Joseph II. George Barany, in a remarkable article, has studied the intimations of an Enlightenment in Hungary; and Marc Raeff has demonstrated that there was an Enlightenment in Russia, French in inspiration at the court and among the high nobility, but influenced heavily by German Enlightenment thought in the rest of Russian society.[4] It might well be argued that in Russia the Enlightenment manifested itself, chronologically, as the last of the several national Enlightenments, being especially visible in the person of the unfortunate Radishchev and in the early years of Alexander I and the proposed reforms of Speransky and Novosiltsev, an Enlightenment movement that came to its climax and disastrous end with Pavel and the Decembrists in 1825.

In addition to these several national Enlightenments, there are two more of special interest. One is the Scottish Enlightenment, which has been receiving in recent years the fond attention (and consequent upgrading) of many historians. The Scottish Enlightenment, writes Peter Gay, "had been developing its own tradition of secular sociological inquiry since the beginning of the eighteenth century. Francis Hutcheson, moral philosopher and student of society, had many disciples, a brilliant assembly of intellectuals—David Hume, John Millar, Adam Ferguson, Lord Kames, Lord Monboddo, William Robertson—followed, in the next generation, by Adam Smith and Dugald Stewart."[5]

The other is the American. Here again, as in the Scottish Enlightenment, present-day historians, more (I think) than ever before, are emphasizing the impact of the Enlightenment upon events in America. "In behalf of Enlightenment liberalism," remarks Bernard Bailyn, "the revolutionary leaders undertook to complete, formalize, systematize, and symbolize what previously had been only partially realized, confused and disputed matters of fact. Enlightenment ideas were not instruments of a particular social group, nor did they destroy a social order. They did not create new social and political forces in America. They released those that had long existed, and vastly increased their power. This completion, this rationalization, this symbolization, this lifting into consciousness and endowing with high moral purpose inchoate, confused elements of social and political change—this was the American Revolution."[6]

Now, where in all this array of national Enlightenments is the English one? As a matter of fact, a recent president of the American Historical Association, writing in 1976, evidently supposed he had dismissed the matter once for all. "The term 'English Enlightenment,'" he wrote, "would be jarring and incongruous if it were ever heard."[7]

However uncommon it may be to encounter any historian using the term "English Enlightenment," I do find it in an article by Giorgio Tonelli, in an introduction written by Adrienne Koch, and in the recent writings of Henry F. May.[8] Sometimes one comes across a reference to "the Enlightenment in England," but this may only imply cultural borrowing, instead of what I believe to be the fundamentally indigenous nature of "the English Enlightenment." Why is the term not used more frequently? Must we accept the implication that the English did not in fact have an Enlightenment of their own, but simply borrowed from other nations? How can we make such an assumption about a country that possessed a Bacon, a Hobbes, a Milton, a Newton, and a Locke?

Let there, then, be tested the following perhaps startling hypothesis: that the English truly had an Enlightenment of their own; that it was, chronologically, the first of all; and that its existence has been obscured by the fact that almost all of it occurred during the seventeenth century, whereas our customary conception of the Enlightenment has been nearly always associated with the eighteenth century.

This hypothesis can be tested, I believe, by identifying the characteristics and phenomenology of the Enlightenment in a country that indubitably experienced it—that is to say, France. Having identified these characteristics, one can turn next to England to find out whether they manifest themselves there. If they do, and if the English phenomena occur a generation or so earlier than the French, then, presumptively, England did experience an Enlightenment—and did so before other European countries.

Let me begin by considering one of the most conspicuous aspects of the Enlightenment everywhere. This was the development and elaboration of its ideas with respect to religion. In the seventeenth century, and increasingly in the eighteenth, the deepening and widening of scientific knowledge inevitably impinged upon orthodox religious beliefs, producing a sort of San Andreas Fault of theological strains, stresses, tremors, and earthquakes. The stress was greatest in countries where the government enforced religious orthodoxy, but the intellectual problem concerned Christian civilizations everywhere. In France the problem is symbolized by the war cry that Voltaire made famous, "Ecrasez l'infame."

The least disruptive of the responses to this emerging threat to revealed religion was the growth of so-called natural religion. The ventilation of this concept was one of the early manifestations of the French Enlightenment. Diderot wrote in 1747 an essay entitled *On the Sufficiency of Natural Religion* (though this was not published until 1770). Previous to that, however, some of the *pensées* in his *Philosophical Thoughts* (1746) had alluded to the persuasiveness of this rival to revealed religion. Rousseau's "Confession of Faith of a Savoyard Vicar," which he interpolated in his *Emile,* published in 1762, is the most notable exemplification during the French Enlightenment of the argument for natural religion. The early and quite general presence of this concept in theological discussions in eighteenth-century France causes me to list it first as a characteristic of the French Enlightenment.

But in England the idea of natural religion had long been familiar to readers of the works of Lord Herbert of Cherbury (1583-1648). And in the latitudinarianism of the Anglican church of the seventeenth and eighteenth centuries one may observe the continuing pervasiveness in English thought of this mild but still genuinely Enlightenment mode of thinking.

More sharply militant, more harshly antagonistic to revealed religion, and much more characteristic of the Enlightenment in France, was the growth of deism. The origins of deistic thought in France go back, to be sure, to the Epicureanism propounded by Pierre Gassendi and his followers.[9] Such "free thinking" or "libertinism" was, of course, highly illicit, and it was still very much so in the early eighteenth century, when unorthodox ideas could be circulated, if at all, only in manuscript.[10] But soon these French ideas began to surface in print. One of the most famous and abidingly influential publications of the century was Diderot's little booklet entitled *Pensées philosophiques*. This was a highly contraband work, deistic in all its implications and declared by the Parlement of Paris, the highest court in the land, to be "scandalous and contrary to Religion and Morals." Voltaire's beliefs, too, were strongly deistic and always remained so. He continued to appeal to a watchmaker God to the end of his life. The inculcation of a belief in deism may be listed as a second characteristic of the French Enlightenment.

But deistic literature in France in the eighteenth century was greatly influenced by the English writers of several decades before. Norman L. Torrey has shown in his *Voltaire and the English Deists* that Voltaire was well aware of the deistic passages in Dryden's early poems, as well as of the writings of John Toland, Anthony Collins, Thomas Woolston, Matthew Tindall, and others. "In his later years," wrote Torrey, "Voltaire plainly adopted the entire spirit and method of the extremists in the English controversy."[11] Perhaps the most seminal work of the whole deistic movement in England was a seventeenth-century one, John Toland's *Christianity not Mysterious* (1696). In fact, deistic thought, which is one of the essential and abiding components of the English Enlightenment, proved to be very export-able. It was destined, as Franco Venturi has remarked, "to be-come a cosmopolitan creed." And Ernst Cassirer, in his *Philosophy of the Enlightenment,* spoke of "the extraordinary effect which English deism had on the intellectual life of the eighteenth century."[12]

Another conspicuous feature of the French Enlightenment was the growth of philosophical materialism, a development associated with the names of La Mettrie, Diderot, Dom Deschamps, and especially D'Holbach. Although deplored by Voltaire (so much so that it caused a kind of "civil war" among the philosophes), it is nevertheless one of the earmarks of the French Enlightenment.[13] But, in point of fact, it was anticipated in England, first of all in the materialistic and mechanistic psychology of Hobbes.[14] Even in John Locke's writings there is a passage that seems to allow for a materialistic view of the universe, a passage that did not go unnoticed by French writers.[15] And an important new element in materialistic thought, namely, the concept that motion is an inherent property of matter, was contributed by John Toland. (It was not for nothing that in 1768 D'Holbach translated Toland's *Letter to Serena,* written in 1704.)[16] Here again, what was really the English Enlightenment foreshadowed the one in France.

A fourth characteristic of the French Enlightenment was the desire for a polity that allowed religious toleration. In a country where the revocation of the Edict of Nantes had forced thousands and thousands of French citizens into exile, religious bigotry continued to be oppressive throughout most of the eighteenth century. Huguenot women were imprisoned for long terms merely because they attended Calvinist services; and, for the same offense, Huguenot men were sentenced to row in the navy's galleys. Unavoidably the philosophes yearned for legal religious toleration. Voltaire was to remark of the British in the sixth letter of his *Lettres philosophiques,* "If there were only one religion in England, we should have to fear despotism; if there were two, they would cut each other's throats; but there are thirty, and they live in peace and happiness."

Powerful currents of English opinion had agitated for religious freedom throughout the seventeenth century. There were Roger

Williams in Rhode Island and Anne Hutchinson in Massachusetts, and there was John Milton's *Treatise of Civil Power in Ecclesiastical Causes: Shewing that It is not Lawfull for Any Power on Earth to Compell in Matters of Religion* (1659). Moreover, by the end of the seventeenth century, the English had already *achieved* legal freedom to worship. They did so through the Act of Toleration of 1689, although it must be granted that toleration did not extend to Roman Catholics or to persons, such as Jews, denying the Trinity. Still, it was a great victory for the Dissenters, who had had their own painful tribulations as late as the punitive Conventicle Acts of the 1660s. What can be spoken of as the English Enlightenment achieved for Britons by 1689 what the Huguenots in France were not allowed to enjoy until almost a century later, 1787.

The French Enlightenment not only desired greater legal guarantees of religious freedom but it also preached the virtues of a general broadmindedness. Here the philosophes followed the example not only of their own Pierre Bayle, but also of Lord Shaftesbury. A translation of Shaftesbury's *Essay on Merit and Virtue* was Diderot's first publication (1745). He prefaced it with an open letter "A mon frère," in which he extolled tolerance and inveighed against bigotry, referring especially to the French civil and religious wars of the sixteenth century. Diderot continued to attack intolerance throughout the rest of his life, a signal illustration of this attitude being his article on that subject in the *Encyclopédie*. As for Voltaire, one of his most famous books was his *Traité sur la tolérance* (1763). Philosophes liked to claim, with Voltaire, that they ran a slight fever every year on the anniversary of the Massacre of St. Bartholomew's Day.

The emphasis on tolerance is in my enumeration the fifth characteristic of the French Enlightenment. But this had been the burden in 1689 of John Locke's argument in his *Letter Concerning Toleration*. And just to show how influential was his *Letter,* which I conceive to be representative of what should be called the English Enlightenment, it might be mentioned that Diderot, in his *Encyclopédie* article "Irréligieux," made the point that religiosity is relative: no one in Paris is going to treat a Muslim as a criminal if he manifests contempt for the law of Mohammed, nor will anyone at Constantinople treat a Christian as a criminal for opposing Christianity—an argument that comes straight out of Locke's *Letter Concerning Toleration,* though Diderot did not choose or did not dare to say so.

Another characteristic of the Enlightenment in France, and one strongly pronounced, was the struggle of the philosophes for freedom of the press. How they did chafe against the elaborate governmental apparatus of censorship! They coexisted with it in a love-hate relationship, for it imprisoned them (as it did Voltaire and the Abbé Raynal)—and it made them famous. What inventive and ingenious subterfuges, many of them illegal, the philosophes used to circumvent the censorship! Even those of their writings that were passed by the censors and then legally published in France always needed, sophisticates knew, to be carefully scrutinized for veiled meanings and Aesopian language.[17] Often the rewards were great.

In England the merits of a free press and the disadvantages of censorship had long since been set forth in history's most eloquent essay on intellectual freedom, Milton's *Areopagitica* (1644). Previous censorship, that is, the official blue-penciling of manuscripts before they are even allowed to go to the printer, was deliberately discontinued in England in 1695, when Parliament intentionally failed to renew the Licensing Act. Thereafter English citizens were spared the anxieties and annoyances and frustrations of censorship that filled the lives and embittered the dispositions of men of letters in France, although, it should be admitted, even after 1695 the English government could still discommode authors by the vigorous execution of libel suits. Nevertheless, legal freedom to publish became for an Englishman a matter of course. He came to take it for granted.[18] So too, apparently, have historians, thus forgetting how effectually, and as early as the seventeenth century, the English achieved one of the greatest blessings of enlightenment.

For men of letters in France (and they, of course, were the class of men most effective in changing public opinion), the most intimidating menace of the apparatus of censorship was the constant threat of arbitrary and indefinite imprisonment. The country had no right of habeas corpus. Consequently, one of the characteristics of the French Enlightenment was a conviction that the fact that *lettres de cachet* were legal was another example of the unfairness and injustice of the whole system of French jurisprudence, demonstrated further in the miscarriage of justice in the cases of Calas and of the Chevalier de La Barre. This, then, may be said to be another characteristic of the French Enlightenment, though not of course so weighty as, say, the love of science or hatred of bigotry. Still, Diderot made a lettre de cachet play a villainous role in the plot of his *Le Père de famille,* and Mirabeau wrote in 1778 his vigorous and trenchant *Des lettres de cachet et des prisons d'Etat* (published in 1782—in Hamburg, and not, one may well imagine, in Paris). Moreover, some of the *cahiers de doléances* of 1789 mention lettres de cachet as a grievance.[19] Meanwhile the English, a shining example to all, had enjoyed the rights of habeas corpus since the act of that name of 1679.

An important element in the thinking of the French Enlightenment, so important that it may here be accounted its eighth characteristic, was the direct influence of Lord Bacon. There was an exciting and stimulating down-to-earthness in Bacon's empirical method and in his philosophy of empiricism. Especially was Bacon associated in France with the *Encyclopédie,* a work that has been called "the most impressive cultural document of the Enlightenment and at the same time the most effective in propagating its ideas."[20] The *Encyclopédie's* famous chart or Detailed System of Human Knowledge, folded into the first volume, was modeled after Bacon: "We have confessed in several places in the Prospectus," wrote the editors, "that our principal obligation for our encyclopedic tree was to Chancellor Bacon." D'Alembert remarked in his "Preliminary Discourse" that "One would be tempted to regard him [Bacon] as the greatest, the most universal, and the most eloquent of philosophers." Diderot, who, according to one of his friends writing in 1756, had been studying Bacon for ten years, modeled his own *Pensées sur l'interprétation de la nature* (1753) on Bacon. In addition, he encouraged his friend Alexandre Deleyre to publish in 1755 the *Analyse de la philosophie du Chancelier François Bacon.* Further, in the article "Encyclopédie," in the fifth volume, Diderot boasted, "I believe that I have taught my fellow citizens to esteem and read Chancellor Bacon; this profound author has been more dipped into the past five or six years than he ever was before."[21] It is both amusing and significant that the arch-conservative Joseph de Maistre, in books like *Les Soirées de Saint-Petersbourg* (1821), devoted much time to singling out and attacking Bacon as the prime originator of what De Maistre regarded as the going-wrong of the eighteenth century.

Naturally, the fellow countrymen of Bacon also felt the impact of his ideas. This was most evident in the motives of the founders of the Royal Society (more precisely styled the Royal Society of London for the Promotion of Natural Knowledge), which was formally established in 1660 and received its charter from the Crown in 1662. It has rightly been said, "The vision of Francis Bacon inspired the founders of the Royal Society in three ways. It laid stress on the communal working of scientists: for example, in the *New Atlantis* there is a College of Natural Philosophy . . . in which the philosophers work together 'dedicated to the study of the works and creatures of God.' It constantly presented science as an activity designed to serve mankind. . . . And it advocated throughout, and for the first time, what is essentially the modern scientific method: the making of experiments, the drawing of general conclusions from them, and the testing of these generalizations in further experiments."[22]

The Royal Society and the French Académie Royale des Sciences, founded six years later, were the prototypes and inspiration of the numerous academies that sprang up in the eighteenth century and which sedulously exchanged their proceedings and transactions in a common desire to spread knowledge. This was part of the cosmopolitanism of the Enlightenment. The impulse to make new scientific discoveries and to impart knowledge concerning them is a conspicuous feature of the whole Enlightenment. In France this impulse especially manifested itself through the activities of the Académie des Sciences and through Diderot's *Encyclopédie*. But so far as priority is concerned, it is well to remember that the Royal Society of London was first in the field.

This brings me to the influence of Newtonianism in the Enlightenment, an influence so enormous and so well known that, paradoxically, there is no need to dilate upon it in a paper of this kind, save to recall that Newton, after all, was English! His name became a shibboleth, and for what? Not only for the magnitude of a past achievement, but also for the promise of things to come. The method of Newton and Newtonianism, which to the French Enlightenment signified what we mean today when we say "science," supported and fortified the zestful and exciting notion inspiring the whole Enlightenment movement, that man's discoveries and man's life on earth were not at an ending, but at a beginning. This euphoria is close to the heart of what enlightenment is, suffusing the era with hopefulness and high morale. I count it as one of the characteristics of the Enlightenment.

It is this faith in scientific reasoning that earned the eighteenth century the title of the "Age of Reason," a faith that was a large part of the "philosophy" that made the philosophes deem themselves philosophers. "The philosophy of the eighteenth century takes up . . . the methodological pattern of Newton's physics. . . . Reason is now looked upon rather as . . . the original intellectual force which guides the discovery and determination of truth . . . ," wrote Cassirer. "The whole eighteenth century understands reason in this sense . . . as a kind of energy, a force. . . ."[23] This is how it is that the eighteenth century could claim that theirs was par excellence the Age of Reason. This faith in reason constitutes the eleventh in my enumeration of the characteristics of the French Enlightenment.

A twelfth characteristic of the French Enlightenment was its great interest in what amounts to psychology. Instances of this interest were the Abbé Condillac's *Essai sur l'origine des connaissances humaines* (1746) and his famous *Traité des sensations* (1754). Such also were Diderot's *Letter on the Blind* (1749) and his *Letter on the Deaf and Dumb* (1751). Also of extreme importance in the history of ideas in the eighteenth century were Helvétius' *De l'Esprit* (1758), which caused a tremendous uproar, and his *De l'Homme* (1773). These books, in turn, prompted Diderot to write his *Réfutation de l'ouvrage d'Helvétius intitulé l'Homme* (1773-1774).

Now, all of this—all this sensationalistic psychology so characteristic of the Enlightenment—stems from John Locke and his *Essay Concerning Human Understanding* (1690). Locke's work is of course a treatise on metaphysics, on epistemology. But Locke was also a physician, besides being a philosopher, and many of his dicta in the *Essay Concerning Human Understanding,* as also in his *Some Thoughts Concerning Education* (1693), depend upon the empirical method and upon actual observation of behavior. Thus, Locke became a kind of intellectual parent of the effort (conspicuous in the French, Italian, and Scottish Enlightenments) to extend the scientific method to social studies and to the study of man.

Locke was emphatic in declaring that there is no such thing as an innate idea, for nothing conceptual is inborn in human beings. All that human beings can ever know they have to learn; all that they can ever know has first to be transmitted to them through their senses. Hence, the name "sensationalist psychology." The banishment of the notion of innate ideas was a giant step forward in the understanding of why we behave like human beings, and it had many implications affecting the French Enlightenment, for, as Cassirer remarked, "On all questions of psychology and the theory of knowledge Locke's authority remained practically unchallenged throughout the first half of the eighteenth century."[24] One of these implications, which most of the philosophes deduced with a logicality that was somewhat overweening, was that nurture is much more important than nature, and that therefore there is almost no limit to the extent that human improvement can be accomplished by education. Faith in the improvement—their own word was "perfectibility"—of man contributed greatly to the dynamism of the Enlightenment, its optimism, its morale, its faith in progress. The psychological doctrines of Locke underlay these happy assumptions. For both in his psychology and in his political theory, Locke took the liberal view of the nature of man.

Another characteristic of the French Enlightenment is that it possessed a quite definite political theory. Until comparatively recent years it was generally supposed that there was not much writing on political theory in the French Enlightenment, save by Montesquieu and Rousseau. But now numerous scholars have changed all that. Thus we have Peter Gay's work on *Voltaire's Politics;* John Lough's and Eberhard Weis's on political theory in the *Encyclopédie;* on D'Holbach, Jeroom Vercruysse and Virgil Topazio; and on Diderot, the writings of Paul Vernière, Jacques Proust, Yves Benot, Paolo Alatri, and Anthony Strugnell.[25] Their researches and analyses confirm a judgment of the *Encyclopédie* made by an English journalist in 1768: "We must observe likewise, to the honour of the authors who have had the conduct of the *Encyclopédie,* that the same manly freedom of sentiment which is observable in the philosophical and other departments of this work, is eminently conspicuous in the political. In short, whoever takes the trouble of combining the several political articles, will find that they form a noble system of civil liberty; and however, as Englishmen, we may have no reason to rejoice at the prospect of a gradual establishment of such a system among our rivals, yet as friends to the rights of mankind, we are delighted to see such a generous system everywhere expanding its influence."[26]

This political theory not only emphasized natural and civil rights for the individual but also was concerned with limiting the powers of overmighty government. Writing on "Autorité, politique" in the very first volume of the *Encyclopédie* — an article which very nearly caused the government's discontinuing the whole enterprise — Diderot declared that "No man has received from nature the right of commanding others. . . . True and legitimate power thus necessarily has limits. . . . The prince holds from his subjects themselves the authority that he has over them; and this authority is limited by the laws of nature and of the State." This, obviously, is an appeal to the ideals of limited monarchy and constitutional restraints, a very bold statement at a time when the monarchy of Louis XV was still vehemently asserting the absolutistic principles of Louis XIV.[27] Yet this is the sort of thing that the English had already achieved as a result of the Revolution of 1688.

And it was from England, rather than from France's own political theorists (say, for example, Jean Bodin) that French political theory was borrowing at that time. It was a foreign importation. English precedents and English political philosophy were heavily drawn upon by the philosophes. In his famous doctrine of the separation of powers — executive, legislative, and judicial — Montesquieu thought, though quite mistakenly, that he was describing the English constitution of his day. Rousseau's *Du contrat social* is an adaptation of the contract theory of government as we see it in Hobbes and Locke. Both with regard to limited, constitutional government and with respect to natural rights, the political theory of Diderot and of the Encyclopedists can be described as closely resembling that of John Locke. As Eberhard Weis has remarked, "Scarcely any work of the eighteenth century contributed as much as did the *Encyclopédie* to the dissemination in France of Locke's political theory."[28]

To say that the political theory of the *Encyclopédie* was Lockean is a shorthand way of saying that it emphasized natural rights and considered these rights as anterior to government. Locke repeatedly stated that the only reason for government — the only reason a human being subjects himself to the constraints of civil government — is the safeguarding of man's natural rights to life, liberty, and estate. In the American phraseology (for Jefferson followed Locke closely, of course) government exists "to secure these rights" — rights that had always existed, before there were any governments, rights which governments could not create, but which it was the function of legitimate government, of good government, to "secure." Diderot adopted the Lockean theory of natural rights, and in his *Encyclopédie* article on "Droit naturel" he used the phrase "inalienable rights."[29]

But Englishmen had already secured most of these. The Bill of Rights of December 16, 1689, extended those that Englishmen already enjoyed, by specifically guaranteeing such things as the right of petition and of trial by jury. It also forbade the imposition of excessive bail and forbade, too, any future attempt to dispense with the law of the land.[30] Thus did the Convention Parliament deal with the claims of overextended royal prerogative or, as President Nixon called it, "executive privilege." In this fashion the English Enlightenment made operative what the French Enlightenment was later to admire and hope to secure.

In the article "Philosophe" in the *Encyclopédie,* the philosophes themselves defined what they meant by "philosophy." Like thousands of its sibling articles in that stimulating work, the article "Philosophe" was controversial. It stated a new philosophical goal (or, perhaps, only restated a very ancient one that is easy for philosophers to lose sight of). "Reason is to a philosopher," it declared, "what grace is to a Christian" — a rather impudent remark. "The philosophical spirit is, then, a spirit of observation and exactness. . . . Man is not a monster who should live only in the deeps of the sea or the depths of a forest . . . his needs and well-being engage him to live in society. . . . The philosopher, then, is an honest man who acts in all things according to reason, and who combines good morals and sociable qualities with a mind disposed toward reflection and preciseness."[31]

This aspect of philosophy, the facet of its dealing with ethics and social philosophy, did indeed develop into a marked feature of French thinking, and I include it here as another characteristic of Enlightenment thought. We see it in Diderot, who said late in life that his greatest desire had been to write a systematic treatise on ethics (the responsibility, he said, had been too great and he referred to the philosophes as constituting a kind of family—a happy analogy, because it allows for hearty family quarrels and for the antipathies, as well as the affection, of siblings and cousins.

It is important to realize that such intellectual interaction—and personal contact—had occurred on the English scene in the seventeenth century. The fact that the Revolution against Charles I had settled so much and yet left a very considerable amount of unfinished business brought it about that the period of the Restoration, the generation between 1660 and 1688, was a happy-hunting time for intellectuals. It is conjectured that Locke knew personally the aged Hobbes; he certainly knew Newton and, as previously mentioned, was the director of Shaftesbury's education. All the members of the Royal Society knew one another: Locke and Newton, of course, and Christopher Wren, and a historian such as Bishop Burnet, the diarists John Evelyn and Samuel Pepys, a statistician in the person of William Petty, a demographer in John Graunt, a chemist-physicist in Robert Boyle, poets like Edmund Waller and John Dryden, astronomers like Halley and Flamsteed, the botanist Hans Sloane, the inventor Robert Hooke, and William Penn.[35]

In the realm of politics there was a brief period in England in 1687 and 1688 when men of every political stripe united in opposition to James II's extreme claims subvertive of the laws of England.[36] Clearly, England had its Party of Humanity too. The crisis once over and the Revolution safely and almost bloodlessly accomplished, England passed into a period of such stability and, on the whole, such conservatism, that it became easy to overlook the fact that the country had indeed had an Enlightenment, and that it was thereafter living serenely on its accumulated capital of political and intellectual achievements.

Thus far my object has been to contend that the English did more than simply influence the Enlightenment—they *had* an Enlightenment. According to this analysis, the characteristics of the French Enlightenment that were also observable, and observable earlier, in England were natural religion; deism; the growth of philosophical materialism; the desire for legal religious toleration, for the spread of tolerance, and for freedom of the press; the intellectual revulsion against arbitrary imprisonment; the influence of Lord Bacon; the founding of scientific societies for the

had given it up); we see it in the books of Helvét:
such a great (and greatly unacknowledged) impac
Bentham and the Utilitarians in England; we see it
of D'Holbach. And we see it in the pronounced hu
of the Enlightenment movement.

Now, the English had had a philosopher like th
influential he was, too, both at home and abroad
thony Ashley Cooper, third Earl of Shaftesbury
whose collected works were published in 1711 und
Characteristicks of Men, Manners, Opinions, Tim
popular that they ran to a fifth edition by 1732. Sh:
had been educated under the supervision of John I
much influenced by the Cambridge Platonists, who
tle way, might likewise be considered as part of tl
lightenment. Shaftesbury was a moralist. His phild
upon the necessity of freedom for any kind of scient
or political achievement; upon the social and mor
man and upon the universal good; upon an optimis
possibilities within any man, given the proper circu
upon the close relationship uniting truth, beauty, a
Such views show him to be an aesthetician as well
but he was a moralist most of all.

This influence had made itself felt early in Fran
tion of Shaftesbury's *Essay on the Freedom of Wit*
was published in 1710. Diderot translated *An Inq*
ing Virtue and Merit in 1745, and Shaftesbury rem:
ing influence in Diderot's thought on eithics and es
thinking on aesthetics.[33] In the article "Génie" (C
Encyclopédie, an article written by the poet Saint-L
is a passage extremely appreciative of Shaftesbury.
the philosophy of the philosophes owed much in i:
only to Locke, but also to Shaftesbury, a leading :
the political and intellectual sides of the English E

I shall terminate this enumeration of the charact
French Enlightenment by alluding to the fact th
sophes developed a sense of kindred feeling that v
like that of a political party. They knew one anothe
acted with one another. In fact, the *Encyclopédie :*
its title page that it was done "by a Society of Me
Peter Gay has called them the Party of Humanity

promotion of knowledge; the prestige of Newtonianism; the faith in reason; the sensationalist psychology; a liberal political theory; the "new" philosophy of Locke and Shaftesbury in its ethical and aesthetic implications; and, finally, a sense of kindred feeling which stoked the movement for enlightenment.

Historians who fail to recognize the existence of a seventeenth-century English Enlightenment will inevitably tend to interpret the whole global movement as somewhat smaller and more restricted than in fact it was. But historians seem to be changing in this regard. I believe that Professor Hatton and other London School of Economics scholars are beginning to speak of the existence of an English Enlightenment. Up to now, however, one cannot find — and I have looked hard to find them — books or articles devoted to a thoroughgoing discussion of whether or not there was an English Enlightenment in and of itself. I have found intimations of it when authors speak of English intellectual *influences* on the Continent, but it is hard to say how sharply and unambiguously these authors had in mind, over and above influences, a fully proportioned English Enlightenment as such.[37] Henry Steele Commager, in his recent book, comes closest when he says, "We can date the Old World Enlightenment from the founding of the Royal Society . . . or perhaps from the publication of Newton's *Principia* in 1687." But even Commager does not speak of an English Enlightenment; on the contrary, he remarks that "England was a bit outside the Enlightenment."[38] And Henry F. May, who does recognize that there was an English Enlightenment, speaks of it as "the Moderate English Enlightenment of the *mid-eighteenth century*" [emphasis mine].[39]

To posit the existence of an earlier Enlightenment in England has the merit of clearing up two historical points that could otherwise be termed paradoxical. The first is this: How does it happen that the Enlightenment in America shows so little evidence of having been much influenced by the Enlightenment in France? The second: How does it happen that English literature of the eighteenth century, a very flourishing and significant literature indeed, does not manifest the characteristics of agitation and turbulence that one would expect to find in literary works associated with an Enlightenment movement?

The answer to the first question is in brief that the American Enlightenment found all the nourishment it needed in its English antecedents. Moreover, it distrusted the religious radicalism of the French movement. The brief answer to the second question is that the literature of eighteenth-century England was supported and sustained by an Enlightenment that, for the most part, had already occurred.

With reference to the first question, it would be hard to find nowadays any American historian who would deny that the North American colonies experienced an Enlightenment, or who would deny that such ideas helped to inspire and foment the American Revolution. As Commager ebulliently remarks, "It was Americans who not only embraced the body of Enlightenment principles, but wrote them into law, crystallized them into institutions, and put them to work." Well and good. But where do we find the influence of the French Enlightenment in all this? Save for the knowledge of Montesquieu's writings, especially the *Esprit des lois,* it is hard to find traces of French influence in Revolutionary American political thought.[40] The influence of Rousseau in America was minimal, according to Paul M. Spurlin, and what there was of it began around 1789.[41]

The only reference in Jefferson's writing or correspondence to Diderot and D'Alembert's *Encyclopédie* was to a second edition published in Lucca and available at Alexandria, Virginia. Jefferson was authorized by the Virginia Council in 1781 to purchase this set "for the use of the Public." The encyclopedia mentioned with great frequency in Jefferson's correspondence was not Diderot's *Encyclopédie,* but the later *Encyclopédie méthodique,* an altogether different (and lesser) work.[42] Nor did Benjamin Franklin or Thomas Jefferson ever act in France as though they were disciples come to sit at the feet of their masters. They treated the philosophes as peers, not as superiors. Both men were irritated by the complacent European assumption, imbibed from the writings of the Abbé Cornelius De Pauw, that "The whole human race is indubitably weakened and rendered degenerate in the new continent."[43] Species of animals likewise, according to the great French naturalist Buffon. Jefferson devoted a considerable portion of his *Notes on the State of Virginia* to confuting Buffon, and, in order to overwhelm his French confrere with evidence, went to great pains and expense to obtain the skeleton of a moose.[44]

If one examines the pamphlet literature written by Americans

in the developing dispute with the mother country, once again
one may well ask, where is the influence of French thought to be
seen in these impressive documents? Not in Jonathan Mayhew's
*Discourse Concerning Unlimited Submission and Non-Resistance
to the Higher Powers* (1750), "the most famous sermon preached
in pre-Revolutionary America." He himself declared that the
great modern teachers of liberty were Bishop Hoadly, Algernon
Sidney, Milton, and Locke.[45] Not in James Otis's *The Rights of
the British Colonies Asserted and Proved* (1764). There the burden of the argument comes from Sir Edward Coke and his celebrated judgment in *Bonham's Case* (1610). Nor in *A Vindication
of the British Colonies* (1765), where Otis relies on Blackstone,
whose *Commentaries on the Laws of England* had been published
that same year. Not in Daniel Delany's *Considerations on the
Propriety of Imposing Taxes in the British Colonies* (1765) or
John Dickinson's *The Late Regulations . . . Considered.*[46] And
when hostilities had started and Americans were considering
whether to declare their independence, Tom Paine, in *Common
Sense,* the most influential pamphlet of all (May 1776), spoke to
the Americans not with the arguments of the French philosophes,
but with the biblical story, from the First Book of Samuel, of how
the Israelites *sinned* in desiring to have a king.

Whence, then, did the colonists derive their ideology? From
their own ancestral traditions, and from the English Enlightenment of the seventeenth century. Colonial thinkers hearkened
back, as research regarding the books they purchased proves, to
the martyred Algernon Sidney and his *Discourses on Government;* to Locke, of course, and to John Trenchard and Thomas
Gordon and the *Independent Whig* and *Cato's Letters.*[47] Most of
all, though, it was simply English revolutions and English religious disputes, especially the complex influence of Puritanism,
and English philosophy and American folkways—but *not* the
French Enlightenment—that provided the Americans with their
ideology.[48]

Let me now turn to the question of what might be termed paradoxical about the nature of eighteenth-century English literature.
The Age of Addison, of Swift, of Pope, of Dr. Johnson, and of
Edmund Burke is a great period in English letters, but its literature does not have the flavor of Enlightenment agitation. Consider, just as an exercise in comparative literature, the difference

in tonality between the books written by these great authors and those written by Pierre Bayle, Voltaire, Montesquieu, Diderot, Rousseau, D'Holbach, and Raynal. The books of an Enlightenment movement carry with them an aura of dissonance and nonconformity and discontent and alienation. Enlightenment books are aggressive, though their aggressiveness and abrasiveness may be wreathed in the gracious rhetoric of seventeenth- and eighteenth-century forms of discourse. They are challenging, they are pugnacious, they are provocative and provoking, and they are antiestablishment. In Enlightenment writings there is a prickliness and irritability ever close to the surface.

But what of a literature written when the time of troubles is past? Of a literature that is free of the stultifications of censorship and the menace of arbitrary punishments; of a literature riding on the crest of an Enlightenment already achieved? This is a literature that can afford to be serene, sedate — and conservative. English eighteenth-century literature was written by enlightened men but it is not Enlightenment in its resonances. Swift is a satirist of overwhelming power, but it is not an Enlightenment trait to despair of the human race nor to think of men as Yahoos. Pope is a poet of infinite grace, but to preach in elegant heroic couplets that "One truth is clear: whatever is, is RIGHT" is not exactly an example of Enlightenment reaching out to new horizons. The formidable Dr. Johnson, "rolling his majestic frame in his usual manner," was an imposing man of letters, but he was also, as the Regius Professor of History at Oxford says of him, a "high-church Tory bigot."[49] Scarcely a man eager to hold out his hand to change.

In eighteenth-century English literature we find urbanity, worldliness (as in Lord Chesterfield or Lord Hervey), some cynicism (as in Chesterfield and, say, in Mandeville), but no manifestations of Enlightenment ferment (save for the deists) until late in the century — with men like Joseph Priestley, Richard Price, Tom Paine, Jeremy Bentham, and William Godwin. Hume frequently spoke with scorn — in his private correspondence with fellow Scots, to be sure — of the intellectual level of all Englishmen of his generation. He made only one exception: Edward Gibbon.

What was the difference: What had happened? The answer is that the English Enlightenment had occurred in a relatively short time and with such decisiveness that no further agitation seemed to the English to be necessary or even very desirable.[50] Whereas the French man of letters had the sensation, throughout the century, of having to live in a kind of pressure cooker, the Englishman quickly accustomed himself to all the considerable gains he had achieved and did not particularly yearn for more. English society became quite conservative. The successes of the English Enlightenment had the paradoxical effect of inducing not only stability but complacency.

If indeed there was an English Enlightenment, occurring mostly in the seventeenth century, how does it happen that that fact has not become one of the commonplaces of historical knowledge and of the vocabulary of historians? The subject invites research. I suspect that the word crept into English from the German *Aufklärung,* perhaps as a result, when Kant's thought eventually began to be studied by the English, of Kant's essay on *Was ist Aufklärung?* Therefore, to insular taste, the word always bore the stigma of being a foreign importation. As recently as 1960, Alfred Cobban, a very sagacious historian, observed that "The term *Enlightenment* is hardly naturalized in English."[51] What had really begun in England came to seem to conservative Englishmen abhorrently foreign, and they were in no mood to claim having had any part in its genesis. Even if Englishmen of the eighteenth century were aware that a special, intellectual, "philosophical" movement was going on in the world, they were happy to attribute it to the French, a nation to which they were delighted to condescend. "Thanks to our sullen resistance to innovation," — it is Edmund Burke who is speaking — "thanks to the cold sluggishness of our national character, we still bear the stamp of our forefathers. . . . We are not the converts of Rousseau; we are not the disciples of Voltaire; Helvetius has made no progress amongst us. Atheists are not our preachers; madmen are not our lawgivers."[52]

This hostile attitude toward the idea of Enlightenment was exacerbated during the French Revolution by fear of the Jacobins and of Napoleon, and made paranoid by the suspicion — I am quoting from a book published in 1798 — that the French Revolution was the result of "a formal and systematic conspiracy against Religion . . . formed and zealously prosecuted by Voltaire, d'Alembert, and Diderot, assisted by Frederick II, King of Prussia."[53]

Anti-French animosities and, later, anti-Enlightenment Romanticism explain the tardiness and reluctance with which

English critics and historians allude to the term. The *Oxford English Dictionary* gives a surprisingly late date—1865—for the first year in which the word "enlightenment" (in the sense of a period in history) is found. Nor is the connotation flattering. In a book called *The Secret of Hegel,* the author refers sarcastically to "Deism, Atheism, Pantheism, and all manner of *isms* dear to Enlightenment."[54] The great editor and Gladstonian liberal, Lord Morley, in his interestingly written and still useful *Diderot and the Encyclopedists* (1878) does not, so far as I can find, use the word "Enlightenment" one single time in his two volumes. And is it not striking that the monumental *Cambridge Modern History,* planned by Lord Acton and published between 1904 and 1910, has no mention of the Enlightenment in its table of contents, its text, or its index?

I have just quoted the *Oxford English Dictionary*'s example of the first use of the term in English. Their own definition of the word "Enlightenment," which was first published in 1887, is, with word order somewhat transposed, the definition they are using today. In the third edition of *The Shorter Oxford English Dictionary on Historical Principles,* published in 1973, it appears as follows: "Enlightenment: Shallow and pretentious intellectualism, unreasonable contempt for authority and tradition, etc., applied especially to the spirit and aims of the French philosophers of the eighteenth century."

No wonder Professor Cobban remarked that the term "Enlightenment" is hardly naturalized in English. No wonder that I could begin this paper by making the observation that there is something anomalous in the way in which historians have treated the role of England in the Enlightenment.

NOTES

1. "Aufklärung ist der Ausgang des Menschen aus seiner selbstverschuldeten Unmündigkeit" (Immanuel Kant, "Was ist Aufklärung?" [1784]).

2. Jean Fabre, *Stanislas-Auguste Poniatowski et l'Europe des Lumières* (Paris, 1952); Robert Howard Lord, *The Second Partition of Poland* (Cambridge, Mass., 1915); Grzegorz Leopold Seidler, "The Polish Contribution to the Age of Enlightenment," *Annales Universitatis Mariae Curie-Sklodowska,* XVIII (1971), 1-31.

3. Richard Herr, *The Eighteenth-Century Revolution in Spain* (Princeton, 1958), pp. 37-85, 154-200, especially 84-85; Jean Sarrailh,

L'Espagne éclairée de la seconde moitié du XVIIIe siècle (Paris, 1954).

4. George Barany, "Hoping Against Hope: The Enlightened Age in Hungary," *American Historical Review,* LXXVI (1971), 319-357. Marc Raeff, "The Enlightenment in Russia and Russian Thought in the Enlightenment," in *The Eighteenth Century in Russia,* ed. J. G. Garrard (Oxford, 1973), pp. 25-47; Raeff, "Les Slaves, les Allemands et les 'Lumières,'" *Canadian Slavic Studies,* I (1967), 521-551.

5. Peter Gay, *The Enlightenment: An Interpretation,* 2 vols. (New York, 1966-1969), II, 332. See also David Daiches, *The Paradox of Scottish Culture: The Eighteenth-Century Experience* (London, 1964); Anand C. Chitnis, *The Scottish Enlightenment: A Social History* (London, 1976); Hugh Trevor-Roper, "The Scottish Enlightenment," *Studies on Voltaire and the Eighteenth Century,* LVIII (1967), 1635-1658; and Roger L. Emerson, "Scottish Universities in the Eighteenth Century, 1690-1800," *Studies on Voltaire and the Eighteenth Century,* CLXVII (1977), 453-474.

6. Bernard Bailyn, "Political Experience and Enlightenment Ideas in Eighteenth-Century America," *American Historical Review,* LXVII (1961-1962), 351; see also Bailyn, *The Ideological Origins of the American Revolution* (Cambridge, Mass., 1967), passim. Consult also Gay, *The Enlightenment,* II, 555-563.

7. Robert R. Palmer, "Turgot: Paragon of the Continental Enlightenment," *Journal of Law and Economics,* XIX (1976), 608.

8. Giorgio Tonelli, "The 'Weakness' of Reason in the Age of Enlightenment," *Diderot Studies XIV* (Geneva, 1971), 217-244: "there are *at least two* basically different Enlightenments: the one dominant first in England and Holland, and later in France, Italy and Spain; the other dominant in Germany and Scandinavia" (ibid., 219-220). Tonelli also alludes to "the Anglo-French Enlightenment" (ibid., 222, 239, 242-243). Adrienne Koch, ed., *The American Enlightenment* (New York, 1965), pp. 36, 39. Henry F. May, *The Enlightenment in America* (New York, 1976), p. 132: "In America the skeptical Parisian Enlightenment had a far less important influence than its moderate, rationalist, English predecessor"; also May, *Enlightenment in America,* pp. 106, 159; and May, "The Problem of the American Enlightenment," *New Literary History,* I (1970), 209, 213. D. H. Meyer, "The Uniqueness of the American Enlightenment," *American Quarterly,* XXVIII (1976), 167, observes that "the English Enlightenment was more moderate than the French."

9. See J. S. Spink, *French Free-Thought from Gassendi to Voltaire* (Oxford, 1960), pp. 85-168; Ira O. Wade, *The Intellectual Origins of the French Enlightenment* (Princeton, 1971), pp. 206-230.

10. Ira O. Wade, *The Clandestine Organization and Diffusion of Philosophic Ideas in France from 1700 to 1750* (Princeton, 1938), passim.

11. Norman L. Torrey, *Voltaire and the English Deists* (New Haven, 1930), passim, especially pp. 2-4, 202-203.

12. Franco Venturi, "The European Enlightenment," in his *Italy and*

the Enlightenment (New York, 1972), pp. 5-8, this quotation p. 8; Ernst Cassirer, *The Philosophy of the Enlightenment* (Beacon paperback ed., pp. 171-177, especially p. 174). For the influence of Toland abroad, see Franco Venturi, *Utopia and Reform in the Enlightenment* (Cambridge, 1971), pp. 49-55, 57-62, 64-67.

13. John Pappas, "Voltaire et la guerre civile philosophique," *Revue d'histoire littéraire de la France,* LXI (1961), 525-549.

14. In the 1760s Diderot became fascinated with Hobbes's philosophy. See Diderot to Naigeon (?), April 1772 (Denis Diderot, *Correspondence,* ed. George Roth and Jean Varlott, 16 vols. [Paris, 1955-1970], XII, 45-46); also Arthur M. Wilson, *Diderot* (New York, 1972), pp. 379-380, 568, 833 n. 49; Leland J. Thielemann, "Thomas Hobbes dans l'Encyclopédie," *Revue d'histoire littéraire de la France,* LI (1951), 333-346; Thielemann, "Diderot and Hobbes," *Diderot Studies,* II (1952), 221-278.

15. John Locke, *An Essay Concerning Human Understanding,* Book IV, chap. iii, sec. 6. For example, Diderot alludes to this passage in his *Encyclopédie* article "Locke, philosophie de" (Denis Diderot, *Oeuvres complètes,* ed. Jean Varloot [Paris, 1975-], VII, 714.

16. Lester G. Crocker, "John Toland et le matérialisme de Diderot," *Revue d'histoire littéraire de la France,* LIII (1953), 289-295; Paolo Casini, "Toland e l'attività della materia," *Rivista Critica di Storia della Filosofia,* XXII (1967), 24-53. See also G. R. Cragg, *From Puritanism to the Age of Reason* (Cambridge, 1950), chap. vii: "John Toland and the Rise of Deism." For a very illuminating discussion of Toland's influence on Enlightenment thought, see Venturi, *Utopia and Reform in the Enlightenment,* pp. 49-67; also Margaret C. Jacob, *The Newtonians and the English Revolution, 1689-1720* (Ithaca, N.Y., 1976), pp. 210-238.

17. See Robert Shackleton, "Censure and Censorship: Impediments to Free Publication in the Age of the Enlightenment," *Library Chronicle of the University of Texas at Austin,* New Series, No. 6 (December 1973), pp. 25-41.

18. See A. V. Dicey, *Introduction to the Study of the Law of the Constitution,* 8th ed. (London, 1920), pp. 256-259; Dudley J. Medley, *A Student's Manual of English Constitutional History,* 6th ed. (Oxford, 1925), p. 481.

19. Beatrice F. Hyslop, *French Nationalism in 1789 According to the General Cahiers* (New York, 1934), pp. 92-93, 160.

20. Ernst Cassirer, in *Encyclopaedia of the Social Sciences,* 15 vols. (New York, 1930-1935), V, 551, s.v. "Enlightenment."

21. Wilson, *Diderot,* pp. 132, 137, 187-190, 244; Howard B. White, "The Influence of Bacon on the Philosophes," *Studies on Voltaire and the Eighteenth Century,* XXVII (1963), 1849-1869.

22. J. Bronowski and Bruce Mazlish, *The Western Intellectual Tradition from Leonardo to Hegel* (New York, 1960), pp. 186-187.

23. Cassirer, *The Philosophy of the Enlightenment,* pp. 12, 13.

24. Ibid., p. 99. Regarding Locke's influence, see also (and espe-

cially) Paul Hazard, *European Thought in the Eighteenth Century from Montesquieu to Lessing* (New Haven, 1954), pp. 42-43. For the great influence of Pierre Coste's translation (1700) of Locke's *Essay Concerning Human Understanding,* see Gabriel Bonno, *La culture et la civilisation britanniques devant l'opinion française de la Paix d'Utrecht aux "Lettres Philosophiques" (1713-1734)* (Philadelphia, 1948), pp. 85-92.

25. See Peter Gay, *Voltaire's Politics* (Princeton, 1959); Arthur M. Wilson, "Why Did the Political Theory of the Encyclopedists not Prevail?," *French Historical Studies,* I (1958-1960), 283-294; *Geschichtsschreibung und Staatsauffassung in der französischen Enzyklopädie* (Wiesbaden, 1956); John Lough, *Essays on the Encyclopédie of Diderot and D'Alembert* (London, 1968), pp. 424-462; Jacques Proust, *Diderot et l' "Encyclopédie"* (Paris, 1962), especially pp. 341-502; Jeroom Vercruysse, *Bibliographie descriptive des écrits du baron d'Holbach* (Geneva, 1971); Virgil W. Topazio, *D'Holbach's Moral Philosophy: Its Background and Development* (Geneva, 1956).

On Diderot, besides Proust and Lough, see Paul Vernière, ed., *Diderot: Oeuvres philosophiques* (Paris, 1956); Arthur M. Wilson, "The Development and Scope of Diderot's Political Thought," *Studies on Voltaire and the Eighteenth Century,* XXVII (1963), 1871-1900; Yves Benot, *Diderot: de l'athéisme à l'anticolonialisme* (Paris, 1970); Anthony Strugnell, *Diderot's Politics* (The Hague, 1973); Paolo Alatri, *Voltaire, Diderot e il "Partito Filosofico"* (Messina-Florence, 1965).

26. Owen Ruffhead, in the *Monthly Review,* XXXIX (1768), 545.

27. Diderot, *Oeuvres complètes,* ed. Varloot, V, 537-539. See also John Lough, *Encyclopédie of Diderot . . . ,* pp. 424-462; and Wilson, *Diderot,* pp. 142-143, 154, 489, 753 n. 30. For an extreme example of Louis XV's assertion of absolutist power, see his scolding of the Parlement of Paris at the "séance de la flagellation," March 3, 1766 (Jules Flammermont and Maurice Tourneux, eds., *Remontrances du Parlement de Paris au XVIIIe siècle,* 3 vols. [Paris, 1888-1898], II, 556-558).

28. Eberhard Weis, *Geschichtsschreibung und Staatsauffassung in der französischen Encyklopädie* (Wiesbaden, 1956) (Veröffentlichen des Instituts für Europäische Geschichte Mainz, Bd. 14, Abteilung universalgeschichte), 176.

29. Diderot, *Oeuvres complètes,* ed. Varloot, VII, 28.

30. Carolyn A. Edie, "Revolution and the Rule of Law: The End of the Dispensing Power, 1689," *Eighteenth-Century Studies,* X (1976-1977), 434-450.

31. Denis Diderot, *Oeuvres complètes,* ed. Jules Assézat and Maurice Tourneux, 20 vols. (Paris, 1875-1877), XVI, 274-277. This article freely plagiarized an earlier anonymous essay first printed in 1743. For a complete discussion, see Herbert Dieckmann, ed., *Le Philosophe Texts and Interpretations* (Washington University Studies, New Series, Language and Literature, No. 18 [St. Louis, 1948]).

32. Caroline Robbins, *The Eighteenth-Century Commonwealthman* (Cambridge, Mass., 1959), pp. 128-132.

33. Wilson, *Diderot,* pp. 50-52, 57, 535, 538, 757 n. 21. See also

Paolo Casini, "Diderot e Shaftesbury," *Giornale Critico della Filosofia Italiana,* XXXIX (1960), 253-273; Stanley Green, *Shaftesbury's Philosophy of Religion and Ethics* (Athens, Ohio, 1967), pp. ix-xi; Dorothy B. Schlegel, "Diderot as the Transmitter of Shaftesbury's Romanticism," *Studies on Voltaire and the Eighteenth Century,* XXVII (1963), 1457-1478; Schlegel, *Shaftesbury and the French Deists* (Chapel Hill, 1956); Wladislaw Folkierski, "Comment Lord Shaftesbury a-t-il conquis Diderot?" in *Studi in onore di Carlo Pelligrini* (Turin, 1964), pp. 319-346; Gordon B. Walters, Jr., *The Significance of Diderot's "Essai sur le mérite et la vertu"* (Chapel Hill, 1971). For an analysis of Shaftesbury's aesthetics, see Cassirer, *The Philosophy of the Enlightenment,* pp. 313-328. For the influence of the Cambridge Platonists on Shaftesbury, see Ernst Cassirer, *The Platonic Renaissance in England* (Edinburgh and Austin, Texas, 1953), chap. vi.

34. Diderot, *Oeuvres complètes,* ed. Assézat and Tourneux, XV, 39.

35. For annual lists of members of the Royal Society, see *The Record of the Royal Society of London,* 4th ed. (London, 1940), pp. 375-516; also Sir Henry Lyons, *The Royal Society, 1660-1940* (Cambridge, 1944), passim.

36. For a study of the "multimedia" by which this consensus was brought about, see the most interesting article by Lois G. Schwoerer, "Propaganda in the Revolution of 1688-89," *American Historical Review,* LXXXII (1977), 843-874.

37. For examples, see Norman Hampson, *The Enlightenment* (Harmondsworth, Middlesex, 1968), p. 56: "Britain and France together provided the main impetus behind the Enlightenment"; Alfred Cobban, *In Search of Humanity: The Role of the Enlightenment in Modern History* (London, 1960), p. 7: "The term 'Enlightenment' is hardly naturalized in English. This is curious, because the intellectual and moral revolution which it describes perhaps obtained its most widespread acceptance and exercised its most lasting influence in Great Britain and the English-speaking world"; Thomas J. Schlereth, *The Cosmopolitan Ideal in Enlightenment Thought* (Notre Dame, Ind., 1977), p. xv, speaks of "the traditional (and, I think, accurate) dates of the Enlightenment which begins with the English Glorious Revolution and ends with the outbreak of the French"; Crane Brinton, in the *Encyclopedia of Philosophy,* 8 vols. (New York, 1967), II, 523, s.v. "Enlightenment": "The English, with Bacon, Locke, Newton, and the early deists like Toland and Tindal, have some claim to being the originators, the adventurers in ideas which the French did no more than spread"; Ira O. Wade, *The Intellectual Origins of the French Enlightenment* (Princeton, 1971), p. 17: "The general view now held would be that the English influence is very important, especially upon France who introduced it throughout Europe. It is thought, however, that in doing this, France enhanced her own importance." Basil Willey, *The Eighteenth Century Background* (New York, 1941), p. 156, comes the closest of all: "Moreover, by the middle of the eighteenth century, after the passing of New-

ton, Locke, and the deists, it was no longer England but France which was conducting the main speculative attack. . . ." However, the remarks of all these authors are, I think, rather incidental and are tangential to the conception that there was, by itself, a distinct and complex English Enlightenment occurring most in the seventeenth century.

38. Henry Steele Commager, *The Empire of Reason: How Europe Imagined and America Realized the Enlightenment* (Garden City, N.Y., 1977), pp. 4, 242.

39. May, *The American Enlightenment,* p. 350.

40. Regarding Montesquieu, see Paul M. Spurlin, *Montesquieu in America, 1760-1801* (Baton Rouge: Louisiana State University Press, 1940), passim. For the incidence of French Enlightenment authors in colonial American libraries, see the tabulations in David Lundberg and Henry F. May, "The Enlightened Reader in America," *American Quarterly,* XXVIII (1976), following p. 271.

41. Paul M. Spurlin, *Rousseau in America, 1760-1809* (University: University of Alabama Press, 1969), pp. 101, 113, and passim.

42. Julian P. Boyd, ed., *The Papers of Thomas Jefferson* (Princeton, 1950-), IV, 168, 211; V, 15, 311; VI, 25. For the *Encyclopédie méthodique,* see ibid., VI, 258 [March or April 1783] and the numerous references indexed in *The Papers of Thomas Jefferson: Index, Volumes 7-12* (Princeton, 1958), and ibid., *Volumes 13-18* (Princeton, 1973), s.v. "Encyclopédie méthodique."

43. Corneille De Pauw, *Recherches philosophiques sur les Américains, ou Mémoires intéressants pour servir à l'histoire de l'espèce humain,* 2 vols., 2d ed. (Berlin, 1777), I, 259. Apparently Franklin himself told Jefferson of a dinner given by Franklin to the Abbé Raynal and a company of other Frenchmen and Americans: "The abbé set off on one of his usual oratorical tirades on the degeneration of men and animals in America. The host, good-humored as ever, suggested that the matter be tested empirically: 'Let us try this question by the fact before us.' He asked his guests to stand up, and it turned out that all the Americans were tall and well built, and all the French singularly tiny: the abbé himself was 'a mere shrimp' " (Antonello Gerbi, *The Dispute of the New World: The History of a Polemic, 1750-1900* [Pittsburgh: University of Pittsburgh Press, 1973], p. 242 and n. 3).

44. Details in Gerbi, *Dispute of the New World,* pp. 264-266; see also Brooke Hindle, *The Pursuit of Science in Revolutionary America, 1735-1789* (Chapel Hill, 1956), p. 322.

45. Bernard Bailyn, ed., *Pamphlets of the American Revolution, 1750-1776* (Cambridge, Mass., 1965), I, 209; for the whole sermon, see ibid., 212-247.

46. For these pamphlets, see Bailyn, *Pamphlets,* I, 419-482, 554-579, 608-658, 669-691. For American political writing from 1765 to 1776, see Clinton Rossiter, *Seedtime of the Republic* (New York, 1953), chap. xii, pp. 326-361.

47. For Trenchard and Gordon, see David L. Jacobson, ed., *The*

English Libertarian Heritage from the Writings of John Trenchard and Thomas Gordon in "The Independent Whig" and "Cato's Letters" (Indianapolis, 1965). Rossiter, *Seedtime of the Republic,* p. 141: "No one can spend any time in the newspapers, library inventories, and pamphlets of colonial America without realizing that *Cato's Letters* rather than Locke's *Civil Government* was the most popular, quotable, esteemed source of political ideas in the colonial period." See also Robbins, *The Eighteenth-Century Commonwealthman,* pp. 115-125; and May, *The Enlightenment in America,* pp. 38-39, 41, 156.

48. The slight influence of French ideas in America before 1776 is emphasized by May, "Problem of the American Enlightenment," p. 210; May, *The Enlightenment in America,* pp. 25, 41, 360; see also Donald H. Meyer, *The Democratic Enlightenment* (New York, 1976), pp. 104-105.

49. Edward Gibbon, *The Decline and Fall of the Roman Empire,* ed. Hugh R. Trevor-Roper (New York, 1963), p. xii.

50. Save for the English deists; see Margaret C. Jacob, "Newtonianism and the Origins of the Enlightenment: A Reassessment," *Eighteenth-Century Studies,* XI (1977-1978), 1-25.

51. See n. 37, above.

52. Edmund Burke, *Reflections on the Revolution in France* (Garden City, N.Y.: Doubleday & Co., Dolphin Book C246, 1961), p. 99.

53. John Robison, *Proofs of a Conspiracy Against All the Religions and Governments of Europe* (New York, 1798), p. 391. Robison's book was republished in paperback (Boston, 1967), under the auspices of the John Birch Society; this quotation, p. 297.

54. I cite the second edition: James Hutchison Stirling, *The Secret of Hegel* (Edinburg, 1898), p. xxxii.

II

CRAW v. *RAMSEY*:
NEW LIGHT ON AN OLD DEBATE

Arthur J. Slavin

1

My subject is the old debate over the nature of the Imperial Constitution before 1775. Few questions in English or American history have attracted the attention of a more distinguished lot of historians than the many Imperialists, Progressives and Neo-Whigs who have kept at the center of their concern related issues of constitutional doctrine, political unrest, and the ideology of rights and liberties.

Coke had anticipated the debate to which I want to draw attention without wandering too widely in the bogs of revisionist historiography, when he said the power of Parliament was so transcendent and absolute as to be unconfined either for causes or persons. Charles Howard McIlwain utterly rejected this doctrine because he found evidence against a legislative sovereignty of the British Parliament over the remote dominions. Robert Livingstone Schuyler firmly upheld the Imperialist thesis of H. L. Osgood: that in law, if not in fact, parliamentary authority over the English in America was as complete as ever it was in any place within England.[1]

The disputants levied contributions from British and American legal precedents, statute books, charters, treaties, and pamphlets, reaching back to the Anglo-Norman period and coming forward to the 1929 Statute of Westminster. McIlwain made much of Calvin's Case, a suit so familiar in textbooks and collections of documents that every English school child knew it. He gave as much space to *Craw* v. *Ramsey,* a suit as obscure as Calvin's Case was well-known. Why he should have done so I hope to show in the main part of my text. But first I should put before you a few commonplace sayings in constitutional and legal history, with some commentary.

The first of these is that in England there is much constitutional law but no constitution. The second is that English constitutional law lies in a province of its own, beyond private law and ordinary public law.

Private law is such that the state has no direct interest in its chief matters: the definition and regulation of torts, contracts, family agreements, and the descent of property. The state has direct concern for public law because that law defines and regulates the mutual obligations of government and subject or citizen, in taxation, military service, the power of arrest, and other delicate matters. One's standpoint determines how the rules are regarded, but even the rules of public law are usually distinguished from constitutional rules.[2]

Constitutional rules regulate the state itself and also its agencies. They arise in the need to settle disputes about structure, function, and relationship in government.[3] Among the problems dealt with are these: How many members make up the Commons? What powers lie in the sovereign's grasp? Who must yield in a dispute between cabinet and Parliament? Maitland spoke wisely therefore, when he said the heart of constitutional law and of constitutional history is the effort to make clear "structure and the broader rules which regulate function."[4]

Unfortunately, when we seek to apply the commonplace distinctions to the actual situation at a point in time, troubles appear. The more remote the point in time the more must we resort to private law to determine public, even constitutional, questions. In the absence of a code or written constitution, and given the meagerness of public law, the rules are obscure.

Consider for a moment rules regulating relations between Britain and the plantations in America toward the end of Charles II's reign. One finds few relevant statutes. A few cases dominate the sources.[5] The dicta of judges, some treaties and customs, and the observations of statesmen are merely useful secondary materials.[6] They cannot command our attention, which turns to *Godfrey* v. *Dixon,*[7] Calvin's Case[8] and *Craw* v. *Ramsey.*[9] Statute did not define "alien" and "subject" with the precision Magna Carta used to require kings to hold pleas in a fixed place.[10] We look to Calvin's Case to know the rules determining the most fundamental relationship between James I's English and Scottish subjects. Because he was unable to get from the Commons all he wanted for his Scottish adherents who came southward with him, James promoted a collusive suit to determine the rights of the *postnati.*[11]

McIlwain fully grasped that great questions had their resolution in petty cases, when the issue in hand was whether a parliament at Westminster had legislative powers in George III's overseas dominions. Nowhere else could he find fundamental notions defined: alien, subject, domicile, nationality. Where the ideas were defined, they were embedded in the language and vocabulary of feudalism. The concept of allegiance governed the others,[12] and understanding allegiance required a journey into the darkest thickets of feudalism, into a veritable *selva oscura,* where the praise of one's colleagues gave immediate courage but little enduring help.[13]

Yet McIlwain was certainly right to follow the path leading from Calvin's Case to *Craw* v. *Ramsey* and to set the one beside the other in his canon of cases. Now, I must say why, in the hope of convincing you to apply to the obscure case what Coke said of the celebrated one: "The least for the value . . . but the weightiest for the consequents."[14]

2

In Calvin's Case the judges in Exchequer Chamber reached this question: is the son of a Scot born in Scotland after the accession of James I to the English throne an alien to England?[15] The Commissioners appointed to draw up an Instrument of Union in Parliament (1606) had distinguished between the *postnati* and *antenati.* They proposed to deal with the antenati by a statute of naturalization. But they intended to seek a declaration that the postnati were in fact naturalized under the common law.[16]

To this there was great opposition in the Commons. Consider that Philip and Mary had left a son who became king of Spain and of England. Were his Spanish subjects in the same case? If yes, how far could they claim the rights of Englishmen? To the point of inheriting lands? Of holding office or a seat in the Commons? Of making a majority to overthrow the Reformation? Say what the lawyers might, the Commons would never say yes to such things.[17] Hence, the resort to Calvin's Case, in which a mere boy postnatus claimed the right to some land in Shoreditch, in an action of novel disseisin against two English brothers.

A dozen judges, among them Coke, Bacon, and Ellesmere, spread their learning at large on every page of Coke's vast report, in giving judgment for the boy and hence for all postnati.[18] There were only two dissenting voices. What the majority found was that the protection of the English law followed from allegiance, which was the obedience a subject owed to his sovereign. This flowed from a subject to the natural capacity of the lord and was the residue of personal homage and liege loyalty which had been at the heart of the feudal idea of dominion. Those who gave allegiance were of two sorts: born and made (*natus et datus*). But they owed it equally and benefited from it without regard to territorial divisions. For allegiance was univocal. Hence no person born in any territory of a sovereign lord after the assumption of that sovereignty could be an alien in any part of that lord's dominions. The laws of the several dominions remained separate. So might their legislatures. But allegiance was owed to none of these, only to the king.[19]

This decision left unclarified the status of the antenati. They had been excluded from the collusive suits, perhaps because even James I could not think they had a case at common law. The king had mercilessly harangued the Commons, however, expressing his deep frustration over the treatment of his fellow Scots who had come southward with him. He had even gone so far as to say he could fully naturalize by prerogative instruments, because *rex est lex*,[20] a point Coke had refuted amply, but only in an *obiter dictum*. The issue had not been reached in Calvin's Case, but Sir Edward took the occasion to fully develop his theory of limitations on the rights conveyable by patent. What the king could do was to make an alien a denizen.[21]

Denizens by patent did differ from naturalized aliens who had the benefit of statute. The former could gain, hold, and transmit property to any heir born after the grant. They lacked all rights in public law. Moreover, the restorative effects of the grant lacked retroactivity; issue born before the grant were excluded from inheritance for the good reason that they could make no pedigree to one then at law an alien. There remained an impediment in their "legal blood." They were in the same case as the antenati excluded from the rule of decision in Calvin's Case.[22] Of that none could have doubt, although there could now be great doubt as to how far the effects of naturalization by statute would carry.[23]

The cloud over the picture of Union led McIlwain straight to *Craw v. Ramsey.*[24] But he knew nothing of the earlier cases of *Foster v. Ramsey*[25] or *Collingwood v. Pace.*[26] Hence he misunderstood the significance of the latter case.[27] I think he did so for another reason: because he had resort to it as a proof-text for his ideas about the imperial connection in the 1770s, in much the same way that James Otis, James Wilson, and John Adams used Calvin's Case to claim independence from the control of Parliament.[28] This together with his ignorance of the full range of *Reports* on *Craw v. Ramsey* gave McIlwain a very poor understanding of the issues and the decision.[29]

3

The following chart shows well enough the line of Robert Ramsey I.[30] He was a Scot antenatus born long before 1603. He sired four antenati sons, in this order: Robert II, Nicholas, John, and George. Robert II's three daughters were Scots by birth. The two sons of Nicholas were native Englishmen, however, as was John Ramsey II, the son of George.[31] You must keep this in mind about Patrick and John II.

John I had been a close follower of James VI in Scotland. He had been knighted there, before being raised to the peerage in England as Viscount Haddington in 1606 and then being further promoted to be Earl of Holderness in 1621. As Sir John had grown richer, amassing much land and other wealth, he had also been naturalized by a private bill enacted at Westminster in 1604.[32] The like favor had been shown to George in 1610, well before the

THE DESCENDANTS OF ROBERT RAMSEY, SCOT

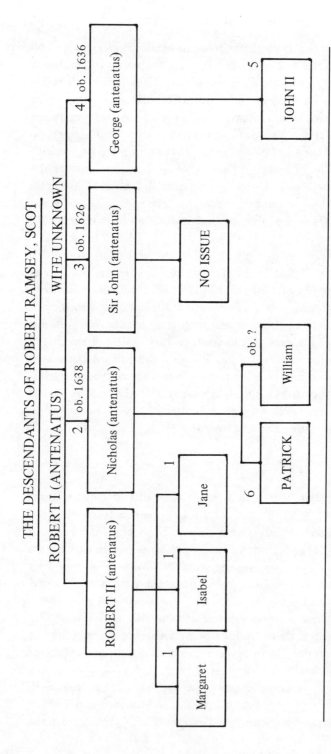

1. Daughters antenatas alive in 1632, 1656, and having living issue born in England who were alive in 1665.
2. Naturalized by statute in Ireland in 1634.
3. Viscount Haddington (1606); Earl of Holderness (1621); naturalized by statute in England in 1604.
4. Naturalized in England in 1610.
5. Born in England ca. 1618, *after* the naturalization of his father.
6. Born in England *before* the naturalization of his father by the Irish Parliament.

birth of his son John II.[33] Thus, when Sir John died in 1626,[34] he was survived by two brothers, Nicholas, an alien, and George, a naturalized Englishman. There were also these survivors: three nieces antenatas[35] and two nephews; Patrick, the son of an alien, and John, the natural born son of a naturalized alien.[36] The date of William's death is unknown, but he never appears as a party after 1626.

The Earl drew a will about 1609, in the light of bad counsel or else in personal ignorance about the effects of Calvin's Case. For in it he devised to Nicholas and his heirs the rectory church of Kingston-on-Thames in Surrey, with many appurtenances. The condition of this bequest was that Nicholas serve faithfully as executor of the will, paying the listed debts and attending to the other terms.[37]

From an office of escheat held in 1632 we know that Sir John had died seised of the church in fee, holding of Charles I in the socage tenure of East Greenwich.[38] He had made an indenture tripartite while he was yet alive, assuring the use of the rectory to himself, with a remainder to his recently acquired wife Martha. She had apparently entered on his death, shortly before marrying Lord Willoughby.[39] It was also found by inquest that Sir John had died without any heir (*obit sine haerede*) whatsoever as well as without issue.

This deserves some attention. It could only be so if the panel had found a bar against Nicholas and George and their own English-born sons. For Nicholas and George were both alive at Sir John's death: the older brother died 31 May 1638, almost two years after George, who died on 10 July 1636.[40] Yet there was a clear statement that they were no heirs to Sir John. The consequence should follow: an escheat. And it did. King Charles took the rectory back into his hands, at least on paper, granting it to his boyhood friend Will Murray on 25 October 1634.[41] The rectory was soon conveyed by Murray in a peculiar way to the Earl of Elgin and Sir Edward Sydnam, by a combination of grantors, including Patrick Ramsey, the dowager Countess, and Lord Willoughby.[42] Many years later, in 1651, there was another conveyance by Patrick and Elizabeth Ramsey to the same grantees.[43]

What thoughts were at the bottom of the office found? And what were the consequences?

First, as to the escheat: It must have been found that Nicholas was an alien and thus incapable of being Sir John's heir. The rule was that there was no heritability where there was no line of descent.[44] This excluded Patrick as well. George must have been barred on the dictum of Coke, that naturalized brothers could not inherit to each other, having no heritable blood between them.[45] Hence John II could be no heir either, by the first rule. Martha's claim to a life remainder was preempted, by one of two possible findings: the precedence of her husband's will over the tripartite indenture; or some imperfection in her alleged entry. Remainders not immediately entered were void at law.[46] In any event, her death on 6 June 1641 removed her from our view.[47]

On the above line of argument, any title later derived from Murray by way of the escheat would be good in law. He was stated to be the conveyor to the Earl of Elgin and Sydnam who may well have been surrogates for the intended heir, Patrick Ramsey. Sir John had been a close friend of King Charles and the saver of the life of James I at Gowrie in 1600. Once the finding was made that Nicholas was no heir, the King perhaps arranged the grant to Murray on the understanding Patrick Ramsey would benefit from it. It is certain that Patrick joined in the first lease and bargain of sale to Elgin and in the second as well. He had ample motive for collusion, because by the will he was to have had £100 p.a. for his maintenance out of the profits of Kingston, with the reversion of the whole estate upon his father's death.[48]

Cousin John was the man in the cold. Patrick might get £1100 from the deal with Elgin,[49] but John had nothing. Yet he considered himself to be inheritable to Sir John as the English son of a naturalized alien. At least he acted on that belief, entering the rectory manor on 30 June 1642 (perhaps so late because he respected Aunt Martha's life interest).[50] And on a special verdict given long afterward he was seised *prout lex postulat*. He could ill afford to rest content, however. For there was a host of third parties ready to claim what John II enjoyed, by way of the Murray patent, and thus to raise again the prickly questions of the will and naturalization. The supreme matter in society was not why was there property, but who should have it.[51]

4

My hypothesis of collusion finds indirect support in *Foster* v. *Ramsey*. There, it is said that Patrick had entered the rectory sometime after the death of Nicholas and George. John had ousted him and been ousted in turn. Patrick then leased to a third party while John leased to Foster. The issue joined was which lessor had the title to give?[52]

Counsel for the plaintiff (Foster-J. Ramsey) argued along three lines. He cited the large words of the naturalization acts: they were "to be held as natural born subjects for all purposes and hence able to make their resorts to any ancestors." Precedents were liberally cited.[53] There was also a common law argument against Patrick's claim through Nicholas: "the son of an alien cannot be heir to any."[54] And there was a technical argument: that the devise to Patrick was void in any event because of an incapacity in the taker. The will had carelessly left out any specific reference to Patrick, speaking only of the heir of Nicholas as the taker. This was an impossibility: no man can have an heir while he is yet in life.[55]

The great Finch argued valiantly for the defense, especially against the strong technical point. He tried to show precedent for allowing an "heir by expectation" in instruments naming executory operants.[56] But the judges finally decided unanimously for Foster, after several adjournments, on the narrowest ground.[57] They avoided the naturalization issue entirely, being content to make a precedent in cases where the person to take as heir might be the issue.[58]

At about the same time as *Foster* v. *Ramsey* was filed (Trin. 1656), John Ramsey made a lease in favor of Gawen Collingwood. The date was 20 July 1656, but there was a clause making the operation retroactive to 1 June. It was to be for seven years. Collingwood was ejected by one Perses Pace after a period of time as occupant not stated. Pace said he acted on the express command of his master the Earl of Elgin.[59] His claim was that he held a valid lease by virtue of the Murray grant.[60]

The justices in Common Pleas quickly agreed on the matters settled in *Foster* v. *Ramsey*. But they split evenly on the great matter avoided in the other case: naturalization. Had Collingwood any title at all? This was to ask whether the act of naturalization for George Ramsey had made John II an heir to Sir John Ramsey. If not, however tainted Patrick might be because of his own alien father, Pace might be a lawful claimant. This amounted to asking whether John II rightfully stood between Murray and the land because the escheat had been unlawful. CJ

Bridgeman and J Tyrell thought the brothers could not inherit one another. Hyde and Brown JJ took the opposite view.[61] All grasped that they had before them a "great case," as Sir Creswell Levinz called it.[62] It touched the king's prerogative. It touched the effects of statutes. And it touched imperial matters beyond the realm.

The case was therefore adjourned from Common Pleas into Exchequer Chamber, where a hearing began in Hilary Term 1662 and was concluded in Easter Term 1664. Numerous reports of the pleadings and arguments survive.[63] And we also have the verdict given in Common Pleas early in 1665.[64] These things deserve attention because the judges refused to be diverted by considerations raised in still other collusive actions,[65] perhaps in the vain hope of settling things finally. In fact they merely opened a new window on the problems.

How so? The answer depends on what was said in Exchequer Chamber. Bridgeman, Tyrell, and Keeling held to the opinion of Bridgeman and Tyrell in Common Pleas, that Sir John and George had no inheritable blood from their father and were in law in a situation parallel to that of the sons of a father who had been attainted before their own births.[66] Against them there was a formidable array: CJ Hyde of the King's Bench, with his brothers Wyndham and Twysden; Brown of Common Pleas; Chief Baron Hales of the Exchequer and his brothers Turner and Atkins, barons there. These seven held the Ramsey brothers to be inheritable one to the other by virtue of naturalization.[67]

This was the argument of the majority. If an alien had two sons born in England, the law made them inheritable to each other but not to their father. Their natural birth overcame the defect in the father and made an "immediate descent" between them. This could be seen from the many cases in which brothers took from brothers by *morte d'ancestor,* without ever breathing a syllable of the father's name. The words of the acts enabled them to inherit to any ancestor "lineal or collateral as if they had been born in England." The seven went against Coke on Littleton 8a, saving Sir Edward's standing by noting how he had spoken in that place, not on his own reading but only saying "some have said." What? That two brothers born in England of an alien father could not inherit to each other but only to their own lines. By this, were it a rule and not merely a saying, the words of the acts were in vain where they said Sir John and George "shall be inheritable to any ancestor" lineal or collateral. If the limitation held, as the three judges argued it should, the brothers in this case could have no ancestors at all in England.[68]

The differing opinions among the judges expose to view an interesting issue of constitutional law and history. Three judges denied that the plain language of a statute had any effects whatsoever. This severely limited the powers of Parliament while elevating a claim to land derived only from an escheat and patent, twin motions of the royal will. That this was so we know from Hales's argument. He frankly asserted the contrary. Parliament had by its power altogether erased any impediment traceable to Sir John or George from their father as well as all incapacities in themselves. Other authorities were of no consequence against an act of Parliament. Naturalization by statute is a much more deep and intricate thing than by patent of denization. It meant that no man or opinion "shall be received against an act of Parliament to say the contrary." This Hales said after reading the statute entirely to the Court.[69] Yes, we must always reverence the dicta of Coke, but all his sayings together do not make a rule of law. *Frater et frater sunt in primo gradu:* that is the law, civil, canon, and English, Hales said.[70]

He then urged his brothers of the several benches to regard Calvin's Case and so make a gentle interpretation in the present one, otherwise they would disturb some noble and many armigerous families of Scottish extract who now enjoy estates in peace in both England *and Ireland.*[71] Serjeant Archer seconded him, saying it would be contrary to the "public faith of the nation" to do otherwise.[72]

What exactly had they in mind? The clue lies in Finch for the defense. He noted that by an Irish statute all Scots antenati in Scotland had been naturalized in Ireland "which doth not extend to England." Yet on the case for the plaintiff, Finch asked, why might natural birth in either kingdom not give capacity in the other? Surely the rights of those natural-born subjects of King Charles I must have been as large, if not larger, than those of the naturalized ones. How can the words as found in the present acts be consistent with a denial of the effects of the Irish statute?[73] If it is argued, as Serjeant Witherington did indeed argue for the plaintiffs, that Sir John and George had for their "civil blood the benefit of the same parent the Parliament at Westminster,"[74] and that Parliament "may enact that the brothers could be heir to a remote stranger,"[75] then how were Englishmen to be safeguarded from the effects of the Irish naturalization of the Scots?

Wyndham might say bravely that those for the defense should neither enlarge incapacities on Coke or bring in Ireland to challenge the powers of the English Parliament.[76] But Brown, in giving his own opinion for the plaintiff, had clearly seen the danger raised by Finch. "There is a danger to our island, in that strength will follow possession."[77] For that cause Edward III had taken the Alien Priories.[78] It might then be argued that Charles I's escheat in the present case was *pro bono publico*. But this was a wrong turn. How was an Englishman's property to be preserved, if the King could by escheat overcome any "weak title whatsoever?"[79] This sparked Tyrell to retort: an absolute power in Parliament is not better than an unfettered prerogative.[80]

But it was Bridgeman[81] who had the privilege of the last word in a case adjourned from his own court. He used the chance brilliantly.

His style was systematic, in the manner of the best commentators of the age of Coke. He laid out the *nomina*: descent, alienship, and naturalization, taking each in turn, both to make rebuttals of the other arguments and also to weave a web of his own making. The question was simplicity itself: whether John II could be styled heir? If no, for want of an heir the escheat had been rightly taken. The point of the case was whether there was any difference in law between the sons of an alien who were born in England and the two sons of the same alien who were aliens by birth but had a "civil birth here by naturalization?"[82]

His brothers were in error to so lightly overthrow Coke. They were likewise in error to suppose their definition of immediate descent settled anything. He believed descent between brothers could only be *mediante patre*. Hence this was itself the matter *ad probandum,* on which unsure foundation no superstructure could be raised.[83] The law of descent requires the absence of impediment not only in those *ad quem* but also in those *a quo*. In a donation it is equally essential that the donor be able to give as the recipient to receive. There had been large words used about the acts of 1604 and 1610, saying these had removed all incapacities, etc. But there is not one word of the father in the acts. How then could it be supposed that Robert Ramsey could transmit a right to make a pedigree for making a descent and taking lands in England?[84] He died an alien.

Foreigners who became denizens or naturalized subjects, Frenchmen for example, did not thereby cease to be *ad fidem regis Franciae*. Even those for Collingwood agreed that alienship and allegiance were in some sense ineradicable. Is faith a perishable thing? Or the pledge of liege homage? Or does it have the character of an indelible mark?[85] If yes, then prudence and caution must govern in the construction of the present acts, indeed all acts of naturalization. It is certain that an escheat was made after an office found that Sir John lacked an heir (*quia obiit sine haerede*). If we overturn that finding, we will make new law touching the prerogative. Yet we can make no demonstrations a priori in this case, because we disagree about first principles. Thus we have resort only to shadowy past adjudications, analogies, and even similitudes.[86]

Therefore, consider the case of a bastard son. His father dies. The son inherits but then dies without issue. Does the natural mother take? No. Why? She is outside the family and stock of the father and has an impediment for which there is no restoration. She lacks legal blood. The son is thus "the commencement of his family and stock."[87] How does this differ from an alien made a denizen by patent? For in patents the words are "he shall be, and so shall his heritors be, as lieges or as Englishmen born." The denizen's sons shall inherit from him. But a brother English born does not by our law do so. Why? Because the aliens cannot inherit from their own father even after they are naturalized. Yet who is he but the *commune vinculum,* the one bridge or link, between brother and brother? The operative words of the present acts do not differ in any material way from the words in the patent of denizenship (exhibiting them to all). If in no sense are they different, how can the effects of the one be larger than those of the other?[88]

Bridgeman answered his own question. It must be that those who favor the plaintiff see in Parliament some hidden power to make things mean what is not said. This would be an absolute power indeed, a power unlimited, greater than any prerogative operating by the mere express word of patent. He then became cautious. "I mean to be observed. I do not deny there is more power able to be given by the Act than by letters patent. . . . But I

say that in this case there is no more power given by the words."
Even acts of Parliament take their effects only from what the
words actually signify.[89] And the words before us signify only
what is signified in denizenship by patent. The greater power in
statute is *the potential* to do things patents may never do. But we
are not to construct words or effects where they are lacking. And
here is no word making the father an ancestor or bridge to the
two brothers. As in the considering of wills we construe them as
judges but make none, so in statutes we must strictly construe
them but not enlarge them beyond what they are by their own
clear words. "If the acts had made the uncle the heir to the nephews expressly, I would say it is so."[90]

Bridgeman then turned more directly to the Acts. In bills of
general effect the assent is "*Le Roi se voet.*" In bills for private
persons, the assent expresses the desire or suggestion of such parties: "*Soit fait come il est desire.*" These are not so much acts of
the Parliament as they are grand charters, acts of grace barring
all other persons from denying the thing expressly conceded.[91]
The words do not signify more than by charter under the Great
Seal because it was never thought that they should so do, or could
so do. "The words carry no significance or sense in such a charter
in Parliament than they could by charter out of Parliament."
Otherwise, a private act could upset the public consequences of
past public acts, for example in escheats and regrants made in
good faith and in good law.[92]

Without mention of the parliamentary history lying behind
Calvin's Case, Bridgeman had set the stage for his argument
about the inconveniences certain to attend on a liberal construction of acts of naturalization. Admit the powers claimed now,
and what dangers ensued. Enemies would discover the secrets of
the realm. Our revenues would be taken and enjoyed by strang-
ers. Things would tend to the destruction of the kingdom, when
aliens were admitted to the heart of the realm. They would
remain *ad fidem* elsewhere but be empowered to do all here. This
is the core of Coke's argument in Calvin's Case, what that great
jurist called the Trojan Horse.[93] It would not always be the case
that the beneficiaries of the acts would be friends to England,
bound to the same sovereign. This consideration had moved the
Romans to distinguish carefully the benefits to be conferred by
naturalization: *jus domicilii, jus honoris, jus civitatis.* "England

must do no less, else it will soon be a question whether a man be not so [able to enjoy the rights of Englishmen] if he be naturalized in Scotland or Ireland."[94] Regard the French and others who use the law of nations. Why else have we made the distinction between those made naturalized by patent and natural born Englishmen? Why else do we levy subsidies on those native born at 2s. 8d in the Pound and 5s. 4d on aliens?[95] Had this not been the case, why did the Irish Parliament resort to a general statute to "encourage the Scots to plant in Ulster by naturalizing all the antenati together?"[96]

In closing, Bridgeman put before his colleagues one final consideration:

I shall conclude this great point with one argument more, which I confess hath some force with me, tho' perhaps not with others. This case concerns the King of the one side in a great prerogative, touching escheats in cases of aliens denized and naturalized, dying without issue. The office of escheator was hitherto considerable, and the revenue of escheats being the principal of his office, reckoned a great branch of the revenue. Escheats, save only in respect of aliens, were very rare and inconsiderable. To hold up the rights and prerogatives of the King in point of Revenue (whatever opinions are taken up) I have always held is the great interest of the People, who are necessitated, on their own safety, to supply what the King's Revenue falls short of to answer the public charge. And, therefore, those rights which concern the King and People in general are to be preferred before the interests of particular subjects.[97]

He continued:

In cases of public concernement, and not formerly resolved, but doubtful, we ought to interpret and declare the law, so as is most in favor of the King *et pro bono publico*.... And it is part of our oath as Judges, according to the Statute of 18 Edward III, that we shall do and procure the profit of the King and of his Crown, in all things, where we may reasonably do the same.[98]

5

The Chief Justice did not move the seven who had spoken before. But some present had carefully listened, with particular interest in the references he had made to the Irish Act of Naturalization passed at Dublin Castle on 4 July 1634. Could it be that its effects could work against both the escheat and the decisions now given, which had the power to deny forever to Patrick Ramsey the consequences of Sir John's will?

It was worth the effort, for those who had spent so much in seeking to drive John Ramsey out of the estates he had occupied in 1642. Calvin's Case and *Collingwood* v. *Pace* had laid down the resotrative effects of naturalization and had established the wholly personal nature of allegiance as well as its immunity to boundaries. Therefore, when Philip Craw, the lessor of Sir Lionel Tolmach,[99] and Humphrey Weld filed an action of trespass and ejectment in 1665, it was possible for Patrick Ramsey to hope the court might now validate his claims. Never mind that the defendant John Ramsey had the best of the jury findings of facts: that Craw had never been seised and had never entered. The earl's agent did show a form of lease from Elgin,[100] and the claim was John Ramsey[101] was a usurper.[102] This allowed the Court to reach the new question: did Patrick Ramsey become an heir in law by the Irish Act?[103]

Let me quickly sketch the case on the main points only, repeating some things you already know. Nicholas Ramsey had been alive on 4 July 1634. The Irish Act had made Charles I's Scottish subjects who were also antenati "to be reputed natural subjects to all intents in Ireland." Did the rights thus created adhere to the Scots in England?[104]

Justices Wylde and Archer quickly pointed out that the Act could do Patrick no good in any case. Like Craw, he had never entered or been seised. He had no standing in court on ejectment. If the effects of the case did extend to England (to make heirs there), then all others must yield to the antenatas, the three daughters of Robert Ramsey II, the first persons in the collateral line.[105] They were found to have been in life on 4 July 1634 and to either be alive in the time of hearing or to have living children. Justices Tyrell and Vaughan (CJ) differed on both points. They were willing to say Patrick intended to enter, and the jury had left that question to the court to find. Moreover, it had never been found that Robert II had been alive at the making of the act. He had not been restored therefore, and the daughters could make no pedigree to him for purposes of inheritance.[106]

Neither point was essential, however. In the chief matter, the extension of the effects of the act to England, Tyrell alone held for the plaintiff. He argued that acts of naturalization by the Irish parliament could not be limited in their scope of effect to any single locale under the sovereignty of Charles I. Calvin's Case had declared allegiance to be personal and not adherent to the "politick person" of the King, or what some called the Crown. *Collingwood v. Pace,* in which he had been in dissent, had shown how large the authority of parliamentary acts must be taken to be. Ireland had a "high Court of Parliament" like that in England. It could naturalize the Scots there, making them one with natural-born Irishmen. Further, because Irish laws received royal assent in England by Poyning's Law, the Irish being under the dominion of England and English laws, it must be thought that the law of England "cooperating with the Act" gave the naturalization effect here as well.

Tyrell further buttressed this breathtaking argument. It was the case that an Irish act of attainder against any lands there caused also the forfeiture of any lands held in England. This followed from the unique character of allegiance. It was also true that a repealer there was restorative here. How could it then be denied that the removal of a like impediment there, alienship, should not have the same effect here, by the rule of parallel reason? One could not very well say the acts of the Irish at Dublin Castle had power but contrary to nature lacked effects or the consequences of that power. Moreover, if any would say: thus an Irish act bound the English; he would answer, not at all. Their act was but *causa remota,* the *sine qua non*; it was the Law of England which set up the Irish Parliament that is the *causa proxima,* the effectual doer, or efficient cause.[107]

The other three judges dissented vigorously in a series of arguments rich in history, recitations of statutes, citing of adjudicated cases, obiter dicta and philosophic speculation. Their immense concern and even greater learning is palpable on nearly every page.[108]

Vaughan argued at length to show the Irish were a conquered nation dependent on England. English writs ran there. English statutes controlled the legislature there. Errors made there were rectified in English courts. It was a subordinate kingdom. It was also against nature to argue that the inferior influenced the superior. Suppose a bill of naturalization were brought in here and rejected, as had been done in James I's time. Afterward, it passed

in Ireland. Should it then have the same effect here? Then, "what
needed the endeavors of King James' Reign to obtain an Act for
the naturalization of all Scots and the Union of the Kingdoms?"
An act could have been procured there with greater facility. On
Tyrell's brief, Vaughan asked, how could the Irish be prevented
from enacting the alienation of any of the King's other dominions? Or the transfer of itself "from the Sovereignty of England?"
It was no good to say assent would not be given; history was rich
in treacherous deeds.

Obviously, such an Act would be void and of no effect in
England. "For their power is merely precarious as to the Parliament of England." Finally, it was true in law the *ligeantia data*
can extend no further than the power of them that gave it.[109]
Otherwise it would not be the case that we are restricted from dis-
solving the bonds of allegiance between King Louis and his subjects, etc.

In effect, Vaughan had argued, the Irish Parliament was subordinate to English rule, as indeed Ireland was under the power
of Parliament. It had its own laws and its own legislature, but
what these could effect derived from the conditions of conquest
and the subsequent legislation restricting the independence of
that kingdom. He had also argued that parliaments can make
civil things at large but not natural things, allegiance for example. Natural things were "not within their powers." It must be
obvious, "for no act of a parliament can make a man a woman,
or a man to be born in any other place than where he was really
born." A natural subject is the correlative to a natural prince.
Hence the antenati are not to be put in the same case with the
postnati. They were first the naturally born lieges of another
prince; and as such "they might have been an enemey to us." But
no Englishman can be an enemy to us, only a traitor.

Vaughan had argued that the point was a "great point of State
interest," as all must know who knew the limitations placed on
what the king himself may do by charter.[110] Wylde and Archer
added chiefly technical arguments to those made by Vaughan.
The most important of these was to point out that the Irish Act
itself could have no effect in the present case, whatever the decision might be on the "great point." It stated specifically that it
was to be of no effect in any case where any land was presently
held by escheat.

Thus the judges split evenly on two minor points, but there was a strong majority on the issue actually joined. The Irish Act was of no consequence in England. Judgment was for the defendant.[111]

6

McIlwain's great interest in *Craw* v. *Ramsey* sprang from his view of the importance of the relations between Ireland and Stuart England to the justice of the American claim to be independent of Parliament one hundred years later. He believed he could show from cases the "validity of the constitutional claim"[112] for Irish independence of Parliament and their subjection only to the king of England. He had in fact somewhat misconstrued Calvin's Case, or at least Coke's *Report* of it, in thinking that Ireland was, in the view of the Stuart judges, subordinate only to its own laws and parliament but dependent on the king.[113] He had studied the tracts of Darcy and Molyneux in that light.[114]

He therefore saw in our case so much grist for his mill. Under the influence of his ideological preference to buttress the case made by the colonial rebels after 1773,[115] McIlwain completely misread Vaughan's brief. It was in fact a refutation of Tyrell on the main point, but McIlwain saw in it a second voice for the plaintiff.[116] Thus he misrepresented the decision in the case, snatching quotations out of context, getting the facts wrong, misplacing the arguments and otherwise doing violence to the record. He did so because he ignored the whole of the legal literature on the case, except for Vaughan's rather poorly printed brief[117] which had been worked up from notes by Vaughan's son after the judge's death.[118] His concourse of errors led him to suppose the antenati had been left out of Calvin's Case for political reasons only.[119] We have seen there were good legal causes for this omission in the common law.[120] It also led him to think his federal theory of empire had great support in the present case,[121] because he misunderstood the points on which the Court was divided. The "Irish" theory of imperial relations[122] had in fact been rejected by the Court and supplied no comfort whatever to McIlwain's thesis, despite his statement to the contrary: that *Craw* v. *Ramsey* made a "concession of considerable significance for our purpose."[123]

The significance of *Craw* v. *Ramsey* for constitutional history and law (and in political history) cannot be grasped apart from the study of the whole string of cases, beginning with *Foster* v. *Ramsey*.

These cases are important because they expose to view early in the Restoration the still-vivid struggle in law and politics about the powers of the prerogative and the powers of parliaments. The cases also make a chapter in the largely unwritten history of the use of statutes as instruments of grace.

These cases show how little had been done to clarify the meanings of ideas at the bottom of modern notions of the state, even as late as 1665. They reveal the still-dominant force of feudal ideas[124] and thus raise the flag of caution against those who, with McIlwain, suppose that by 1500, or even by 1700, "the whole structure of the English national state had developed at the expense of Feudalism,"[125] or that "the King had become really *Rex* rather than feudal *dominus.*"[126]

Finally, *Collingwood* v. *Pace,* like *Craw* v. *Ramsey* and even *Foster* v. *Ramsey,* became an important part of the constitutional law of the state and of the empire; but not in the sense alleged by McIlwain. The cases helped to make the fundamental distinction between aliens and subjects, without which there could be no useful modern notion of either the state or the nation.

We need only turn to a number of other, later, landmark cases to see how important our cases have been. For they were always set out with Calvin's Case as the determining precedents. I wish we had the space to fully explore *De Geer* v. *Stone,*[127] *Isaacson* v. *Durant,* [128] and *Rex* v. *Markwald.*[129] But we do not.

Hence I must leave them to another place, while being content here to have pointed out how dangerous it is to argue about the imperial constitution without a very careful study of difficult and scattered sources. Our cases give no comfort whatsoever to the idea that Parliament lacked fundamental powers over the plantations under the dominion of the king of England. That authority ran down through the decade of the American Revolution itself, and when it was ended, the issues involved were decided in great cases about the rights of Englishmen in America who had thrown off their allegiance to George III and Parliament together: for example, could they still take property in England by inheritance?[130]

NOTES

1. Osgood may be said to have started the modern debate in his "The American Revolution," *Pol Sci Q,* XIII (1898), 41-59; see also his *The American Colonies in the Seventeenth Century,* 3 vols. (New York, 1904-1907), III, 9. McIlwain's argument in *The American Revolution: A Constitutional Interpretation* (New York, 1923) was anticipated by R. W. Adams, *Political Ideas of the American Revolution* (Durham, N.C., 1922). But it was McIlwain who condemned the Imperialist school, with their "unhistorical and unconstitutional British doctrine" of Westminster's legislative sovereignty over "the autonomous dominions." Charles Andrews made a rejoinder in "The American Revolution: An Intepretation," *Am Hist Rev,* XXXI (1925-1926), 219-232, but the most detailed rebuttal came from Schuyler's pen in *Parliament and the British Empire* (New York, 1929) and also from Arthur B. Keith, *Constitutional History of the First British Empire* (London, 1930).

McIlwain never abandoned the position he took in 1923 despite the all but universal agreement among historians, that Schuyler had done great damage in the attack first made in "The Britannic Question and the American Revolution," *Pol Sci Q,* XXXVIII (1923), 104-114. For McIlwain's defense and reiteration see his AHA Presidential Address, "The Historian's Part in a Changing World," and also "Whig Sovereignty and Real Sovereignty," pp. 5-25 and 61-85 in *Constitutionalism and the Changing World: Collected Papers by C. H. McIlwain* (Cambridge, Mass., 1939); see also his contribution to the symposium edited by Roscoe Pound, *Federalism as a Democratic Process* (Rutgers, 1942), pp. 31-48: "Some Sources of our American Federalism." McIlwain there sets out his "federal theory" of early relations between Crown and Dominions, against the "unitary theory" of the Osgood-Andrews-Keith school.

The most thorough consideration of the vast literature down to about 1965 is in the third part of volume XIII of Lawrence H. Gipson's *The British Empire Before the American Revolution* (New York, 1968), in "Historiography." For more recent bibliographic surveys, historiographical essays, and other important works, see the numerous entries in John Shy, *The American Revolution* (Northbrook, Ill., 1973), a volume in the Goldentree Bibliography series of American History, particularly under the entries for Edmund P. Morgan, Bernard Knollenberg, Jack Greene, Merrill Jensen, W. F. Craven, Bernard Bailyn, John Alden, Richard B. Morris, and Robin Winks.

2. E. W. Ridges and G. A. Forrest, *Constitutional Law* (London, 1950), chap. 1; also Thomas Ernst and H. H. L. Bellot, *Leading Cases in Constitutional Law,* 8th ed. (London, 1927), chaps. 1 and 2; F. W. Maitland, *Constitutional History of England* (Cambridge, 1908), pp. 526-539, for an effective criticism of the views of Austin and Holland.

3. Ridges and Forrest, *Constitutional Law,* pp. 2-4.

4. *Ibid.,* p. 535, criticizing the sharp distinction made by Holland (cf. *Jurisprudence,* pp. 359 ff.) between constitutional and administrative law.

5. Sir William Anson, *The Law and Custom of the Constitution:* Part II, *The Crown* (Oxford, 1892), II, vi.

6. E. S. Corwin, "The Higher Law Background of American Constitutional Law," *Harvard Law Review,* XLII (1929), 365-409.

7. More properly called *Godfrey and Dixon's Case* (16 Jac. I, King's Bench rol. 374), in which an alien born in Flanders had a son naturalized by Parliament, the son claiming thereby the rights of Englishmen to inherit in England.

8. *4 Rep. 1; 2 State Trials* 559; and *English Reports,* KB VI, 77, pp. 378-410, for the great case reported by Coke in 7 Co. Rep. fols 1b-28a.

9. 1 K. B. 617; 87 L. J. K. B. 620; see also *Markwald* vs. *Attorney General* (1920) 1 Ch. 348; 89 L. J. Ch. 225. For the importance of this case see n. 129 below.

10. Article 17.

11. James I desired that the union of the two crowns should completely naturalize the subjects in England and Scotland. The Commons balked at this, and two collusive actions arose in behalf of Robert Calvin, a postnatus of Scotland. It was claimed in King's Bench that Calvin was able to inherit certain freehold lands in England. In Chancery the suit was for the title deeds to the estate. The defendant pleaded in abatement that Calvin was an alien, arguing thereby that all other questions were "out of the case." When plaintiff demurred, the case was heard in Exchequer Chamber (see note 15) by the Lord Chancellor and the twelve judges of the courts of common law. Judgment was for Calvin.

There are excellent treatments of the importance of Calvin's Case in all basic case law books and treatises on constitutional law: see Ernst and Bellot, *Leading Cases in Constitutional Law,* pp. 50-58, under the heading "Allegiance," and also Forrest and Ridges, *Constitutional Law,* chap. 21 ("Allegiance and Alienage"), pp. 359-369, as well as the comprehensive discussion in Herbert Broom, *Constitutional Law* (London, 1885), pp. 3-56 ("Relation of the Subject to the Sovereign").

On the parliamentary background of the case itself see Wallace Notestein, *The House of Commons, 1604-1610* (New Haven, 1971), pp. 78-85 and 211-255.

12. There is a competent survey of the question in Sir William Holdsworth, *A History of English Law,* 16 vols. (London, 1903-1963), IX, 72-104. There, Holdsworth shows how little there was to go on before the period ca. 1400-1600; how Calvin's Case *began* a period of clarification and consolidation, setting up the doctrines essential to a modern state but without abandoning feudal ideas of allegiance; and how wholly territorial ideas have failed to force out personal elements, even in modern statutes.

13. McIlwain was awarded this in 1924, specifically for his *The American Revolution*. My reference is to the disappearance of any interest in McIlwain's argument from the modern bibliography on the nature and origins of the American Revolution. I have made an exhaustive survey and have found that there is no serious discussion of McIlwain in any of the modern works, with two notable exceptions. One is Harvey Wheeler's "Calvin's Case (1608) and the McIlwain-Schuyler Debate," *AHR*, LXXIII (1968), 587-597; it contains a good summary of the dispute. The other is a full-length study by Nicola Matteucci, *Charles Howard McIlwain a la Storiografia sulla Rivoluzione Americana* (Bologna, 1965). This important work has had no impact on recent American scholarship.

14. *7 Co. Rep. 4a; English Reports* 77, p. 381 (hereafter cited as *ER*, with volume preceding and pagination following).

15. On the special weight attached to decisions by all of the judges in this "court of discussion" see T. F. T. Plucknett, *A Concise History of the Common Law*, 2d ed. (Rochester, N.Y., 1936), pp. 154 and 310-311. Plucknett followed the treatment of A. Hemmant's "Introduction" to *Select Cases in Exchequer Chamber* (London, 1919), p. xiv. Cases requiring mature consideration and authoritative decision, often because questions touching the monarchy were involved, were heard there. Decisions were considered binding precedent by Coke, Bacon, and other great seventeenth-century judges. The same authority did not adhere to a decision by any other bench.

16. Notestein, *The House of Commons*, pp. 213 and 214. This recommendation of the Commissioners who drew up the Instrument of Union rested on legal opinions given in 1604. James resented the treatment accorded the *antenati* of Scotland and also the clause restricting postnati from office-holding. There were grave misgivings on both sides, even when the question of naturalization was given to the Lords (ibid., pp. 218-219). The lid came off early in 1607, when a vote in committee declared the king's proclamation in favor of the postnati to be contrary to common law (pp. 225-226). The Commissioners had said that James could naturalize by proclamation.

17. Ibid., pp. 228 ff., even after it was conceded that there would be limitations on inheritance, officeholding, and other personal rights among Scots in England. James would have no power to levy taxes on Scots as king of England. Why should Scots hold English lands but escape the charges paid by Englishmen? The king's speech to Commons at Whitehall, on 31 March 1607, did not help. He berated the members over the naturalization issue.

18. The judges had given opinions to the Conference Committee late in February 1607, favoring the king's cause. This probably accounts for the odd comment in Coke's report of Calvin's Case. On the last folio, he said "no commandment or message by word or writing was sent or delivered from any whatsoever to any of the Judges" to incline them toward any opinion in the case: *7 Co. Rep.* 28a. Coke claimed the judgment

was unanimous (ibid.). In fact, two judges ruled for the defendants: Walmsley and Foster.

19. See Clive Parry, *British Nationality, Including Citizenship of the United Kingdom and Colonies and the Status of Aliens* (London, 1951), pp. 1-7, with references to Calvin's Case; there is a definitive annotation of the case in Broom, *Constitutional Law,* pp. 25-55 ("Note to Calvin's Case").

20. Notestein, *The House of Commons,* p. 243.

21. *7 Co. Rep.,* 6a; see also Bacon's argument to the same effect, in J. Spedding, ed., *Works,* VII, 649. The principle was alleged in 1365, in *Molyns* vs. *Fiennes, Select Cases Before the Council,* pp. 48-53; and it was made definite early in the next century: *Year Books 3 Henry VI Trinity Term,* pl. 30.

22. On this point see *7 Co. Rep.* 6a and 25b as well as *Co. Littleton,* 8a and 129a. Coke probably relied on *Y.B. 9 Edward IV,* Trinity term, pl. 3 (pp. 11-12).

23. On the argument that a naturalized subject was quasi natural born there would be no limitations on either pedigree or heritability than those arising from convictions for treason or acts of attainder. This was pursued at length in the three cases treated here as parts of *Craw* v. *Ramsey;* see below for citations.

24. There are several reports: Sir Thomas Jones, *Les Reports de divers special cases. By the assigns of Ric. and Edw. Atkins, for Samuel Keble* (London, 1695); the 1729 edition has an English translation of the Law French; see also Keble, work cited in n. 26 below, and *84 ER;* Anonymous, *A General Abridgement of Cases in Equity, Argued and Adjudged in the High Court of Chancery, etc., 1667-1744* (London, n.d.) and *21 ER;* S. Carter, *Reports of Several special Cases argued and resolved in the Court of Common Pleas in the XVI, XVII, XVIII, and XIX Years of King Ch. II, to which are added some cases adjudged in the time of CJ Vaughan* (London, 1688) and *124 ER;* Ventris, *Reports* (1716 and 1726) and *86 ER;* Sir John Vaughan, *The Reports and Arguments [1665-1674] of that learned judge, Sir John Vaughan, Kt.*

25. The only report is in Thomas Siderfin, *Les Reports de divers Special Cases Argue et Adjudge en le Court de Bank le Roy et auxy en le Co. Ba. et l'Exchequer, en les primier dix ans apres le Restauration del Son Tres-Excellent Majesty le Roy Charles le II. Colligees par Thos. Siderfin Esq., Jades de Melieu Temple* (London, 1704). This is reprinted in 82 *ER,* 1235-1238, 1251-1252, 1304-1306. The discontinuity in pagination in this source and others stems from the several adjournments in the reported case. Hereafter cited as 2 *Sid* and 82 *ER.* etc.

26. There are several reports: Thomas Siderfin, *Le Second Part (mes les primier en Temps) de les Reports du Thomas Siderfin Jades del Middle-Temple Londres, Esq. esteant plusiers Cases comes ils estoyent Argue at Adjudges en le Court del Upper Banck, en les Ans 1657, 1658 and 1659. La Seconde Edition Corrigee* (London, 1714) and reprinted in *82 ER;* hereafter cited as *1 Sid.* Also, Sir Creswell Levinz, *The*

Reports of Sir C. L., Knt. Late One of the Judges in the Court of Common Pleas at Westminster (London, 1793) and reprinted in *83 ER.* Joseph Keble, *Reports in the Court of King's Bench at Westminster, from the XII to the XXX Year of the Reign of our Late Sovereign Lord King Charles II. Taken by Jos. Keble of Grey's Inn Esquire. The first Part: Containing the 13th, 14, 15, 16 and 17th Years* (London, 1685) and reprinted in *83 ER;* Sir Peyton Ventris, *The Reports of Sir Peyton Ventris, Kt, late one of the Justices of the Common Pleas. in two Parts. Part I—Containing Select Cases Adjudged in the King's Bench in the Reign of K. Charles II. Part II—Containing Choice Cases Adjudged in the Common Pleas, in the Reigns of K. Charles II and K. James II. and in the first three years of their late Majesties K. William and Q. Mary. Also several Cases and Pleadings Thereupon in the Exchequer Chamber, upon writs of late lord chief justice of the Court of Common Please, being all of them special cases* (London, 1677) and reprinted in *124 ER.* The 1706 edition is to be preferred; it contains important corrections. McIlwain used the earlier edition, unfortunately, complaining of the "rough state" of Vaughan's "confused notes" (*The American Revolution,* p. 98 n).

27. McIlwain, *The American Revolution,* pp. 96-108. Other writers, among them Wheeler, who treated the legal issues specifically, ignored *Craw v. Ramsey.*

28. The best example is James Wilson, *Considerations on the Nature and Extent of the Legislative Authority of the British Parliament,* in R. G. Adams, *Selected Political Essays* (New York, 1930), especially pp. 66, 75-82. For others, see Bernard Bailyn, *The Ideological Origins of the American Revolution* (Cambridge, Mass., 1976); and also the references given by McIlwain to the works of Dickinson and John Adams, *The American Revolution,* p. 107 n. 1.

29. Indeed, McIlwain used the same technique as had Wilson, who merely strung together quotations from Coke's report on Calvin's Case. Most of McIlwain's treatment consists of a series of quotes from Vaughan's report, taken out of the context of the arguments in *Craw v. Ramsey;* see *The American Revolution,* pp. 98-104.

30. The date of his birth is unknown and appears to be unknowable.

31. This is not agreed upon by the various reporters, but seems to be the best inference from conflicting evidence. The younger son, William, died sometime before 1638: cf. n. 36.

32. *124 ER 1072;* on 9 May 1604. *Bridgeman* 415 gives 19 March 1604. The sources agree on the time of this act. Sir John had been a close supporter of the king in Scotland well before 1603. On his involvement in the Ruthven Murder at Gowrie see David Mathews, *James VI and I* (London, 1967), p. 89; see also p. 167, for evidence of the King's favor; and William McIlwee, *The Wisest Fool in Christendom* (London, 1958), p. 173.

33. There is some discrepancy on the date of the act for Sir George. *124 ER 1072* gives the date 19 February 1621 (Vaughan's *Reports* 274),

and finds support elsewhere: *Carter 184*. But *86 ER* 274 (*2 Ventris 2*) gives the date 1610, with support from *Bridgeman* 415 (*124 ER* 664). But there is no doubt the naturalization took place before the death of Sir John, Earl of Holderness, in 1626. From circumstances in the cases, 1610 seems the proper date.

34. All sources agree on this date: 24 January 1626.

35. *Vaughan* 274 (1677 ed.) states the sisters were *antenatas* who were "living 1 October 14 Car. I (1638) and have issue at Kingston." This appeared from the special verdict in *Foster* v. *Ramsey,* as a finding of fact by the jury.

36. The only point of confusion concerns the relationship of Patrick and William. In some reports they are stated to be brothers: *2 Sid* 23, *1 Sid* 194, and *1 Lev.* 59. In others William is clearly said to be Patrick's son, the grandson of Nicholas: *Vaughan* 275, *2 Ventris* 1, *Carter* 184, *Bridgeman* 415, 1 *Ventris* 412 and 1 *Keble* 174. The Siderfin reports are not independent sources. Hence the weight of evidence is for Patrick to be William's father. In any event, Patrick was always said to have been born at Kingston 1 May 1618. All reports agree John II was born a native Englishman after 1610, but provide neither place nor date.

37. *Bridgeman* 411 states the will was made in 6 Jac., but gives no exact date to place it in 1609 or 1610; the will is in PCC 13 Skynner/ PRO, Prob 11/151; it was proved 6 January 1627.

38. There is again a dispute as to fact here. Bridgeman 415 says the tenure was "in fee as of the manor of East Greenwich, in Socage." Other reporters spoke of the tenure simply as "in knight's fee": *Carter* 184, *2 Sid.* 23, *1 Sid.* 194. Bridgeman alone quotes the will and IPM. Hence I follow him. The date of the IPM is given there as 29 February 7 Car. I.

The extant manuscripts bearing on this and other disputed points are the will noted in n. 37 and also certain writs and findings preserved in Chancery and Wards; there are no surviving Exchequer copies of the case. See PRO C 142/436, No. 68 and C 142/473, No. 17; also Wards 7/100, nos. 156 and 167; Wards 7/80, no. 91.

A manor held "in fee as of the manor of East Greenwich" was a beneficial tenure, in that it was not subject to most of the feudal incidents, wardship for example. It was in effect a freehold, with the reservation of a small annual rent, but remained subject to escheat. See Joel Hurstfield, "The Greenwich Tenures of the Reign of Edward VI," *Law Quarterly Review,* LXV (1949), 72-81. In the *Queens Wards* (London, 1958), pp. 19-24, Professor Hurstfield has demonstrated the powerful reasons behind the Crown's increased resort to this fiction and the extension of the practice in time as well as from England to Ireland and the American colonies.

39. Martha was the daughter of Sir William Cockayne, the Alderman of London who was also the notorious "projector" in the great dislocation of the cloth trade: for the father, see A. Friis, *Alderman Cockayne's Project and the Cloth Trade* (London, 1927). Holderness married Martha Cockayne 27 September 1624, after promising to levy a fine

securing a remainder for life to Sir William's daughter. The indentures tripartite were made 1 July 1624, and the fine was levied on Michaelmas 1624. For these and other details see *Vaughan* 275 (1677). Charles Lord Effingham was the third party. C 142/436, no. 68 recites the indenture in favor of Martha. The new will also makes clear her claim, in a marginal note on her marriage to Lord Willoughby (Prob 11/151, fo. 105).

40. See *2 Ventris 2, Carter* 185, and *1 Lev.* 59, for references to the IPM in detail. The problem in fixing a date of death for Nicholas is this: *Bridgeman* 415 gives the date 31 May 1638, while reports of *Craw* v. *Ramsey* give the date as 1 September 10 Car. I, or 1634. Bridgeman gives the date of George's death as 16 July 1636, but only he gives a sequence for the death of the brothers. It is clearly the case that George died before Nicholas. Hence I prefer the date 31 May 1638 for Nicholas' death.

41. This escheat appears in the findings of the office (1632) and was confirmed as a special finding in *Foster* v. *Ramsey:* Trinity 1656, Chancery Roll 1618, membrane 1 (quoted in part in *2 Sid.* 23). Will Murray, the grantee of the presumably escheated lands, was a Gentleman of the Bedchamber, an "inveterate wire-puller," according to C. V. Wedgewood, *The King's Peace, 1637-1641* (London, 1955), pp. 149, 460-461. The letters patent were dated 25 October 1634.

42. The date cannot be precisely determined, but this conveyance must have been made *after* the death of Patrick's father, Nicholas, on 31 May 1538 (*Bridgeman* 415); and before the day of Martha's death on 6 June 1641 (*124 ER* 664).

43. The jury in *Collingwood* v. *Pace* found the facts of the conveyance to the Earl of Elgin and Sydnam to be such that the Rectory was part of the estate conveyed: *1 Keble* 35 and *1 Ventris* 413.

44. Littleton, *lib.* 2. *cap.* 14; *7 Co. Rep.* 18b.

45. *Bridgeman* 418: "And I take the rule for it set down by my Lord Coke to be good; viz. for there was never any inheritable blood between the parents and them; and where the sons by no possibility can be heir to one of the parents, no one of them shall not be heir to the other." This is to argue that naturalized sons can transmit, but cannot take, a pedigree; they have no "ancestral legal blood" and are thereby debarred, on the axiom *"nemo dat quod non habet" (Bridgeman* 427).

46. It is certain that the office found an escheat. The cause may well have been some finding other than the rule I have alleged [see John Reeve, *The History of English Law* (Philadelphia, 1786), III, 7]. Sir John's will might be held to preempt the terms of the subsequent indenture.

47. *124 ER* 664.

48. PRO, Prob 11/151, 13 Skynner, fo. 104.

49. For the sum of £1100; see *124 ER* 1073; 16 February 1651.

50. *Bridgeman* 415. The land in question included one messuage, one garden, 500 acres of arable, 500 acres of meadow, 500 acres of pasture, with the appurtenances in Kingston and the rectory Church.

51. John Locke, *Two Treatises of Civil Government,* ed. Peter Laslett (Cambridge, 1963), I, xi, 106. The title of ch. xi is "Who Heir;" the exact quotation is "the great question which in all ages has disturbed mankind . . . is not whether there should be Power in the world, nor whence it came, but who should have it."

52. The only report is in *2 Sid.* 23-27, 51-52 and 148-151.

53. Shafto relied on Bukley's Case, concerning the Act for Naturalization of Wales; Magdalen College Case; Jo. Marquess of Winchester's Case.

54. Citing Coke in *3 Co. Rep.,* Ratcliff's Case. See also *Littleton,* 133 and *Co. Littleton,* 128a.

55. See *Co. Littleton,* f. 3.

56. Thus anticipating Bridgeman's argument in *Collingwood* v. *Pace: Bridgeman* 418. C. J. Glyn would have allowed the devise, if the will had called Patrick the "reputed heir" of Nicholas, S. N. "Devises," in *1 Eq. Ca. Abr.* 213, Case 10.

57. *2 Sid.* 151.

58. *21 ER* 998.

59. *124 ER* 663-664.

60. *Bridgeman* 416.

61. *1 Lev.* 59.

62. *83 ER* 296. The case was apparently entered as an action on ejectment in 1661. Hence Collingwood either was ousted that summer or had bided his time before seeking a remedy at law. This, and other details, appear in the manuscript notes of C. J. Bridgeman in the British Library, Hargrave Mss. 55, fol. 52: "This term, Tr. 13 Car. 2, the great case of Collingwood vs. Pace was argued by the Judges." There is another comment indirectly referring to *Foster* v. *Ramsey* as being settled "in the time of the Commonwealth." Trinity Term in 1661 ran from about 2 June through 8 July. There is also a report in *1 Keble* 35 (*83 ER* 814).

63. By Levinz, Ventris, Keble, Bridgeman and Siderfin.

64. *1 Lev.* 60; *1 Sid.* 194 and 201.

65. Our only knowledge of the satellite cases derives from references made to them in Exchequer Chamber: on *Dawson* v. *Pace* (1655) see *1 Keble* 220; this was a nonsuit, for want of entry proved. See also *Davise* v. *Pace,* another nonsuit, in *1 Keble* 578.

66. *1 Lev.* 59, with the citations there to *1 Coke Inst.* 8a and Hobbies Case, in *Noy* 158-159.

67. *1 Sid.* 201.

68. *1 Lev.* 60; on the point of *morte d'ancestor* see Serjeant Allen for the plaintiff, in *1 Keble* 217.

69. *86 ER* 262-272, an undated argument by Sir Matthew Hales, Chief Baron (1660-1671) of the Exchequer. The quote is found in *1 Ventris* 419, in regard of Parliament; for Hales on Coke, see *1 Keble* 423.

70. See Littleton *On Tenures,* 20; *1 Keble* 423.

71. *1 Keble* 428. The interest of Scots in this case was reported by

Siderfin, in *1 Sid.* 194: *"ils fueront divide in cest po que fuit de cy grand concern al tants les escois que fueront nee devant le Coron d'Angleterre discend sur le Roy Jacques."* Bridgeman ridiculed this contention, asking how many Scots *antenati* now upward of sixty years old could be in a similar situation: *Bridgeman* 459.

72. *1 Keble* 266.

73. Sir Heneage Finch (1621-1682), M.P. for Oxford in 1661, a celebrated lawyer, made Chancellor 1674, after serving as attorney general (1670-1673); then Earl of Nottingham. See *1 Keble* 267. Finch's reference is to a decision given in K. B., YB 1 (1486) Henry VII, the famous Merchants of Waterford case.

74. *1 Keble* 535.

75. Maynard, for the defense; *1 Keble* 536.

76. *1 Keble* 582.

77. *1 Keble* 585.

78. On this see 42 Edward III, c. 2; also, Marjorie Morgan, "The Suppression of the Alien Priories," *History* (1941), XXVI, 204-212. Suspicion of foreigners and potential enemies was more the cause than any alleged greed on the part of the Crown.

79. The question was put by Brown, in his own brief: *1 Keble* 585.

80. For this reply see *1 Keble* 589. He was rebutting an argument by Turner about the largeness of statutory powers. Turner, one of the barons of the Exchequer, who in a flight of philosophic rhetoric claimed for statute the power to return men "to the law of nature," when all things were in common. Then, "property was introduced by assent only," flowing from the power to give where there was a kind of love.

81. Sir Orlando Bridgeman (1606?-1674), son of John (1577-1652) Bishop of Chester, Lord Keeper 1667-1672. This great judge had had a most distinguished career in the law. He had been closely attached to Charles II, when the future king was Prince of Wales, serving as Solicitor General to Charles. He sat in the Oxford Parliament (1644) for Wigan and avoided the practice of law during the Commonwealth. He presided at the trial of the Regicides and was CJ of Common Pleas (1660-1667).

82. Ibid., 417.

83. Ibid., 419.

84. Ibid., 420.

85. Ibid., 421; this argument was a good one. It was not until the early nineteenth century that English law unambiguously recognized the cease of allegiance, in cases deriving from the establishment of the United States of America.

86. Ibid., 424-425.

87. See *49 Edward III,* c. 12.

88. *Bridgeman,* 426.

89. Ibid., 428, quoting the formula again. He also put in the record the words of patents reaching back to *YB 9 Edward IV,* Bagot's Case.

90. Ibid.

91. Citing 1 Henry VII, c. 2.

92. *Bridgeman,* 429. Bridgeman also made an elegant comparison between pardons by patent and Acts of Oblivion. A man attainted by Parliament could be pardoned in either manner, but not with removal of the corruption of blood, rules that were made specifically in the Act, with public forms of assent. The reason was that the attainder had public consequences, escheat for example.

93. Ibid., 429-430; *7 Co. Rep.* 18b. These were familiar dangers cited in statutes passed in time of war: 2 Henry V, c. 2 and 4 Henry V, c. *ultimo.* 1 George I, c. 2 laid down that foreigners could not hold English public offices.

94. Ibid., 432.

95. Ibid., 433; for example, in the subsidy act of 15 Charles II.

96. Ibid., 459; the act referred to was penned in 10 Charles I (1634).

97. Ibid., 459-460.

98. Ibid., 461.

99. Sir Lionel was a close associate of Sir William Murray and also Sir William Compton. Tollemach's sister Lady Alington married Compton. The brothers-in-law were somewhat involved in the Royalist conspiracies of the 1650s, particularly the Sealed Knot. Tollemach's Ipswich quarters were a meeting place, as he was the husband of the Countess of Dysert, the staunchly Royalist Elizabeth Murray who was the daughter of Sir William Murray. Murray had ended his life as first Earl of Dysart (d. 1651). After Tollemach's death Elizabeth married John Maitland and so became Duchess of Lauderdale.

100. The sequence was this: Patrick Ramsey to Elgin and Sydnam in 1651; Elgin and Sydnam to Anabel Dowager Countess of Kent in 1662; she to Simon and Pullen Neale in the same year; the Neales to Sir Lionel and Mr. Weld on 20 January 1665; they to Craw on the very same day, on which he claimed to both conclude and enter. There are difficulties of two kinds: in the sources; and in the alleged events. *2 Ventris* 2 and *Vaughan* 275 put the transactions back a decade in each case, incorrectly. It is obvious that this chronology is impossible, otherwise this string of tenants would have been involved in the cases arising in the Commonwealth courts. They were not. *Carter* 906 and *Bridgeman* 185 (1688) give the correct sequence of dates. On the second point see n. 103.

101. *Vaughan* 301 claims this was the *grandson* of George, son of John II. Ventris, Carter and other reporters do not.

102. All reporters agree on these essential facts: see *2 Ventris* 2; *2 Keble* 602; etc.

103. That this was the only question reached is most clearly stated in Sir Thomas Jones, *Les Reports de divers special cases* (London 1695), p. 10: "Sur un especial verdict, le sole matter en ley fuit, an un Antenate del Scotland naturlize per act de Parliament del Ireland soit inheritable al terres in Engleterre." Jones did not hear the serjeants, but he was able to record the views of the judges. See also *Carter* 906; *2 Keble* 602; *Vaughan* 277; and *2 Ventris* 2.

The case is hence another collusive suit. The purported lease and entry to Craw took place early in January 1665, just before the verdict on *Collingwood* v. *Pace* was entered in Common Pleas and after it was mandated by the decision in Exchequer Chamber toward the end of 1664.

104. *2 Ventris* 1.

105. *2 Ventris* 2; *Vaughan* 277.

106. *86 ER* 274; *2 Ventris* 3. Serjeant Brome argued this point at length *pro defendante, ER 124* 909.

107. The fullest report of this argument by Tyrell, which had been made also by Serjeant Maynard: see *2 Ventris* 3-4 and *Carter* 185-188.

108. *2 Ventris* 4; *86 ER* 275; *Jones* 10-13.

109. *Vaughan* 280 on the last point specifically; for the fabric of the whole argument, ibid., 279-301.

110. Ibid., 279.

111. *2 Keble* 602: "The Court delivered their opinions in ejectment yesterday that one naturalized in Ireland after the Union of that with England cannot inherit to a brother born in England as is naturalized there he might per Vaughan, CJ, Wylde and Archer, JJ; contra Tyrell that held he may, and judgment *pro defendant*." See also *2 Ventris* 8 and *Jones* 10.

112. McIlwain, *The American Revolution,* pp. 95 and 106 especially, but 90-119 inclusive. See Appendix A.

113. *7 Co Rep* 18a. Interestingly enough, Coke grasped the importance of the issue raised much later in *Craw* v. *Ramsey*: "Grant, in that case, while the Realm of England, and not of Ireland were governed by several laws, any that was born in Ireland was the alien to the Realm of England." See Wheeler, "Calvin's Case," 588-591.

114. McIlwain, *The American Revolution,* pp. 35 ff.

115. Ibid., p. 95; see also "Whig Sovereignty and Real Sovereignty," op. cit., 67-79.

116. "Vaughan . . . conceded to the Irish Parliament a power of naturalizing for the Kingdom of England . . . and held for the plaintiff in that case." For this conclusion see McIlwain, *The American Revolution,* p. 106.

117. McIlwain complained of this: ibid., 98: "Some of the cases [in Vaughan *Reports*) are clearly in the form of rather rough notes," a fn. comment to simplify his particular comment in the text: "The report is far from clear in many points." Actually, the printed brief lacks clarity only when one fails to see it for what it is, a responsive rebuttal to the points carefully laid out by Maynard and Tyrell.

118. This is stated on the title page of the 1706 edition.

119. McIlwain, *The American Revolution,* pp. 95-96, especially fn. 1, which begins on p. 95 and carries on overleaf.

120. Ibid., pp. 3-5 with the authorities in the notes.

121. McIlwain's most complete expositions of the supposed seventeenth century contrast between a "federal" and a "unitary" theory of

imperial relations are in attack on Austin, in "Whig Sovereignty and Real Sovereignty."

122. The arguments of Darcy and Molyneux. For a careful study, see Francis Godwin James, *Ireland in the Empire* (Harvard, 1973) especially pp. 27-50, 111-133 and 277-312 ("Ireland's Place in the Old Empire").

123. McIlwain, *The American Revolution,* p. 99.

124. On the force of such ideas in the seventeenth century, see J. G. A. Pocock, *The Ancient Constitution and the Feudal Law* (Cambridge, 1957).

125. McIlwain, *The American Revolution,* p. 94 (great *Isaac v. Durant*), p. 65.

126. Ibid.

127. *22 Law Reports Chancery Division* (1883) 243-254. Sir Matthew Hales's brief and argument in *Collingwood* v. *Pace* is there cited to "overturn decisions to the contrary," in a case to decide the right to inherit in England of an Englishman born abroad of naturally born English parents. By 7 Anne, c. 3; and 4 George II, c. 21; and 13 George III, c. 21, the status of natural-born British subjects had been conferred on the children and grandchildren of such parents; but it was a merely personal status by the acts, not transmissible to the descendants of the persons to whom the status was given. The case had its origin in fact in 1691, when a Scottish peer's English-born son (Aeneas Mackay), the great grandfather of the testator in *De Geer* v. *Stone,* went abroad in 1691 in King William III's war against France. Mackay "married a Dutch lady" and had a child in Holland, etc.

128. *17 Law Reports Queen's Bench Decision, Court of Appeals* (1886), 54-66. This case arose because of a petition to set aside the Stepney Election of an M.P. Isaacson claimed the seat, asking to be certified to the Speaker. Petitioner claimed the votes actually making the majority for Isaacson were not valid because: (1) Nine were votes of persons born in the Kingdom of Hanover before the accession of Queen Victoria, and not naturalized; (2) thirteen were votes cast by persons born in Hanover since the accession, but of parents born in Hanover *before* 20 June 1837; (3) one was the vote of a person born in Prussia since the accession, but of parents born in Hanover in 1802, and not naturalized. The question was whether any of the three classes of persons were aliens, within the meaning of the election laws. Isaacson claimed the antenati were not aliens, because this would clearly bring in the postnati. Durant counterclaimed, on certain dicta in Calvin's Case. Coke had said "persons born under one natural allegiance while realms were united should remain subjects natural-born and no aliens," if the realms were subsequently divided. But this was found to be merely a *dictum* and no part of the rule of decision in Calvin's Case. In 1837 the succession of Hanover and England had been divided, and Hanoverians came under the protection of the King of Hanover, owing allegiance to him. *Craw* v. *Ramsey* was cited in favor of the antenati, but after long arguments the

case was decided for Durant because the parallelism of the present case to either Calvin's Case or *Craw* v. *Ramsey* was demonstrated to be falsely alleged.

129. *1 King's Bench* 617 (1918); *87 L. J. King's Bench* 620 (1920). Markwald was born in Germany in 1859 and immigrated to Australia in 1878. In 1908 he obtained a certificate of naturalization there, taking the oath of allegiance under the Australian Act of 1903. He came to London to reside before 1914. He failed to register as an alien and in 1916 was arrested. He defended himself, under counsel alleging he was no alien by virtue of his oath of allegiance, etc. It was held the 1870 Naturalization Act had empowered the dominions and possessions to naturalize with effects of a local character only. Therefore taking the oath and gaining the certificate in Australia did not dissolve alienage in England. Hence a man was "held to be a liege subject of the King in some part of his dominion but not in all," as in *Craw* v. *Ramsey*. There was an appeal in *Markwald* v. *Attorney-General* (1920): *1 Chancery* 348; *89 Law Journal* Ch. 225. But Markwald's conviction and imprisonment was upheld.

130. *Doe d. Thomas* v. *Acklam* [in 2 B. and C 779]. This decision rested on one set of facts, the Treaty ending the American Revolution; and a theory, that of the link between protection and allegiance. *Doe d. Thomas* v. *Acklam* is the case of children born in America, since the severance of the two countries, of persons born there before. The parents chose to remain in America when it ceased to be a part of the dominions of the king of England. The decision depended on the terms of the Treaty of Paris, which refused the rights of Englishmen to those who remained in America and gave allegiance to the new United States. This was contested on the theory of Coke in Calvin's Case and Hales in *Craw* v. *Ramsey*: that an antenatus (i.e., before the severance) continues to be a British subject. *Doe d. Auchmuty* v. *Mulcaster* posited now that but for the provisions of a treaty a British subject cannot divest himself of allegiance. The father of the claimants in the case had not done so within the time limited by the Treaty of Paris. Hence it was held that they were not aliens but British subjects under the meaning of *4 George II,* c. 21. This held that persons born abroad where fathers were natural-born subjects are themselves natural-born subjects: see the Case, in *5 B. & C.,* 771. On the American side, the U.S. courts approached the same issue in *Bright's Lessee* v. *Rochester*.

III

POVERTY, PROTESTANTISM, AND POLITICAL ECONOMY: ENGLISH ATTITUDES TOWARD THE POOR, 1660-1800

Daniel A. Baugh

The printed edition of the *Liverpool Vestry Books,* published in 1912, contains an interesting footnote on the first page of the introduction. The author, who had published the piece separately in a local history journal two years earlier, now felt the need to offer a general criticism of it:

...I think [he wrote in this footnote] that I took too narrow a view of the question of poor relief, and in praising the select Vestry's firmness, ignored the fact that poverty and pauperism are not synonymous expressions. The Vestry probably reduced the one without affecting the other to a proportionate degree, and . . . [there are indications that] the vigour of the official tests may have driven many poor people, not into independent labour, but only into the streets. The Vestry was no doubt efficient in administering its principles; but those principles were not generous enough to enable it to solve the real problem. That problem, how to abolish not pauperism but poverty, remains unsolved to this day.[1]

His self-criticism was justified, for indeed he had approved the stingy severities of the Liverpool Vestry in a most unguarded

manner. The author was a barrister—whose politics were Liberal
—named W. Lyon Blease. He was not a major figure, but as a
matter of curiosity one would like to know what influenced his
change of outlook, because his footnote is a small indicator of an
important shift in the current of opinion respecting a fundamental issue of social policy.[2] The current became a tide. R. H. Tawney's attack in the 1920s on nineteenth-century views on the cure
of poverty was part of it; his writings enjoyed widespread approval
in humanitarian cirles;[3] and of course the economic events of the
1930s discredited nineteenth-century views not only in the eyes of
humanitarians but also of the public in general. That the welfare
policy of England today substantially rejects nineteenth-century
views, and is indeed in some measure a reaction against them,
hardly needs saying. Nevertheless, our historical understanding
of the poverty question in England down through the centuries
remains strongly influenced by scholarly works that, though they
were published between 1900 and 1930, were in one way or another in the grip of nineteenth-century views.[4]

Our concern here will be not with welfare policy but with attitudes toward the poor (a word that should be understood to refer
throughout to both employed and unemployed persons); in
examining the evolution of these attitudes we shall be conscious
of the extraordinary power of the views that dominated nineteenth-century thought. What interests me chiefly about W. Lyon
Blease is not his sudden change of outlook but the fact that as late
as perhaps 1909 an intelligent, well-informed, and public-spirited
man brought to his original interpretation of early nineteenth-
century Poor Law policies the same attitude that has served to
justify the harsh measures of that earlier time. It is one instance
among thousands demonstrating the longevity of an outlook that
jelled about the year 1820 and survived, without significant
amendment, through a century of massive industrial and social
change. Its influence on Poor Law policy during the period is
obvious. Against this prevailing outlook the handful of reformers
with differing perceptions struggled in vain. Such was its intensity
and power that we may appropriately call it a consensus.

The purpose of my inquiry is to try to understand the origins of
this powerful consensus and to account for its eventual triumph.
My approach will be to view the problem from a long perspective.[5] The result will, I hope, persuade the writers of general his-

tory to renounce the well-rooted practice of tracing nineteenth-century English attitudes toward the poor directly to the seventeenth century. In such writings the eighteenth century is curiously left out of the picture. My aim is to put it back in. But first something should be said about the nature of the nineteenth-century consensus.

THE NINETEENTH-CENTURY CONSENSUS

Nineteenth-century solutions to the problem of poverty emphasized individual motivation. Self-maintenance or self-betterment, through the "independent labour" that Mr. Blease mentioned, was essential. Traditional charity was in the long run detrimental. The aim of law and of charitable activity therefore had to be, as the Sturges Bourne committee of 1817 asserted, to discover a way of

setting again into action those motives which impel persons, by the hope of bettering their condition on the one hand, and the fear of want on the other, so to exert and conduct themselves, as by frugality, temperance and industry . . . to ensure to themselves that condition of existence in which life alone can be otherwise than a miserable burthen.[6]

As the Labourers' Friend Society put it, the object was to appeal to "the honest feelings of independence that would disdain any other source of supply than that which arises from self-exertion." The aim of the Society was

to elicit, by appropriate encouragement, the productive industry of the labourer, to an extent that shall proudly raise him above parochial aid; it is exclusively to cast him on his own manual powers, and to render him altogether superior to charitable assistance. What the Labourers' Friend Society contemplates is in no sense eleemosynary, but intended to promote such permanent habits of lucrative industry as may afford the best security against deficiency and want.[7]

The virtues described are those that we readily associate with Victorianism. They are also recognizable as aspects of the Protestant ethic. The nineteenth century did not originate the idea of "self-help." Neither did the seventeenth century, although the Puritans gave it a strong boost. Encouraging people to avoid poverty by working is of course a very old idea, certainly as old as the Old Testament. What the nineteenth century did was wed itself to the ideal of self-help to an exclusive degree, forsaking all others.

Therefore the distinguishing features of the nineteenth-century consensus are: first, the conviction that there was *no other solution* to the problem of poverty than individual motivation;[8] and second, the belief that the requisite willpower and desire for economic independence could be found in any man, however humble.[9]

There was a further assumption, namely, that it was economically possible for poor people to support themselves by "independent labour" alone. This raised questions about economic reality that were not much talked about at the time. Such questions were thrust aside by an orthodoxy convinced of the indispensability of free volition. Nassau Senior, the economist who was responsible more than any other for drafting the report on which the New Poor Law of 1834 was based, expressed the simple and unbending logic that underlay this view as follows:

The [traditional] poor laws of southern England are an attempt to unite the irreconcilable advantages of freedom and servitude. The labourer is to be a free agent, but without the hazards of free agency; to be free from the coercion, but to enjoy the assured subsistence of the slave.[10]

The nineteenth-century consensus, to its credit, was founded on a vision of the moral potentialities of ordinary people, but it tended to deny compassion, to promote contempt for human weakness, and to be blind to hazards of personal misfortune and constraints of economic facts. The blindness was willful, for it was supposed that the system would not work if there was a catch-net.

PROTESTANTISM

In tracing the origins of this powerful consensus we must go back to the seventeenth century. The reason is the apparent kinship of Puritan and Victorian attitudes. It requires no great historical sophistication to see a connection. Indeed, this connection has been generally stressed beyond reasonable proportion, thanks to some impressive and highly readable works of scholarship. Max Weber pointed the way with his study of *The Protestant Ethic and the Spirit of Capitalism*. Tawney's *Religion and the Rise of Capitalism* has commanded the attention of three generations of

English-speaking readers, and more recently Christopher Hill has set forth ideas along similar lines.[11] That Puritanism was responsible for injecting severity and harshness into attitudes toward poverty is a corollary of the Weber thesis, but Weber did not explore the question. Tawney did, and his book lays so much stress on seventeenth-century developments as to obliterate those of the eighteenth. It is the enormous influence of Tawney's book that accounts for the tendency of modern surveys to overlook what happened in the eighteenth century, for Tawney leapt over the eighteenth century with scarcely a nod at it. That century was not one of his fields of interest. He projected seventeenth-century social ethics forward to the heartless principles of the nineteenth century—and perhaps nineteenth-century principles back into seventeenth-century religion. All in all, it is not hard to understand why the idea that it was a straight course from Puritan discipline to Mr. Gradgrind has such a strong grip on our historical imagination.

It is my purpose, as I mentioned, to fill in the intervening history, but it is impossible to avoid grappling with the problem of Protestantism, and particularly its most virulent expression, Puritanism. Because it was not Weber, but Tawney who explicitly argued the case for Puritan influence on attitudes toward the poor, it is with Tawney's argument that we shall be concerned. The argument is not easy to dissect; most of it may be found in a section of the book labeled "The New Medicine for Poverty," but it can only be understood in the context of the whole book. As is the case with all of Tawney's writings, it is presented with an eloquence, persuasiveness, and historical awareness that must command the deepest admiration. The book may be criticized as history but not as historical literature.

Tawney believed that something important—and deplorable— happened in English society during the second half of the seventeenth century. Christian authority and influence over economic relations collapsed. The churches gave up their ethical claims in this sphere; the "territory within which the writ of religion was conceived to run" contracted, and the "world of commercial transactions" became a "closed compartment with laws of its own," indifferent to religious values. The ethics of economic life, hitherto considered "part of the province of religion," ceased to be so considered.[12]

The purpose of *Religion and the Rise of Capitalism* was to

explain how this happened, and it is here, in this sharply defined historical thrust, that the book differs fundamentally from Max Weber's work. Whereas Weber saw the spirit of capitalism as an outgrowth of Puritanism, Tawney saw it as preexistent and outside religion; it was "as old as history" and, like the devil, ready to conquer if given half a chance.[13] This secular spirit got its chance in the wake of the civil war, when disillusionment enveloped England. At that historical moment "the force of common things prevailed."

Puritanism's role in this was both tragic and ironic. For although Puritans had sought a regimen of religious discipline, they had also "repudiated as anti-Christian the [traditional] organs through which such discipline had in fact been exercised." The all-encompassing edifice of English ecclesiastical authority was thereby shattered — a wholly unintended result.[14] In addition, Tawney argued, Puritanism shredded the fabric of the old paternalistic economic system of England. Indeed, the effect of its doctrines was "to revolutionize all traditional values" respecting society. The Puritan vision saw "the entire world of human relations . . . in a new and wintry light," and this vision influenced English social ethics long after the religious ardor that had given it birth disappeared.[15]

Respecting the attitudes toward poverty and charity that attended this vision, Tawney stressed two points. The first was the inclination of the Puritan mind, which readily connected prosperity and success with hard work, sobriety, prudence, dedication, and uprightness, to see poverty not as "a misfortune to be pitied and relieved, but a moral failing to be condemned." The second was the orientation of Puritan teaching toward "individual responsibility, not social obligation."[16]

In sum, Tawney argued that economic ethics ceased once and for all to be under the influence of religion. Puritanism broke the power of religious authority in England, diverted Englishmen's minds away from social obligation, and reinforced with its peculiar sense of human virtue the uncharitable features of the secular system of economic thought that thereupon came to the fore. Although in the broad view he saw a new harshness insinuating its way into English society's view of the poor from the sixteenth century onward, owing partly to the authoritarian social policy of the Tudors and partly to the spreading influence of commercial mores, the main point of his book was that the critical period came in the late seventeenth century and that the role of Puritanism was crucial.

Let us examine these arguments. Certain points are indisputable. It is a fact that most of the institutional authority of religion in England did terminate at this time, and it is undoubtedly true that the Puritan movement contributed mightily to that end. Leonard Trinterud, in a Clark Library lecture a few years ago, called this "the end of the clerical world" in England. "Thirteen centuries during which the mission and function of the church was understood in terms of the clergy reigning over the people of the entire nation" in God's name and supported by the power of the state, came to an end with the civil war. There was a subsequent effort, from 1660 to 1689, to reaffirm ecclesiastical discipline over the laity, but it failed.[17] Certainly it is also true that secularly inspired economic ideas were at the same time rapidly gaining influence; their roots lay chiefly in political philosophy, experimental science, and disputation over commercial policy. Finally, it is impossible to deny that Puritanism gave a religious sanction to the notion that poverty was the natural consequence of idleness, improvidence, and vice.

Tawney's view of the permanent influence of all this on English attitudes toward the poor is, however, seriously defective. His argument that Puritanism's emphasis on individual character annihilated social obligation rests on a one-sided view of the movement. There was another side of Puritanism, a side that stressed social obligation. Tawney was well aware of it, and, indeed, found fault with Weber on precisely this ground. Weber, he noted, had glossed over the fact that Calvin's teachings stressed Christian responsibility for the general welfare and improvement of the godly community (and there was, in principle, no earthly limit on the size of that community). This responsibility, when melded with the Puritan injunction to be active in the world, thus to carry on God's work, pointed not toward the annihilation of social obligation but most intently toward the opposite. It had to be acknowledged that in the sixteenth century Calvinism had "savoured more of a collectivist dictatorship than of individualism";[18] at that time English Puritan divines insisted that man's place was in a community and that a community was responsible for the welfare of its members.

With this problem in mind, Tawney decided to substitute a dynamic view of Puritanism for Weber's static one: Puritanism had been transformed. During the seventeenth century the "collectivist . . . aspect . . . quietly dropped out of notice," and "individualism congenial to the world of business became the distinctive characteristic of a Puritanism which had arrived."[19] Therefore when religious fervor subsided and the clerical world passed from the scene, what was left was an individualistic rather than collectivistic discipline.

By this means Tawney was able to overcome a number of historical objections to the Weber thesis.[20] But because the argument required him to discriminate between an earlier Puritanism and a later version, it led him into the temptation of categorizing parts of "the Puritan mind which looked backward," or forward, in ways that savor of the self-fulfilling hypothesis.[21] Indeed, the theory of transformation entails a major historical difficulty when it comes to the question of poverty. For while it is true that Puritan individualism and the concept of self-discipline that attended it must have served to encourage a censorious and unsympathetic attitude toward the poor, there is no evidence that individualism's importance in Puritan thought changed during the seventeenth century.[22] In this regard Weber's view is closer to the evidence than Tawney's. The historical validation of Tawney's theory of transformation must therefore be sought on that side of the argument that stresses the annihilation of social obligation.

But here too the evidence fails. Puritan clergymen of the later seventeenth century preached a code of ethics that showed just as much concern for social obligation as that of their predecessors. Regarding charity, Samuel Clarke, ejected in 1662, argued that it should be extended not just to the physically helpless but also to "the honest labourer, and poor house-keeper, who either, through greatness of their charge [i.e., number of dependents], or deadnesse of trade, crosses, losses, sicknesse, &c. are not able to get their bread." He felt that giving to the poor was a duty, and that bounty to the poor was the best way to prevent poverty.[23] Richard Steele, also ejected in 1662, opposed assisting "idle beggars," but felt, like Clarke, that both the unemployed and housekeepers with too many children were proper objects of charity, so long as they did not beg.[24] Richard Baxter, the best known of these later seventeenth-century Dissenting clergymen who published ethical advice, insisted on Christian standards in market transactions. His requirements amounted to what today the SEC calls "full disclosure"; one must not profit from the ignorance of one's neighbor, and when one is buying from poor people "charity must be exercised as well as justice."[25] In his chapter on charity Baxter stressed "our obligation to do good to others." He commended missions, schools, loans to young tradesmen, and the like, but also reminded his readers that the task "for every one, is to relieve the most needy which are next at hand. To know what poor families are in greatest want, and to help them as we are able; and to provoke the rich to do that which we cannot do our selves; and to beg for others." "*Giving* according to our ability," he wrote, "is as sure and great a duty as *Praying,*" and should be done as regularly.[26]

There is nothing in these Christian advice-books written by "later Puritan" clergy to suggest that poverty was a crime, or that economic dealings ought to be considered as independent of religious concerns, and Tawney knew it, for these were the sources that he used himself. But he said that such books had no lasting influence: "The rules...elaborated by Baxter were subtle and sincere. But they were like seeds carried by birds from a distant and fertile plain, and dropped upon a glacier. They were at once embalmed and sterilized in a river of ice."[27] Tawney's explanation for this sterilization involves subtleties of social psychology that we need to examine here. (Clearly, in view of the fact that *The Christian Directory* was published in 1673, we are required to regard Richard Baxter as backward-looking.)

Thus the notion of transformation lacks empirical foundation. The harshness toward the poor that is implicit in Puritanism's linkage of misfortune to moral failing is as discernible at the beginning of the movement as at its end. And if there was a trend toward a diminishing emphasis on social obligation, it lies for historians in the realm of the ineffable; it can only be traced by deduction or perhaps through evidence of a kind that Tawney did not consult, such as the diaries and letters of laymen. For it is almost impossible to discover anything from the pulpit or in the Christian advice-books of the late seventeenth century to suggest that it happened. (On the contrary, the men of the cloth of that time, aware as they were of the insidious implications of Hobbes's egotistically based political geometry, and afraid that religious toleration would yield a godless society, apparently took the enhancement of a Christian social conscience to be one of their main tasks.) And there is of course — Tawney would have granted this — no evidence that the collapse of institutional religious authority influenced the content of religious teaching on the subject of poverty.

Indeed, by the late seventeenth century, when the storms had passed, the heirs of the Puritan tradition appear to have emerged with views on charity that were not materially different from those of Anglicans on the main points. Both groups adhered to the doctrine of stewardship (i.e., no Christian's possessions were truly his own to dispose of as he pleased, but rather the Lord's to be disposed of as the Lord would wish);[28] that the helpless should be helped; that the poor man should be content in his station; that relief to vagrants and professional beggars should be given only with the greatest caution; and that the deserving should be discriminated from the undeserving. But none would allow a poor person, however undeserving, to perish.[29] Since they all read the same Bible, and recognized scriptural authority as paramount, it is not surprising that they agreed on the main points. None could overlook the numerous messages relating to charity in both testaments, especially Matthew 25:40.[30]

Of course there were differences in emphasis. Puritans (whom we shall take to include their heirs, the Dissenters, in this discussion) paid more attention than Anglicans did to the effect of alms on the recipient; this arose chiefly from their fundamental concern for the spiritual health of all men, poor as well as rich.[31] Since righteous conduct was not only essential for the preservation of the soul, but was also the means, Puritans believed, "whereby we may know our selves to be the adopted Children of God" and distinguished "from the Children of the devil," it was logical for them to place a great emphasis on behavior. (However, the idea that poverty was often, but not always, the consequence of vice and laziness occurred to both Anglicans and Puritans, perhaps because it seemed obvious in fact.)[32] Puritans also tended to be more concerned about the regularity of giving;[33] more programmatic in their approach; more active in planning for a better society; more inclined to believe that useful reforms could be instituted; more hopeful of finding eventually a solution to the poverty problem. This accorded with their sober rational outlook as well as their aim of fashioning a godly society.

Anglicans, in contrast, saw almsgiving as perpetual. The poor would indeed always be with us. The author of that long-lived Anglican manual, *The Whole Duty of Man*, remarked on "how prime and fundamental a part of Christianity this of Charity is."[34] This was a traditional feature of Anglicanism, but became accentuated toward the end of the seventeenth century by the absorption "into Anglican theological method [of] a practicality which expresses itself in a concern with charitable objects." The Latitudinarians, who were the main carriers of this notion, "contrived to convey the impression that religion was chiefly a matter of acquiring and practising justice, honesty, sincerity and charitableness."[35]

As is well known, charity in Anglican eyes was a means of grace. On the day of judgment the testimony of the poor would be heard; thus, by charitable acts, a person could improve his chances of salvation. Strict Calvinists held no such view: benevolent conduct was at best an indicator of regeneracy.[36] Anglicans made much of the joyfulness of beneficence; Puritans would not allow themselves such indulgence. Baxter required his readers to give until it hurt, and he really meant it.[37] For Puritans, charity was always a duty but never a delight. Anglicans could aspire to follow "the example of the Son of God, who out of pure charity" embraced "extreme poverty and want for our sake."[38] This inclination and ability to imitate Christ, at least in some degree, was a gift from God, and a natural sympathy for those in distress was a symptom of it; charitable actions, by enhancing this attribute, enhanced happiness. Isaac Barrow, who gave up the Lucasian chair in mathematics at Cambridge so that the young Newton could have it, put this vividly:

God and nature therefore within us do solicit the poor man's case: even our own ease and satisfaction demand from us compassion and kindness towards him; by exercising them . . . we become not only more like to God, but more perfectly men: by the contrary practice . . . we do weaken, corrupt, and stifle that which is best in us; we harden and stupify our souls; so monstrously degenerating from the perfection of our kind, and becoming rather like savage beasts than sociable men; yea, somewhat worse perhaps than many beasts; for commonly brutes will combine to the succour of one another, they will defend and help those of the same kind.[39]

The Puritanical mind allotted no such instincts to fallen men. Even a regenerate man could gain satisfaction from charitable acts only through a realization that he was executing God's commands as expressed in scripture. Finally, there was a universalism in Anglicanism that had no counterpart in Puritanism. The Anglican church purportedly encompassed all Englishmen, not just some of them. Puritans, in contrast, although sometimes acknowledging the obligation to succour *in extremis* even the enemies of Christ, looked first to the needs of the regenerate, to their own religious community, to the sect.[40]

The differences in emphasis and motive were of course accented at the two extremes of the religious spectrum, but there was a large middle ground that seems to have been occupied by increasing numbers of clergymen. These men bequeathed to the eighteenth century an attitude toward charity and poverty that was united on the essentials, in other words, a Protestant attitude. Historians who doubt this should read through the sermons and pamphlet literature of the early eighteenth century dealing with charity, poverty, and regulation of the poor, and see how well they can identify without labels (after the fashion of a blind wine-tasting) which ones were written by Dissenters. If one turns from texts to activity, one finds that eighteenth-century Dissenting sects looked after the poor of their congregations in a manner that reflected the attitudes of the country as a whole. The Quakers, who struggled hard to maintain their separateness from the rest of English society, provide an interesting example. They not only insisted on each local meeting's responsibility for its own poor, but also developed a rather elaborate "settlement law" to deal with migrations from one meeting to another. In other words they set up a scheme that mirrored the Poor Law system of the society from which they so earnestly wished to remain alienated.[41]

In articulating the Protestant view of charity in the early eighteenth century the Church of England's voice was dominant.[42] Churchmen, as we have seen, considered relief of the poor to be an essential part of Christianity. "It is vain for him to pretend to love either God or Man, who loves his Money so much better, that he will see his poor brother (who is a Man, and bears the image of God) suffer all extremities, rather than part with anything to relieve him." Those are the modulated phrases of *The Whole Duty of Man*. Isaac Barrow put it more bluntly: "[H]e that appears hard-hearted and close-fisted towards his needy brother, let him think or call himself what he pleaseth, he plainly is no

Christian, but a blemish, a reproach, and a scandal to that honourable name."[43] But the established church did not monopolize the theme. Throughout the eighteenth century Dissenting ministers stressed the Christian's obligation to the poor. For Calvinists there was no doctrinal inconsistency in this: if the pursuit of an earthly calling was in truth the work of God, then the fruits of that work were to be disposed of not for personal pleasure but in ways pleasing to Him.[44]

A crucial question arises, however. We have been speaking of the teachings of clergymen. Since, as we have noted, clerical authority disappeared from the English scene in the late seventeenth century, were these fine sentiments of even the slightest importance in the eighteenth? The answer is that they were of great importance, although admittedly they had to swim with other, perhaps more powerful, currents. To say that clerical institutional authority disappeared is not to say that religious conscience became of no account. Tawney's portrait of a society suddenly smothered in secularism, and of a church readily abandoning the task of criticizing the conduct of economic relations "to the rationalist and the humanitarian," does not accord with the facts. Moreover, it presupposes a fundamental and complete antithesis of religious and secular ideas that clergymen of the late seventeenth and early eighteenth century were not disposed to accept, especially Anglicans. On the contrary, churchmen of the time endeavored to shore up their intellectual authority by melding reason and humanity with Christian charity. Drawing on all three, they elaborated a code of conduct which they believed was pleasing to God as well as salutary for mankind. Its guiding principle was benevolence, and it assumed, as did most English Enlightened philosophy, the existence of a benevolent deity. With this code they addressed the "main army" that Tawney said they had ignored.[45] Whether the eighteenth century in England deserves to be called, as Hannah More called it, the Age of Benevolence may be disputed, but there can be no doubting that the ideal of benevolence was ubiquitous throughout the century; nor can it be doubted that religious teaching was the main contributor to its influence.[46]

We shall return to the role of benevolence presently. It is time to turn to the secular views and influences that were in the ascendant in the early eighteenth century.

POLITICAL ECONOMY

The "river of ice" upon which, Tawney said, Richard Baxter's kindly seeds of economic morality fell and withered was "lay opinion," secular in its inspiration but well chilled by the bleak attitudes toward character and conduct that Puritanism had bequeathed. The main stream of that river was mercantilism, which dominated English economic thought between 1650 and 1750. Its doctrines respecting the laboring poor were brilliantly portrayed in a long essay by Edgar Furniss published in 1920.[47] Essentially they may be reduced to a principle that Furniss called "the utility of poverty." The broad underlying assumption was that wealth and power depended on large numbers of poor laborers, who were looked upon as units of industrial machinery would be today, and valued as such. The relationship between labor and wealth seemed simple and direct. Labor was the measure of total product value. Hence the prime object of social policy was to "set the poor on work" and to insure that drudgery became habitual to them. Prudence dictated that some method of relief should exist to prevent these "low and . . . illiterate" creatures, who were "the most useful people in the common-wealth,"[48] from dying off when their circumstances became peculiarly hard. But aside from the fact that their poverty put them in danger of death or debilitation, it was seen as generally beneficial. Only poverty, it was supposed, induced people to work steadily in the "meanest employments" at wages low enough to keep English manufactures competitive with foreign goods. Thus early eighteenth-century economic thought endorsed poverty and pointed toward a policy of strict and oppressive regulation of the poor. Although many, perhaps most, economic writers of the time sincerely believed that such methods were the only route to any lasting amelioration,[49] it is nevertheless clear that mercantilistic economics offered a rational excuse for viewing misery with complacency and an argument for limiting charitable assistance.

Mercantilism was the age's most notable and comprehensive body of economic doctrine. But we should bear in mind that its influence was supplemented by various diffuse notions about the causes of progress of nations. Englishmen of the late seventeenth century always had one eye on the envied and admired Dutch. Sir William Petty noted that the Dutch, because they were a "crowded" people, had to work hard and to trade, and thereby built a civilization. Thinly populated Ireland, by contrast, was uncivilized because the lazy Irish were able to earn enough for a week's food in two days.[50] The notion that drudging labor was the kind most essential to the wealth of nations and progress of civilization was reinforced by a revived awareness of the economic benefits of slavery. The press and popular literature were filled with allusions to the dazzling new wealth generated across the Atlantic by black slaves, and high culture was on familiar terms with the image and example of the ancient world's slave economies. The lesson seemed simple: prosperity and civilization depended on a large population of menial laborers.[51]

Keeping this population poorly paid and confined to menial tasks amounted of course to keeping them in their place. That was a policy which needed no particular economic justification. The long-standing conception of a hierarchy of nature and society, arraying rich and poor in a scheme ordained, as some believed, by Divine Providence, still held sway. But economic considerations gave this tradition powerful reinforcement. Sir William Petty thought that when employment was lacking, it would be best to have people working even if they only moved the "Stones at *Stonehenge* to *Tower-Hill,* or the like; for at worst this would keep their mindes to discipline and obedience, and their bodies to a patience of more profitable labours when need shall require it."[52] Anything that might detract from this was generally considered dangerous: children were thus to be inured to deprivation, discipline, and hard labor from an early age and were to be brought up to expect nothing else.

If we examine Bernard Mandeville's writings, we may see these various ingredients displayed. (Mandeville was a clever sounding board for what passed as hardheaded thinking in his day.) "[I]t is manifest," he asserted, "that in a free Nation where Slaves are not allow'd of, the surest Wealth consists in a Multitude of laborious Poor; for besides that they are the never-failing Nursery of Fleets and Armies, without them there could be no Enjoyment, and no Product of any Country could be valuable." The problem was to keep them working. His view was: "If nobody did Want no body would work; but the greatest Hardships are look'd upon as solid Pleasures, when they keep a Man from Starving." Mandeville pushed the logic of the utility of poverty to its extreme, urging that "great Numbers" of people "should be Ignorant as well as Poor," so that they would never look beyond menial labor. The quotations above are taken from his "Essay against the Charity Schools," attached to *The Fable of the Bees;*[53] but his argument against those schools is most vividly displayed in the Sixth Dialogue, Part II of *The Fable,* where Cleomenes (who is Mandeville talking) explains that the poor who are "least wretched as to themselves, as well as most useful to the Publick" are those who "submit to the Station they are in with Chearfulness;" he also makes the totally unfounded assertion that those who send their children to charity schools are the worst sort, "idle, sottish People, that ... are neglectful of their Families, and only want ... to shake off the Burden of providing for their Brats from their own Shoulders." When Horatio answers that "it is barbarous, that the Children of the labouring Poor should be for ever pinn'd down ... to that slavish Condition," Cleomenes brushes it aside by saying that it does not always happen because some, by hard work and saving, will inevitably rise. But the point that Cleomenes hammers home is that the proponents of the charity schools have something else in mind, namely an ambitious plan by which "universal Benevolence" would "every where industriously lift up the indigent Labourer from his Meanness," which of course would be "injurious to the whole Kingdom." To show this, he goes off into one of those back-of-the-envelope calculations that are so characteristic of the age. He supposes that "the hard and dirty Labour throughout the Nation requires three Millions of Hands," and that if one-tenth of the children of the poor were "to be exempt from the lowest Drudgery," the work must either remain undone or be done "by the Children of others, that had been better bred." Horatio sees the light, noting that charity for some brings cruelty to others.[54] Mandeville's sympathies, it appears, lie with the "better bred" children who might be forced downward.

To people of liberal inclinations who have acquired an affection for the eighteenth century, Mandeville makes for uncomfortable reading. He has Voltaire's cynicism without Voltaire's instinct for the underdog.[55] Some have argued that Mandeville was really a moralist who, like Swift, used satire as his weapon to fight the good fight, and is therefore not to be taken at his word. Others have viewed him as a realist who went beyond accepting social evil to arguing the inutility of amelioration. The second view is the essentially correct one. Most of his ideas about the poor were not controversial at the time, and it is therefore impossible to suppose they were meant satirically. What was controversial was his effort to demonstrate the futility of ameliorating the condition of the poor or educating their children. Mandeville found satisfaction in making his readers realize the full implication of their attitudes, and sought to rub their noses in it. We have every reason to believe that, on this subject at least, he meant exactly what he wrote.[56]

But how can we be sure that his attitude toward the poor represents the commonplace attitude of his time? Even if there were space here to string out quotations from other writers, the result would not be conclusive. What we shall do instead is confront Mandeville with an opponent, the Rev. Dr. Isaac Watts, a Dissenting minister. Grandson of a Commonwealth navy captain, son of a Southampton clothier and chapel deacon, Watts is best known as a hymn writer; he wrote "Joy to the World," "Oh God, Our Help in Ages Past," and numerous others, about a dozen of which have found their way into the Anglican hymnal. His prose works encompassed theology, education, logic, and natural philosophy.[57] In him we have an articulate Christian humanitarian embodying the enlightened outlook of his age, whether one thinks of it as the Age of Benevolence or the Age of Newton.

In 1728 Watts published a pamphlet entitled *An Essay Towards the Encouragement of Charity Schools*. (We may reasonably infer from the timing that it was provoked by Mandeville's attack.) It includes of course a Christian warning:

Now if the Poor know nothing at all, but are bred up in gross Ignorance, and constant Stupidity, 'tis supposed they are fitter to become *Beasts of Burden* all their Lives, without ever thinking that they are *Men*. If this be the Case, I pity the Slaves indeed; but wo to their Lords and Masters, who keep them all their lives in such profound Ignorance upon such wretched and inhumane Motives. There is a Day coming when the Rich and the Poor shall appear without Distinction before that God who is no *Accepter of Persons*.[58]

However, practical questions predominate. Watts asks whether Englishmen want their land to be peopled with slaves and heathens or with men who worship God and value liberty. Do they want to live among brutes or "reasonable Creatures"? May not charity schools serve to educate young people to work hard and diligently? If the poor "have no manner of Learning bestowed upon them," how can anyone expect "Truth, . . . Honesty and Faithfulness" from them? "How little Sense will Servants have of the Honour and Obedience that is due to their own Masters?" Moreover, is not a servant who can read and write far more useful to his master, especially if his master must be absent from the household from time to time? Recognizing how difficult it is to find constant employment for young people, is it better that they should be allowed to go their own way, "in Danger of growing idle and slothful" as they "wander about the Streets and Lanes, and lie exposed to all manner of Iniquity?" And if it should happen that occasionally some good brains should be discovered among the charity-school pupils, "why should not such sprightly Children . . . have their Chance to rise in the World? . . . Why should the World be deprived of all the Benefit that might be drawn from such ingenious Minds, under the Care of a happy education?"[59] Watts did not share, as Mandeville did, the common supposition of his age that menial labor was the foundation of wealth: " 'Tis not menial Servants," he wrote, "but Mechanicks and Manufacturers that increase the Commodities, and thereby the Riches of the Nation."

But let us observe certain other points that this practical Christian humanitarian made in the same tract. Either because of personal conviction or recognition of the invincible prejudices of his readers, Watts accepted the hierarchical social system. There is no mistaking this. Among the propositions which he laid down at the outset were these: that "Great God has wisely ordained in the Course of his Providence in all Ages, that among Mankind there should be some Rich, and some Poor: And the same Providence hath alloted to the Poor the meaner Services"; that the "Children of the Poor (especially such as need the Charity of their Neighbours) should not be generally educated in such a Manner as may raise them above the Services of a lower Station"; but that an exception should be made for children of parents who formerly "enjoyed plentiful Circumstances in Life" but since then "have been reduced to great degrees of Poverty." And so, like Mandeville, Watts indicated a special concern for those reduced in rank. "Such misery," he commented, "has somewhat a Sacred Tenderness belonging to it, and seems to claim the Regards of Sympathy and Compassion from those who now enjoy plentiful Circumstances, while they meditate on the Uncertainty of human affairs, and remember that they are liable to the like Calamity." So the stations in life were substantially fixed; they were ordained by God. It was also ordained that the lower orders should "gain their Bread by the Sweat of their Brows"; their children should not be bred "too high for that Station in Life, for which their Birth has designed them," and the schools should make every effort to include manual labor in the curriculum. Indeed, one practical benefit was that the schools would *discourage* habits of idleness. The clothes given to the charity children should be "of the coarsest Kind, and of plainest Form" in order to distinguish them "from Children of better Rank, and they ought always to be so distinguished." The "Sons of Tradesmen and Mechanicks" who paid "Publick-Taxes and Parish-Dues" and sometimes gave to the poor had "a Right" to be employed in all the "Stations, as Clerks or Servants to Merchants and others, wherein there is a Prospect of Advancement in Life," and charity pupils should not be preferred to them.[60]

One senses from all this that Watts was in an uphill battle. His purpose in writing the tract was to encourage the development of Dissenting charity schools by answering objections which he acknowledged to be "common and popular."[61] Essentially he was pleading for humane treatment of a mass of people who, according to a social system that he accepted, were bound to be regarded as despicable. His acceptance of that system meant that he and Mandeville occupied a great deal of common ground (in regard to the poor) which encompassed the common prejudices of his age.

This form of social prejudice was probably reinforced by economic circumstances peculiar to the time. It appears that labor-market conditions in the first half of the eighteenth century, dismal as they may seem to us today, favored manual workers in England to a degree which at the time was unprecedented. Watts alluded to this and expressed the familiar complaint himself in these words: "Do they not claim larger Wages and at the same time refuse to do the servile Works that belong to their Place?" His answer was not a denial that this happened, but a denial that schools could be the cause of it.[62] To understand why workers seemed to be particularly unwilling to work at this time, as compared with former times, we must explore briefly some economic history.

Between 1660 and 1740 real wages rose in England. Prices of wheat and most manufactured goods declined while nominal wages were slowly inching up.[63] The decline of food prices was momentous. The reason for the long-term downward trend was probably agricultural improvement, although there were admittedly some decades of fine grain-growing weather and the "sunspot theory" cannot be entirely ruled out.[64] The important point is that wages did not follow food prices downward. A diarist recorded in 1732: "plentyfull of all provisions, corn cheap and trade good, soe that labouring people lived well." Although low agricultural prices "broke many" small farmers, there were "great wages for spining and other labouring people" in such years of plenty.[65] The most bountiful decades brought especially good times to wage earners, but the whole period was broadly favorable to them. Between 1660 and 1740 the growth of population in England was quite slow,[66] and this prevented the gains in real income from being nullified by pressure of excess population on wages.

Obviously, with abundant food — England was a net exporter of grain at this time — and slow population growth, fears like those Malthus later evoked could not thrive. This helps to explain why a great mass of laboring poor was viewed as an asset rather than a menace; and it also helps to explain the optimism with which various projects for employing and training the poor were put forward. Naturally, the fact that workers and servants were not always easy to get, tended to deaden charitable instincts and intensify resentment of idleness and insubordination. London absorbed a substantial portion of the nation's population increase, and manufacturing and pastoral areas took the rest.[67] Although there was a great deal of seasonal unemployment, there appeared to be a "great Want of Ploughmen and Labourers in the Country,"[68] and industry could not count on the steady services of a class of manufacturing wage earners. Pastoral and forest people, as well as many miners and industrial journeymen, worked at mixed employments: modest farming of a specialized sort was intermingled with weaving, spinning, knitting, mining, metal handicrafts, and countless other occupations. "As the market for industrial goods expanded, it met labour shortages which peasant-workers could not, or would not, satisfy, and which are reflected in the rapid rise in textile wages in the first half of the eighteenth century."[69] Thus, the trend of economic developments may have had an impact on attitudes toward the laboring poor. Against this background we may easily see why the employing classes bewailed the traditional leisure preference of the labourer so loudly and why there was so marked an emphasis on bringing up the children of the poor in the habit of steady, arduous labor. The abundance and cheapness of food added a practical dimension to the notion of the utility of poverty.

In summing up the situation in 1750, we may observe that there were two widely held attitudes toward the poor existing side by side. Although they were not mutually exclusive, they were grounded on different premises and in many respects pointed toward different policies, so that well-meaning and humane Englishmen at the time were in constant danger of contradicting themselves on the subject. The dominant one supposed that the poor should never have misery lifted from them, nor their children be encouraged to look beyond the plough or loom. It reflected traditional notions of social hierarchy and was reinforced by economic theories about labor and motivation. The other attitude was derived chiefly from Christian ethics. It held that the duty of the rich was to treat the poor with kindness and compassion, and to aid them in times of distress. This benevolent attitude did not provide a suitable basis for policy making; rather it was a reminder of conscience, of the fact that the ill-clad, filthy laboring masses, habitually viewed with contempt by their betters, were equally God's creatures, whom a Christian community could neither exclude nor ignore. It was an attitude less visible in the world of politics, and its role therefore appears to have been subordinate.

Before we leave this period and turn to the later eighteenth century, we must take a moment to reemphasize the point that the foundations of the dominant attitude were secular. Tawney made the point himself, but he also tried to argue that Puritanism intensified the attitude's implicit hardheartedness by its emphasis on individual responsibility; therefore Puritanism left in its wake a sense of self-discipline that sharpened awareness of the distinction between deserving and undeserving poor. Against this view it may be pointed out that individualism — indisputably an important ingredient of eighteenth-century social thought — had political as well as religious roots, and also that the distinction between deserving and undeserving poor was not invented in the seventeenth century.[70] The most one can say is that there were elements in both the political and the religious culture of the seventeenth century that firmly imprinted the importance of distinguishing between deserving and undeserving poor on the English mind.

But we should not forget how little bearing this distinction had on the idea of the utility of poverty. Mandeville was not concerned with who was deserving or undeserving. The attitude he mirrored treated the lower orders as a race apart, to be manipulated and conditioned, and regarded as not even remotely capable of responding to individualist incentives. The laboring poor were to be dealt with much as one would deal with domesticated animals, and Mandeville rested his case, as did all those who argued the utility of poverty, on sheer animal instinct for survival.[71] The contrast with Puritanism's stress on self-betterment and the shamefulness of indolence could hardly be more striking. The dominant theory regarding the laboring poor in the first half of the eighteenth century was essentially fashioned from nonreligious materials.[72]

THE LATER EIGHTEENTH CENTURY

The theory of the utility of poverty could not last. A nation that had brought off the Glorious Revolution of 1688, thereby embracing the doctrine that government existed for the benefit of individuals, and had become persuaded that individual incentives were the real guarantors of freedom, prosperity, and civilization, could not forever allow its economic theory to exhibit the primacy of such incentives in every sphere except that in which the poor man offered his labor. Early eighteenth-century England's economic beliefs about the laboring poor were not only at odds with its religious conscience but also with the rationale of its most treasured political achievement.

This circumstance did not elude Samuel Johnson's sharp eye for hypocrisy. When Soame Jenyns wrote something that echoed Mandeville's arguments against charity schools, Johnson answered thus:

To entail irreversible poverty upon generation after generation only because the ancestor happened to be poor is in itself cruel, if not unjust, and is wholly contrary to the maxims of a commercial nation, which always suppose and promote a rotation of property, and offer every individual a chance of mending his condition by his deligence.[73]

When we see a staunch Tory advancing the fitness of equality of opportunity—this was in 1757—we may suppose that change was in the air. But the change in attitudes took time.[74] It was not a simple matter of generational reaction, nor can it be satisfactorily explained by a vague reference to the arrival of a "wave of humanitarianism."[75]

The major breakthrough came in 1776, when a philosopher of great learning, penetration, and literary persuasiveness published his *Inquiry into the Nature and Causes of the Wealth of Nations.* Adam Smith did not mince words: "No society can surely be flourishing and happy, of which the far greater part of the members are poor and miserable." This was unmistakably a riposte to Mandeville, Jenyns, and the rest of them. *The Wealth of Nations,* widely recognized as an attack on protectionism, colonialism, and bullionism, was much more than that: it was a calculated revision of certain principles that dominated English economic thought in the earlier eighteenth century, most notably the premise that wealth had to be based either on slave labor in the Indies or on its next of kin in Britain. After a lengthy argument in favor of the "liberal reward of labour" Smith remarked, "To complain of it, is to lament over the necessary effect and cause of the greatest public prosperity."[76] He even offered an explanation of why employers tended to imagine that laborers worked best when pressed by poverty:

Masters of all sorts, therefore, frequently make better bargains with their servants in dear than in cheap years, and find them more humble and dependent in the former than in the latter. They naturally, therefore, commend the former as more favourable to industry.[77]

Smith's argument against low wages was of course an economist's argument, founded on economic incentives, that is, on self-interest: "It is not from the benevolence of the butcher, the brewer, or the baker, that we expect our dinner, but from their regard to their own interest." His matrix of bargains and incentives *encom-*

passed everyone, including the humblest laborer. It answered the utility-of-poverty theory on its own ground.[78]

Adam Smith's great book clinched victory for a revisionist argument that had been gaining influence over four decades. Berkeley and Hume had been seconded by a growing body of economic writers who reasoned that high wages and a high standard of living for laborers and craftsmen meant economic progress for the nation.[79] It is important to realize that these writers perceived and were impressed by recent developments in the British economy. Smith was too. The vigor and confidence that spill off the pages of *The Wealth of Nations* tell us of an author who feels he has seen the world firsthand and knows how it works. He has observed the productive efficiency that arises from the application of capital and proper division of labor, and he knows that the goods produced by English workers are fully competitive with goods produced by miserable wretches in other countries.[80] Still, we may wonder about the optimism that pervades the book, and why such economic indicators were not suspected by Smith of signaling a merely temporary or contingent advance. The best answer is a fundamental one: that there was in the middle decades of the eighteenth century an emerging sense that the basic conditions affecting life, work, well-being, safety, and prospects of progress in Britain had changed.[81] This change altered the terms in which the problem of poverty could be viewed and thus cleared the way for a resolution of eighteenth-century England's contradictory theories of freedom and wealth.

We may describe this change, using the words of Dr. Eversley, as the advent of the "non-catastrophic world." Referring to England, he observes: "After 1740, for the first time, more people live in a non-catastrophic world. Food, shelter, and clothing became a certain expectation. Calamitous deaths became rare."[82] There is no disputing this (assuming that "calamitous deaths," natural or manmade, refers only to large surges of mortality). The noncatastrophic world arrived in England by the mid-eighteenth century because three major catastrophes that had always frustrated material progress—war, pestilence, and famine—virtually disappeared.[83]

For the disappearance of the threat of war, we may call on architectural evidence. Cities like Lincoln and Durham were not built on hills for the view, nor were other English cities encircled by walls for convenience. The dilapidation of English town defenses has not, to my knowledge, been systematically studied, but it is known that many boroughs still had their walls in the civil war or refurbished them at that time. It also appears that during the later eighteenth century English burghers generally viewed their ancient walls and gates as traffic-clogging nuisances. In city after city they were demolished by a citizenry who thought they had seen the last of baronial anarchy, rurally based depredations, civil war, invasion, and plunder.[84] By midcentury it had become clear that their first line of defense could repulse the best that France could throw at them, and for various reasons the problem of domestic disorder had become one to which city walls did not offer much of an answer. From invasion Englishmen had been delivered by their navy, and from internal strife by their political settlement.

In 1723 they could also congratulate themselves on having avoided the bubonic plague that swept through the south of France in 1720-22. It was expected to hit Britain and never did. Perhaps they were just lucky, some natural alteration in the propagation of the disease serving to spare them, but perhaps they had a right to believe that their own effort in mounting a strict quarantine had walled it out.[85] At any rate, eighteenth-century England was free of plague—the last massive epidemic was in 1665—and there was no serious cholera until the nineteenth century.[86] Smallpox was the most prevalent epidemic disease in the eighteenth century, but its effects were localized, and the occasions when more than 15 percent of any particular community died seem to have been rare.

Although England had not experienced a serious famine in centuries, fear of shortage had never been eradicated from the popular mind. Many English towns had public granaries in the sixteenth century. The biblical account of lean years and fat years touched on a matter that was close to home in seventeenth-century England, for when consecutive crop failures occurred, the desperate populace at that time tended to consume some of the seed corn.[87] In the eighteenth century the state of the grain crop continued to be noted everywhere and by everyone, because its manifold effects on economic life were realized;[88] but as midcentury approached, the subject stirred up less apprehension. As we have seen, low prices were the rule, high prices the exception;

England's substantial exports of grain from 1700 to 1750 signified reserve capacity.[89] By midcentury, Englishmen could reasonably believe that famine had been banished from the country. Not only was there copious domestic production of food but there was a capitalist marketing system that enticed food from one part of England to another according to need; there were turnpikes, coasting vessels, and canals to move it; and there were municipal and Poor Law authorities, whose action was essential to compensate, in times of temporary scarcity, for the high prices upon which the capitalist marketing mechanism depended.[90] These things did not suddenly spring up in the mid-eighteenth century, but they now seemed to work effectively.

War, pestilence, famine—the elimination of any one of these was a giant step. The elimination of all three was momentous. Yet the transformation has not been much noticed, partly because it is so difficult to pinpoint, and partly because history has a bias toward what starts rather than what stops. The catastrophic world, with its attendant need for magic and superstition, was gone. In 1650 Englishmen opposed census taking on the ground that numbering the people was forbidden by Scripture and might bring on the plague; in 1750 they opposed it because they feared it might be an instrument for collecting taxes more efficiently. In 1650 life insurance was viewed as a form of betting, and the church objected to betting on a thing so sacred as human life;[91] in 1750 insurance had become a recognized means of converting (Renaissance) risk enterprise into (Weberian) sober enterprise, and life insurance was seen as an adjunct to this sort of business prudence. (Today, of course, it is the uninsured person who is thought to be betting.)

Obviously, in that earlier world there had been no hope of eliminating poverty; at best it could be ameliorated until Divine retribution or inscrutable wisdom—however you saw it—once again laid society on its back. Therefore it did not seem sensible to suppose that individual initiative had much bearing on the earthly fate of the lower orders. Struggle as they might, they would be overwhelmed sooner or later by the disruption of peace or the forces of nature; their behavior reflected this outlook.[92] In the catastrophic world, fatalism and resignation pervaded the attitudes of both rich and poor. The Reformation undoubtedly initiated a change in outlook. The concept of an omniscient, omnipotent God who knew exactly what he was doing ruled out mere chance and vitiated the allure of ecclesiastical magic: "people were now taught that their practical difficulties could only be solved by a combination of self-help and prayer to God."[93] But we should not carry the implications of this new viewpoint too far too soon. The Puritans, who were its chief promoters in England, were well aware that God did not always punish the idle, improvident, or wicked, and did not confine his punishments to them. It was a fact that gave them much trouble. The Almighty dealt terrible blows to individuals, communities, and nations, some of the blows apparently deserved, others completely mystifying. All that godly men could do was search out the sins that provoked His displeasure and try to be grateful for His warning.[94] Theirs was a dilemma of belief confronting realities of life in a catastrophic world. This explains why the idea of *managing* the lower orders was firmly in place in the later seventeenth and early eighteenth centuries, but optimism about permanently bettering their condition was not. Optimism depended on the arrival of the non-catastrophic world.

The social optimism that came to the fore during the later eighteenth century was expressed in three broad currents of thought, one religious in inspiration, the other two secular. The religious one was Methodism, which assumed that although human beings were inherently vicious and depraved, the human will had immense potential if assisted by divine power, the availability of which was revealed by Christ's life and mission. Wesley picked up the loose strands of English Dissent that were lying in disarray in the earlier eighteenth century.[95] His object was saving souls. His movement, however, not only carried the Protestant ethic to the poor but also, as the major force in the Evangelical revival, caused it eventually to pervade the outlook of many of the rich. Another current was Benthamism, which envisioned a set of laws that would be perfectly tailored to the achievement of utilitarian goals; the laws would incite people to choose to act in ways that accorded with the general improvement of society as a whole. There was an inherent assumption that any conflicts as to what was beneficial could be overcome by legislative "fine-tuning." The third current was political economy as expounded by Adam Smith, which we have already discussed. It was perhaps less optimistic than the others about general and permanent betterment of the human condition.[96] All three of these currents credited the lower orders with an instinct for patient self-help, or at least a capacity to develop that instinct. Indeed, the more hopeful outlook was premised upon it.[97]

All three of these eighteenth-century currents, plus the seventeenth-century legacy of liberty, played a powerful role in early nineteenth-century English thought. But the ingredients of the nineteenth-century consensus were not yet determined. An important development intervened. Against these intellectual currents there flowed during the later eighteenth century, gently at first but with great force in the last decade or two, a new tide of economic facts, and these economic facts played a major role in shaping attitudes toward the poor as the century neared its close.

After about 1750, perhaps 1760, the trends of prices and wages began to move against the laboring poor. Population growth, which had registered a minuscule net increase on the order of 0.2 percent per year in the first half of the century, rose to 0.5 percent after 1750, and jumped to 1.0 percent after 1790. The increasing supply of labor tended to hold down wage rates.[98] At the same time, food prices rose, possibly under the influence of population growth; after the late 1760s they rose more steeply; in the dearths of 1795 and 1800-1801 they soared. The real wages of ordinary laborers thus went into a declining trend. High prices were hard on both agricultural laborers and the people who divided their time between farming and industrial pursuits. The latter in particular had been favored by the low price of breadcorn before 1750; now the situation was reversed. In certain industries where employment opportunities were favorable, total family income was well above the subsistence level;[99] here the maxims about frugality, hard work, and self-discipline seemed to be borne out in practice. But for most of the laboring poor they were irrelevant.

Mandeville had remarked that although the poor "ought to be kept from starving," they "should receive nothing worth saving."[100] The strong tendency of social thought seventy-five years after he wrote was that they should be encouraged in every possible way to save, to lay up a reserve against hard times. The irony of history was that at the same time such encouragement was on the rise, the trend of prices and wages was making it harder and harder for most of them to save anything. Whatever may have been put aside for a rainy day—and no laborer with three or more children was likely to save anything anyway—was wiped out during the next run of bad harvests.

These harvest crises displayed poverty in the most visible form and thus gave great stimulus to the spirit of benevolence. The workers themselves may have been aware of a gradual erosion of living standards—it is hard to know—but they were certainly aware of the sharp deterioration that occurred in the years of dearth, and let the authorities know it, sometimes by rioting. The humane answer, perhaps the easiest, was public assistance. Poor Law authorities paid rents, distributed coals, and provided family allowances, especially in times of dearth. In these measures they were impelled by necessity as well as benevolence.[101] As such expedients became regular practice, laborers were gradually pauperized, especially in rural southern England. Thus, at a time when the ideal of self-sustaining independence with a view toward self-betterment was becoming among the intelligentsia the recognized key for solving the problem of poverty, the laboring poor were becoming increasingly dependent on charity and public assistance. Naturally this circumstance prevented the accent on individual responsibility from overcoming traditional Christian benevolence. As a result, both ideals were ascendant at the end of the century, although theoretically they were incompatible, or at least largely so.[102]

The nineteenth-century consensus, as outlined earlier, is not conceivable without either a sharp curtailment of the influence of traditional benevolence or a transformation of the meaning of benevolence. Both occurred. The key intellectual blow was struck by Thomas Malthus as the century closed. The famous *Essay on Population* fell upon a nation beset by severe scarcities and inflating prices. Malthus's main point about geometric growth of population and arithmetic growth of the means of subsistence is well known. His specific criticism of public relief boiled down to one argument: it was self-defeating. Its beneficial effects would always be offset by inflation of food prices, lower production (because the amount of labor offered would be reduced), and expanding population (stimulated by guaranteed subsistence). But giving regular relief to the poor was worse than throwing money away. In the long run, it spelled disaster because it would nullify all efforts to inculcate in laborers a sense of the virtues of the

Protestant ethic. Malthus did not use these terms, but this is what he meant.[103] Since the only hope of amelioration lay in self-reliance, the Poor Laws were in effect a fraud. True benevolence called for the curtailment of relief.

However contradictory Malthus's various arguments may be, his main point about population had an enormous influence.[104] In effect, what Malthus did was to reinstate the mentality of a catastrophic world in a new guise. The source of catastrophe was now the uncontrollable force of sexual lust (which Southey jeeringly referred to as "menstrual pollution").[105] Hobbes had imagined the possibilities of an overpopulated world, and his simple comment upon it suited the outlook of that earlier age: "And when all the world is over-charged with inhabitants, then the last remedy of all is War, which provideth for every man by victory or death."[106] In contrast, Malthus's view was historically directional; his promise of creeping deterioration resonated with his era's sensitivity to gradual social transition.[107]

Malthusianism accounts for the fanatic quality of the nineteenth-century outlook on poverty, for the fact that people of professed good will could convince themselves that ordinary workers ought to be able to guard, without external assistance, not only against predictable vicissitudes of life, such as old age, sickness, or the burden of raising young children, but also against unpredictable catastrophes like death of the breadwinner, incapacitating injury, prolonged unemployment, or suddenly surging food prices. The influence of Malthusianism explains why the inculcation of the laboring poor with the virtues of the Protestant ethic, which had been seen in the late eighteenth century as an avenue toward brightness and hope, was seen in the nineteenth as an indispensable bulwark against darkness and disaster.

In summing up, we should redirect our attention to the early decades of the eighteenth century. At that time the vision of social progress was chiefly focused on the strength, prosperity, and cultural elevation of English civilization, none of which, it was believed, could be sustained without the blessings of Protestant Christianity. This vision excluded the poor, or, more accurately, its glance in their direction saw only the problem of keeping them orderly and productive. Although some Christian activists were deeply concerned about the spiritual and moral improvement of the poor, their benevolence was constrained from encompassing material improvement. Where material benefi- cence was to be directed toward nonspiritual ends, it was thought to be properly confined to answering the calls of distress, a policy that was consonant with the prevailing sense of the incurability of poverty. A century later the vision of social progress was in many respects not very different, but, for reasons that we have sur- veyed, there was one profound change: the poor were no longer regarded as mere handmaidens of society, but as constituent ele- ments of the civil order. Society was now seen as the sum of its human parts, and each part was potentially capable of respond- ing to the same set of incentives. To be sure, not all the parts were considered equal, but the mass of smaller ones seemed imposing enough to determine the outcome—to carry society to new heights or new depths. The hopes of the optimists and the gloom of the Malthusians both rested on a numerical equation.

The foregoing is an essay in the history of ideas, aiming to identify attitudes that were ascendant at particular times, place them in a correct relationship, detect their sources of inspiration, and display the circumstances that permitted them to flourish.[108] It cannot pretend to be comprehensive. Nor can the inherent un- certainty of the undertaking be denied: the validity of its results must rest on an array of texts rich enough to display both intellec- tual invention and enduring tradition, and for this very reason the timing of the phases cannot be established beyond doubt. Yet the discovery of "that objective mind which controls the thinking and doing of an age," as G. M. Young put it,[109] is the supreme goal of historical inquiry and represents its most humane aspect. It is also, as Young's formulation indicates, an indispensable pre- requisite of any causal explanation of decisions and events.

This raises the important question of how these attitudes that we have traced affected the treatment of the poor. It is not our purpose to answer this, but the complexity of the problem posed by it deserves a brief closing comment. When Christopher Hill writes, "Thought about charity was changing rapidly in the six- teenth and seventeenth centuries, and changing to the detriment of the poor," he offers a simplistic assertion that can only cause confusion when the facts are examined; the literary dexterity with which he applies interesting information to support the assertion serves only to make confusion enjoyable.[110] For if we consider no more than the problem of the impact of ideas and attitudes on policy, as if no other influences existed, we must at the very outset try to discover what ideas the policymakers held. It will not do to suppose that the dominant national currents whose shifts have been traced in this essay were influential everywhere or even in the majority of localities; and this is a point of special importance when considering the English Poor Law prior to the nineteenth century, when policy was fashioned in the parishes much more than in Parliament. Indeed, one of the main purposes of the great Poor Law Amendment Act of 1834 was to make possible the imposition of the dominant national attitude on localities that either did not share it or did not wish it to govern their management of the poor. Therefore, to take the early years of the eighteenth century for the purpose of illustration, although we may confidently relate the enactment of workhouse legislation to the then dominant national attitude toward the poor, we may not assume that workhouses were widely established and kept up along the lines intended by the legislation. The same period provides another example of a different kind: the foundation of charity schools. Unquestionably there was a strong connection between religious imperatives and the charity-school movement, but the historian must be wary because, as noted earlier, one of the distinctive features of early eighteenth-century English Christianity was its inclination to incorporate secular wisdom wherever possible. There are other kinds of pitfalls, but it is not necessary to pursue them. The point, which ought to be obvious, is that in history generally, and especially the history of the poor, an explanation that attributes policy and practice to some apparently dominant idea or attitude, without further inquiry, is certain to be defective. And this holds true even for Britain in the nineteenth century, when a particular attitude toward treatment of the poor enveloped the public mind to a degree unequalled in modern history.

NOTES

In preparing this lecture for publication I have inserted some illustrative material and close argument that it seemed wise to omit when I presented it at the Clark Library in December 1977. The questions from that well-informed audience, and particularly the private comments of

Professor Gary B. Nash, indicated ways in which I might clarify my arguments, and I am very grateful to them for their assistance. I am especially grateful to William Sheasgreen, Cornell Ph.D. candidate, who supplied valuable suggestions during the early stages of this work. In the notes below, place of publication is London, unless otherwise noted.

1. Henry Peet, ed., *Liverpool Vestry Books, 1681-1834,* with introduction by W. Lyon Blease, 2 vols. (Liverpool, 1912-1915), p. xxii. Blease's introduction was originally published in *Transactions of the Historic Society of Lancashire and Cheshire,* LXI (1910), 97-182.

2. Blease became a lecturer in law at the University of Liverpool in 1910 and a professor in 1919. He was a member of the Liverpool Reform Club and wrote *A Short History of English Liberalism* (1912), which he dedicated to *The Manchester Guardian.* The period of his change of heart coincides perfectly with the Liberal government's move toward a progressive social policy, which is interesting; but we should not disregard the possible influence of taking up academic employment and writing a general history. Indeed, the sentiments of the *Vestry Books* footnote are mirrored on p. 175 of the *Short History.*

3. R. H. Tawney, *Religion and the Rise of Capitalism* (1926); based on lectures given in 1922; reprinted with a new preface in 1936. Tawney's viewpoint had been made clear in *The Acquisitive Society* (1920), especially in the opening chapters. For the impact of these books on churchmen, see E. R. Norman, *Church and Society in England 1770-1970* (Oxford, 1976), pp. 316-317.

4. E. M. Leonard, *The Early History of English Poor Relief* (Cambridge, 1900; repr. 1965); Dorothy Marshall, *The English Poor in the Eighteenth Century* (1926; repr. 1969); Sidney and Beatrice Webb, *English Poor Law History. Part I: The Old Poor Law* (1927, repr. 1963). (Tawney's work, I believe, was also in the grip of the nineteenth century in the sense that his Christian socialism was partly a reaction to the century's chief tenets.) Elizabeth Leonard's book is closely bound to legislative and administrative evidence, and the evidence controls her conclusions. She was careful to warn her readers (p. 302) of the possible irrelevance to modern market conditions of her findings concerning the economic consequences of poor relief in the period she studied (1514-1644). The other two books, however, are unmistakably biased. I am not saying that either the Webbs or Dorothy Marshall were blind to the flaws of nineteenth-century social thought, but they believed that severe reforms, such as the New Poor Law of 1834, had been necessary. This belief stemmed from an almost naive faith in the cleansing power of centralized bureaucracy, a common faith among English progressives at the time the books were written. (This is muted in Leonard's book, but her "heroic age" is clearly the period of conciliar government under Charles I.) Their sense that "untrammelled parochial responsibility" (Marshall, *English Poor,* p. 14) was an evil in itself, heavily influenced their interpretation of the era of the Old Poor Law. One might be

tempted to say that a new historiographical era dawned in 1934 when Ethyl M. Hampson—interesting how much women figure in this—published *The Treatment of Poverty in Cambridgeshire* (Cambridge, 1934), which is entirely free of the centralization mystique. But that carefully researched study never had the impact it deserved.

5. There already exists a very fine study of the more immediate influences: K. R. Poynter, *Society and Pauperism: English Ideas on Poor Relief, 1795-1834* (1969).

6. Quoted by E. W. Martin in "From Parish to Union: Poor Law Administration, 1601-1865," in Martin, ed., *Comparative Development in Social Welfare* (1972), p. 53.

7. Taunton Committee of the Labourers' Friend Society. Quoted in D. C. Barnett, "Allotments and the Problem of Rural Poverty, 1780-1840," in E. L. Jones and G. E. Mingay, eds., *Land, Labour and Population in the Industrial Revolution: Essays presented to J. D. Chambers* (1967), pp. 173-174. However, the Labourers' Friend Society, which sought to provide garden plots in rural areas, had to steer carefully between encouraging self-betterment and disturbing either the social order or the labor market. I owe this point to Mary Ann Quinn, Cornell Ph.D. candidate.

8. This belief, as we shall see, became widespread among philanthropists before the end of the eighteenth century. "Count Rumford's science, Sir Thomas Bernard's evangelical morality and Arthur Young's concern for agrarian reform all tended towards an emphasis on self-help rather than public charity" (Poynter, *Society and Pauperism*, p. 85).

9. "Let us give effect," wrote Sir Thomas Bernard, "to that master spring of action, on which equally depends the prosperity of individuals and of empires—the desire implanted in the human breast of bettering its condition" (ibid., p. 92).

10. From *Three Lectures on the Rate of Wages* (1830), quoted by Martin in *Comparative Development*, p. 43.

11. Max Weber, *The Protestant Ethic and the Spirit of Capitalism* (1930); trans. by Talcott Parsons, with a foreword by R. H. Tawney; first published in German in 1904-1905. Tawney's book was published in 1926. Christopher Hill's writings on this subject may be found primarily in "William Perkins and the Poor," repr. in *Puritanism and Revolution* (1958), pp. 215-238; and *Society and Puritanism in Pre-Revolutionary England* (1964), esp. chapters 7, 12, and 14.

12. Weber, *Protestant Ethic*, pp. 226, 238, 277-280.

13. Ibid., p. 226; also pp. 319-320. Weber was a comparativist. For him the problem that needed explaining was why some societies took to zealous capitalistic accumulation while others did not. He found capitalism to have existed in lots of places in early modern Europe, but did not find the capitalist *spirit* in all of them. The thrust of his concern permitted him to be rather careless of chronology. For these reasons, and because Weber did not really take up the questions of poverty or philanthropy, I have not addressed his work here.

Christopher Hill has inclined toward the Marxist view that Puritanism's spread was owing its attractiveness to a rising commercial class (e.g., "William Perkins and the Poor," p. 236). Tawney allowed this position some credence, but did not consider it a sufficient explanation (*Religion and Rise*, pp. 202 ff.). Hill's writings are highly readable and informative, but his arguments on this subject are not sufficiently coherent to warrant careful examination.

14. Tawney, *Religion and Rise*, pp. 183, 187-188, 212, 219.

15. Ibid., pp. 197, 199, 228, 254.

16. Ibid., pp. 231, 253-255, 264-267, 271-273.

17. Leonard J. Trinterud, "A.D. 1689: The End of the Clerical World," in Winthrop S. Hudson and L. J. Trinterud, *Theology in Sixteenth and Seventeenth-Century England* (Los Angeles, 1971), pp. 34-39.

18. Tawney, *Religion and Rise*, p. 113.

19. Ibid., pp. 234, 280, 320. He raised the issue in footnote 32, where he took up his differences with Weber, and repeated it in his foreword to the translated edition of the *Protestant Ethic* (p. 10).

20. For instance, the evidence of public-spirited Puritan charitable activity in the earlier seventeenth century—there is no significant conflict between Tawney and W. K. Jordan on this point—is thus explainable in terms of the origina Calvinist emphasis on discipline and community responsibility. (Wilbur K. Jordan has rhapsodized on the generosity of Puritan merchants in their charitable deeds; see especially his *Philanthropy in England, 1480-1660* [1959]. Although the statistical hull on which these praises float is, as reviews by D. C. Coleman and Lawrence Stone pointed out, seriously defective, one cannot be sure that the seventeenth-century Puritan was typically ungenerous to the poor.) Tawney's ascription of such charitable activity to traditional "reverence" for poverty (*Religion and Rise*, p. 263) may, for all I know, be closer to the mark than Jordan's notions about Puritan charitable impulses, but it reveals a certain diffuseness of argument, because his notion of a transformed Puritanism does not require it.

21. Tawney, *Religion and Rise*, p. 239.

22. The connection between Puritan theology and the Puritan view of the poor may be summarized as follows: Because Puritans craved assurance of election and regeneration, and could only find such assurance in action—in work understood to be God's work—they laid stress on individual conduct and character. Their God was a stern taskmaster, who viewed idleness and moral weakness not with compassion but scorn. Believing as they did in the omnipotence and omniscience of God, and in day-to-day Providential intervention in the affairs of the world, they were disposed to see penury and misery as manifestations of divine justice. (This is a simple outline of a complex problem, on which see J. Sears McGee, *The Godly Man in Stuart England: Anglicans, Puritans, and the Two Tables, 1620-1670* [New Haven, 1976], esp. pp. 29, 36, 63-67, 91, 207.) This connection is implicit in Weber's discussion of

the work ethic, but his only explicit statement is a passing remark (*Protestant Ethic,* p. 178). On the importance of work see also Stephen Foster, *Their Solitary Way: The Puritan Social Ethic in the First Century of Settlement in New England* (New Haven, 1971), pp. 105-109.

23. Samuel Clarke, *Medulla Theologiae, or The Marrow of Divinity* (1659), pp. 231, 246.

24. Richard Steele, *The Tradesman's Calling* (1684), p. 124: "poor Tradesmen and House-keepers that often want Work, and so want Bread, or are overstock'd with Children, yet are loth to complain, and asham'd to beg." Tawney (*Religion and Rise,* p. 266) quoted Steele's severe position on idle beggars (*Tradesman's Calling,* p. 22), but ignored his passage on "Mercy to the Poor" (ibid., pp. 123-124).

25. Tawney, *Religion and Rise,* p. 222.

26. Richard Baxter, *A Christian Directory* (1673), IV, "Christian Politicks," pp. 190-193.

27. Tawney, *Religion and Rise,* p. 226.

28. See Isaac Barrow's sermon on "The Duty and Reward of Bounty to the Poor" (1671) in Alexander Napier, ed., *The Theological Works of Isaac Barrow, D.D.* 9 vols. (Cambridge, 1859), I, 31. Steele (*Tradesman's Calling,* p. 125), said men were "Stewards of God's stock." Barrow was an Anglican; Steele was not.

29. Samuel Clarke (*Medulla Theologiae,* p. 231) favored severity for the undeserving and found Scriptural authority for refusing relief to "sturdy rogues" and "profuse prodigals"; such "should not eat." In case of extremity, however, they had to be relieved, but it was to be considered as given "not to the person, but to the common nature of mankind." In general, clergymen of Puritanical persuasion were more outspokenly censorious of beggars. Thomas Gouge, for instance, thought of them as robbers and social outcasts; see Richard B. Schlatter, *The Social Ideas of Religious Leaders, 1660-1688* (Oxford, 1940), p. 156. But this attitude was not the sole property of Dissenters and Puritans. Robert Sanderson, one of Charles I's chaplains, who became Bishop of Lincoln at the Restoration, said that beggars and vagrants were dangerous because they tended to rob "the truly poor, to whom properly all the fruits of our alms are due." Quoted by H. R. McAdoo, *The Spirit of Anglicanism: A Survey of Anglican Theological Method in the Seventeenth Century* (1965), p. 44.

30. "And the King shall answer and say unto them, Verily I say unto you, Inasmuch as ye have done it unto one of the least of these my brethren, ye have done it unto me."

31. Baxter, for example, urged the "seconding" of all relief "with spiritual advice and help" (*Christian Directory,* IV, 191). Thomas Gouge used handouts as bribes for attendance to his catechetical lectures (*DNB,* "Gouge"). See also McGee, *Godly Man,* pp. 189-200, 221. I am indebted to McGee's book not only for some of the particular points in this paragraph but also for its incisive formulation of the historical problem.

32. The quotation is from Clarke, *Medulla Theologiae,* p. 11. Clarke,

however, specifically warned his readers against using the supposed laziness of poor people as an excuse for denying them alms (Schlatter,
Social Ideas, p. 143). But Robert South, an outspoken foe of Dissenters
and a friend of the Non-Jurors, said that poverty was often the direct
effect of sin and vice (ibid. and *DNB*, "South").

33. Baxter made the practical point that to give "deliberately and
prudently" rather than impulsively or occasionally made charity "more
extensive" and caused proper objects of charity to be effectively sought
out. He also likened "occasional Giving" to "occasional Praying" (*Christian Directory*, IV, 192-193).

34. *The Whole Duty of Man, Laid Down in a Plain and Familiar
Way for the Use of All, but especially the Meanest Reader*, Sunday 17,
sect. 10. It was first published in 1658 and probably written by Richard
Allestree, who was made Regius Professor of Divinity at Oxford after
the Restoration. He once refused to accept the fee from the corporation
of the City of Oxford for some lectures he gave, ordering instead that it
be distributed among the poor (*DNB*, "Allestree"). Isaac Barrow said
that charity was "the main point of religion" and "mercy and bounty . . .
the chief parts of charity" ("Duty and Reward," I, 21).

35. McAdoo, *Spirit of Anglicanism*, pp. 160-161.

36. But it is interesting that Samuel Clarke and Richard Baxter both
felt that charitable acts influenced an individual's heavenly fate. Baxter
said that good works "much tend to . . . salvation" and that on the last
day we would be judged "according to our works, and especially our
works of Charity." (Clarke, *Medulla Theologiae*, p. 252; Baxter, *Christian Directory*, IV, 190.)

37. The rich, he said, are "bound not only to give all that the flesh
can spare," but also to mortify the flesh (Baxter, *Christian Directory*, I,
194).

38. Barrow, "Duty and Reward," I, 86.

39. Ibid., I, 62. I have cited Barrow's sermon extensively; as Charles
II remarked, he was "an unfair preacher, because he exhausted every
topic, and left no room for anything new to be said by any one who
came after him." The story is told that once when he ran overtime in
Westminster Abbey, the vergers signaled the organs to play "till they
had blowed him down" (*DNB*, "Barrow"). For the importance of the
imitation of Christ in Anglican teaching, see McGee, *Godly Man*, pp.
107-113.

40. McGee, *Godly Man*, chap. 5.

41. Quaker rules for removals and settlements appear to have been
set out most comprehensively in the year 1737. See Norfolk Record
Office, Norwich, King's Lynn Museum Deposit T176D: "Christian and
Brotherly advices given forth . . . by the Yearly meeting in London.
Alphabetically digested under Proper Heads," by Richard Reckover in
1755, who gave it to the monthly meeting of Wells, Fakenham, and
Holt. I have been unable to find these rules recorded in a printed edi-
tion of the epistles from the London meeting.

42. This was generally the case with social questions; see Norman,

Church and Society, p. 7. Halévy believed that many Dissenting preachers, unable to stomach the rantings of their congregations, returned to the fold in the early eighteenth century; see Elie Halévy, *The Birth of Methodism in England*, translated and edited by Bernard Semmel (Chicago, 1971), pp. 46-47.

43. *Whole Duty*, Sunday 17, sect. 2; Barrow, "Duty and Reward," I, 85.

44. Tawney was silent on this point, but it holds whether Calvinism is seen as collectivist or individualist. See M. G. Jones, *The Charity School Movement: a Study of Eighteenth-Century Puritanism in Action* (Cambridge, 1938), p. 7, for a clear-cut statement of the argument. Obviously I sympathize with her inclination to use the word Puritan in a comprehensive manner that encompassed practically anyone in the eighteenth century who was an earnest Christian, and included High Church Anglicans, but it has to be granted that, for all its shock value, her choice of that term has caused confusion.

45. Tawney claimed that the eighteenth-century Church provided only "succour for the non-combatants and for the wounded," and sidestepped the task of "inspiring the main army." He felt that the Church should have fashioned a social policy according to "an independent standard of values" (*Religion and Rise*, pp. 192-193, 277). In historical context this is scarcely imaginable. The Church of England has generally endeavored to stay in touch with major intellectual forces, and certainly did at this time (see McAdoo, *Spirit of Anglicanism*, esp. p. 5; Norman, *Church and Society*, pp. 10-11). It did not choose to ignore the growing influence of rationalism. But even if it had contrived to do so, any attempt to enjoin a doctrinal social policy on the nation in an age of toleration would have met with great resistance and could have been quite damaging to the Church's other concerns. For better or worse, eighteenth-century Anglicans generally looked on their accommodation of Christianity and reason as a triumph (*Church and Society*, p. 15). Halévy is worth quoting in this connection: "So far as the established church is concerned, it is usual to stress the spiritless rationalism of preachers at that time and the absence of zeal and culture among the country parsons. . . . However, let us not exaggerate the decline of the religious spirit in the Anglican church" (*Birth of Methodism*, p. 41).

46. Jones, *Charity School Movement*, chap. 1 contains a good discussion. A number of studies of English thought in this period have emphasized rational deists like Shaftesbury while ignoring the pulpit; A. O. Hirschman, *The Passions and the Interests* (Princeton, 1977) is an extreme example. Whatever utility this method may have for tracing the history of thought, it is useless for describing the history of England.

47. Edgar Furniss, *The Position of the Laborer in a System of Nationalism* (New York, 1920).

48. Richardson put these words in the mouth of Clarissa Harlow; quoted by Christopher Hill in "Clarissa Harlowe and Her Times," in *Puritanism and Revolution*, p. 379.

49. See Charles Wilson, "The Other Face of Mercantilism," in *Economic History and the Historian* (1969), pp. 73-93. On the subject of low wages the indispensable study is that by A. W. Coats, "Changing Attitudes to Labour in the Mid-Eighteenth Century," *Economic History Review,* 2d ser. XI (1958), 35-51. Before 1750 most writers favored low wages; the exceptions were John Cary, Daniel Defoe, Dudley North, Jacob Vanderlint, Bishop Berkeley, and David Hume ("Changing Attitudes," pp. 35-37, 46). To this list may be added the philanthropist, Lawrence Braddon; see his *A Proposal for Relieving, Reforming and Employing all the Poor of Great Britain* (1721), pp. 52-55.

50. James Bonar, *Theories of Population from Raleigh to Arthur Young* (1931, repr. 1966), p. 96.

51. So did national security. Without poor people the army and navy could not amount to anything. In the early eighteenth century this consideration was underlined by the experience of twenty years of warfare against Louis XIV, so that one seldom finds an English writer on the subject of managing the poor failing to mention the needs of the fighting forces, especially the navy.

52. Charles Henry Hull, *The Economic Writings of Sir William Petty,* 2 vols. (Cambridge, 1899), I, 31. The notion of psychological conditioning received a tremendous intellectual boost from Locke's *Essay Concerning Human Understanding.*

53. Bernard Mandeville, *The Fable of the Bees,* ed. F. B. Kaye, 2 vols. (Oxford, 1924), I, 287-288. Or, as he put it in one of his best-known epigrams: the lowest orders "have nothing to stir them up to be serviceable but their Wants, which it is Prudence to relieve but Folly to cure" (from "Remarks," ibid., I, 194). The "Remarks" were published with the original edition in 1714; the "Essay against the Charity Schools" was added to the 1723 edition.

54. Ibid., "Sixth Dialogue," II, 351-353.

55. Voltaire once wrote, "It seems to be essential that there be ignorant wretches." The great majority of poor children, he reasoned, should not be taught to read and write "because you need only one pen for every two or three hundred arms;" nevertheless, he had the children of the peasants on his own estate educated. See Harry C. Payne, *The Philosophes and the People* (New Haven, 1976), pp. 96-97.

56. This does not make him a moralist. Mandeville lived in an age when it was fashionable to lament the decline of morality. Every age has done this, but Mandeville's age was particularly prone to it because it had witnessed the decline of religious authority. Dissenters, gazing at the burnt-out carcass of Puritanism, and High Churchmen bewailing the godlessness of the post-1688 constitution, however they may have differed in assigning the blame, agreed that the kingdom had gone to the devil. This gave Mandeville both audience and inspiration. Like many cynical people, he set inhumanly high standards for those who would try to do good. This is especially evident in the opening essay of the *Fable:* "An Enquiry into the Origin of Moral Virtue" (I, 41-57). It

might be supposed that because this essay describes the power of the upper classes as partly depending upon a moral confidence trick played on the workers, that Mandeville was taking the side of the underdog. But his purpose was simply to call any pretensions to superior moral behavior into question; for his philosophical position rested on the free functioning of a cunning sort of behavior that he believed to be natural.

Mandeville's aim and sincerity are central questions in studies of his work; there are two recent book-length inquiries: Richard I. Cook, *Bernard Mandeville* (New York, 1974) and Hector Monro, *The Ambivalence of Bernard Mandeville* (Oxford, 1975).

57. *DNB*, "Watts." The powerful influence of Watts's *The Improvement of the Mind* on a young nineteenth-century scientist is observable in L. Pearce Williams's *Michael Faraday* (New York, 1965), pp. 12-13.

58. Isaac Watts, *An Essay Towards the Encouragement of Charity Schools, Particularly among Protestant Dissenters* (1728), p. 22.

59. Ibid., esp. pp. 12, 17-18, 20-21, 26-29, 32-33, 40, 47. Lawrence Braddon made similar points about the real alternative to charity education: "[T]he Children of the poorer sort being (at present generally) bred up in a most wretched State of Ignorance of their Duty, both to God and Man; and in a Habit of Idleness, Begging, and (too often) Stealing, Lying, Cursing, and Swearing" were a "National Curse"; whereas children might be "Industriously bred up, and by their Religion taught, that Industry becomes their indispensable Duty" (*The Miseries of the Poor* [1717], pp. xxxviii, 66).

60. Watts, *Essay*, pp. viii, 14, 22, 28, 36-38, 42.

61. Ibid., p. 13.

62. Ibid., p. 25.

63. D. C. Coleman, *The Economy of England, 1450-1750* (Oxford, 1977), 102-103.

64. Ibid., pp. 117-124, 199. See also A. H. John, "The Course of Agricultural Change 1660-1760," in L. S. Pressnell, ed., *Studies in the Industrial Revolution* (1960), pp. 125-155; and Joan Thirsk, "Seventeenth-Century Agriculture and Social Change," repr. in Paul S. Seaver, ed., *Seventeenth-Century England* (New York, 1976), p. 77. There was a stretch of bad harvests in the 1690s, and one of the worst food scarcities in modern English history in the year 1740. That year, however, was a singular exception: for most of the 1730s and 1740s the grain-growing weather was exceedingly fine; the 1730s was perhaps the best decade for harvests that England had ever seen.

65. J. D. Marshall, ed., *The Autobiography of William Stout of Lancaster, 1665-1752* (Manchester, 1967), pp. 211, 213.

66. N. L. Tranter, *Population since the Industrial Revolution: The Case of England and Wales* (1973), p. 41.

67. See E. A. Wrigley, "A Simple Model of London's Importance in Changing English Society and Economy 1650-1750," *Past and Present,* no. 37 (1967), pp. 46-49; Tranter, *Population,* p. 47, citing J. D. Chambers's study of the Vale of Trent; Thirsk, "Seventeenth-Century Agriculture," p. 98.

68. Watts, *Essay,* p. 21. Watts was aware of the large migration of laborers to London, and was inclined to blame the upper classes for setting the trend (pp. 22-23).

69. Thirsk, "Seventeenth-Century Agriculture," p. 102.

70. On the political roots of individualism, see J. A. W. Gunn, *Politics and the Public Interest in the Seventeenth Century* (1969), esp. pp. xi, 326. The distinction between deserving and undeserving was hashed out by medieval canonists. See Brian Tierney, *Medieval Poor Law: A Sketch of Canonical Theory and Its Application in England* (Berkeley and Los Angeles, 1959), esp. pp. 54-61, 118-119, 130. For details see Tierney, "The Decretists and the 'Deserving Poor,'" *Comparative Studies in Society and History,* I (1958-1959), 360-373.

71. On Mandeville's naturalism I strongly concur with M. R. Jack, "Religion and Ethics in Mandeville," in *Mandeville Studies* (The Hague, 1975), pp. 34-42.

72. Perhaps some sort of secularized Calvinism induced Englishmen to divide their nation into humans and humanoid animals, but there is scarcely any evidence to support this line of causation, and lots of evidence indicating that, instead, beliefs about the laws of nature inspired the attitude. Compare, for example, the effective evidence that C. B. MacPherson uses to show that Locke believed the working class to be "incapable of living a rational life" with the conjectural deductions that he employs to argue the influence of Calvinist election on attitudes about the poor (*The Political Theory of Possessive Individualism* [Oxford, 1962], pp. 223-228).

73. Quoted in John Wain, *Samuel Johnson* (1974), p. 198.

74. Just as the contradictions that arose a century later (which G. M. Young pointed out with words that inspired the rhetoric of the preceding paragraph) stood for a long time before they were resolved (G. M. Young, *Victorian England: Portrait of an Age* [Oxford, ed. 1960], pp. 16-17). Perhaps the most notorious of the holdouts were Arthur Young and Joseph Townsend. In 1771 Young wrote: "...every one but an ideot [*sic*] knows, that the lower classes must be kept poor, or they will never be industrious." His view did not change until the end of the century. See John G. Gazley, *The Life of Arthur Young 1741-1820* (Philadelphia, 1973), pp. 22, 73, 415 ff. Joseph Townsend, who called himself "a Well-Wisher to Mankind" on the title page of his *Dissertation on the Poor Laws* (1786), gave the utility of poverty a central role in maintaining the hierarchy of society which he believed to be natural and necessary. See the modern edition with a foreword by Ashley Montagu and an afterword by Mark Neuman (Berkeley and Los Angeles, 1971), p. 8.

75. As Dorothy Marshall has done (*English Poor,* p. 223).

76. *Wealth of Nations,* Bk. I, chap. 8 (ed. Cannon, 1950, I, 82-91). That this argument is no byway is evident from Smith's Introduction. He premised that the "annual labour of every nation is the fund" which originally creates its total consumable product; the proportion of laborers to consumers determines a nation's relative supply of these consumables. This proportion was regulated by two circumstances: "the skill,

dexterity, and judgment with which its labour is generally applied" and the proportion of those usefully employed to those not. "The abundance or scantiness" of the supply of consumables seemed to Smith "to depend more upon the former of those two circumstances than upon the latter." Therefore he undertook to investigate the causes of the improvement in the application of labor in civilized lands, which formed "the subject of the First Book" of his *Inquiry* (ibid., I, 1-2).

77. Ibid., I, 93.

78. Bk I, chap. 2 (I, 18). By this I mean that he answered it within the orbit of calculated self-interest. Smith had directly addressed Mandeville on purely philosophical grounds in *The Theory of Moral Sentiments* (1759), Pt. VII, Sect. 2, chap. 3.

79. There is no need to supply details of this movement of economic thought here; Professor Coats in his "Changing Attitudes to Labour" (n. 49 above) has done it admirably. After I wrote this essay there came to my attention a recently published paper in which he develops his analysis still further: A. W. Coats, "The Relief of Poverty, Attitudes to Labour, and Economic Change in England, 1660-1782," *International Review of Social History*, XXI (1976), 98-115.

80. C. P. Kindleberger argues, against Jacob Viner and Max Lerner, that Smith was not a "keen observer of his surroundings" ("The Historical Background: Adam Smith and the Industrial Revolution," in *The Market and the State: Essays in Honour of Adam Smith*, ed. by Thomas Wilson and Andrew S. Skinner [Oxford, 1976], pp. 3-8). While it is true that Smith failed to see the industrial revolution coming, and misread more than a few social and economic realities in Great Britain in his lifetime, so did lots of intelligent men. It does not mean that Smith was "a literary economist . . . who drew his examples from books, not from the world around him" (p. 6). He drew from both, as befits a man whose instincts were not only historical but also anthropological.

81. It may be contended that the change in basic conditions merely confirmed the optimistic position staked out by the Enlightenment in Britain with its premise of a beneficent deity. That Smith's optimism was grounded fundamentally in the conception of a well-intentioned deity, who had supplied mankind with a nature and a natural world in which morals favorable to human happiness would tend to develop, is evident in *The Theory of Moral Sentiments*. My point is, however, that one must address the further question of why Smith could think along these lines whereas Hobbes, for example, could not.

82. D. E. C. Eversley, "The Home Market and Economic Growth in England, 1750-1780," in E. L. Jones and G. E. Mingay, eds., *Land, Labour and Population in the Industrial Revolution: Essays presented to J. D. Chambers* (1967), p. 255.

83. In this sort of global history, timing is the great difficulty. Underlying shifts of this kind involve both conditions and perceptions. Hence historians may readily agree that such a change did occur, but not on when, or when it was realized.

84. According to Malcolm Falkus, "Lighting in the Dark Ages of English Economic History: Town Streets before the Industrial Revolution," in D. C. Coleman and A. H. John, eds., *Trade, Government and Economy in Pre-Industrial England: Essays presented to F. J. Fisher* (1976), p. 265, walls were breached and gates permanently opened chiefly between 1760 and 1800. The scattered clues I have come across generally accord with this timing.

85. Charles F. Mullett, *The Bubonic Plague and England* (Lexington, Ky., 1956), pp. 266-308, discusses the English reaction to the French epidemic; of course it took a while before the nation could be reasonably confident that plague would not recur. The causes of the natural withdrawal of the plague from northwest Europe in the eighteenth century are succinctly discussed in Christopher Morris, "The Plague in Britain," *Historical Journal,* XIV (1971), 212-213.

86. Estimates vary, but it is possible that each time the plague hit London with epidemic force in the seventeenth century (1603, 1625, and 1665), it killed about one-sixth of the inhabitants.

87. W. G. Hoskins, "Harvest Fluctuations and English Economic History, 1620-1759," *Agricultural History Review,* XVI (1968), 17.

88. William Stout (1665-1752) recorded each harvest and its impact. In his old age he witnessed years of plenty, but the scenes of his youth left a different impression (Marshall, ed., *Autobiography*). David G. Hey has commented that fear of bad harvests was a major reason why so many seventeenth- and early eighteenth-century diaries mentioned the weather (*An English Rural Community: Myddle under the Tudors and Stuarts* [Leicester, 1974], p. 49).

89. A. H. John, "English Agricultural Improvement and Grain Exports, 1660-1765," in *Trade, Government and Economy,* p. 51. See also John's interesting comments on the significance of these surpluses (pp. 45-46).

90. The bad harvests of the 1690s caused great distress in England and outright starvation in Scotland. The difference in the development of the Poor Law in England and Scotland probably caused the difference in results; see Rosalind Mitchison, "The Making of the Old Scottish Poor Law," *Past and Present,* no. 63 (1974), pp. 75-79.

91. See Bonar, *Theories,* pp. 79, 112.

92. On the contrasts with the modern Western outlook, see Peter Mathias, "Adam's Burden: Diagnoses of Poverty in Post-Medieval Europe and the Third World Now," *Tijdschrift voor Geschiedenis,* 89 (1976), esp. pp. 152-156.

93. Keith Thomas, *Religion and the Decline of Magic* (1971), pp. 111-112, 277-279.

94. McGee, *Godly Man,* pp. 25-42. Isaac Barrow spoke to this point ("Duty and Reward," I, 64): "The great incertainty [*sic*] and instability of our condition doth also require our consideration. We, that now flourish in a fair and full estate, may soon be in the case of that poor creature, who now sues for our relief; we, that this day enjoy the wealth

of Job, may the morrow need his patience: . . . all our weal is surrounded with dangers, and exposed to casualties innumerable: violence may snatch it from us . . . ; mischance may seize thereon . . . ; the wisdom of Providence for our trial, or its justice for our punishment, may bereave us thereof."

95. Halévy, *Birth of Methodism,* pp. 45-50.

96. See E. A. Wrigley, "The Process of Modernization and the Industrial Revolution in England," *Journal of Interdisciplinary History,* III (1972), 237-242.

97. It may be observed that I have avoided the term *humanitarianism.* Dorothy Marshall's reference to a "new humanitarianism" (*English Poor,* pp. 53-54, 159, 223, 252) muddles the issues. Raymond G. Cowherd, in *Political Economists and the English Poor Law* (Athens, Ohio, 1977), pp. 1-23, follows the same path. It is a well-worn one. The trouble with the word is that it can cover two different things: (1) compassion for those who are helpless, destitute, and miserable; and (2) the sort of sympathy that "calls for a much deeper regard for the individual and a profound respect of his freedom to shape his own life in his own way — and to make his own mistakes. It means that people should be treated as responsible beings" (Thomas Wilson, "Sympathy and Self-Interest," in *The Market and the State,* p. 94). In the eighteenth-century English context, the first is identical with traditional Christian benevolence. The second, which expresses the humanitarianism of Adam Smith, involved a "respect for individuality" and "an ability to share in the sense of frustration that a person must feel" ("Sympathy and Self-Interest," p. 93) when pushed around by his governors. Perhaps it might be called *radical humanitarianism* because it credited the lower orders with the same motives that actuated their betters. Professor Coats avoided the word *humanitarianism* in "Economic Thought and Poor Law Policy in the Eighteenth Century," *Economic History Review,* 2d ser. XIII (1960), 39-51, and analyzed the ingredients of the "generous thinking" whose development he traced (p. 49).

98. Tranter, *Population,* p. 41. The figures are reasonable estimates; there was no census at this time. Eversley ("Home Market and Economic Growth," pp. 213-220) argues that rising population had little adverse effect on living standards until 1780.

99. Neil McKendrick, "Home Demand and Economic Growth: A New View of the Role of Women and Children in the Industrial Revolution," in McKendrick, ed., *Historical Perspectives: Studies in English Thought and Society in Honour of J. H. Plumb* (1974), pp. 175 ff.

100. Mandeville, *Fable,* I, 193.

101. For a brief discussion of the circumstances, see J. D. Chambers, *The Vale of Trent 1670-1800 (Economic History Review Supplement III* [1957]), p. 58.

102. It might be imagined, as some historians have done, that the "benevolence" of this epoch was nothing more than an upper-class reaction to dire necessity and dangerous rioting. However, that knowledge-

able and humane reformer, Sir Frederick Morton Eden, did not think so. He commented: "If there is a defect in British benevolence, it is, that it is too unbounded and indiscriminate" (*The State of the Poor,* 3 vols. [1797, repr. 1966], I, 458).

103. See Poynter, *Society and Pauperism,* pp. 152-160.

104. As students of Malthus know, later editions of the *Essay,* as well as other writings by its author, amply testify, by curious omissions or otherwise, to his awareness of some — but not all — of the contradictions in his views on the Poor Laws. Poynter's critical insights are extremely valuable in this regard. But Poynter notes: "The Malthusian influence on attitudes to the problem of pauperism was greatest where it was most vague" (*Society and Pauperism,* p. 185).

105. Quoted ibid., p. 168.

106. Hobbes, *Leviathan,* chap. 30, quoted in Bonar, *Theories,* p. 36.

107. The triumph of Malthusianism over benevolence is illustrated by Cowherd in *Political Economists,* pp. 27-46.

108. An alternative mode of explanation might be to link the ascendancy of such attitudes to the ascendancy of certain classes. A scenario of this kind could portray the triumph of the nineteenth-century consensus as a byproduct of the ascendancy of the middle class, and might explain the rise of benevolence in the eighteenth century in terms of an aristocratic resurgence. My sense is that this scenario fits the facts only at a very superficial level, if then, and I would point out that for it to mean anything historically, the classes must be defined in socioeconomic terms (which is not easily done in the period from 1660 to 1800). For if classes are to be defined in terms of a class consciousness which exhibits itself in certain shared ideals, the mode of explanation becomes essentially tautologous.

109. Young, *Victorian England,* p. 185.

110. Poynter, *Society and Puritanism,* p. 268. Rapidly indeed if we take note of the legislation of the first year of Edward VI's reign, which laid down that "if any man, or woman, able to work, should refuse to labour, and live idly for three days, that he or she should be branded with a red-hot iron on the breast with the letter V, and should be adjudged the slaves, for two years, of any person who should inform against such idler." Quoted in Eden, *State of the Poor,* I, 101. To be sure, this regulation was soon modified. C. S. L. Davies, in "Slavery and Protector Somerset: the Vagrancy Act of 1547," *Economic History Review,* 2d ser. XIX (1966), 533-549, has laid its harsh slavery provisions to the "sheer incompetence" of Somerset's social policy, but the point I am making here is not affected by that conclusion. My point is that *at the very outset* of the Protestant era in England, influential men were willing and able to introduce extremely harsh measures.

IV

THE GLORIOUS REVOLUTION AS SPECTACLE: A NEW PERSPECTIVE

Lois G. Schwoerer

The Glorious Revolution as a spectacle is the new perspective on the Revolution of 1688-89 which I want to develop in this essay.[1] The Glorious Revolution is not usually thought of as having the characteristics of a spectacle. Perhaps this is because historians have focused attention on the origins and results of the revolution rather than on the revolution itself. Thus they have treated only in a perfunctory way the processions, ceremonies, bonfires, and fireworks that filled the day, February 13, 1689, when the revolution was publicly brought to an end. On that day the Declaration of Rights was carried through the streets in grand procession to the Banqueting Hall at Whitehall Palace. There it was read to Prince William and Princess Mary of Orange and the crown was offered to them. Then, ancient officers of the state and political leaders again in grand procession marched to four places in London to proclaim William and Mary king and queen. I believe that an examination of these proceedings may not only vivify the revolution, but also deepen understanding of the political process underlying it and clarify aspects of the Declaration of Rights. I will argue that the principals in the revolution contrived a stylized ceremony, organized the two elaborate processions, promoted the use of bonfires and fireworks, and encouraged the appearance of printed written and pictorial materials. Their purpose in so doing was to create certain political impressions and to win from Prince William an implicit commitment that could not be obtained directly—a commitment that assured that this revolution would change not only the English king but also the kingship.[2]

Ten years ago, it might have been necessary to justify using certain ceremonies and processions as evidence for understanding the political process. Today, thanks to pioneering work by both historians and anthropologists,[3] ceremonies and processions, bonfires and merrymaking have become recognized as legitimate parts of the historical record, properly regarded as cultural artifacts capable of being "read," just as conventional documentary evidence is read. They were important aspects of political life in Early Modern Europe. We in the twentieth century have no trouble understanding the significance of ceremonies for conveying political messages. Similarly, we should have no difficulty, I think, in accepting that in the late seventeenth century, when the literacy rate[4] was low and the means of communication limited, political leaders communicated with the public by means of symbols and symbolic acts in the form of ceremonies, processions, and bonfires.

Admittedly, direct evidence is a bit thin for some of the points I will make. Indeed, I found in searching through the archives that information on the kind of wine William and Mary preferred for washing their feet was easier to come by than data on what they wore at the presentation ceremony, what was served at the gala that evening, how much the ceremony cost, and who paid for it![5] Surely the absence or thinness of some material is explained by the haste with which the proceedings were devised, the breakdown of the administrative machinery during this "interregnum," and, probably, the reluctance of some men to preserve the evidence of their intimate involvement in elevating the new monarchs. There is, however, much circumstantial evidence and a lot of direct data, including the architectural record (for, of course, the Banqueting Hall survives and has recently been refurbished)[6] —enough, I believe, to permit legitimate inferences.

The ceremonies of February 13 came at the end of several months of deepening crisis. From the time William landed in England with an army of about 15,000 men on November 5,

1688, political maneuvering had escalated and tension had sharpened.[7] Although closely related as nephew and son-in-law to James II, the Roman Catholic king of England, the Protestant William of Orange had no direct claim to the English throne.[8] James's flight in mid-December to the court of England's enemy, the French king Louis XIV, was calculated to deepen confusion in England; it created a new and unexpected situation. Rejecting advice to declare himself king on the grounds of conquest, as Henry VII had done—in which case there would have been, very likely, no ceremony in the Banqueting Hall and almost certainly no Declaration of Rights—William and English political leaders entered into delicate political negotiations. All parties jockeyed for advantage. The prince's initial popularity waned. The threat (real and alleged) to England and The Netherlands from Ireland and France added urgency to a complex situation.

In January, pursuant to an agreement reached between William, on the one hand, and English peers and members of the Parliaments of Charles II on the other, a Convention was elected to settle the crisis. Although efforts were made to preserve legal forms, the Convention was an illegal assembly, a revolutionary tribunal. In the weeks prior to its meeting, no broad consensus of opinion about settling the government emerged, and after members assembled on January 22, the situation became so tense both within and between the two houses that bloodshed was feared. The prince was fully aware of the differences of opinion among Englishmen and sensitive enough to ask a Dutch emissary in London not to report them in his letters to Holland. Members of the Convention, however, reached agreement on February 6 that King James I had "abdicated" the government and that the throne was "vacant." On the ninth they agreed to link their offer of the crown to William and Mary to a declaration of the nation's rights.

On the declaration, as on the question of the king, there was no immediate agreement, as sometimes thought. The statement was promoted by a small number of men in the House of Commons who wanted to change the kingship as well as the king. It was reluctantly accepted by others in both Houses who wanted only to change the king. During these days, some men at the center of events expressed a pessimistic view of affairs. For example, the prince himself, who was reported to look worried, remarked that now it was "hosanna," but soon he could expect to be "cruci-

fied."[9] Lord Halifax, the Speaker of the House of Lords, confessed that he had "noe great hopes of a lasting peace."[10] Indeed,
J. P. Kenyon has estimated that less than 5 percent of the govern-
ing class would have agreed to the settlement if they had realized
clearly what they were doing.[11] Perspective observers from all
walks of life could have known about the difficulties. Despite the
"closed doors" policy of both Houses and their efforts to preserve
the confidentiality of their affairs, oral, written, and printed
sources circulated news of what was happening in Westminster.[12]
The arrangements for the ceremony and proclamation, then,
were made against a background of tension about the terms of
the settlement and of relief that bloodshed had been avoided.

The proceedings, moreover, were contrived in great haste, in
tandem with the larger political decisions of the Convention. In
fact, arrangements were not completed until the early morning of
the thirteenth.[13] Swiftness of action, however, need not imply
absence of calculated purpose or prior consideration. Prince William and his close friends had already used deliberately and skill-
fully every available device, including printed tracts, broadsides,
pictures, and commemorative medals, to mold the opinion of a
broad spectrum of society.[14] One may assume their intense interest in this first major public event. The surviving record does not
specify a "committee on arrangements," but indirect evidence
suggests that the men in the House of Commons who were responsible for drafting the Declaration of Rights helped to design the
ceremony and, as will be shown, they were deeply concerned
about what should be presented. The fact that politically-con-
scious people looked for certain specific things in the ceremony—
some hoped that Mary, if not William, would apologize for dis-
placing James—strengthens the conclusion that the proceedings
were of more than casual interest to persons in and out of the
Convention.[15] Moreover, the absence of any report of a misstep, a
misspoken word, a hesitation, or an embarrassment of any kind
in these stylized events reinforces the idea that men practiced
what one writer calls "impression management." But, whatever
the degree of calculation of the persons involved in a public
event, it has been argued that their actions, including nonverbal
actions, and the unfolding of the event create impressions and
help shape the response of witnesses.[16] And, in this case, the positive public response had been prepared by the propaganda effort
just mentioned.

What were the purposes underlying the processions, ceremonies, and bonfires, and what impression did these events convey? The major function of the proceedings was, of course, to
proclaim the prince and princess of Orange king and queen of
England. A closely related aim was to demonstrate to people in
England and abroad the joyous unanimity of a united nation at
this resolution of the crisis. The day's events were also designed as
a spectacle to entertain participants and spectators and express
relief that the upheaval was over. These purposes served the interests of both William and the Convention.

There was apparent concern to carry out the proclamation in
the traditional way and uncertainty how, in the existing circumstances, when the requisite administrative structures had collapsed, this could be achieved. One M.P. pointed out (in clouded
language) that the usual procedures for proclaiming a new king
called for the privy council to meet, name the heir, confer with
the lord mayor of London, and order the proclamation. But
there was no Privy Council in being to do that. Drawing an analogy from the law of property, this member compared English
subjects to a tenant who might "attorn" to a new lord.[17] The
point of interest is not the analogy, which was farfetched and
never repeated, but rather the confusion it suggests about how
the Convention might proceed. The Dutch ambassador reported
that since February 8 the Convention had been "continually occupied in planning in what manner" the prince and princess would
be proclaimed.[18] In the event, the House of Lords, at the very last
moment, ordered the proclamation to be performed "in the usual
manner and at the usual places accustomed on like occasions."
They specifically declared that their order was a sufficient warrant.[19] The generality of the language and the specific assertion
that the order was a sufficient warrant would seem to reflect their
anxiety about the matter. Concern was also expressed over which
local officer in the counties should receive the proclamation.
Sheriffs would customarily be addressed, but since so many of
them were Catholic, left over from James II's remodeling of local
government, it was decided to direct the document to the coroner.[20] Moreover, members labored over drafting the official
proclamation. The text they finally agreed upon is significantly
different from that of the documents proclaiming earlier Stuart
kings. The Privy Council is not named, but the House of Commons and "others of the commons of the realm" are specifically

mentioned along with the Lords Spiritual and Temporal and the Lord Mayor and Citizens of London as the persons proclaiming the new monarchs.[21] Clearly, the drafters broadened the base of persons responsible for the proclamation and, by so doing, implied wide support for the step.

At the same time these political and constitutional aspects of the proclamation were troubling people, the duke of Norfolk, who simply continued to function as the earl marshal, took steps, without any warrant apparently from the Convention, to ensure that the public ceremonies traditionally associated with proclaiming a new monarch would be carried out. Thus, beginning on February 7 and in a rising flurry on the twelfth, written and verbal orders went out, calling upon the heralds "to be ready (when commanded) to proclaim" the new monarchs, instructing the Jewell House to recall all maces, ordering the repair and assignment of maces, and alerting the high constable of Westminster and the keeper of the Tower as to their responsibilities for the proclamation.[22] There must have been many such orders and perhaps many meetings, notice of which is lost, to arrange the logistics of the proclamation ceremony. One should not underestimate the attention to details which the smooth carrying out of the proclamation reveals nor the interest in fulfilling prescribed formulae it suggests.

In point of fact, the proclamation was very grand, on the whole traditional and evocative of the past. An officer of the ancient Order of the Garter, Garter Principal King of Arms, carried the document in a splendid procession from Westminster to the Banqueting Hall. Following the ceremony there (discussed below), the assembled company of peers and M.P.s joined the Heralds, Sergeants-at-Arms, trumpeters, and others at Whitehall Gate. The trumpets sounded three times and at the last blast were answered by a "great Shout" from the crowd. Whereupon Knight Garter read the official document "in short periods or sentences," the people replying with "several repeated Shouts." Then, moving in another brilliant procession, with kettledrums, bugles, and trumpets, he proclaimed them four more times in London in the presence of the lord mayor, other city officials, and "vast multitudes." The streets of London were lined on both sides by members of the Orange, Green, Blue, and White Regiments of the city Militia.[23]

It should be noted, however, that an untraditional and polemical note was injected in the proclamation by a curious exchange at Temple Bar. Upon the knock at the gate an officer therein inquired, "Where is King James II?" And someone thereout "thrice-over" responded, "He is dead. He is dead. He is dead." Others heard, "He has abdicated the government."[24] These statements clearly aimed to justify the elevation of the new monarchs. A sensitive observer might also have noticed that the latter comment supported the "abdication" and "vacancy" formula, which had caused such bitter fights in and between the two houses of the Convention just the week before. Surely that comment was uttered by a partisan of the formula in order to underline it in public.

At the same time these proceedings announced that England had a new king and queen, they also expressed joy, unanimity, and relief. The procession, the banners, the stirring sounds of trumpets, bugles, and kettledrums, the presence of ancient officers of the crown in gorgeous regalia, and so on, must have been, for the seventeenth-century viewer, just as they seem to the twentieth-century observer — splendid and inspiriting. All contemporary reporters testify that masses of people turned out, lining the streets, standing on balconies, and leaning from windows.[25] A large number of persons took part in the official proceedings; upward of fifty persons are specifically mentioned and many others are implied by the official account preserved in the *Journals of the House of Commons*.[26] A broadside, *The Manner of the Proclaiming of King William, and Queen Mary, at White-Hall, in the City of London, Feb. 13, 1688/89,* stresses the point that the crowds "filled the air" with "such shouts as were scarcely ever heard." The people, it was said, were transported with delight, "each striving to exceed" the other in "publick demonstration thereof."

The reputedly large and enthusiastic crowd invites comment. It is possible that the official accounts exaggerated the numbers and zeal of people to magnify the occasion. But the confirmation of these points by private reports makes that unlikely. Assuming then that there was a huge crowd, the question is: were people "encouraged" to appear? There is no direct evidence that they were, and the turnout may have been spontaneous. But it should be recalled that William and his English and Dutch friends had made the most concentrated effort in England's history to shape the opinion of a broad spectrum of society in favor of the prince. Printed and visual materials were aimed at people far outside elite categories. If the people appeared spontaneously, some credit must go to this unprecedented propaganda campaign. Moreover, it is not unreasonable to think that an immediate effort was made to bring out a substantial number of people and to instruct them in their response. The success achieved just ten days earlier in rounding up signatures to a petition to the Convention—it was said some 15,000 names were subscribed in two days and 10,000 men were ready to deliver the petition—supports the hypothesis.[27] The certainty that the shouts of the crowd had to be orchestrated with the steps in the proclamation adds strength to the idea. And the weather was cold and "tempestuous," as it had been for days.[28] This too might have discouraged the appearance of some people, if an effort had not been made to bring them out. Further, it is reasonable to suggest that men took into account the likelihood that a large number of people and the excitement of the processions would blunt the impact of the absence of a great many peers. Despite an effort to ensure a good turnout of lords, only 35 out of a possible 153 peers attended, and of the 35 only 3 bishops appeared in the procession.[29] The archbishop of Canterbury was absent, and Henry Compton, the bishop of London, was called on to preach a sermon that afternoon. A fortnight later, a member of the House of Commons excoriated the spiritual peers for absenting themselves at the proclamation.[30] Moreover, the comment of a Tory observer that although there were many expressions of joy, "a great many [people] looked very sadly upon it,"[31] reinforces the thought that the hearty shouts and the competition among individuals to excel one another in the "publick demonstration" of their approbation may have been to some degree contrived. Finally, if any person were inclined to a contrary expression—as by the end of the month the street songs clearly showed that some were—the presence of members of the Orange, Green, Blue, and White regiments of the city Militia along both sides of the streets of London would have discouraged that expression.[32]

In the evening, just as at earlier critical moments in the Revolution, bonfires burned all over the city.[33] They were the blazing visible symbols of approval of the settlement, and appeared at "particular persons' doors" to signify that approval. Some of the bonfires were ingeniously devised to convey political messages. One of "extraordinary great height" was placed in St. James's Square. It depicted the Pope and the Devil before whom an effigy of Sir George Jeffreys, King James's hated lord chancellor, manipulated by an "engine," pleaded his "great service." Then, all the figures were cast into the fire and burned.[34] The most elaborate and costly of all the bonfires was four stories high; at its summit was an effigy of Father Edward Petre, James's detested Jesuit adviser and confessor. As the bonfire was consumed, Father Petre was blown up, "even as he would have done the nation," explained one admiring account. Placed outside Watts Coffee House in German Street, the scene of earlier political discussions and of previous bonfires, this bonfire, designed by a Captain Silver, was "contributed to" by peers and members of the Convention Parliament.[35] Such complicated creations cost money, required gun powder, and must have taken time to design and construct. Precisely how much money was expended on the displays is not known but the fireworks celebrating the Treaty of Ryswick eight years later reportedly cost £10,000. It is a tantalizing thought that some of these bonfires may have been partly fueled with papers that one looks for in vain in the Public Record Office.[36] Not only bonfires but also rockets and fireworks, timed to go off at intervals, illuminated the city throughout the evening.

Written, printed, iconographic, and oral accounts carried news of the proclamation all over England and to persons abroad. The official proclamation, upon the order of the Convention, appeared in print immediately.[37] It went through five editions in February. A lengthy account of the proclamation was entered in the *Journals of the House of Commons,* the only time such a step was taken in the seventeenth century. Entering the record of the proclamation invested it with legality and regularity. *The Manner of Proclaiming,* just mentioned, was on the streets of London by February 15.[38] It identified persons, described their regalia, and provided a detailed account of the processions and ceremonies. Pictures also appeared. An anonymous Dutch print (see figs. 1, 2) was published in Amsterdam within the year, clearly conveying to viewers the idea of the joyous unanimity of the nation in elevating William and Mary to the throne. It shows a grand procession of peers, members of the Convention Parlia-

Fig. 4.1. The grand procession.

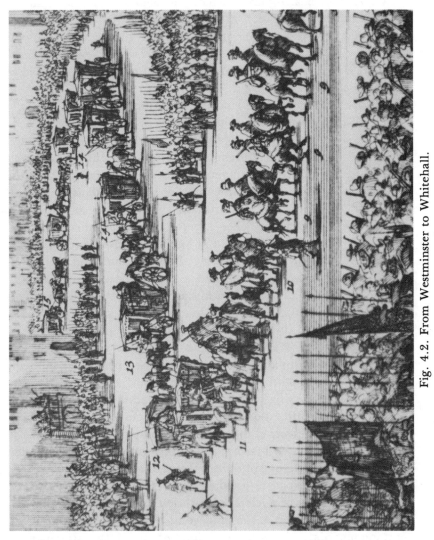

Fig. 4.2. From Westminster to Whitehall.

ment, Pursuivants, Garter Principal King of Arms carrying the proclamation of the new monarchs, trumpeters, and others, dressed resplendently—we know from written accounts—in blue and scarlet, bearing large maces, on foot, on horseback, and in coaches. The procession makes its way with banners held aloft and flags flying from Westminster to the Banqueting House at Whitehall. The print depicts a confident English "establishment" on its way to a settlement of the political crisis while a crowd of people applauds the event.[39]

Appealing to another kind of public taste, a song, *The Subject's Satisfaction: being a new song of the proclaiming of King William and Queen Mary the 13th of February,* was printed beneath a picture of William and Mary sitting under two angels holding one crown.[40] One verse stressed the joy with which the ceremony was received, and another discounted as a "Popish rumor" that the House of Lords and the House of Commons had ever been "at variance." The *London Gazette,* formerly the official newspaper of Charles II and James II, broke its self-imposed silence and printed a full account of the proclamation. Several of the new newspapers, which had all along been sympathetic to William, ran detailed and enthusiastic stories.[41] In all, observers described the proclamation as having been done in "the accustomed manner" and regarded it "as splendidly performed as ever any was before."[42] Such was the impression conveyed by the Dutch ambassador and by the prince himself who wrote immediately to persons on the continent disclaiming any ambition to be king.[43] The carrying out of the proclamation in the traditional way, with the officers of the crown, the members of the Convention, and the officers of the city of London participating, with the bugles and trumpets blaring, and the crowds shouting, concealed the significant change in the royal succession that had occurred. These things helped to legitimize the revolution and create the impression that the ancient constitution had not been breached.[44]

Another function of the proceedings was to present publicly a statement of the rights of the nation and to link that statement to the offer of the crown. In the Banqueting Hall (fig. 3) about 10:30 in the morning of that Ash Wednesday, a stylized ceremony was held. It was witnessed only by members of the Convention and close friends of the Prince.[45] Preceded by the Gentleman Usher of the Black Rod, the Speakers of both Houses led the peers

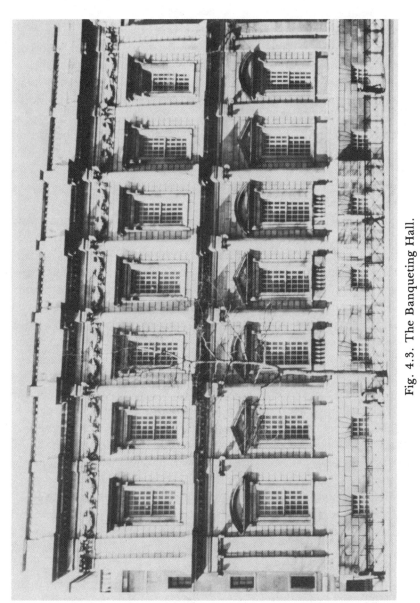

Fig. 4.3. The Banqueting Hall.

and Commoners across the length of the great hall (fig. 4), lined with Yeomen of The Guard, made at intervals three deep obeisances and approached Prince William and Princess Mary as they sat hand-in-hand under a canopy of state. In this close setting, as a later print (fig. 5) shows and contemporary accounts confirm, the Declaration of Rights, "fairly written in parchment," was read by the Deputy-Clerk of Parliament.[46] Then the crown of England was offered to William and Mary. Rising to respond for them both, while the princess signified her assent by "her looks and a little curtsy,"[47] Prince William accepted the crown and acknowledged the Declaration of Rights in brief remarks. His "acceptance speech" was greeted inside with a great shout and masses of people outside echoed the cry.[48] William and Mary then left the Hall.

This ceremony was the unique aspect of the day's events. Many times before (especially in the seventeenth century), Parliament had presented to a reigning king instruments, in the form of petition, remonstrance, advice, and address, which set forth the grievances and the rights of the subject.[49] Six times before 1689 the English had removed their king, each time justifying the step in apologias that defined the authority of the monarchy.[50] But never before had an instrument, in any form, been presented to a person *before* he was king and *at the time* he was offered the crown. Nor before had such an instrument been shaped to suggest that acceptance of it was the condition for the offer of the crown and that its terms restricted the prerogatives of the crown. The reading of the Declaration of Rights before the crown was offered reflected a political victory of men who favored changing the kingship as well as the king over those who wanted only to change the king. Clearly, if the latter had had their way, a ceremony simply proclaiming the new monarchs would have been all that was necessary. Nevertheless, there was more symbolism and image making than legal substance in this unique ceremony.

The story of the contest between these two points of view is set out in detail in my book, *The Declaration of Rights, 1689.* In brief, then, the contest was implicit from January 29, when the House of Commons appointed a committee to identify the "heads" of things that were absolutely necessary to secure the nation's religion, laws, and liberties, the first step leading to the Declaration of Rights.[51] Outside the Convention, pamphleteers,

Fig. 4.4. The Great Hall.

Fig. 4.5. Declaration of Rights being read to
William and Mary.

taking advantage of a virtually free press, urged members to place "terms or conditions" on the kingship, in other words, to do more than simply change the person of the king.[52] But the draft statement about rights which the committee prepared did not move smoothly through the Convention. It was threatened on February 2 by the effort to present the petition, already mentioned, which called for proclaiming William and Mary immediately, without any reference to a statement of rights. It was shortened and reordered to make it less of a reform package. And it took a "long"[53] debate the morning of February 7 to persuade the House of Commons to defer declaring William and Mary king and queen, which the House of Lords had proposed be done, until the draft statement of rights could be reported.[54] The committee drafting that statement was "revived" and ordered to bring in its report that afternoon.[55] This order was an important victory for members who wished to change the kingship as well as the king.

The committee submitted a new report that afternoon, and in the ensuing debate members stressed for the first time that the statement about the rights of the subject should be linked to the resolution about the headship of the state. Said one, "A Declaration of the Rights of the Subject . . . [should] go along with the Declaration of filling up the Throne."[56] The House of Commons accepted the report, but reached no conclusion on how to handle it.[57] Men outside the Convention, however, who all along had interpreted earlier drafts of the statement of rights as "stipulations," "limitations," and "conditions" and reported that the new monarch(s) would "subscribe," or "swear," or "promise" to observe the rights before they were crowned continued to describe the draft report of February 7 in similar terms, referring to it as "acts which had to precede the offer of the crown," or the "new articles of Government to be laid before the new King, that he might know upon what terms he was to have the crown."[58] Significantly, the report was in print that very evening, surely for the purpose of arousing public opinion for it and assuring that it not be lost.[59]

The next day, February 8, another determined effort was made to preserve the statement of the subject's rights. In the course of preparing amendments to the Lords' resolution making William and Mary king and queen, a committee of the Commons apparently perceived that an opportunity was at hand to advance the statement of rights.[60] John Somers (the past counsel for the defense in the trial of the Seven Bishops and the future lord chancellor) returned to the House to ask their direction.[61] In response, some members urged that the statement of rights be joined to the offer of the crown. One argued strenuously against filling the throne and "nothing with it."[62] The House finally agreed, giving another victory to men who wanted to change the kingship as well as the king.

Thus instructed, Somers's committee "tackt" together into one statement all the resolutions the Convention had passed.[63] Three aspects of this statement require comment. First, the report linked a claim to rights and liberties to earlier claims of rights through the phrase that the Lords and Commons were acting "as their Ancestors, in the like Case, have usually done." Surely the intent was to recall the Petition of Right and other remonstrances and addresses with which men of political experience, legal training, and historical bent were well acquainted and, thus, underscore the traditional nature of their actions and claims. Second is the explicit reference to, indeed the very borrowing of words from William's *Second Declaration*,[64] which with his *First Declaration* had been an important instrument in his propaganda campaign. In the *Second Declaration* appeared the sentence that the "only means for obtaining a full redress and remedy of the [nation's] grievances" was by a "Parliament in a Declaration of Rights of the subject." In the committee's draft, a sentence avers that members were "particularly invited" to make "demand of their rights" by the prince's *Declaration,* which had said—citing exactly—that "the only means for obtaining a full redress and remedy" of grievances was by a "Parliament in a Declaration of Rights of the subject."[65] Later, on February 12, in arguing against one of the lords' proposed amendments to the draft, Somers again referred to the prince's *Declaration;* he said it confirmed the opinion of the committee and declared candidly that the committee had "followed" the words of the manifesto.[66] Now, William's declarations had been widely distributed throughout England and had become the basis for discussing solutions to the crisis. Thus, to appeal to the prince's manifesto as the justification for their claim of rights was to put great pressure on William to accept that claim. Should he be inclined to reject it, he would be faced with the embarrassment of publicly disavowing his own well-known manifesto. Clearly, members of this committee in the House of Commons were playing political hardball.

Third, the several resolutions were "tackt" together in such a way as to suggest that the offer of the crown was conditional upon William's accepting the itemized rights. There was nothing inevitable about how the parts of the draft should be arranged. A different sequence from the one chosen was certainly possible. For example, the crown could have been offered first, the offer justified by the misdeeds of James II, and then the nation's rights asserted. Such an arrangement would not have implied that the crown was conditional upon the prince's accepting the statement of rights. The committee, however, used such words as "vindicating," "asserting," "declaring," "claiming," "demanding," and "insisting upon"—all those things!—with respect to the statement of rights. Then they connected the statement of rights and the offer of the crown by the word "accordingly." That word means and was so used in the seventeenth century "in accordance with the sequence of ideas; agreeably or conformably to what might be expected; in natural sequence, in due course; so." The text reads that the Lords Spiritual and Temporal and the Commons "do pray the said Prince and Princess of Orange to accept [the crown] accordingly."

What is one to make of these words and the arrangement of the parts of the statement? Did Somers's committee regard their draft as a condition on the offer of the crown and as a restriction on the prerogatives of the king? Unfortunately, no written record of their intention survives, and anyone who considers the matter has to base his conclusions upon inferential judgments. Recently these questions have been raised by scholars, three of whom (Pinkham, Frankle, and Nenner) concluded that the Declaration was not a condition and two (Carter and Horwitz) that it was.[67] Nenner's analysis, which is the most extensive and is based upon a close reading of the legal meaning of the language, argues that the language is not legally binding; it is precatory rather than obligatory. I concur with Nenner's conclusion about the language, but my reading of what happened goes farther. It is this: men who endorsed the Declaration of Rights did, indeed, want to make it a condition on the offer of the crown and a restriction on the prerogatives of the king. They wanted to change the kingship as well as the king. Persons outside the Convention so interpreted their actions and purposes. Pamphleteers emphatically urged this course. But, trained in the law as these M.P.s were, they realized that, legally, anything William signed before he was king could not bind him thereafter, and they appreciated that they could not hope for even so much as Charles I gave in 1628 when he signed the Petition of Right.[68] They also accepted that in strictly legal terms the Convention could not make a law, notwithstanding the claims which some publicists advanced that it had as much or more power than a regular Parliament.[69] For many reasons, the Committee's final report was a much watered-down version of the first draft, but it did retain sections that changed the monarchy in two fundamental points: the king's lawmaking power (the power to suspend or dispense with the law) and his military prerogatives (the power to keep a standing army in time of peace).[70] These were the crucial points, touching the essence of sovereignty. The Declaration of Rights changed them fundamentally, although the changes were disingenuously described as old rights restored. With greater awareness of the power of symbolic action, with greater sensitivity to public opinion, and with greater willingness to employ an elaborate pretense than has been fully appreciated, these men insisted upon a public reading, in a stylized ceremony, of the statement of rights *before* the crown was offered. And, with calculated purpose, they chose the words and arranged the text of the document to imply that the Declaration was a condition to the offer of the crown and a limitation on the powers of the crown. There was no doubt in the minds of contemporaries that such was the nature of the draft. One among several observers described it as a "new instrument of government," which the Convention "intended to lay before the Prince . . . at the same time that they offered him the crown of England."[71]

Somers's report precipitated a crisis during the evening of February 8 and the next day, which laid bare William's views on the matter. In brief, William Bentinck, the prince's closest Dutch adviser, told a member of the House of Commons that William did not like the "restrictions and limitations" that were being placed upon the crown.[72] Rumors circulated that the prince was "very angry with those that had made mention of them," and that men close to him shared the view that he should not accept any "stipulations."[73]

In the meantime, a number of unidentified bishops (all of whom were said to be against redressing grievances) and temporal peers attempted to exploit the situation.[74] In a private meeting with the prince, they told him that the stipulations were indeed restrictions upon the crown, and that if he would depend upon them they could make him king without any statement of rights.[75] William's response is not reported, but, clearly, the prince did not reject this proposition out of hand that evening, for the crisis deepened the next morning when the news of William's disapproval circulated in Westminster, filling men who favored the statement of rights "with consternation and despair."[76] They rushed about to try to save the situation. An important spokesman for rights importuned one of William's advisers.[77] An unidentified person asked a member of William's Dutch entourage to intervene with William.[78] A group of men, among them Sir Henry Sidney (at this time William's closest English confidant), hastened directly to the prince.

Unfortunately, this interview with William is imperfectly reported, but, apparently, Sidney argued that the proponents of the statement of rights were the prince's "most faithful servants." Using a threat, he pointed out that opposing the statement would have "dangerous consequences," and he asserted persuasively but disingenuously that the terms "contained nothing . . . but the known laws." One may speculate that in return for William's consent that the statement be read, it was agreed that he would not be asked to sign or take a formal oath to uphold it, as reports earlier had asserted. For his part, William denied that he had ever "expressed his sense one way or another," disavowed any person who had suggested the contrary as one who "had done him a very great injury," and declared that he was "satisfied with whatever they did for their own security."[79] In view of William's later disinclination to transform the Declaration of Rights into statutory form and make it the Bill of Rights—he said in April that "he had no mind to confirm [all the articles in the Declaration], but the condition of his affairs overruled his inclinations"—his disavowal of Bentinck must be seen as a political retreat not an expression of his true feelings.[80] Surely William backed down because he wanted the crown, because he overestimated at this time the power of men who supported the statement of rights, and because it would have been extremely awkward, given the image of his policies created by his propaganda, for him to have rejected the Declaration.[81]

The Resolution of this crisis was a victory for men who wanted to change the kingship as well as the king. One described William's capitulation as a "special instance of divine providence."[82] From February 9, it was certain that a special ceremony would be needed to present the statement of rights and offer the crown. It was equally certain that, although differences were papered over, profound disagreement with the statement of rights existed.

Against this background of tension, crisis, and disagreement, members of the Convention made preparations for a unique presentation ceremony. Their actions reveal a concern to underscore in subtle ways the importance of the statement of rights. First, a title to the statement, a matter on which the committee could not agree earlier, was settled.[83] By February 11, the draft was referred to as a "Declaration," a stronger term than "Address" or "Petition," which had been mentioned earlier. The phrase "Declaration of Rights of the subject" had, it will be recalled, appeared in William's manifesto, so the choice of words may be seen as another public link to the prince's manifesto as well as an effort to convey the idea that the Convention was stating already established and accepted rights.[84] Second, in requesting an interview with the prince to settle the details of the time and place of the ceremony, the lords specifically stated that the purpose of the ceremony was "to wait on [the prince] with their Declaration." No mention was made of the crown.[85] Third, at the initiative of the lords, both Houses, surely in an effort to give the document as much status and legal force as possible, ordered that the Declaration be engrossed in parchment, enrolled in the rolls of Parliament, and entered in the Court of Chancery "to remain in perpetuity."[86] Although the Declaration was not a bill, they treated it as if it had properties of a bill. A pamphlet printed shortly after the ceremony argued that since the Declaration of Rights was engrossed and enrolled it was "conclusive and binding."[87] Fourth, the presentation copy of the Declaration of Rights—the one the clerk read in the Banqueting Hall—was given marks of importance. Either the scribe on his own initiative or at the prompting of an unidentified person selected a piece of parchment two and one half inches wider than normally used for bills and applied two red lines on either side of the text.[88] It was—and is—a handsome document. Fifth, the House of Lords agreed to meet at 8 A.M. the morning of February 13 in their chamber and "go in a body" with the Declaration to the Banqueting Hall. Further, they suggested that the members of the House of Commons do likewise, recommending that M.P.s "go along" with them.[89] Such an arrangement for peers and commoners to meet first at Westminster, rather than at any other place, and to arrive at the Banqueting Hall as a body, rather than individually, may be seen as an effort to give public testimony to the corporate nature of Parliament and its importance in the proceedings to follow. Most important of all, no changes of significance were made in the language or arrangement of material in the draft presented by Somers on February 8. Thus, the conditional relationship between the nation's rights and the crown was clearly articulated. In sum, all these details suggest that, whatever the actual legal force of the Declaration, the Convention did many different subtle things to underline the importance of the document and to create the impression that it was a precondition for receiving the English crown and that it limited the royal prerogative.

Although the initiative in arranging the events of February 13 remained with the Convention, William and his close friends played a role in the preparations. The prince must have considered his first major public ceremony with some care. His demonstrated interest in shaping public opinion argues as much. The immediate background of tension and crisis and William's reluctant acceptance of the Declaration of Rights would have intensified his concern. Further, the almost certain fact that William bore much of the expense of the affair would also have concentrated his attention and that of his close advisers.

It fell to William to choose the time and place of the presentation ceremony.[90] He chose the Banqueting Hall. There were other possible sites: for example, Westminster Hall or Westminster Abbey (the likely choice if an emphasis upon Anglicanism were desired), or the House of Lords chamber (where the Petition of Right had been presented).[91] There is no "minute" that reveals why the prince selected the Banqueting Hall, but it had been, throughout the century, the center of the Stuart court's activities and used for manifold purposes. A good-sized hall, measuring 110 feet long by 55 feet wide and high, its ceiling gorgeously decorated by Rubens, the Banqueting Hall was ideally suited for public ceremonies. Here, Stuart kings had received members of parliament and ambassadors presented their credentials.[92] Here Charles II was joyfully received on May 29, 1660, upon his return to the throne. It is interesting that lords and members of Parliament had approached and addressed him in a manner very like that used in 1689.[93] Finally, it could hardly have been lost on any sensitive observer — especially since the specter of civil war had influenced the debates — that just forty years before, on January 30, 1649, Charles I had walked through this same hall on his way to the scaffold outside the window. This revolution, the choice of Banqueting Hall seemed to say, has brought no such bloodshed and divisions, as occurred in 1649, but rather has brought a reconciliation as in 1660.

It was also William's decision to hold the ceremony on Ash Wednesday, a day more important in the religious calendar of the Anglican church than for the Calvinist faith in which William had been raised. It is a nice question whether Mary, whose boat was already in the Thames when the decision was made, would have urged her husband, had she been present, to postpone the ceremony until Thursday in deference to the sensibilities of devout Anglicans. The argument in favor of holding the ceremony on Ash Wednesday, according to Gilbert Burnet, at this time the prince's principal propagandist and later to become the Bishop of Salisbury, was that it "had a particular decency in it, that princes immediately when they were set on the throne should come and humble themselves in dust and ashes before God."[94] Did William choose the day to signal his religious inclinations and indicate his sympathy with Dissenters? The point is moot. But one may speculate that the choice of day implied just that. And the idea is reinforced by the service of Thanksgiving held later in the afternoon in the Chapel Royal. The service, conducted (as already noted) by Henry Compton, attracted a "very great audience," which delighted, reported one newspaper, "to see a King and Queen of England together Worshipping GOD in the Reformed Religion."[95]

In addition to deciding the day and place of the ceremony, William surely thought about how to present himself. For the first time he would appear before the members of the Convention. What was he to wear? How was he to act? Less than four months ago, William had made a dazzling entry into Exeter mounted on a "milk white palfrey armed cap a pied, a plume of white feathers on his head."[96] He could not appear in that oufit, indeed military dress of any kind would not conform to the image that he had taken pains to project. It is interesting that none of the prints of the occasion shows him wearing so much as a sword.[97] Iconographic material portrayed him as an Orange Tree, a Lion, and a Roman senator, none of which was appropriate to the occasion. For the ceremony William probably wore a simple cinnamon-colored suit, interlined with flannel to protect his chest, racked by a deepening of his asthmatic cough, against the cold.[98] Probably his waistcoat was a rich gold and silver brocade with gold buttons, also interlined with flannel. William West, his embroiderer, very likely embroidered on his coat the star seen in the print.[99] Sitting under the canopy, a symbol of nobility which, of course, he claimed in his own right, William presented a rather modest, certainly civilian, surely benign picture. As the ceremony unfolds, he plays a passive role. The Speakers of the two Houses approach him. They begin the exchange. He signifies assent to their request to present their Declaration. The deputy clerk of the Parliament reads the Declaration. William responds. That is all. William plainly was content that he and Mary should leave the hall immediately after the speeches were concluded. They make no further public appearances until late in the afternoon at Compton's sermon and in the evening at a party at Whitehall. All of this is, I suggest, entirely consistent with the image of a selfless Deliverer who came only with a "Force sufficient" — as his *Declaration of Reasons* insisted — in response to the call of the nation to restore England's laws, religion, and liberties.

In addition, William surely instructed Mary how she should present herself during the ceremony — even as he had told her what attitude to assume when she reached England.[100] Her actions in the Banqueting Hall are too highly stylized to be spontaneous. William and Mary enter, you will recall, hand-in-hand and sit holding hands. Surely this posture was designed to placate the Maryites and to underscore the dual nature of the monarchy, notwithstanding the fact that William had insisted that the administrative powers be vested in himself alone. Mary said nothing during the ceremony. Indeed, anything she might have said would have been liable to misinterpretation, and there is no evidence at all that the hopes of some Englishmen that she would apologize for what was happening were ever discussed with her or William. "Her looks and a little curtsy," her acknowledged beauty, above all her presence by her husband's side were her contributions to the ceremony.[101] If she had any feeling about the ceremony she failed to note it in her memoirs.[102]

Another major contribution William made to the ceremony was to respond for himself and Mary to the reading of the Declaration of Rights and the offer of the crown. The speech that prompted such shouts of joy repays study. William, surely by design, reversed the order of things as they had been presented in the Declaration. Two could play this game. He accepted the crown *first* and then referred to the statement of rights. Moreover, William's oral remarks about Parliament were, apparently, different from the official version. Observers reported that the Prince declared not only that he would preserve the nation's rights and maintain the Protestant religion but also that he would place no obstacle in the way of Parliament's privileges, prefer their advice to his own views, and consult them often.[103] The official version of the speech, a holograph copy of which is preserved in the House of Lords Record Office, is more restrained. In it William is reported to have said only that he would "endeavor to support" the nation's religion, laws, and liberties, and would concur in "anything" that shall be for the "good" of the kingdom.[104] Both accounts agree that the prince took no solemn oath, made no binding pledge, signed no paper. But both accounts show that William did not ignore the statement of rights. However his remarks are reported, he probably said more than he really wanted to. In a high and serious moment, the prince made a public commitment to "endeavor to support"—at the least—the nation's religion, laws, and liberties. And he did this before a body whose authority was confirmed within a fortnight by a statute transforming it into a regular Parliament. As the next nine months showed, despite continuing reluctance, William felt himself obliged, because of the circumstances of his affairs, to go forward with transforming the Declaration into the Bill of Rights. Surely part of those "circumstances" that obliged him was his public commitment to the Declaration.

The Convention's immediate handling of William's acceptance speech suggests their concern to hold him to his commitment. On

February 14, the Speaker of the House of Commons requested a written copy of the speech "to prevent any mistake," and the next day introduced the official version, which, of course, was entered in the record of the house. On February 15 the House of Lords, upon receiving the official version, ordered William's response to be printed and published with the Declaration of Rights. And more, they ordered it to be added to the engrossed Declaration in parchment and enrolled in Parliament and Chancery.[105] A contemporary observer complained about the date — the fifteenth — under which William's answer appeared in the printed document. Describing it as a "great mistake," he pointed out that a reader might think that the answer had been made on the fifteenth rather than the thirteenth, and implied that a precedent had been set for the king to exercise royal power without the restraints of the Declaration of Rights.[106]

Other printed pieces carried news of the ceremony and the Declaration of Rights. The official proclamation referred to the Declaration. *The Manner of the Proclaiming of King William and Queen Mary* specifically noted that the prince and princess had accepted the crown "pursuant" to the Declaration and that the document had been presented "in writing." The entire text of the Declaration also appeared in the body of a pamphlet that was printed and reprinted in the spring.[107] The *London Gazette* and the new newspapers reported the ceremony, one declaring that the "Grand Convention" had presented their Declaration in writing and that William had "promised to perform to the utmost" all it required.[108]

At least one medal commemorating the ceremony of February 13 was cast (fig. 6). Measuring two and one half inches across, this large coin (one of which survives in the collection of the British Museum) was designed by Anton Meybusch, a medallist of German origin active in Stockholm, Paris and Copenhagen.[109] It is not known whether or not the medal was commissioned, but it seems likely that neither the new king nor his friends had anything to do with it. Meybusch probably made the medal in Stockholm for the collectors' market. Thus, it is of interest for what it shows about a continental medallist's understanding of events in England. That understanding was clouded. First, only William is depicted; no reference is made to Mary. On one side is only a bust of William, a patent insult to English Maryites and a clear mis-

Fig. 4.6. Medal commemorating ceremony of February 13.

representation of the settlement. There is no proof of a polemical intent in the omission of Mary and it may be, simply, that Meybusch thought of William as the major figure in the revolution and so represented him alone. Second, the obverse of the medal shows William dressed as a Roman, standing with a spear in one hand. He proffers a cap of liberty to three kneeling female figures, who symbolize England, Scotland, and Ireland. The cap of liberty was a well-established device, used by the Dutch for over a hundred years as a symbol signifying their fight for liberty from Spanish overlords in the sixteenth century. The cap had appeared on many other medals in 1688-89 to indicate that William had come to restore England's laws, liberties, and religion.[110] On this present medal, broken yokes symbolizing Catholicism and tyranny strew the ground, while rays from the Eye of Providence bathe the scene. The overall message reiterates the major theme in William's propaganda, namely that he had come to restore the nation's rights. The medal also implies that the nation is suppliant to the prince and that their rights derive from him. The use of the word "Vici" in the legend heavily reinforces this impression. The legend reads, "Veni, Vici, Libertatem redidi"—"I came, I conquered, I restored liberty." Probably Meybusch was not aware of the delicacy surrounding the point of whether or not William was a conqueror. Although both William's friends and foes used various versions of conquest theory to justify the revolution, the Prince himself had gone to lengths around this time to avoid the image of conqueror, denying such an idea in his manifesto, refusing to claim the crown on those grounds, and ordering any soldier who intimated as much to be punished.[111] The suggestion on the medal that William gave rights rather than responded to the nation's demand for them would have suited the prince's view of the Declaration of Rights, but it is doubtful that this medal could have pleased the new king.

In any case, oral, written, printed, and visual material carried news of the ceremony, proclamation, and Declaration of Rights to England and Europe. Anyone with the slightest interest in public affairs could have known of the event and formed the impression that William and Mary accepted the crown on terms set out in a written instrument devised by the peers of the realm and the nation's elected representatives.

What are the implications of looking at the Glorious Revolution as a spectacle? Of accepting that the ceremonies and processions were an integral part of the political process by which the revolutionary crisis was resolved? Such a new perspective may assist in understanding first that the ceremonies, processions, and merrymaking helped to legitimize the revolution. The use of traditional forms, the bright colors and brilliant sounds of pageantry and pomp, and the presence of so many people all combined to that end. In the face of disagreements and tension in and between the two Houses in the Convention, among English political leaders, and between them and the Dutch prince, news of which circulated, the ceremonies suggested national unanimity and harmony. They conveyed the impression that the corporate body of Parliament had taken the initiative in making a settlement and that Prince William had passively concurred in it. Intimating only that William was to exercise administrative authority alone, the ceremony in the Banqueting Hall underlined the *dual* nature of the monarchy, thereby reinforcing the legitimacy of the settlement and placating those who favored Mary. They wrapped change in traditional forms and thus minimized it. In so doing they made it easier for persons who were disappointed at the outcome to feel comfortable about accepting it. At the same time the processions, bonfires and merrymaking were an emotional catharsis to those who had conspired for so many months to bring about a change in government.

Second, the presentation ceremony in the Banqueting Hall testified to the importance of the claim of rights which the two Houses insisted upon presenting to the prince and princess of Orange in a public ceremony. The reading of a document—which had been given marks of distinction—in a structured ceremony invested that document with importance. Leaders of an irregular assembly presented a written Declaration in which they claimed specific rights of the subject, some of which were new law, and *then* offered the nation's crown.[112] The unfolding of the ceremony reinforced the impression created by the choice of words and the arrangement of the parts of the document: namely, that the claim of rights was a condition—a condition which William had to accept to win the crown and a condition on the powers of the kingship. Only in the last decade or so have historians recognized that the Declaration of Rights was just that: a declaration, a claim that according to strict law carried no legal force. We know that at no time did English political leaders say to William that if he did *not* accept the Declaration of Rights they would withdraw the offer of the crown.

Moreover, the ceremony underscored the skill and determination of a small number of men in the House of Commons. It represented a political victory over persons who wanted simply to change the king and also over William. Although traditional in form, this ceremony implied, in terms of seventeenth-century political notions, a libertarian idea, the preeminence of Parliament in England's mixed government.[113]

Third, the events of February 13 show that the principals were sensitive to public opinion and displayed skill in shaping it. The ceremony, processions, and so on, reinforce the argument that Englishmen and Dutchmen together mounted the most sophisticated and extensive propaganda campaign thus far in the history of Western Europe. They appealed to persons outside socially and political elite categories. They made a deliberate attempt to engage the attention of such persons and to involve them as participants in the events that marked the end of the most critical phase of the revolution, even as they had appealed to such persons through tracts, pamphlets, and visual materials for at least the six previous months.

In sum, the "spectacles" of February 13 are properly seen, I believe, as an integral part of the political process by which the revolutionary crisis was resolved. These proceedings did not just happen. They were organized by members of the Convention and to a lesser extent by Prince William—men who knew full well what they were doing. When they are examined closely not only can they vivify the Revolution but also help us to understand it more deeply and accurately.

NOTES

1. The idea for this paper originated in 1975 in connection with a larger study of the Declaration of Rights and Bill of Rights for which I held a Senior Fellowship from the National Endowment for the Humanities. The research was completed in the summer of 1977 during a visit to England funded by the Graduate Schools of Arts and Sciences of George Washington University. I am deeply grateful for this support. Isabel W. Kenrick helped locate iconographic material and otherwise

expedited the research in England. The staffs of the Print Room and Numismatic Room at the British Museum and of the Guildhall Library clarified certain technical points, and Natalie Rothstein and Hugh Murray Bailey generously shared their knowledge of dress, etiquette, and furnishings. The London Meteorological Office supplied a photocopy of the relevant portion of the Rawlinson MSS Weather Diary. I thank them as well as the staffs of the British Library, the House of Lords Record Office, the Public Record Office, the Bodleian Library, Henry E. Huntington Library and, especially, the Folger Shakespeare Library. Jop Spiekerman of the University of Leiden and Margaretha Arlman aided in translating from the Dutch. The Trustees of the British Museum and of the Guildhall Library granted permission to reproduce the pictures of the prints and the medal. The recent photographs of the Banqueting House are British Crown Copyright and are reproduced with permission of the Controller of Her Britannic Majesty's Stationery Office. I also thank Robert Kenny, Joseph Martin, Howard Nenner, Barbara Taft and Irving Wechsler for their constructive comments on a version of this paper. I am grateful to the Regents of the University of California for permission to use this paper, in substance, in chapter 15 of my book, *The Declaration of Rights, 1689* (Baltimore, 1981). I presented a version of this essay at the annual meeting of the Anglo-American Conference of Historians, London, 1981.

2. Jennifer Carter, "The Revolution and the Constitution," *Britain After the Glorious Revolution,* ed. Geoffrey Holmes (London, 1969), p. 40, posed the key question of the Revolution of 1688/89: "whether it established a new king on the throne, or a new type of monarchy?"

3. See such provocative studies as Victor Turner, *The Ritual Process, Structure and Anti-Structure* (Chicago, 1968), and Erving Goffman, *Interaction Ritual: Essays in Face-to-Face Behaviour* (London, 1972) and *The Presentation of Self in Everyday Life* (London, 1959). Also, Sidney Anglo, *Spectacle, Pageantry, and Early Tudor Policy* (Oxford, 1969); Natalie Z. Davis, *Society and Culture in early Modern France: eight essays* (Stanford, Calif., 1975); Ralph Giesey, *The Royal Funeral Ceremony in Renaissance France* (Droz, 1960); Gerard Reedy, "Mystical Politics: The Imagery of Charles II's Coronation," *Studies in Change and Revolution: Aspects of English Intellectual History 1640-1800* (New York, 1972), pp. 19-42; and Roy Strong, *Splendour at Court: Renaissance Spectacle and Illusion* (London, 1973).

4. Lawrence Stone has estimated literacy for this period at about 40 percent of the adult males nationally and at about 67 percent of the adult males in the cities: "Literacy and Education in England, 1640-1900," *Past and Present,* 42 (1969), 109, 112, 125, 128. Also David Cressy, "Illiteracy in England, 1530-1730," *The Historical Journal,* 20, 1 (1977), 1-23.

5. The records of the Lord Chamberlain, the Lord Steward, and the Master of the Robes at the Public Record Office (hereafter P.R.O.) are full of gaps for the months of January and February 1689. Mary preferred Palme wine and William champagne: LS 1/32.

6. See the useful pamphlet, John Charlton, *The Banqueting House, Whitehall* published by the Department of the Environment, Ancient Monuments and Historic Buildings (Edinburgh, n.d.).

7. Of several scholarly biographies that by Stephen Baxter, *William III* (London, 1966) is the most persuasive and coherent. Nesca A. Robb, *William of Orange: A Personal Portrait* (London, 1962, 1966), 2 vols. is also useful. Two recent popular studies, beautifully illustrated, are John Miller, *The Life and Times of William and Mary* (London, 1974) and Henri and Barbara van der Zee, *William and Mary* (London, 1973). The size of the army is given by Baxter, p. 237.

8. See Lois G. Schwoerer, "Propaganda in the Revolution of 1688/89," *American Historical Review*, 82, 3 (1977), 846-847, 872 for the following points.

9. "Journaal van Constantyn Huygens, den zoon, van 21 October 1688 tot 2 September 1696," *Werken Uitgegeven door het Historisch Genootschap* (Utrecht, 1876-1878), n.s., 23: 85; and J. G. van Terveen, ed., "Uittreksels uit het Bijzonder Verbaal Nopens de Deputatie en Ambassade Daarop Gevolgd in Engeland, 1689, Gehouden Door Mr. Nicolass Witsen, Burgemeester te Amsterdam," *Geschied-en Letterkundig Mengel werk van Mr. Jacobus Scheltema* (Utrecht, 1823), Derde Deel, pt. 2, 134. Also P. L. Müller, ed., *Willem III von Oranien und George Friedrich von Waldeck* (The Hague, 1873-80), 2:137.

10. Sir John Reresby, *Memoirs of Sir John Reresby*, ed. Andrew Browning (London, 1936), p. 553.

11. J. P. Kenyon, *The Stuart Constitution, 1603-1689: Documents and Commentary* (Cambridge, 1966), p. 1.

12. Lois G. Schwoerer, "Press and Parliament in the Revolution of 1689," *The Historical Journal*, 20, 3 (1977), 545-567.

13. House of Lords Record Office (hereafter H.L.R.O.), Braye MSS 43, f. 31 v. The excitement of the moment is shown in the "scribble" books of the clerk. Words are repeated or omitted, the handwriting is hasty, and two black slashes run across the page.

14. Schwoerer, "Propaganda in the Revolution of 1688/89."

15. John Evelyn, *The Diary of John Evelyn*, ed. E. S. deBeer (London, 1955), 4:624.

16. Goffman, *Presentation of Self in Everyday Life*, p. 11.

17. Lois G. Schwoerer, "A Jornall of the Convention at Westminster begun the 22 of January 1688/89," *Bulletin of the Institute of Historical Research* (hereafter B.I.H.R.), 49 (1976), 253-254. No such exact formula for proclaiming a king existed prior to the seventeenth century. The speaker was Sir Robert Sawyer.

18. British Library (hereafter B.L.), Add. MSS 38, 496, f. 19.

19. *Journals of the House of Lords* (hereafter *L.J.*), 14:127.

20. B.L., Add. MSS 40, 621, ff. 18, 24; B.L. Add. MSS 34, 515, p. 2. Also, see an oblique reference, perhaps to this point, in H.L.R.O., Hist. Coll., Willcocks Coll. VI, 20. Letters for electing members of the Convention had also been directed to the coroner: *Journals of the House of Commons* (hereafter *C.J.*), 10:7.

21. Robert Steele, ed., *Bibliography of Royal Proclamations of the Tudor and Stuart Sovereigns and of others published under authority, 1485-1714* (Oxford, 1910), 1:476-77; cf. pp. 107, 166, 343, 384, 437, 512 for proclamations of other Stuart kings. In the proclamation of Charles II, dated 8 May 1660, the Commons are also mentioned. The question of which persons should have the authority to proclaim a king surfaced again in June in debates on the Act of Succession: Anchitell Grey, *Debates of the House of Commons From the Year 1667 to the Year 1694* (London, 1763), 9:345-346, 351-352.

22. P.R.O., L/C 9, ff. 43, 73, 73v; Bodleian Library (hereafter Bodl.), MSS Rawlinson D 1079, f. 14v; Bodl., MSS Ballard 45, f. 28; The *Universal Intelligence*, #12, 13 Feb. 1688/89; *Orange Gazette*, #12, 12-15 Feb. 1688/89.

23. The official proclamation was printed under date of 13 February. *The Manner of the Proclaiming of King William, and Queen Mary, at White-Hall and in the City of London, Feb. 13, 1688/9*, a broadside, supplies many details. Also, Narcissus Luttrell, *A Brief Historical Relation of State Affairs from September 1678 to April 1714* (Oxford, 1857), 1:501; Bodl., MSS Rawlinson D 1079, f. 17; *Orange Gazette*, #12, 12-15 Feb. 1688/89. Sir Thomas St. George was garter principal king of arms. The lord mayor, Sir John Chapman, was ill and confined to his coach, a circumstance doubtless explaining the passive role of the lord mayor.

24. Roger Morrice, "Entr'ing Book, Being an Historical Register of Occurrences from April Anno 1677 to April 1691," Q, 467. The original is in Dr. Williams's Library in London. I have used a photocopy at the Folger Shakespeare Library (hereafter F.S.L.).

25. A member of William's Dutch entourage specifically noted that he saw the proceedings from his window: "Journaal van Constantyn Huygens," p. 86. See also fig. 1, discussed below.

26. *C.J.*, 10:29.

27. The petition urged the Convention to declare William and Mary king and queen immediately. A manuscript copy of the petition without signatures (the only one, apparently, to have survived) is at the Hertfordshire County Record Office, D/EP F26. For a brief account of the petition, see Schwoerer, "Press and Parliament in the Revolution of 1689," pp. 551-552.

28. London Meteorological Office, Rawlinson MSS Weather Diary, n.p.

29. Reports of the number of peers attending the ceremony vary: see *L.J.*, 14:127; H.L.R.O., Braye MSS, ff. 31v. 32; H.L.R.O., MSS Minutes 13 Feb. 1688/89. The average attendance in the Lords was 95, ranging from a low of 56 on 24 January to a high of 112 on 7 February. The average attendance in the House of Commons, based on the days when a division was reported in the *Journals*, was 360: see *C.J.*, 10:16, 20, 21, 24. My figures are a little different from those given in Andrew Browning, ed., *English Historical Documents, 1660-1714* (London, 1966), p. 956. A modern study of the House of Lords for this period is

needed to replace Arthur S. Turberville, *The House of Lords in the reign of William III*, in *Oxford Historical and Literary Studies*, vol. 3 (Oxford, 1913). See Henry Horwitz, *Parliament, Policy and Politics in the Reign of William III* (Manchester, 1977), passim.

30. Grey, *Debates*, 9:112.

31. Reresby, *Memoirs*, p. 554.

32. Van Terveen, "Verbal... Witsen," p. 142; On 25 February, Witsen noted that "taunting songs are sung in the street; the Butterboxes [i.e., the Dutch] have given us a King." The term "Butterboxes" was pejorative; it had been used in 1650s in vicious pictorial satire against the Dutch. See M. Dorothy George, *English Political Caricature to 1792: A Study of Opinion and Propaganda* (Oxford, 1959), 1:42, 50. By the end of February desertion in the army had decimated the ranks: Luttrell, *Brief Relations*, 1:505; Reresby, *Memoirs*, pp. 557-58; Morrice "Entr'ing Book," Q, 474.

33. A bonfire celebrating William's acceptance in late December of the administration of the government was also placed outside Watts Coffee House and was contributed to by persons who were elected to the Convention. See *Orange Gazette*, #1, 31 Dec. 1688, and the *London Courant*, #6, 25-29 Dec. 1688. The news that the House of Lords had accepted the "abdication" and "vacancy" resolution was greeted with bonfires the night of February 6. See Morrice, "Entr'ing Book," Q, 459, 462; Bodl., MSS Rawlinson D 1079, f. 13. The night of Mary's arrival, bonfires were so numerous that people thought the city was on fire. See *London Mercury*, #12, 12 Feb. 1688/89; Algemeen Rijksarchief, Collectie van Citters, Brieven van den Ambassadeur van Citters, 1688 tot 1690, no. 25, 12/22 Feb. 1688/89.

34. Morrice, "Entr'ing Book," Q, 467; *London Mercury: or, Moderate Intelligencer*, #12, 11-14 Feb. 1688/89.

35. *Orange Gazette*, #12, 12-15 Feb. 1688/89. Earlier cartoons and medals had featured Jeffreys and Petre in the most unflattering terms. See Schwoerer, "Propaganda in the Revolution of 1688/89," pp. 861-865.

36. The figure is reported in John Eliot Hodgkin, *Rariora, Being Notes of some of the Printed Books, Manuscripts, Historical Documents, Medals, Engravings, Pottery, Etc., Etc.* (London, 1902), 3:vi (second page so numbered). This volume contains engravings of firework displays and a list of books on fireworks. John Carswell speculates that many English sources for this period were burned. *The Descent on England: A Study of the English Revolution of 1688 and Its European Background* (London, 1969), preface.

37. The Lords made specific arrangements about the printing of the proclamation both before and after the Prince was proclaimed: H.L.R.O., MSS Minutes, 12 Feb. 1688/89.

38. The date is written on the copy of the broadside in the British Library.

39. Courtesy of Guildhall Library, Print L. 22.2: "Uyt-roeping tot de

Krooning van Willem de III en Maria de II tot Koning en Koninginne van Engeland, Schotland, Vrankryk en Ierland den 23 [N.S.] February 1689, binne, Londen." The print appeared in an anonymous work, *Engeland Beroerd onder de Regeering van Koning Jacobus de II* (Amsterdam, 1689). For maces, see P.R.O., L/C 9, ff. 43, 72v, 73, where their value is given as over £300.

40. The tune for the song was used two months later for a coronation song: *The Protestants Joy; An Excellent New Song on the Glorious Coronation of King William and Queen Mary, which in much Triumph was Celebrated at Westminster on the 11th, instant April.* Licensed according to Order.

41. The new newspapers are discussed in Schwoerer, "Press and Parliament in the Revolution of 1689."

42. *London Mercury: or, Moderate Intelligencer,* #12, 11-14 Feb. 1688/89; Reresby, *Memoirs,* p. 554; *Calendar of State Papers, Domestic, William and Mary,* 1:1; Add. MSS 38, 496, ff. 19v, 23, 23v. But one disgruntled onlooker thought he had never seen a "worse sight." B.L., Add. MSS 36, 707, f. 57.

43. Algemeen Rijksarchief, Brieven van den Ambassadeur van Citters, no. 25, 15/25 Feb. 1688/89; B.L. Add. MSS 38, 496, ff. 21, 21v; Müller, ed., *Willem III . . . und . . . von Waldeck,* 2:137, 139.

44. For the power of the idea of the "ancient constitution," see J. G. A. Pocock, *The Ancient Constitution and the Feudal Law* (London, 1957).

45. The two doorkeepers of the House of Commons were ordered to allow none but members of the Convention to enter the Hall: *C.J.,* 10:28.

46. *C.J.,* 10:29. F.S.L., Anon., "A Short Account of the Revolution in England in the year 1688." Bound in Sir Robert Southwell's Collection of MSS Material on the Glorious Revolution, V.b. 150, f. 15. John Walker was cousin and Deputy to John Browne, Clerk of Parliament, who was absent presumably because of illness and old age. See H.L.R.O., MSS Minutes, Feb. 13, 1688/89. The print is one of three undated prints of the ceremony found in the British Museum Print Room. None is contemporary; they all date from the late-eighteenth or nineteenth century.

47. F.S.L., "The Newdigate Newsletters, Addressed to Sir Richard Newdigate, 1st Bart., and 2nd Bart., 1673/74-1715," L.C. 1976.

48. Ibid.; Konigl. Geh. Staat-Archiv. Acta betr. des Residenten Bonnet relat. aus England 1689 Jan.-June. Rep. XI.73 Engld. Fast 1, 15/25 Feb. 1688/89, f. 60. I have used a microfilm of this collection kindly supplied by the University of Kansas Library (hereafter KUL). Frederic Bonnet was the representative from Brandenburg.

49. The Petition of Right of 1628 and other petitions are discussed by Elizabeth R. Foster, "Petitions and the Petition of Right." *Journal of British Studies,* 14 (Nov. 1974), 21-45.

50. See William Huse Dunham, Jr. and Charles T. Wood, "The

Right to Rule in England: Depositions and the Kingdom's Authority, 1327-1485," *American Historical Review,* 81 (Oct. 1976), 738-61. The dates were 1327, 1399, 1460, 1483, 1485, and 1649.

51. Grey, *Debates,* 9:29-37; J. Somers, "Notes of what passed in the Convention . . . Mr. Hampden in the Chair, 29th January," *Miscellaneous State Papers, from 1501 to 1726,* ed. P. Yorke, 2d Earl of Hardwicke, 2 vols. (1778), 2:413-425.

52. John Humfrey [?], *Advice Before It be too Late: or A Breviate for the Convention* (London, 1689), p. 4 [unpaginated]. For assignment to Humfrey, see Douglas Lacey, *Dissent and Parliamentary Politics in England 1661-1689* (New Brunswick, 1969). For the press, see Frederick S. Siebert, *Freedom of the press in England 1476-1776: the rise and decline of government control* (Urbana, 1952), esp. chaps. 9, 10, 13, 17.

53. Grey, *Debates,* 9:70-71.

54. The House of Lords agreed to the "abdication" and "vacancy" resolution the night of February 6 and immediately moved to declare William and Mary king and queen, without any reference to a statement of rights. See *L.J.,* 14:118-119.

55. *C.J.,* 10:20; F.S.L., "The Newdigate Newsletters," L.C., 1970.

56. Grey, *Debates,* 9:74.

57. *C.J.,* 10:21-22.

58. Grey, *Debates,* 9:35; Bodl., MSS Rawlinson D 1079, ff. 3v, 14; Reresby, *Memoirs,* p. 564; Historical Manuscript Collection, *The Manuscripts of His Grace the Duke of Portland, Preserved at Welbeck Abbey,* 3:425; Morrice, "Entr'ing Book," Q, 445, 447, 448, 461. "Journaal van Constantyn Huygens," p. 83; S. W. Singer, ed., *Correspondence of Henry Hyde, Earl of Clarendon, and of His Brother, Laurence Hyde, Earl of Rochester* (London, 1828), 2:262.

59. H.L.R.O., Willcocks Coll., VI, 20; Lord Yester to Lord Tweeddale, 7 Feb. 1688/89 specifically refers to this draft as being in print, but no copy seems to have survived. The first draft, a committee report entitled *The Publick Grievances of the Nation adjudged necessary, by the honorable the House of Commons to be redressed,* appeared on either February 4 or 5. The penultimate draft prepared by the House of Commons on February 11 was also printed under the title *The agreement of the House of Lords, during this session, with the concurrence of the House of Commons, to this present eleventh of February, in the great affairs of these nations.* Despite the title, the Lords amended this draft. Copy at the Huntington Library.

60. Eighteen members of this committee of twenty-one M.P.s were also members of the committee responsible for drafting the statement of grievances and rights. A study is needed of the committees of the Convention Parliament like that undertaken by T. K. Moore and H. Horwitz for the parliamentary sessions of 1691-92 and 1692-93 — "Who runs the House? Aspects of parliamentary organization in the later 17th century," *Journal of Modern History,* xlii (1971), 202-227.

61. See William L. Sachse, *John Lord Somers* (Manchester, 1975).

62. Grey, *Debates,* 9:79-80.

63. Bodl., MSS Rawlinson D 1079, f. 14v; the same remark appears in F.S.L., "The Newdigate Newsletters," L.C. 1944.

64. The full title was *Declaration of His Highness William Henry, Prince of Orange, of the Reasons Inducing Him to Appear in Armes in the Kingdom of England for Preserving of the Protestant Religion and for Restoring the Lawes and Liberties of England, Scotland, and Ireland.* The first declaration was dated 1/10 October 1688; the second appeared two weeks later. See Schwoerer, "Propaganda in the Revolution of 1688/89," pp. 851-54.

65. The word was later changed to "encouraged" at the insistence of the Lords.

66. *C.J.,* 10:26.

67. Lucile Pinkham, *William III and the Respectable Revolution* (Cambridge, Mass., 1954), pp. 234-235; Robert Frankle, "The Formulation of the Declaration of Rights," *Historical Journal,* 17 (1974), 270; Howard Nenner, "The Convention of 1689: A Triumph of Constitutional Form," *American Journal of Legal History* (October 1966), p. 295. Prof. Nenner kindly allowed me to read in typescript his article, "Constitutional Uncertainty and the Declaration of Rights," *After the Reformation: Essays in Honor of J. J. Hexter,* ed. Barbara Malament (Philadelphia, 1980), pp. 291-308; Henry Horwitz, "Parliament and the Glorious Revolution," *B.I.H.R.,* 47 (1974), 47-49. Carter's article is cited in n. 2, above.

68. Morrice, "Entr'ing Book," Q, 447. Also, Foster, "Petitions and the Petition of Right," pp. 43-44.

69. Grey, *Debates,* 9:34. Among the tracts are: Humfrey, *Advice Before It Be Too Late,* pp. 2-3 [unpaginated]; Anon., *A Brief Collection of some Memorandums: or, Things humbly offered to the consideration of the great Convention and of the succeeding Parliament* (London, 1689), p. 7; Anon., *Four Questions Debated* (London, 1689).

70. Carolyn Edie, "Revolution and the Rule of Law," *Eighteenth-Century Studies,* 4 (Summer, 1977), 434-450 deals with the dispensing power in the Declaration of Rights. For an extended study, see J. J. R. Greenberg, "Tudor and Stuart Theories of Kingship: The Dispensing Power and the Royal Discretionary Authority in Sixteenth and Seventeenth Century England" (Ph.D. diss., Univ. of Michigan, 1970). For standing armies, Lois G. Schwoerer, *"No Standing Armies!" The Anti-army Ideology in Seventeenth-Century England* (Baltimore, 1974) and her "'The Fittest Subject for a King's Quarrel' An Essay on the Militia Controversy 1641-1642," *Journal of British Studies,* 9 (Nov. 1971), 45-76.

71. Singer, ed., *Correspondence of. . . Clarendon,* 2:262; H.L.R.O., Hist. Coll., Willcocks Coll., VI, 21; Reresby, *Memoirs,* p. 552; also Morrice, "Entr'ing Book," Q, 463; *The London Intelligence,* #8, 5-9 Feb. 1688/89; F.S.L., "The Newdigate Newsletters," L.C., 1974; "Journaal van Constantyn Huygens," p. 84; Bodl., MSS Rawlinson D 1079, f. 14 v.

72. H.L.R.O., Willcocks Coll., VI, 21.

73. Morrice, "Entr'ing Book," Q, 463, 464. Jacobite tracts written in the 1690s asserted that William threatened to return to Holland if he were offered a crown "upon conditions." See [Nathaniel Johnston], *The Dear Bargain: or, a true Representation of the State of the English Nation under the Dutch. In a Letter to a Friend.* (1690), in Walter Scott, ed., *A Collection of Scarce and Valuable Tracts... Somers Tracts* (London, 1812), 10:369-70; and [Sir James Montgomery], *Great Britain's just Complaint for her late Measures, present Sufferings, and the future Miseries she is exposed to* (1692), in ibid., p. 440.

74. B.L., Add. MSS 40, 621, ff. 18, 22. The role of the bishops in the spring of 1689 still needs investigating.

75. Morrice, "Entr'ing Book," Q, 463.

76. Ibid., p. 464.

77. "Journaal van Constantyn Huygens," p. 84. The spokesman was Sir Richard Temple.

78. Van Terveen, "Verbaal... Witsen," p. 141. Witsen refused, fearing the Prince's temper, but reported that Everard van Weede, heer van Dijkvelt, urged William to accept the Declaration.

79. Morrice, "Entr'ing Book," Q, 465; B.L., Add. MSS 40, 621, f. 20; H.L.R.O., Hist. Coll., Willcocks Coll., VI, 21.

80. H. C. Foxcroft, *Life and Letters of the First Marquis of Halifax* (London, 1898), 2:217 (The Spencer House Journals).

81. Ibid., p. 203.

82. B.L., Add. MSS 40, 621, f. 20.

83. *C.J.,* 10:21.

84. Morrice, "Entr'ing Book," Q, 466; Bodl., MSS Rawlinson D 1079, f. 16; H.L.R.O., Braye MSS 43, f. 30v; F.S.L., Anon., "A Short Account of the Revolution of 1688," f. 15. See Esther Cope, "The King's Declaration concerning the Dissolution of the Short Parliament of 1640: An Unsuccessful Attempt at Public Relations," *Huntington Library Quarterly* (August 1977), p. 326, for different kinds of "declarations" issued in the seventeenth century.

85. *L.J.,* 14:126-127; H.L.R.O., MSS Journal, 61:78.

86. *C.J.,* 10:26, 27; *L.J.,* 14:126; H.M.C., *House of Lords Mss.,* 1689-90, p. 30; H.L.R.O., Main Papers contain the original draft of this recommendation. For treatment of earlier petitions see Foster, "Petitions and the Petition of Right," pp. 38-40.

87. Anon., *The Present Convention a Parliament* (London, 1688 [before March 25, 1689]), p. 18. A second edition in 1689.

88. Locating the presentation copy of the Declaration of Rights was difficult; no copy is marked as such in the Archives. I thank Maurice Bond, Clerk of the Records, H.L.R.O., and the Deputy-Clerk, H.S. Cobb, for discussing the matter with me. They agree that the document, tagged #1, Statues of William and Mary, is almost certainly the one used at the presentation ceremony. Two red lines were customarily placed on either side of the text of documents in the Garter Rolls at the time; letter from Cobb dated 26 March 1975.

89. *L.J.*, 14:127; *C.J.*, 10:28; H.L.R.O., Braye MSS 43, f. 31v; H.L.R.O., MSS Journal, 61:81.

90. *C.J.*, 10:28; *L.J.*, 14:126-127.

91. Foster, "Petitions and the Petition of Right," p. 2.

92. See Charlton, *The Banqueting House,* where the uses are detailed. The sovereign received members of Parliament here in the early part of the century, also: Esther Cope, letter to the author, 13 January 1977.

93. *C.J.*, 8:49; *L.J.*, 11:46.

94. H. C. Foxcroft, ed., *A Supplement to Burnet's History of my own time* (Oxford, 1902), p. 311. The decision on whether the proclamation should follow immediately after the presentation ceremony was left to the Convention: B.L., Add. MSS 38, 496, ff. 19v, 21v; Algemeen Rijksarchief, Collectie van Citters, Brieven van den Ambassadeur van Citters, no. 25, 15/25 Feb. 1688/89.

95. The *Universal Intelligence, #12,* 13 February 1688/89. Compton's text was taken from Galatians 6:15—"For in Christ Jesus neither Circumcision availeth any thing, nor Uncircumcision, but a new creature." The sermon was not printed and no written copy has, apparently, survived. Edward Carpenter, *The Protestant Bishop. Being the Life of Henry Compton, 1632-1713, Bishop of London* (London, 1956) does not comment on it. A study of preachers and their sermons in London and elsewhere during the Revolution of 1688/89 is needed.

96. B.L., Add. MSS 34, 487, f. 42. Two printed accounts are *A True and exact relation of the Prince of Orange his publick entrance into Exeter* (London, 1688); and *The Expedition of His Highness the Prince of Orange for England, Giving an Account of the most remarkable Passages thereof, from the Day of his setting sail from Holland to the first Day of this instant December, 1688* (London, 1688).

97. The Prince's *Declaration of Reasons* disclaimed the idea of conquest. William issued an order on 2 January 1688/89 that any of his soldiers who suggested that he had conquered England be punished; see the *Orange Gazette, #4,* 7-10 January 1688/89.

98. William had a heavy cough in mid-January and a bad cold ten days later. Mary described him on 12 February as in "very ill condition," with a violent cough and very thin. R. Doebner, ed., *Memoirs of Mary, Queen of England (1689-1693) Together with her Letters* (Leipzig, 1886), p. 10; Morrice, "Entr'ing Book," Q, 425; "Journaal van Constantyn Huygens," pp. 68, 71.

99. P.R.O., L/C 9/386, pp. 47, 57, 66, 68. Natalie Rothstein kindly allowed me to go through her photocopies of this collection. The identification of the cinnamon-colored suit, the first one ordered in the period beginning 13 February 1689, as the one William actually wore at the ceremony is reasonable, but not certain. The print shows William dressed in a suit such as that described in the Lord Chamberlain's accounts.

100. See DeBeer, ed., *Evelyn's Diary,* 4:624-625 n. 3.

101. At the Coronation two months later, it was remarked that there

had never been a more ugly king or a more beautiful queen: "Journaal van Constantyn Huygens," p. 112; F. J. L. Krämer, ed., "Mémoires de Monsieur de B . . . ou Anecdotes, Tant de la cour du Prince d'Orange Guillaume III, que des principaux seigneurs de republique de ce temps," *Bijdragen en Mededeelingen van het Historisch Genootschap*, 19 (Utrecht, 1898), 82.

102. There is no mention of the ceremony in either Doebner, ed., *Memoirs of Mary*, or *Lettres et Mémoires de Marie Reine D'Angleterre*, ed. Mechtild, Comtesse Bentinck (The Hague, 1880).

103. K.U.L., Bonnet, Acta, 15/25 Feb. 1688/89; Algemeen Rijksarchief, Collectie van Citters, Brieven van den Ambassadeur van Citters, no. 25, 15/25 Feb. 1688/89. See H. M. C., *Portland Mss.* 3:428. See also Leopold von Ranke, *A History of England principally in the seventeenth century* (Oxford, 1875), 4:519 and n.

104. The speech was not very different from that of 28 Dec. 1688 when William agreed to take on the administration of affairs until a Convention was elected: *C.J.*, 10:7.

105. *C.J.*, 10:30; *L.J.*, 14:128.

106. F.S.L., Anon., "A Short Account of the Revolution of 1688," f. 17.

107. Anon., *An Account of what was done between the time the Prince of Orange came to London, till the Proclaiming him King of England*, reprinted in *A Compleat Collection of Papers, In Twelve Parts: Relating to the Great Revolution in England and Scotland, From the Time of the Seven Bishops Petitioning K. James II, against the Dispensing Power, June 8, 1688, to the Coronation of King William and Queen Mary, April 11, 1689* (London, 1689). See also n. 59 above.

108. The *London Gazette*, #2427, 11-14 Feb. 1688/89; The *London Mercury: or, Moderate Intelligencer*, #12, 11-14 Feb. 1688/89; *Universal Intelligence*, #12, 13 February 1688/89.

109. I am grateful to Dr. G. van der Meer, Koninklijk Kabinet, The Hague, for supplying information about Meybusch. The best biography is in Georg Galster, *Danske og Norske Medailler og Jetons ca. 1533 - ca. 1688* (Copenhagen, 1936), pp. 103-234.

110. At least ten medals bearing the device appeared at this time. See Nicholas Tindal, *The Mettalick History of the Reigns of King William III and Queen Mary, Queen Anne, and King George I* (London, 1947), Volume 3 of his edition and translation from the French of Paul Rapin de Thoyras, *The History of England*. Plates I, II, III. See Schwoerer, "Propaganda in the Revolution of 1688/89," p. 865 n.

111. Mark Goldie, "Edmund Bohun and *Jus Gentium* in the Revolution Debate, 1689-1693," *The Historical Journal*, 20, 3 (1977), 569-583 treats conquest theory.

112. For a discussion of the clauses that embodied new law, see my book, *The Declaration of Rights, 1689*, chapters 4 and Conclusion.

113. Clayton Roberts, "The Constitutional Significance of the Financial Settlement of 1690," *The Historical Journal*, 20, 1 (1977), p. 73.

V

BRITAIN AND VICTOR AMADEUS II:
OR, THE USE AND ABUSE OF ALLIES

Geoffrey Symcox

In this essay I intend to analyze the relations between the British
government and Victor Amadeus II of Piedmont-Savoy from
1690 to about 1720, to demonstrate from one specific but crucial
example how Britain went about the business of fighting wars in
Continental Europe during this period.[1] I shall devote particular
attention to an aspect of British policy which I consider a factor
of prime importance in bringing about Britain's rise to world
power in the century or so following the Glorious Revolution: the
judicious payment of subsidies to carefully chosen Continental
allies who carried much of the burden of the war on land, freeing
British forces to pursue objectives elsewhere. The workings of this
policy can be studied with special clarity in Britain's relations
with the Savoyard state during this period. At the same time, I
hope to show the close relationship between the two fundamental
elements in British foreign policy, so often treated as separate
and unrelated: the pursuit of a strategic and political balance of
power in Europe, and the thrust toward commercial expansion. I
would argue that successive British governments in this period
saw war as a means of promoting commercial growth and sought
to achieve a military and diplomatic equilibrium as the essential

151

condition for maintaining and extending trade. Again the Savoyard alliance offers an excellent illustration of how this worked in practice. From 1690, and even more so after 1703, Victor Amadeus's state became the fulcrum of British policy in the Mediterranean, and—landlocked and agrarian though it was—a point of growing interest for British commerce. The alliance worked well because of the basic community of interests that underlay it. Both parties benefited handsomely, and in 1713 it was crowned by Victor Amadeus's acquisition of Sicily, engineered by the British government to enhance the political and military weight of the Savoyard state within the framework of the balance of power, and as a means of safeguarding vital commercial interests in the Mediterranean.

The establishment of a British presence in the Mediterranean, and in Italy in particular, is still a largely unexplored topic. Sir Julian Corbett's classic work deals only with the political and naval aspects of the process, and the development of trade— apart from the Chartered Companies—was neglected until Fernand Braudel observed the movement of English and Dutch merchant shipping into the Mediterranean after about 1590.[2] Since then a number of studies, notably by Ralph Davis, have outlined the general development of English trade in the Mediterranean; Davis has shown convincingly how it grew rapidly after about 1660, overtaking Dutch competition.[3] The Italian market played an important part in English commercial growth, and in fact English (and Dutch) exports have been invoked as a factor responsible in part at least for the decline of Italian shipping and manufacturing in the seventeenth century.[4] Already before the end of the sixteenth century the free port of Leghorn had become the base for English merchants trading in the western Mediterranean, as well as the chief staging-post for the Levant trade.[5] By the beginning of the eighteenth century the volume of British trade there had attained impressive proportions. A Parliamentary Report of 1708 noted that, even without the Turkey trade, "the customs of Leghorn, Venice and Genoa did amount to about £300,000 sterling per annum."[6] Of this total, Venice and Genoa controlled a small and diminishing share: in 1705 the British ambassador at Turin estimated that twenty of his nation's ships called at Leghorn for every one that put into Genoa.[7] The trade with Sicily and southern Italy—especially in silks—had also been growing steadily during the seventeenth century; consulates had been set up at Naples, Messina, and other ports, and the commercial agreement signed with Victor Amadeus II in 1713, when he took possession of Sicily, confirmed the privileged position of the English merchants there.[8] Much of the trade between Britain and the Italian states went by sea although a large volume of goods also moved overland, down the Rhine and over the Alps.[9] But this traffic, which in wartime, at least, was probably more extensive than the seaborne trade, exposed to the ravages of French privateers, remains at present largely unknown and uncharted. We might note in passing, however, that Victor Amadeus's position, controlling several of the biggest Alpine passes, made him an object of more than cursory interest to British policy.

It is clear that by the end of the seventeenth century—the period that concerns us here—Mediterranean trade had become a factor of moment, to be given careful consideration by any British government. By then it was realized that informal bridgeheads like Leghorn were not enough; allies were needed, to prevent any single power—first Louis XIV, subsequently the emperor—from establishing political and commercial hegemony in the area. Moreover, as we shall see later on, the British government also sought to use its political and military alliance as the thin end of the wedge of commercial penetration. After 1690, therefore, the Savoyard state under its wily duke became Britain's principal—and from 1703, Britain's only—ally in the western Mediterranean, an essential instrument for the conduct of military policy, and a prime target of British mercantile expansion. Far from being a mere cat's-paw of British interests, however, Victor Amadeus in his turn profited from the alliance to pursue the traditional goals of his dynasty: territorial expansion and military strength, the better to negotiate the perpetual tightrope stretched for him by the great powers that hedged his state on all sides. And by pursuing a policy of protectionism, he resisted British attempts to dominate his state's economy. In the long run, therefore, the British alliance helped him to enhance his power and prestige at a critical moment in the development of the Italian state system. Between 1690 and 1748 a series of violent upheavals wiped dynasties and states off the political map, and replaced Spanish dominion by a Bourbon-Habsburg dyarchy.

Out of this chaos Piedmont-Savoy emerged a compact, central-ized state, with a reputation for diplomatic expertise and military durability. The vital point in this process, which in the end en-abled the rulers of Piedmont-Savoy to cut a figure not only in Italian politics but on the wider stage of European affairs as well, is undoubtedly the War of the Spanish Succession, when Victor Amadeus fought for his survival and ended by reaping substantial rewards at the Peace of Utrecht. Without the backing of British subsidies, naval power, and diplomatic influence, the story would have ended very differently for him.

For the British government, Victor Amadeus II's primary mili-tary function lay in fighting Louis XIV, a function which he needed little urging to fulfil. Since the treaty of Cherasco in 1631 Piedmont-Savoy had been a French satellite, its rulers' obedience guaranteed by a French garrison at Pinerolo, a few miles from Turin, and after 1681 by another French garrison at Casale, to the east. For Victor Amadeus, therefore, the British alliance offered the way to reassert his independence and throw off French control. But what could he offer in return? What made his rather small, remote state a desirable ally from the British point of view? Until 1690 there had been only the most fleeting contacts between the two states: mainly a commercial treaty in 1669, which had produced no tangible result, and whose only real significance was as an indication of the duke of Savoy's eager search for allies to offset the oppressive tutelage of France.[10] But the outbreak of war against Louis XIV in 1689 forced Britain to cast about for allies able to threaten the French flanks. Among the Italian states, Piedmont-Savoy alone could figure as a credible ally. Venice, the only other state of any significance, was economically decrepit and militarily exhausted by long wars with the Turks. Piedmont-Savoy alone had the capacity to pursue an independent military policy from its own resources: though small and economically undeveloped, it could field an effective little army.[11] More impor-tant still, geography made Victor Amadeus the natural ally of any enemy of France. His state straddled the Alps on Louis XIV's southern flank, where the frontier defenses were spread more thinly than in the great fortified arc that Vauban had built from Dunkirk to the Rhine, and where the large Huguenot populations of Dauphiné and Languedoc were ripe for revolt since the revoca-tion of the Edict of Nantes in 1685. An added attraction for the

British government was Victor Amadeus's proximity to Toulon, the only French naval base of any size on the Mediterranean. From 1690 onward the idea of a strike against Toulon, led by the duke of Savoy, was always present in the minds of the British ministers as perhaps the single most damaging blow that could be delivered against the rival maritime power of France.

The Savoyard alliance thus offered real strategic advantages for Britain in a war with Louis XIV. At the same time, if we may look ahead for a moment, it would later offer a useful way to curb the pretensions of Britain's constant but often unsatisfactory ally, the emperor. By 1690 Leopold I had already begun to stake out dynastic and feudal claims in Italy, anticipating the day when the Spanish succession would fall vacant. After 1706, when the French were expelled from the peninsula, his successor Joseph I occupied Milan, Mantua, and Naples and put forward claims as heir or suzerain to most of the other Italian states. British policy, as we shall see, did not view the establishment of Habsburg hegemony in Italy with favor, and therefore bolstered Victor Amadeus II as the best obstacle to it. For the British government, the Savoyard alliance served as a fine double-edged weapon for maintaining the equilibrium of forces, first by threatening Louis XIV, and then by restricting Habsburg expansionism. In the latter instance, as in the former, Victor Amadeus needed no prompting to uphold the balance of power by resisting the encroachments of a great neighbor who threatened his independence and limited his chances of territorial acquisition in the future.

At this point a brief digression is in order to examine a special factor that had traditionally helped focus British attention on the Savoyard state. This was the presence in the Alpine valleys above Turin of a sizeable colony of Waldensians, sole survivors of the movement founded by Peter Waldo of Lyon in the twelfth century.[12] Protected by their mountains, the Waldensians had resisted successive persecutions unleashed by their rulers, but at Easter 1655 a particularly savage blitzkrieg was launched against them, threatening to wipe them out. Together with the other Protestant powers, Cromwell intervened to call a halt to the atrocities and send relief to the victims.[13] The plight of the Waldensians touched a responsive chord in English public opinion, as the contemporary literature attests: they became the subject of numerous tracts, pamphlets, and histories, and of Milton's great sonnet "On the late massacres in Piedmont," which sprang directly from his work as Cromwell's Latin secretary, drafting addresses to the duke of Savoy, and whose imagery echoed the contemporary pamphlet literature in its evocations of the violence and bloodshed. The poem also hints at the reason for the special veneration accorded to the Waldensians: their supposed antiquity, dating from a putative apostolic origin.[14] This erroneous belief, which first apparently gained currency in the early seventeenth century, was enshrined in the most influential contemporary English work on the Waldensians, Samuel Morland's *History of the Evangelical Churches of Piedmont* (1658). Its author had served as Cromwell's envoy to the court of Turin after the massacre of 1655, and at Archbishop Ussher's instigation he had collected materials bearing on the history of the Waldensians. In his *History,* Morland declared them to be an offshoot of the Primitive church, founded by the Apostles, thus lending his authority to an error that would not be laid to rest until the nineteenth century.[15] By this argument, the Waldensians of Piedmont became a fossil remnant of the Apostolic church, founded in the Alps—perhaps by Saint Paul, who was presumed to have passed that way on his journey to Spain—and miraculously preserved from the Romish innovations that had corrupted the rest of Christendom. The Waldensians' acceptance of the doctrines of the reformers, in 1532 to 1535, thus vindicated Protestant claims to have restored the Church to its pristine state, which the Waldensians alone had preserved, and linked Luther and his fellow reformers in an unbroken historical chain to the Apostles. If the Waldensians were wiped out, Rome would have eliminated the only living witnesses who substantiated the reformers' claim to be the true heirs of the Apostolic church. These arguments, which recur in the pamphlets of the period, gave the Waldensians a special claim on English Protestant sympathies. A renewed persecution in 1686 thus provoked a fresh outpouring of pamphlet literature—distinguished by such contributors as Bishop Burnet—even though James II did not feel impelled to intervene as Cromwell had. After the Revolution, however, William III reverted to the traditions of the 1650s and actively aided the Waldensians, making the alleviation of their religious and judicial disabilities a condition for signing the alliance with Victor Amadeus in 1690.[16] William III's intervention produced the Edict of Toleration of

1694, by which Victor Amadeus restored the Waldensians' privileges which had been abrogated during the persecution of 1686. From this time, as diplomatic contacts between London and Turin grew closer, it became standard practice for every British ambassador's instructions to contain a clause enjoining him to succor "the poor Vaudois."[17]

Feelings of Protestant solidarity were reinforced by more mundane political and military considerations. Support for the poor Vaudois became part of a wider design to aid the oppressed Protestants in France and stir them to righteous rebellion. Here we touch once more on the fundamental strategic factor that made Victor Amadeus such a desirable ally from the British point of view, and we come to the point where the poor Vaudois take their place in a grand strategy for attacking France from the south. For these Protestant mountaineers had a military value as well. In their heroic return to their valleys in 1689 — the "Glorieuse Rentrée" — the Waldensians had proved themselves indomitable guerrilla fighters. Victor Amadeus was happy to enroll them as irregulars in his army, where they fought loyally and well. British and Dutch subsidies helped support several regiments of Waldensian irregulars, intermingled with Huguenot refugees, both during the 1690s and in the War of the Spanish Succession. It was a constant dream of the British government that Victor Amadeus would lead his army, spearheaded by these Protestant regiments, to raise the Huguenots in revolt. The rising of the Camisards of Languedoc in 1703 seemed to promise real success for the plan, and British correspondence of the period is filled with references to this grand design, in which military and evangelical goals so happily merged.[18] Apart from a few shiploads of arms and recruits sent to the Camisards, most of which never got through, nothing ever came of the plan, but it remained a serious objective of British policy until the failure of the Toulon expedition in 1707 and the collapse of the Camisard revolt a year or so later.

The reasons why this grand design never took shape reveal some of the limitations and tensions in the Anglo-Savoyard alliance. British zeal for the poor Vaudois caused a certain amount of strain, for Victor Amadeus could justifiably construe it as unwarranted meddling in his efforts to control recalcitrant heretics. Moreover, as a Catholic prince he could hardly feel comfortable about leading his Waldensian irregulars into France to foment a

Huguenot rebellion. As it was, his Edict of Toleration in 1694 led to grave repercussions; it was condemned by the Pope and was used by the French to stir up trouble among ultra-Catholics in Piedmont.[19] So although he stood by the letter of the Edict of 1694, Victor Amadeus deferred to domestic Catholic opinion by allowing it to be interpreted in the most restrictive sense, and while he led two invasions into France, in 1692 and 1707, on neither of them did he display any crusading enthusiasm. His religious reservations were corroborated by his sense of the profound practical difficulties involved in mounting an invasion over the Alps. His misgivings were borne out in the abortive invasion of 1692, and by the failure at Toulon: a full-scale invasion of France from the south was not feasible, given the difficulties of terrain and logistics, and from 1708 the grand design for penetrating the soft underbelly of Bourbon power was scaled down to a series of diversionary raids to tie down as many French troops as possible and to achieve minor but realistic territorial gains.

But in spite of these crosscurrents, the alliance proved of great value to both parties. While for Victor Amadeus it offered a springboard to greater power, on the British side is provided a classic instance of how the payment of subsidies to well-placed allies — one thinks of Frederick II of Prussia in a later war — could yield military and political dividends far in excess of the original outlay. The essence of the successful use of subsidies lay in timing and placement rather than in the volume of cash deployed.[20] Everything hinged on finding an ally whose interests harmonized as closely as possible with Britain's and whose strategic position made it a key element in the current alignment of forces on the Continent. Mere payment to an unwilling ally could never produce results: foot-dragging and evasion would have been the only consequences. The trick lay in using money to reinforce existing ties of mutual interest and to provide the means — when these were lacking — for carrying out policies that benefited both parties. In effect the subsidy policy, exemplified in British dealings with Victor Amadeus II, amounted to paying a carefully selected ally to do pretty much what he wanted to do anyway, because this would automatically serve British interests. The flow of cash merely served to speed up the action and give the paymaster some control over the choice and timing of operations. Sometimes — as in the great plan for an invasion of France — the allies might not see eye to eye on the objectives to be achieved, and the results would be below expectations. Sometimes it was impossible for Victor Amadeus to comply with the British government's demands, as in the years from 1703 to 1706, when he was too hard pressed by French armies in Piedmont to contemplate the attack on Toulon that he was being urged to launch. But so long as he was being paid to do what his own self-interest dictated—to resist the French armies that threatened his state—he provided a formidable diversion in return for a relatively small outlay of the British government's cash. Let us now see how this worked in practice.

The outbreak of the Nine Years War provided Victor Amadeus with a chance to escape from French domination. In June 1690 he declared war on Louis XIV and concluded alliances with the emperor and Carlos II of Spain, then, on October 20, with William III. The Allies promised to secure the restoration of Pinerolo to Victor Amadeus, as the real key to independence for his state; as long as it was held by the French, Piedmont lay open to invasion and its ruler would perforce remain a client of Louis XIV. In addition the British and Dutch government agreed to pay a subsidy of 30,000 écus per month (over and above the sum already promised by Spain). Two-thirds of this sum was to be paid by Britain, one-third by the United Provinces. The Allies were to remain united until all their common aims had been achieved; there was to be no separate peacemaking. Finally, a secret clause in the alliance with William III bound Victor Amadeus to revoke all the punitive measures taken against the Waldensians since 1686 and to restore them to the conditions under which they had lived before the persecutions of that year.[21]

This first Anglo-Savoyard alliance lasted until the summer of 1696. The opening of a new front in Piedmont diverted French troops from the Netherlands and the Rhine, and forced Louis XIV to give careful thought to the problem of internal security posed by the dissident Huguenots of the southeast. In William III's mind the great strategic design now took shape for an attack on the south of France by armies from Spain and Piedmont, linked by the Anglo-Dutch fleet. The scheme was never carried out in this war, for conditions were never right. The Allied forces in Catalonia and Piedmont remained almost continuously on the defensive, except for the isolated invasion of Dauphiné by Victor

Amadeus in 1692, and even when the Allied fleet controlled the Mediterranean in 1694 and 1695, nothing could be achieved beyond shoring up the Catalan front and giving moral support to the troops in Italy. Toulon did not fall; the Huguenots did not rise. William III's grand strategy had to wait until the next war, when Marlborough, his chosen successor, could profit from more favorable conditions to implement it. Nevertheless, it is important to remember that this grand strategic design dates from the 1690s, despite the disappointments that dogged William III's efforts to put it into practice, and that from the first Victor Amadeus was called upon to play a key role in it. Even though William III and the Allies never achieved the spectacular results that this southern strategy seemed to promise, it is still fair to say in the words of a recent commentator that "in the long run the Italian and Mediterranean fighting was to return the Allies a substantial profit."[22]

Victor Amadeus meanwhile was reduced to fighting a bitter defensive war. The duchy of Savoy itself and the county of Nice were quickly overrun by the French, and year after year Piedmont was ravaged by their armies. Traveling through Piedmont in 1703, Joseph Addison observed that "notwithstanding this Interval of Peace, one may easily trace out the several Marches that the French Armies have made thro' their Country, by the Ruin and Desolation they have left behind 'em."[23] The devastation wrought by the French armies was compounded by a series of bad harvests that reached their peak in the terrible famine of 1694 and 1695, which undercut the state budget and weakened Victor Amadeus militarily. Furthermore, he had twice been defeated in battle by Catinat (Staffarda 1690; La Marsaglia 1693), and had failed in his efforts to besiege and capture Pinerolo. By 1695, therefore, the cost of the war was becoming unbearable for him, in spite of the Anglo-Dutch subsidies (the Spaniards hardly ever paid) and the support of extra troops provided by the Allies.[24] All this needs to be borne in mind when we come to consider Victor Amadeus's defection from the Alliance in 1696.

William III never forgave Victor Amadeus for this betrayal, and from this time the latter acquired the reputation for shiftiness and bad faith that would bedevil his future dealings with his Allies. In June 1696 he concluded a separate peace with Louis XIV, prepared after long and tortuous negotiations, then joined forces with him and forced the Allied armies in Italy to capitulate.[25] This was the signal for the collapse of the whole Alliance. In a negative sense, the value of the Savoyard alliance was proved by the consequences of its abrupt termination: the strategic situation changed overnight, and the Allies were obliged to sue for peace. In extenuation of Victor Amadeus's conduct we may note that he had kept the other Allies informed, in a general way, of his negotiations with Louis XIV, and that as the war went on he had come to the realization that the Allies either could not or would not make good on their promise to obtain Pinerolo for him. Pressed on this point by the Savoyard ambassador in 1695, William III had admitted that he saw little hope of securing it.[26] Moreover, the Allies tended to dismiss Victor Amadeus's pleas for aid, occasioned by the very real damage inflicted by the French armies in Piedmont, as blackmail aimed at extorting larger subsidies. We may understand, therefore, although we may not excuse, Victor Amadeus's decision to take matters into his own hands and seek the separate peace with Louis XIV that gave him Pinerolo. Finally—and for Victor Amadeus this was probably the decisive factor—Austrian influence in northern Italy was growing, under cover of aiding the Spaniards to defend Milan. All Victor Amadeus's future hopes centered on Lombardy, the only avenue of expansion open to him, and he had no desire to fight a costly war merely to see the flaccid Spanish dominion there replaced by the rising military power of Austria.[27] Hence his decision to join his armies to those of France, late in 1696, in order to expel the Habsburg forces and obtain the neutralization of Italy.

The unsavory aftertaste of Victor Amadeus's defection lingered on in the years after the war. William III's hostility effectively excluded him from the Partition Treaty negotiations, despite his undoubted claims to a part of the Spanish succession.[28] When war broke out again in Italy at the beginning of 1701, Victor Amadeus found himself diplomatically isolated and accordingly with no choice but to join the Bourbon coalition. Sandwiched between France and the duchy of Milan, which had declared for Philip V, he was deprived of all freedom to maneuver, and was reduced once more to the condition of vassaldom from which he had only just escaped. Victory for the Bourbon cause, which he had been forced unwillingly to support, would doom him to gradual absorption, like another duchy of Lorraine. Consequently, he remained open to the secret counteroffers that the Allies at once began to make to him.

At first these approaches were not substantial enough to tempt Victor Amadeus into the very risky step of breaking with Louis XIV. But by the summer of 1703 this changed.[29] The Habsburg armies in Lombardy had been forced onto the defensive, and the only chance of success for the Allies there now lay in securing Victor Amadeus's support. Pressed by the British and Dutch governments, Leopold I therefore nerved himself to pay the price and sacrifice certain territories in the duchy of Milan to meet Victor Amadeus's demands. At the end of September, Louis XIV—who had been aware of these negotiations for some time—suddenly declared war on Victor Amadeus, precipitating the conclusion of the alliance between the latter and Leopold a month or so later. The Maritime Powers, although not yet formally parties to the alliance, at once promised subsidies of 80,000 écus a month, plus an initial payment of 100,000 écus, and from December 1703 the money began to flow, aiding Victor Amadeus at a critical moment when he was beset on all sides by French armies.[30] The emperor for his part agreed to cede Monferrato and a number of districts in the western Milanese, once he had conquered the duchy. This was to prove a bitter source of discord after the French were expelled in 1706. Finally, we might observe in passing that the Allied leaders (and most subsequent historians, except the French) who had so roundly condemned Victor Amadeus for his change of sides in 1696 regarded this new *volte-face* as a logical, even admirable, display of enlightened self-interest.

The duke of Savoy had embarked upon the most dangerous gamble of his adventurous career. For the next three years he fought desperately for his survival as the French moved systematically to overrun his territory and block every avenue by which help could reach him. In the summer of 1706, Louis XIV's armies moved in for the kill. Turin was besieged, but at the last moment an Imperial army under Prince Eugene joined Victor Amadeus and the tattered remnants of his army, defeated the French, and then moved on to expel them from Piedmont. The victory was complete, and for the remainder of the war Victor Amadeus was able to assume the offensive, leading the attack on Toulon in 1707, and mounting invasions over the Alps in the following years.

At this point it would be as well to assess the significance of the subsidies paid to Victor Amadeus, and to see what they achieved. It is fair to say that the payments from the Maritime Powers — and chiefly England — played a decisive part in assuring Victor Amadeus's survival and ultimate victory. A very complete picture of how the subsidies worked, and of the part they played in the state budget, is contained in the painstaking study of Savoyard finance published by Luigi Einaudi over seventy years ago (table 5.1), but still unsurpassed, even though in my opinion Einaudi underestimates the total contribution made by the Maritime Powers.[31] To begin with, it is important to remember that for the decade of war from 1703 to 1713 the Anglo-Dutch subsidies represented a very sizeable addition to the Savoyard budget — one-fifth of the total, according to Einaudi; but actually more like one-quarter, when one considers real revenue, as opposed to budget estimates. These payments were the only external support that Victor Amadeus received; otherwise he had to fight this very costly war from his own resources. In the desperate years between 1703 and 1706, as the French conquered more and more of his territory and steadily eroded his tax base, a significant amount of Victor Amadeus's budget came from the Allied subsidies, until by 1706 they accounted for about 40 percent of his total expenditure, as a glance at the table will indicate. Without this support, he would have been unable to pay his troops and continue fighting. But the percentages are only part of the story. In the critical years down to 1707 and even 1708, the Anglo-Dutch subsidies provided a regular supply of hard cash that was used to raise loans when all other expedients had failed. Victor Amadeus's astute finance minister, Gropello, borrowed large sums from local bankers, meeting the interest payments out of the bimonthly Allied subsidies.[32] Without these loans Victor Amadeus would not have been able to carry on the war and defend his capital. In 1706 the garrison of Turin was paid by money raised on the security of the Allied subsidies. The Maritime Powers thus underwrote the Piedmontese state's credit, which would otherwise have collapsed. And in overall terms, the money generated by borrowing was far in excess of the actual subsidy payments, which merely provided the means for raising far larger sums.

The regular subsidy payments did not, however, represent the entire Anglo-Dutch contribution to Victor Amadeus's war

TABLE 5.1

THE ALLIED CONTRIBUTION TO VICTOR AMADEUS II's WAR FINANCES, 1704-1713

	A Allied subsidies	B Total budget	C A as % of B	D Actual revenues collected	E A as % of D
1704	4,346,620	15,111,857	29	13,361,246	33
1705	4,685,506	15,716,105	30	13,322,455	35
1706	4,508,525	13,498,289	33	11,069,417	41
1707	3,929,645	20,047,009	20	16,937,964	23
1708	5,814,989	21,266,293	27	18,671,087	31
1709	4,480,834	17,622,573	25	15,196,391	29
1710	3,682,060	16,237,246	23	13,601,084	27
1711	3,148,460	15,130,733	21	12,528,871	25
1712	2,208,270	14,396,059	15	11,826,390	19
1713	478,026	14,903,680	3	12,378,993	4
			20.5		26.7

(NB: subsidies paid only for Jan.-Mar. 1713)

Figures modified from L. Einaudi, *La finanza sabauda all'aprirsi del secolo XVIII e durante la guerra di successione spagnuola* (Turin, 1908). Figures above are in Piedmontese lire.

Note:

Einaudi calculates the contribution of the Allied subsidies as a percentage of the total budgeted revenue (column B). It seems more accurate, however, to calculate it on the basis of revenues actually collected (column D), since the Allied subsidies came in the form of ready cash; columns A and D are actual revenue, not budgetary totals or paper figures.

finances. Various other payments were made for different reasons. Thus, in January 1707 Parliament voted a special grant of £50,000 sterling to finance the attack on Toulon, and then in 1708 voted a bonus of £100,000 to Victor Amadeus for leading it.[33] Other payments, distinct from the subsidies, maintained various detachments of hired troops fighting in Italy, either directly or indirectly in support of the duke of Savoy.[34] Then a part of the subsidies paid by the Maritime Powers to the emperor were earmarked to support the Habsburg troops fighting in Lombardy, although at least until 1706, little or none of this money seems to have reached its destination. At times, however, infusions of cash could galvanize the lethargic Viennese government into action: in 1706 Prince Eugene's dash to save Turin was accelerated by a special British loan of £250,000.[35] Altogether, therefore, the financial assistance from the Maritime Powers to Victor Amadeus II far exceeds the amount paid in direct subsidies. And of this, Britain paid by far the larger share, since the Dutch paid less regularly—even though their share was only one-third—and were less generous with bonus payments and extraordinary grants. It is therefore probably correct to assume that of the total amount paid in subsidies to Victor Amadeus throughout the war, the British government contributed at least three-quarters, and perhaps even more. Converting Einaudi's total of 37,282,935 Piedmontese lire (the figure for all the subsidy payments received during the war) into sterling at the rate of just over 17 lire to the pound, gives a global figure of about £2,180,288 sterling. The British government's contribution, in round figures, would thus amount to between £1,500,000 and £1,700,000 for the decade of war, in direct subsidies and extraordinary payments, exclusive of the sums spent on troops who were not paid through the Piedmontese government. All in all a crude total for British payments to Victor Amadeus II for the duration of the War of the Spanish Succession might be in the region of two million pounds.[36]

What did the British government receive in return for this outlay of cash? Down to 1706 the subsidies helped ensure the survival of a very valuable ally, to maintain an important diversion that tied down several French armies and prevented them from defeating the small Habsburg army in Lombardy. Victor Amadeus's successful resistance, stiffened by the Maritime Powers' gold, thus paid a dividend far beyond the sums of cash involved, and created the conditions for the French defeat and loss of Lombardy in 1706-07. Then, in 1707, the subsidy payments and bonuses provided the means for executing the long-meditated strike against Toulon. Although the attack failed to destroy the city and its port as planned, it brought about the destruction of the French warships in the harbor and delivered a damaging blow to Louis XIV's already tottering naval power. From this point, the Toulon fleet ceased to pose a threat to operations in the Mediterranean.[37] Then from 1708 until the end of the war, the subsidies helped the duke of Savoy launch a series of annual incursions across the frontier into France, forcing Louis XIV to keep an army in readiness there. Even in the later years of the war, Victor Amadeus continued to play a key role in the Allies' southern strategy, offsetting to some degree the decline of their fortunes in Spain.

From 1707 the duke of Savoy was called upon to fulfill a new function as Great Britain's only Italian ally by curbing the advance of the Habsburgs, which the British government viewed with mounting disquiet. This was a role that exactly suited Victor Amadeus's inclinations, for Habsburg hegemony in Italy was a far more immediate threat to him than it was to the British government. By 1707 a serious divergence of purpose began to appear between the emperor and the other Allies. In March 1707 his commissioners negotiated a cease-fire in Lombardy, allowing the French forces there safe passage home, contrary to the wishes of the British and Dutch governments. This gave the emperor undisputed control of Milan. At the same time he confiscated the duchy of Mantua, whose ruler had ill-advisedly backed the Bourbons. In the summer of that year the Habsburg armies were sent to conquer Naples. This gave the emperor a commanding position throughout the Italian peninsula, but delayed the attack on Toulon. British opinion held the emperor responsible for the ensuing failure at Toulon, while exonerating Victor Amadeus II. Meanwhile the emperor's commissioners were levying war contributions from the lesser Italian states, friend, foe, and neutral alike, and this fiscal pressure, backed by military threats, was accompanied by the resurrection of feudal and dynastic claims to most of the lesser states, a matter of more than antiquarian interest in view of the imminent demise of the ruling houses of Parma and Tuscany. In a short while it seemed as though the emperor had secured for himself the dominant position in Italy enjoyed by his Spanish cousins before 1700. To the British government, it looked as though Habsburg hegemony would open the way for economic control: with Naples, Leghorn, and most of the other ports in Austrian hands, with Venice and Genoa intimidated by the encircling Imperial presence, British commercial interests would inevitably suffer. The British government thus sought to oppose any further extension of Habsburg power in Italy. The obvious instrument for carrying out such a policy lay ready to hand in Victor Amadeus II, whose own interests demanded that he resist any extension of Imperial territory and influence.

So just as before 1706 Victor Amadeus had provided the means for preserving the balance of power in Italy by blocking the Bourbon bid for hegemony, in the later period he was called upon to counter the new threat to equilibrium presented by the Habsburgs. Almost from the moment of their joint victory at Turin, he and the emperor had been at loggerheads over the cession of the territories promised by the treaty of 1703. Although Victor Amadeus had occupied most of these lands, including Monferrato, late in 1706, the emperor delayed granting him formal investiture and specifically withheld the Vigevanasco, promised in a secret article that Leopold I had refused to ratify. Nor would the emperor (Joseph I, Leopold's successor) recognize the duke of Savoy's rights to various fiefs in Le Langhe (the southern part of Monferrato) earlier ceded to him.[38] This territorial dispute continued for the rest of the war, and throughout it the British government steadily backed Victor Amadeus II, putting diplomatic pressure on the court of Vienna, sending a special envoy to mediate, and finally arbitrating (with the Dutch) in favor of the Savoyard claims.[39] This anti-Imperial trend in British policy culminated in the granting of Sicily to Victor Amadeus in 1713.

Sicily had never figured on the duke of Savoy's list of war aims. The instructions he drafted for his envoys to the peace conference at Utrecht reveal what he hoped to obtain: the recognition of his claim on the Spanish succession, guarantees for the newly won lands in the Milanese, cession of the Vigevanasco or its equivalent, and the redrawing of the Alpine frontier with France to include the districts conquered in 1708.[40] From the first abortive peace conferences the British government had steadily supported these demands: in 1709 the British plenipotentiaries were instructed that "Her Majesty is likewise very intent that the Duke of Savoy should have full satisfaction at the ensuing peace."[41] The change of ministry in 1710 led, if anything, to still greater solicitude on behalf of Victor Amadeus, who was by now clearly Britain's preferred ally. This pro-Savoyard bias, in part the consequence of British disenchantment with the emperor and the Dutch, was reinforced by Queen Anne's personal partiality for Victor Amadeus, whose wife Anne-Marie d'Orléans had been excluded from the English succession as a Catholic by the Act of 1701.[42] British championship of Savoyard interests must be largely ascribed to growing concern over the advance of Habsburg power in Italy, but this geopolitical motive was given greater immediacy by what we might term Queen Anne's sense of dynastic guilt, which had to be assuaged by some form of compensation for the frustrated Savoyard claims on the English crown: Sicily, which brought with it a royal title, would serve this purpose very well. So when the Utrecht negotiations settled into their decisive phase of hard bargaining between Britain and France, St. John stated to Torcy that "of all the Allies there is none whose interest the Queen has so much at heart as the Duke of Savoy's."[43]

The initiative in the Sicilian affair seems to have come entirely from the British side. Originally, however, the British government had even greater plans for Victor Amadeus; for a time he was put forward as a candidate for the Spanish empire. Early in 1712 a series of deaths in the French royal family brought Philip V perilously close to the French throne once more, and raised the specter of the union of the two Bourbon crowns. The British government therefore demanded that Philip either keep Spain and renounce his rights to the French succession, or abandon Spain, retain his claims on France, and meanwhile content himself with a conglomerate kingdom made up of Naples, Sicily, and Piedmont-Savoy: the Spanish Empire would then pass to Victor Amadeus in return. Preferring a bird in the hand, Philip chose Spain and the proposal fell through. But its failure, which became known at London in the first days of June 1712, meant that Sicily was once more available as a bargaining piece, and from that moment the British government determined that the island would be awarded to Victor Amadeus, even before he had been consulted.[44] Sicily had been untouched by the war and still owed allegiance to Philip V at this time, although without a navy his hold on the island was at best nominal; in the same way, the Habsburgs had not been able to complete their conquest of Naples by annexing Sicily in 1707 for lack of a fleet. Britain, as the dominant naval power in the Mediterranean, had Sicily in its grip. Apparently without even securing Victor Amadeus's consent, St. John demanded Sicily for him during his negotiations with Torcy in August 1712. Louis XIV then extorted Philip V's agreement to the transfer, and Sicily passed to Victor Amadeus II at the Peace of Utrecht. With the naval bases acquired by Britain at the same time, at Gibraltar and Minorca, it became a foundation of British maritime supremacy in the Mediterranean.

In the language of dynastic diplomacy, Victor Amadeus received Sicily in compensation for his claims on the Spanish succession. But there was more to it than that. In the first place the transfer of Sicily to Victor Amadeus II reveals how far Britain's relations with the emperor had deteriorated: to sever Sicily from the kingdom of Naples, of which it historically formed a part, and to award it to a bitter rival of the Habsburgs, constituted a deliberate affront. After the death of Joseph I in 1711, Britain had been faced with the obligation to continue the war in order to conquer Spain for its Habsburg claimaint, the Archduke Charles, who had now inherited the Imperial title and thus stood to reunite the Habsburg empire as it had been before 1555 — a manifestly unpalatable prospect for the British government. In response to this, the British ministry wound down the war in Spain, concluded its notorious separate truce with Louis XIV in the summer of 1712, and bolstered the duke of Savoy as the only effective counterweight to Habsburg power in Italy. The transfer of Sicily to Victor Amadeus II was intended as an obstacle to any further extension of the emperor's power in Italy and the western Mediterranean. On July 12/23 St. John wrote to Torcy: "It is neither for the interest of Great Britain nor France, that the Kingdom of Sicily be given to the House of Austria, and he therefore demands it for the Duke of Savoy, and declares that the Queen will not desist from this demand."[45] Concern for the balance of power was reinforced by fears for British trade. Mellarède, one of the Savoyard plenipotentiaries at Utrecht, was told by the British ministers that Sicily in the emperor's hands would be "trop préjudiciable au commerce du Levant." If the emperor were to control Sicily as well as Naples, "leur commerce de ce côté dépend de lui seul": British interests therefore required "un prince leur ami en Sicile, ou sont les meilleurs ports, et ou se fait le plus grand commerce."[46]

Victor Amadeus reacted with surprise and even dismay to the news that he had become the lucky winner in this diplomatic sweepstake.[47] He would have preferred a slice of Lombardy to the remote and rather alien island that he received, but this was not in the British government's power to give. And the gift came with strings attached. It could be held only by grace of the British navy, for as long as the British government chose — as it happened, no more than five years. Victor Amadeus was well aware that he had been appointed caretaker of British interests there, on Britain's terms. Certainly the island was desirable, with its substantial revenues and its royal title, but in return Victor Amadeus had to provide secure naval bases and a privileged trading position to Britain, and see his already tense relations with Vienna poisoned still further by an acquisition coveted by the emperor. The British government had presented Victor Amadeus with an apple of discord; moreover, he was expressly forbidden to give it away or exchange it.

Late in 1713 he sailed aboard a British fleet to take possession of his new island kingdom, and remained there a year, endeavoring to set things in order. But by then the conditions that had made possible his acquisition of Sicily were already changing. The Hanoverian succession and the change of ministry began to produce a complete reversal of British policy: championship of Victor Amadeus II gave way to cooperation with the emperor. The fundamental reason for this shift, in Mediterranean politics at least, was the revanchism displayed by Bourbon Spain, accompanied by a disquieting resurgence of Spanish naval power; the target of Philip V's and Alberoni's ambitions was the lost Spanish dominion in Italy, and the thrones of Parma and Tuscany, soon to fall vacant. Anglo-Spanish relations were further exacerbated by wranglings over trade and the possession of Gibraltar. In these circumstances, British policy swung round to a rapprochement with the emperor, as the best insurance against Spanish attempts to upset the Utrecht settlement: a more solid counterpoise than Victor Amadeus was deemed necessary. In return for the emperor's support, the British government was willing to consent to some territorial adjustments in the interests of maintaining stability in the Mediterranean, and it soon became evident that the cost of these adjustments would be borne by Victor Amadeus, the prime object of Habsburg resentment in Italy. The growing estrangement between Victor Amadeus and the British government was aggravated by some unseemly bickering over the arrears of subsidies still unpaid from the war years. Finally a shady deal was worked out by which Victor Amadeus was obliged to settle for a fraction of his original claims.[48] Meanwhile the Convention of Westminster (May 1716) had already marked the first stage in the new Anglo-Imperial alignment, and the conclusion of a formal alliance was finally precipitated by Spanish aggression in the Mediterranean. In July 1717, Alberoni's new fleet seized Sardinia and then a year later moved on to capture Sicily. The result was the conclusion of the Quadruple Alliance in August 1718. Britain, France, and the United Provinces were joined by the emperor, and together the powers sought to impose a new peace settlement in the Mediterranean. A new stable order was to be achieved by rewriting the Treaty of Utrecht to take account of Bourbon and Habsburg claims, thus, it was hoped, heading off the danger of a full-scale war. The emperor's claim on Sicily had to be gratified, to balance the right of succession to Parma and Tuscany granted to the Spanish Bourbons. (The treaty, we may note, specifically guaranteed that Leghorn's status as a free port would in no way be affected by any change of dynasty; this in the interests of English trade).[49] Victor Amadeus was to be given Sardinia — which also conveniently carried a royal title — as compensation for the loss of Sicily. To the very end he sought to evade this unattractive bargain by proposing alternative territorial arrangements, but George I and the emperor rebuffed his approaches.[50] On November 8, 1718, he adhered unwillingly to the Quadruple Alliance, signing away Sicily for the depressed and poverty-stricken island of Sardinia. As an English officer sent to supervise the transfer of the island to its new sovereign observed, "It is hardly of any other advantage to the Prince that possesses it than giving him the title of king."[51] British policy, after engineering Victor Amadeus's triumph at the Peace of Utrecht, had left him in the lurch as cynically as he had deserted his allies in 1696.

From its high point during the War of the Spanish Succession, the Anglo-Savoyard alliance had thus deteriorated to the point of almost complete rupture. But it remained an underlying necessity for both parties; rapprochement followed in the 1730s and the alliance was resurrected during the War of the Austrian Succession.[52] In the meantime the political and military alliance had helped to foster a more durable commercial relationship, beneficial to both sides. For Victor Amadeus and his advisers, the forging of commercial ties that would lessen their economic dependence on France was a matter of prime importance. The British government for its part sought to use the military alliance as a way to penetrate an area hitherto outside Britain's economic orbit.

Let me conclude by describing the commercial relations that developed during this period between Britain and Piedmont-Savoy, and that survived the virtual collapse of the political alliance in 1718.

British policy from the start strove to oust the French from the favored position they held in the Piedmontese economy and was facilitated by the disruption of trade over the Alps after the onset of war in 1690. The aim was to replace the French as the chief suppliers of high-quality woolen cloth, and to divert to England the large exports of raw and spun silk (the latter wound into skeins called "organzines") which had hitherto passed from Piedmont to the great manufacturing center of Lyon. The English silk-weaving industry was in a period of rapid growth, aided by the influx of Huguenot silk workers in the 1680s, and the chief obstacle to its expansion seems to have been a shortage of raw material. Much of the silk used in Britain already came from Italy, which produced a finer type than that obtained from the other traditional source of supply, the Levant.[53] The war aggravated the problem of securing raw material, and matters were further complicated by a tug-of-war between the various commercial interest groups involved. In 1690 the Levant Company obtained passage of a bill restricting the import of Italian silks; so in 1692-93 the silk weavers, insisting on their need for the finer Italian silks, mounted a successful campaign to secure passage of a bill reversing the previous one.[54] Behind these contenders the various cloth-manufacturing interests lined up: those involved in exporting to Turkey backing the Levant Company, and those producing cloths sold in the Italian market lending their weight to the silk weavers' demands, since the cost of imported silk would be met by increased sales of cloth. Then, as import of Piedmontese organzines began to increase, the silk-spinning interests entered the fray, seeking to ban the import of all but raw silk, while, however, preferring the Italian to the Turkish product.[55]

British commercial expansion into Piedmont was, thus, far from being a simple, cut-and-dried issue. The interplay of all these different interests probably explains why the government failed to pursue a consistent line of policy. At the same time, it had to contend with Victor Amadeus's own policy of protectionism, aimed at developing his state's economy in accordance with mercantilist principle. He welcomed English trade as a means of escaping the virtual commercial monopoly that France exercised over his states, but he had no intention of allowing Britain to secure a similar commanding position. So, despite the British government's demands, he maintained high tariffs on English goods and made full use of the leverage provided by British dependence on Piedmontese silk. As he observed to the British ambassador, "On ne peut pas se passer de nos organsins."[56]

The first real indication of the British government's intentions seems to have come in 1695. Three years before, the government had given its blessing to the formation of a consortium known as the Lutestring or Lustring Company, which produced fine silken cloths after the French fashion.[57] In 1695 this company was given the task of developing trade with Piedmont, in part as a way to offset the drain of money caused by the payment of subsidies, in part as a way to break Victor Amadeus loose from his close economic relationship with France and force him to replace French goods with English in his home market. The Lutestring Company was chosen as the standard-bearer of the British commercial advance because it was a large user of Piedmontese silks. The government now remitted part of the duty on these, and in return the company was ordered to press the sale of English woolens in Piedmont.[58] But the results were disappointing. Victor Amadeus did not lower his tariffs on English cloth, which still paid more duty than French, and when Richard Hill visited Turin in 1699 as envoy extraordinary, he noted the continued French predominance in the Piedmontese economy and the multiple obstacles to English trade.[59]

With the renewal of the alliance in 1703 the British government resumed its efforts to break into the Piedmontese economy and oust the French from their favored commercial position, this time with greater success. Hill, sent out again to Turin in 1703, was instructed to spare no pains in promoting trade.

In this conjuncture, it is very likely that the Duke will not be averse to anything that the Queen can reasonably desire. . . . You may remember how very popular a thing it is to clothe the armies of our allies and it cannot be proposed to any prince with greater likelihood of success than to the Duke of Savoy, because it may be made very plain to him, that we can do it for him much cheaper than it can be done for him from other parts.[60]

Or, more bluntly, "It is to be hoped that he will make no difficulty in choosing to be supplied at cheap rates from his friends, rather than at dear rates from his enemy."[61] The resultant export of English cloth would serve several purposes: it would help balance the payment of subsidies and the cost of imported silk; it would compete with French goods; most significant, in the long run it "will encourage our merchants to send our commodities thither, and begin a trade, which, in time, will increase to the mutual benefit of both."[62] From this and other instructions to Hill in these years, it is clear that the government was consciously exploiting the potentialities inherent in the military alliance with Victor Amadeus II as a weapon in its economic war with France, and as a way to establish a commercial foothold in Piedmont. Here the parallel of the Methuen Treaty springs at once to mind, but the Piedmontese economy proved a tougher nut to crack than the Portuguese. Victor Amadeus refused to join in the Allied embargo on French goods, arguing that many of his merchants depended on the French trade for their livelihood. The most he would do was to reduce the duties on English imports to the same level as those on French goods, which, as Hill observed, "is more than we could obtain all the last war."[63]

But after the French defeat in 1706 conditions began to change. Louis XIV imposed a temporary embargo on trade with Piedmont, which soon had to be revoked because of protests from the merchants of Dauphiné and Lyon, who warned that

Il y a actuellement a Turin des Anglois, qui proposent d'enlever des soies de ce pays, et d'y porter des draps, des bas, des chapeaux. . . . Si les Piémontois s'accoutument à ce commerce, il sera impossible de retablir celuy de la ville de Lyon, les manufactures du Royaume en souffriront.[64]

Periodically, however, the French embargo was reimposed, and the Alpine campaigns after 1708 further disrupted trade, while in that year Victor Amadeus at last acceded to British pressure and banned trade between his states and France, agreeing at the same time to buy the cloth required for his army's uniforms from English suppliers.[65] The result was a steady increase in the volume of trade with Great Britain, and a corresponding diminution in trade with France. By 1712 the merchants of Lyon were seriously concerned by the loss of some of their market to English and Dutch competition.[66] Nor did Piedmont revert to its former dependence on French trade, once peace was restored and normal relations were resumed. The tariffs on French cloth were raised, and imports from Lyon decreased. But France's loss was not England's gain. Although a considerable volume of English cloth was now being sold in Piedmont, it by no means dominated the market, and its sale was hedged about with restrictions aimed at protecting the nascent local cloth industry. The place in the Piedmontese cloth market lost by the French was not filled by the English, but was largely taken over by high- and medium-grade cloth produced domestically.[67] Subsequent British efforts to increase sales of cloth in Piedmont met with little success. A commercial bridghead had been won during the War of the Spanish Succession, but it could be expanded only with difficulty.

The tariffs levied on cloth imported into the Savoyard state led to periodic complaints from the British government for the rest of Victor Amadeus's reign and after, but a more serious dispute in the years after the Peace of Utrecht — when political relations were deteriorating rapidly, as we have seen — centered on the export of Piedmontese silks and organzines. The Piedmontese export trade was initially threatned by the establishment in 1717-19 of a factory at Derby to produce organzines in the Italian manner.[68] The brothers Thomas and John Lombe, who had built the factory, obtained the raw silk needed for their organzines from Italy, much of it coming from Victor Amadeus's domains in Monferrato. From the first, they encountered serious difficulties in procuring the raw material they required, for the Italian states naturally restricted the export of raw silk to this new competitor who threatened their traditional primacy in the production of organzines. Moreover, Victor Amadeus was interested in developing his own silk-weaving industry, and in years when the silk crop was meager, he restricted exports of raw silk and organzines to ensure that domestic producers were not starved of raw material.

In 1722 one of these periodic bans was imposed, and the British government at once protested, for by now roughly half the silk imported from Italy came from Piedmont, and the loss of such a quantity of raw material would have very serious effects for the British silk weavers. Victor Amadeus replied that the ban was occasioned by a temporary shortage that was affecting his own manufactures as well, but it is also true that he had a definite interest in hamstringing the Lombes's silk-throwing operation, which competed directly with the growing Piedmontese production of organzines.[69] After a while, the ban was revoked and silk exports were resumed, and by the end of Victor Amadeus's reign the value of Piedmontese organzines shipped to Britain had risen to about £85,000 sterling per year. Imports of cloth, the main British commodity sold in Piedmont, by then amounted to about £70,000 per year.[70]

Strictly speaking, therefore, the balance of trade seems to have been in favor of Piedmont-Savoy. But the silk trade provided Britain with a vital raw material to be worked up and sold in other markets at a high profit. And the most important point to bear in mind was that in 1690, before the conclusion of the first Anglo-Savoyard alliance, trade between Britain and the Savoyard domains had been virtually nonexistent. By 1730 it had attained a respectable level; English cloth had found a useful market where none had existed thirty years before; the French hold on the economy of Piedmont-Savoy had been broken; Piedmontese silk, which had formerly gone almost entirely to Lyon, now found its way in growing quantities to the developing British silk industry. The military alliance and the payment of subsidies to Victor Amadeus II had been used, consciously and deliberately, as a means of opening up trade between the two states, and to a considerable degree this policy had been successful. Certainly the volume of trade was not as large as might have been hoped, and the obstacles to the sale of British cloth in Piedmont-Savoy had proved stiffer than expected. But a foothold had been established, and at the same time the Piedmontese economy had undergone a major reorientation away from its dependence on France, Britain's commercial and political rival. In the long run, the commercial ties forged in the matrix of political alliance outlasted the diplomatic breakdown of 1718 and provided a basis for the resumption of political relations in later years.

NOTES

1. I shall be using the terms *Savoy* and *Piedmont-Savoy* interchangeably; the latter, to my mind, is more accurate, since it draws attention to the fact that Victor Amadeus's state was composite of different entities (it also included the county of Nice). Already by the sixteenth century the economic and political center of gravity of the state was located in Piedmont, while the duchy of Savoy itself, the historic heart of the state, was declining in relative importance. Victor Amadeus II ruled from 1675 to 1730, first as duke of Savoy (down to 1713), then as king of Sicily (1713-1720), and finally as king of Sardinia (1720-1730). A more extensive discussion of Victor Amadeus's foreign policy will appear in my forthcoming study of his reign. For general background on Anglo-Savoyard relations in this period, see S. J. Woolf, "English Public Opinion and the Duchy of Savoy," in *English Miscellany*, vol. 12 (Rome, 1961). Apart from this, the literature is scanty.

2. J. S. Corbett, *England in the Mediterranean 1603-1713*, 2 vols. (London, 1917); F. Braudel, *La Méditerranée et le monde méditerranéen a l'époque de Philippe II* (Paris, 1949; 2d ed., 2 vols: Paris, 1966). The discussion of Anglo-Dutch trade is to be found in vol. 1 of the 2d ed., pp. 557 ff.

3. R. Davis, *English Overseas Trade 1500-1700* (London, 1973), pp. 20-23; "England and the Mediterranean 1570-1670," in F. J. Fisher, ed., *Essays in the Economic and Social History of Tudor and Stuart England in Honour of R. H. Tawney* (Cambridge, 1961), "English Foreign Trade 1660-1700," in *Economic History Review*, n.s., vol. 7 (1954).

4. C. Cipolla, "The Economic Decline of Italy," in his *The Economic Decline of Empires* (London, 1970). The article originally appeared in the *Economic History Review*, n.s., vol. 5 (1952). See also D. Sella, "The Rise and Fall of the Venetian Woollen Industry," in B. Pullan, ed., *Crisis and Change in the Venetian Economy in the Sixteenth and Seventeenth Centuries* (London, 1968), and A. Tenenti, *Piracy and the Decline of Venice 1580-1615* (London, 1967).

5. On Livorno see F. Braudel and R. Romano, *Navires et marchandises à l'entrée du port de Livourne 1547-1611* (Paris, 1951).

6. W. Cobbett, *Parliamentary History*, 36 vols. (London, 1806-19), 6:631-632, gives a date of February 1708 with this information, and also that, between September 1703 and October 1704, 91 running galleys reached England from Livorno without convoy. There was also a considerable trade in wine and oil from Livorno; see F. Venturi, *Settecento Riformatore* (Turin, 1969), pp. 14-15 for statistics from the 1730s.

7. W. Blackley, ed., *The Diplomatic Correspondence of the Rt. Hon. Richard Hill . . .*, 2 vols. (London, 1845), 2:565, on the general question of trade to Genoa and Livorno; see also G. Giacchero, *Storia economica del Settecento genovese* (Genoa, 1951), chap. 3; L. Bulferetti and C. Constantini, *Industria e commercio in Liguria nell'età Risorgimento 1700-1861* (Milan, 1966), p. 121 ff.; C. Morandi, ed., *Relazioni di am-*

basciatori sabaudi, genovesi e veneti durante il periodo della grande alleanza e della successione di Spagna 1693-1713 (Bologna, 1935), pp. xviii-xix, xliv-xlix; J. Meuvret, "Louis XIV et l'Italie," in *X VIIᵉ Siècle,* no. 46 (1960), pp. 87-88.

8. H. G. Koenigsberger, "English Merchants in Naples and Sicily in the Seventeenth Century," in *English Historical Review,* vol. 62 (1947), reprinted in his *Estates and Revolutions* (Ithaca, 1971). The trade treaty of 1713 appears in Comte Solar de la Marguérite, ed., *Traités publics de la royale maison de Savoie. . . ,* 3 vols. (Turin, 1836), 2:276-278.

9. On this, some information in Giacchero, *Storia economica,* chap. 4; also L. Bulferetti, "Les communications entre Turin et Lyon au XVIIIe siècle," in *Cahiers d'Histoire* (Clermont-Lyon-Grenoble), vol. 5, pt. 4 (1960).

10. Treaty in J. Dumont, ed., *Corps universel diplomatique du droit des gens,* 8 vols. (The Hague, 1731), vol. 7, pt. 1, pp. 119-122; a Latin version is in G. Duboin, ed., *Baccolta per ordine di materie delle leggi, editti, patenti, manifesti ecc. emanati negli Stati Sardi sino all'8 dicembre 1798,* 31 vols. (Turin, 1818-1868), 15:1304-1313, with useful notes and ancillary documents. See also G. Prato, "Le ambizioni commerciali e maritime di un ministro piemontese del sec. XVII," in *Miscellanea di studi storici in onore di Giovanni Sforza* (Turin, 1923).

11. On the Piedmontese army at this time see C. Contessa et al., *Le campagne di guerra in Piemonte 1703-1708 e l'assedio di Torrino,* 10 vols. (Turin, 1907-1933), vol. 1, Intro; cf. also the remarks in G. Quazza, *Il problema italiano e l'equilibrio europeo 1720-1738* (Turin, 1965), pp. 28, 82.

12. The nonspecialist treads warily among the literature in this field, which even in the present ecumenical age is shot through with sectarian bias on both sides. The most recent general survey of the Waldensians is A. Molnar and A. Armand-Hugon, *Storia dei Valdesi,* vols. 1-2. (Turin, 1974), vol. 3 not yet published.

13. Details on Cromwell's intervention in T. Birch, ed., *A Collection of the State Papers of John Thurloe, Esq. . . . ,* 7 vols. (London, 1742), 3:361 ff.; S. R. Gardiner, *History of the Commonwealth and Protectorate,* 4 vols. (London, 1903), 3:406 ff.

14. Lines 3 and 4: "Even them who kept thy truth so pure of old/ When all our fathers worshipped stocks and stones" seems to me to refer to the contemporary belief in the apostolic origin of the Waldensians; this is the interpretation offered by D. Bush, ed., *The Complete Poetical Works of John Milton* (Boston, 1965), p. 198, and by J. S. Smart, *The Sonnets of Milton* (Glasgow, 1921), pp. 99-106. J. Carey and A. Fowler, eds., *The Poems of John Milton* (London, 1968), p. 411, however take these lines to refer to the English church before the Reformation. Lines 6 and 7: "Slain by the bloody Piemontese that rolled/ Mother with infant down the rocks" refers to an incident frequently mentioned in the contemporary pamphlets, e.g., in S. Morland, *The*

History of the Evangelical Churches of Piedmont (London, 1658), pp. 344, 363.

15. On Morland, see the article in the *Dictionary of National Biography*. See also R. Buck Knox, *James Ussher, Archbishop of Armagh* (Cardiff, 1967), pp. 108-109, 168. In the sixteenth century the myth of the Apostolic origin of the Waldensians had not yet appeared: Foxe's *Book of Martyrs* dates their origin correctly from Peter Waldo. J. Perrin's *Histoire des Vaudois* (1616: translated into English by S. Lennard 1624, and republished 1711) is ambiguous, giving both accounts of the Waldensians' origin — on p. 1 of the 1711 ed. they are dated from ca. 1160, but elsewhere (p. 13) are described (in a quotation from Beza) as the "offspring of the purest part of the Ancient Christian Church." The preface to J. B. Stouppe, ed., *A Collection of the Several Papers sent to His Highness the Lord Protector... concerning the Bloody and Barbarous Massacres... committed on many Thousands of Reformed, or Protestants dwelling in the Vallies of Piedmont...* (London, 1655), accepts the Apostolic origin, as do nearly all subsequent writers, e.g., W. Wake, *The Case of the Exiled Vaudois and French Protestants Stated...* (London, 1699), pp. 14-18. On this whole question see J. H. Todd, *The Books of the Vaudois* (Dublin, 1865), especially p. 210 ff.; M. Viora, *Storia delle leggi sui Valdesi di Vittorio Amedeo II* (Bologna, 1930), Intro.

16. On William III's intervention and the Edict of 1694, see Viora, *Storia...*, p. 174 ff.

17. They are described thus in the Instructions for Hill in 1703. Essex's Instructions, 11 Mar. 1730 (quoted by Quazza, *Problema italiano*, p. 145 n. 35) require him to give "the best assistance to the Vaudois and other Protestants yet remaining within the Dominions of that King."

18. Thus Hill to Nottingham, 2 Nov. 1703 (NS), in Blackley, *Diplomatic Correspondence*, 1:276; Marlborough to Godolphin, 8/19 July 1703, in H. Snyder, ed., *The Marlborough-Godolphin Correspondence*, 3 vols. (Oxford, 1975), 1:218. Similar references continue to 1706, after which they become less frequent.

19. D. Carutti, *Storia della diplomazia della corte di Savoia*, 4 vols. (Rome, 1875-1880), 3:591.

20. In a sense, the payment of subsidies was similar to the payment of gratifications to ministers at foreign courts in that it tended only to produce results when it reinforced prior inclinations on the part of the recipient. See the remarks by A. Lossky in *Cambridge Modern History* (Cambridge, 1970), 6:183-184; also R. M. Hatton, "Gratifications and Foreign Policy: Anglo-French Rivalry in Sweden during the Nine Years War," in R. M. Hatton and J. S. Bromley, eds., *William III and Louis XIV. Essays 1680-1720 by and for Mark A. Thomson* (Liverpool, 1968). It is also important to establish the distinction between a subsidized ally like Victor Amadeus II, who kept command of his own troops, and the various states which hired out contingents of mercenary troops that were

incorporated directly into the armies under British command; in the latter instance, the states' rulers remained technically neutral and were not allies.

21. Treaty in Dumont, vol. 7, pt. 2, pp. 272-275. The secret clause is also printed in Blackley, *Diplomatic correspondence,* 2:764-765.

22. S. B. Baxter, *William III* (London, 1966), p. 289.

23. Quoted by Woolf, *English Public Opinion,* p. 222.

24. Besides the regiments of Vaudois and Huguenots paid for by Britain and the United Provinces, a corps of Bavarians was paid from 1691 to support the Allies in Piedmont. See Max Emanuel of Bavaria to William III, 20 June 1691 (NS), in N. Japikse, ed., *Correspondentie van Willem III en van Hans Willem Bentinck, eersten Graaf van Portland,* 2 vols. in 5. (The Hague, 1927-37), vol. 2, pt. 3, p. 241. At other times there were also contingents of Swiss troops, Württembergers and other Germans fighting in Piedmont.

25. The most recent account of this is R. D. Handen, "The End of an Era: Louis XIV and Victor Amadeus II," in R. M. Hatton, ed., *Louis XIV and Europe* (London, 1976).

26. These arguments are made by Carutti, *Storia della diplomazia,* 3:248-249.

27. Victor Amadeus's mistrust of Austrian intentions is shown in his insistence that Casale be returned to its owner, the duke of Mantua, after its French garrison surrendered in 1695, to prevent its being taken over by the Habsburgs. In May 1695, Victor Amadeus sent a special envoy to Madrid, charged with trying to obtain the governorship of Milan for him, in an effort to forestall the Austrians. See Morandi, *Relazioni di ambasciatori sabaudi,* pp. xxxiii-xxxiv.

28. The claim derived from Charles Emanuel I's marriage to the Infanta, daughter of Philip II, in 1585, and had been confirmed in Philip IV's will. For a sample of William III's (and Louis XIV's) attitude to Victor Amadeus at this time, see Portland to William III, 17 May 1698 (NS), in Japikse, *Correspondentie van Willem III,* vol. 1, pt. 1, p. 307.

29. For these negotiations see Contessa et al, *Le campagne di guerra,* vol. 5, Introduction and passim; Carutti, *Storia della diplomazia,* 3:327 ff. The treaty is printed by Solar de la Marguérite, *Traités publics,* 2:203-219; this version differs somewhat from that in G. de Lamberty, *Mémoires pour servir à l'histoire du XVIIIe siècle...,* 14 vols. (The Hague, 1728-1740), 2:547-562.

30. Details on these negotiations in Blackley, *Diplomatic Correspondence,* vol. 1, passim; cf. Marlborough to Godolphin, 2/13 Aug. 1703, in Snyder, *Marlboro-Godolphin correspondence,* 1:229: "If the Duke of Savoy coms [sic] into our interest, there is nothing but our folly and knavery in England that can save France." Text of the treaty in Blackley, *Diplomatic Correspondence,* 2:770-797; signed by Hill Aug. 1 1704.

31. L. Einaudi, *La finanza sabauda all'aprirsi del secolo XVIII e durante la guerra di successione spagnuola* (Turin, 1908), especially pp.

278-292. Einaudi gives similar figures in the tables appended to his *Le entrate pubbliche dello stato sabaudo nei bilanci e nei conti dei tesorieri durante la guerra di successione spagnuola* (Turin, 1909), which is vol. 9 of the series *Le campagne di guerra in Piemonte.*

32. Einaudi, *La finanza sabauda,* pp. 386-387.

33. Cobbett, *Parliamentary History,* 6:550-551, 610; *The Journals of the House of Commons,* 75 vols. (London 1803 ff.), (hereafter referred to as *JHC*) 15:245A-B, 485B.

34. It is virtually impossible to trace all the detachments of hired troops which served in Piedmont at one time or another. The largest contingent seems to have been that of 8,000 Prussians hired by Marlborough in December 1704, at 300,000 crowns a year (the Dutch paying 1/3); see Marlborough to Heinsius, Sept. 12, 19, 26, 1704 (NS), in B. van't Hoff, ed., *The Correspondence 1701-1711 of John Churchill, Duke of Marlborough, and Anthonie Heinsius, Grand Pensionary of Holland* (The Hague, 1951), pp. 133, 135, 137. There were also about 4,000 Württembergers; see Marlborough to Godolphin, 25 Jan./5. Feb. 1704, and Godolphin to Marlborough, 11 Sep. 1705, in Snyder, *Marlborough-Godolphin correspondence,* 1:264, 491. For a contingent of Hessians, see Marlborough to Heinsius, Sept. 27, 1706, in van't Hoff, *Correspondence 1701-1711,* p. 270. In addition there were the regiments of Huguenots and Vaudois, and some Swiss. A careful search of the correspondence would no doubt reveal others.

35. Cobbett, *Parliamentary History,* 6:542.

36. This averages out to about £200,000 p.a. for the decade. Such a figure, reached by using Einaudi's figures, is confirmed by working back from the normal payments recorded in the *JHC,* which were £160,000 p.a. (e.g., *JHC,* 15:25A: payments for 1706). The addition of bonus payments and other extraordinary sums would raise the average to roughly the £200,000 p.a. worked out from Einaudi.

37. For the Toulon expedition, see J. H. Owen, *War at Sea under Queen Anne 1702-1708* (Cambridge, 1938), chap. 6; the contemporary account in B. Tunstall, ed., *The Byng Papers,* 2 vols. (London, 1930), 1:216-235, is very favorable to Victor Amadeus. Godolphin held the Imperial forces responsible for the failure; see his letter to Marlborough, 1 Sep. 1707 (OS), in Snyder, *Marlborough-Godolphin correspondence,* 2:899. See also the debate in Cobbett, *Parliamentary History,* 6:966-968, 976, 991-997.

38. On the dispute with the emperor, see Carutti, *Storia della diplomazia,* 3:367 ff.

39. Among the numerous examples of pro-Savoyard sentiment in this dispute, see Marlborough to Heinsius, 20 Jan. 1710 (NS), and Heinsius to Marlborough, 22 Feb. 1710, in van't Hoff, *Correspondence 1701-1711,* pp. 480, 484. Major-General Palmes was sent to mediate the dispute at Vienna in 1708; some information on his mission is in *Historical Manuscripts Commission, 11th Report, Appendix, pt 4: Manuscripts of the Marquess of Townshend* (London, 1887), pp. 53 ff., 61, 74, 80. In

1712 the Anglo-Dutch mediators found in Victor Amadeus's favor on all counts in the territorial dispute: see the Decree of the Commissioners, 27 June 1712 (NS), in Solar de la Marguérite, *Traités publics,* 2:272-275.

40. M. Gasco, "La politica sabauda a Utrecht nella 'Relazione Mellarede,'" in *Rivista Storica Italiana,* 4th series, 6 (1935), 321.

41. Boyle to Marlborough and Townshend, 24 May 1709 (OS), in L. G. Wickham Legg, ed., *British Diplomatic Instructions 1689-1789,* 2: *France 1689-1721* (London, 1925), 14.

42. Thus Carutti, *Storia della diplomazia,* 3:429n, quotes the *Relation* by Mellarède, one of the Savoyard negotiators at Utrecht: "La reine d'Angleterre a dit à quelques personnes de confiance qu'elle était engagée en conscience de procurer un aggrandissement considérable à la Maison de Savoie, parce qu'elle l'a privée de l'espérance de la Couronne de la Grande-Bretagne... par l'exclusion... des princes Catholiques à la succession de la dite Couronne." The Duchess of Savoy's Protest against the Act of Succession, dated 11 April 1701, is printed by Dumont, *Supplement au corps universel diplomatique,* vol. 2, pt. 2, p. 5, and by Lamberty, *Mémoires pour servir,* 1:503.

43. In a letter of July 12/23 1712, printed in *A Report of the Committee of Secrecy relating to the Negotiations of Peace and Commerce, Chairman Robert Walpole* (London, 1715), p. 26. That this was not just a fabrication of Whig propaganda can be seen from J-B. Colbert, marquis de Torcy, *Mémoires,* 3 vols. (The Hague [actually Paris]: 1756), 3:285 ff., which describes this phase of the negotiations. On this question, see H. N. Fieldhouse, "A Note on the Negotiations for the Peace of Utrecht," in *American Historical Review,* vol. 40 (1935), and "St John and Savoy in the War of the Spanish Succession," in *English Historical Review,* vol. 50 (1935); D. McKay, "Bolingbroke, Oxford and the Defence of the Utrecht Settlement in Southern Europe," EHR, vol. 86 (1971).

44. For the background to this, see A. Legrelle, *La diplomatie française et la succession d'Espagne,* 2d ed., 6 vols. (Braine-le-Comte, 1895-1899), 6:93-97. On June 6 (OS) the Queen's Message to Parliament noted that the disposition of Sicily had not yet been decided, Cobbett, *Parliamentary History,* 6:1143, but next day she informed Maffei, the Savoyard ambassador, that Sicily would go to Victor Amadeus II. Carutti, *Storia della diplomazia,* 3:427-430. The treaty between St. John and Torcy alloting Sicily to Victor Amadeus was signed on Aug 11/22 1712: Wickham Legg, *British Diplomatic Instructions,* 2:25.

45. *Report of the Committee of Secrecy,* p. 26.

46. Gasco, "Politica sabauda," p. 336.

47. Thus when Peterborough broached the subject with Victor Amadeus in Sept. and Nov. 1712, he was by no means pleased, and had to be warned that if he refused Sicily he would incur the Queen's displeasure, *Report of the Committee of Secrecy,* p. 26.

48. Einaudi, *La finanza sabauda,* pp. 283-285. Between 1713 and 1716 Victor Amadeus claimed £347,000 in unpaid subsidies; he re-

THE USE AND ABUSE OF ALLIES

ceived £80,000 and this only through the help of a group of M.P.'s described by the Savoyard ambassador, Trivié, as his "souterrain," or "une cabale avide de proffiter qui avoit assez de credit à la Cour et au Parlement pour faire réussir ce qui lui convenoit." Payment was finally made unofficially, without the authorization of either king or cabinet. Lord Chados was specifically mentioned as one of those involved. In 1719 another payment of £35,000, again unofficial, settled all other claims. Evidently considerable sums of money voted for subsidies during the war years had been diverted to other uses.

49. Quazza, *Problema italiano,* p. 17.

50. On Victor Amadeus II's policy at this time, see Carutti, *Storia della diplomazia,* 3:510-551. See also E. Robiony, "Un'ambizione mal nota della Casa di Savoia," in *Archivio Storico Italiano,* 5th series, vol. 32 (1903); G. C. Gibbs, "Parliament and the Treaty of Quadruple Alliance," in Hatton and Bromley, eds., *Essays by and for Mark A. Thomson;* B. Williams, *Stanhope, a Study in Eighteenth-Century Diplomacy* (Oxford, 1932), pp. 276-278, 290, 310. Idem., "The Foreign Policy of England under Walpole," in *English Historical Review,* vol. 15 (1900) is full of errors and misconceptions about Savoyard policy.

51. J. L. Cranmer-Byng, ed., *Pattee Byng's Journal* (London, 1950), p. 292.

52. See the recognition of this in Victor Amadeus's Instructions for Ossorio, his ambassador to England, 25 Nov. 1729, printed by Quazza, *Problema italiano,* p. 136.

53. Davis, "England and the Mediterranean 1570-1670," notes that by about 1669 approximately one-third of British silk imports came from Italy. For a general idea of the scale of the trade with Italy, see E. B. Schumpeter, *English Overseas Trade Statistics 1697-1808* (Oxford, 1960), which however does not give a detailed breakdown of provenance or destination.

54. *JHC,* 10:359, 363, 366 for the 1690 Bill; ibid., p. 698 ff., and 11:9 ff., for the Bill of 1693.

55. This line-up of interests can be observed after the submission of a petition in Feb. 1727 by the silk-throwers to curtail the import of Italian silk, in *JHC,* 20:748 ff.

56. Quoted in L. Bulferetti, *Agricoltura, industria e commercio in Piemonte nel secolo XVIII* (Turin, 1963), p. 300.

57. On the foundation of the Company, see *JHC,* 12:117-118.

58. Ibid., pp. 210-235 contains an Enquiry into the Company's affairs in April 1698, and prints (p. 230) Shrewsbury's Proposals to the Company for trade with Piedmont. The aim was to ruin French trade; to export goods and manufactures in return for oil, silk, soap and paper; to cut off the silk trade between Piedmont and Lyon; to profit from the opening of the Mediterranean by the Allied fleet "to make some Experiments how our English Manufactures would go off in Piedmont." See also *Calendar of State Papers, Domestic Series, William III,* 6 (London, 1908), 16, for "Lord Galway's letter to Lord Godolphin about settling the trade in Piedmont for their silks; this was chiefly

thought of to save the returns of money thither for paying the subsidies."

59. Blackley, *Diplomatic Correspondence,* 2:811-814.

60. Nottingham to Hill, Nov. 19 1703 (OS). Blackley, *Diplomatic Correspondence,* 1:62.

61. Blackley, *Diplomatic Correspondence.*

62. Nottingham to Hill, Dec. 10 1703 (OS). Blackley, *Diplomatic Correspondence,* 1:66.

63. Hill to Nottingham, 14 Mar. 1704 (OS). Blackley, *Diplomatic Correspondence,* 1:336.

64. Report of d'Angervilliers, intendant of Dauphiné, 10 Dec. 1706 (NS), in A. de Boislisle, ed., *Correspondance des contrôleurs-généraux des finances avec les intendants des provinces,* 3 vols. (Paris, 1874-97), 2:369. For this whole question see P. Léon, "Economie et diplomatie: les relations commerciales delphino-piémontaises au debut du XVIIIe siècle (1700-1713)," in *Cahiers d'Histoire* (Clermont-Lyon-Grenoble), vol. 5, pt. 3 (1960).

65. On the serious effects of the ban in France, see Ravat (prévôt des marchands of Lyon) to the Controller-General, 8 March and 11 April 1708, in Boislisle, *Correspondence des contrôleurs-généraux,* 3:4-5. The first consignment of English cloth for Victor Amadeus's army was sent aboard the warships leaving for the Mediterranean in Sept. 1708: Tunstall, ed., *Byng Papers,* 2:268-269, 277.

66. See the *Mémoire sur le commerce* of 1712, in Léon, "Economie et diplomatie," p. 284.

67. On the development of the Piedmontese woolen cloth industry, see V. Castronovo, *L'industria laniera in Piemonte nel secolo XIX* (Turin, 1964), chap. 1.

68. On the Lombes, see the article in the *Dictionary of National Biography;* also G. H. Jones, "English Diplomacy and Italian Silk in the Time of Lombe," in *Bulletin of the Institute of Historical Research,* vol. 34 (1961).

69. G. Prato, "L'espansione commerciale inglese nel primo Settecento in una relazione di un inviato sabaudo," in *Miscellanea di studi storici in onore di Antonio Manno,* 2 vols. (Turin, 1912), describes these negotiations. See also Bulferetti, *Agricoltura, industria e commercio in Piemonte,* p. 146, for the ban of 1722.

70. Quazza, *Problema italiano,* p. 56 says that ca. 2 million lire worth of organzines were exported to England in the 1720s, which agrees roughly with the figures in Duboin, 16:109n: average 1,941,575 lire p.a. for 1721-1725. Jones, *English Diplomacy,* pp. 185-186 says that in 1722, 255,090 lbs of Italian silk were imported, half of this from Piedmont: this is presumably raw silk rather than organzines. Prato, "L'espansione commerciale," p. 58n gives 130,955 lbs of silk imported from Piedmont in this year, corroborating Jones's figure. Bulferetti, *Agricoltura, industria e commercio in Piemonte,* p. 300, estimates the balance of trade as quoted here; p. 379 he says the average value of English cloth imported 1721-1725 was 579,676 lire p.a.

VI

PARTY AND PATRONAGE IN LATER STUART ENGLAND

Clayton Roberts

In a celebrated aphorism Mao Tse-tung once declared that power springs from the barrel of a gun. Twice in the seventeenth century Englishmen proved this brutal assertion to be true, once in 1642, again in 1688. But it is a measure of the civility of the English that they thereafter proved it to be false, and it is a measure of the greatness of English political theory that both Hobbes and Locke should proclaim that in a political society—whatever might be true in the state of nature—power does not spring from the barrel of a gun.

But if power in a political society does not spring from the barrel of a gun, whence does it spring? To this question the most obvious answer is the power of the purse: he who pays the piper calls the tune. Indeed, it would not be saying too much to assert that English constitutional history is but a commentary on the power of the purse. Throughout English history, as the financial independence of the crown waxed and waned, so did its power. William the Conqueror possessed the land necessary to support his independence. Edward III, wasting his treasure in wars abroad, sank into bankruptcy and a dependence on Parliament. Edward IV restored the solvency of the crown and thereby its independence. The Tudors walked a precarious line between solvency and insolvency and so retained a precarious independence. Charles I stepped over the line into bankruptcy and catastrophe. Charles II possessed enough revenue to live "of his own" and to be able to send contumacious Parliaments packing. James II enjoyed so great an income and used it so wretchedly that Englishmen had to resort to the power that springs from the barrel of a gun to drive him from the realm. They thereupon resolved never to vote another king sufficient revenues to "live of his own." The power of the purse, which had been slipping from the king's hand for a century, now fell irremediably into the hands of Parliament.

The power of the purse having fallen from the king's hand, the struggle for power now took on a different shape, neither military nor financial, but political. It was now a struggle within Parliament, not outside it, a struggle to gain control of the formidable legislative and financial powers of the two Houses. To this struggle the king brought the allegiance and reverence men owed him as king. But if allegiance and reverence were not enough to bind a man to him, he might seek to do so by granting him an office at court, or a title, or a regiment, or a pension, or a deputy lieutenancy, or a government contract. The king, however, soon found himself opposed by the politician, who brought to the struggle his skill in debate, his popularity in the House, his leadership of a party. A contest arose between the king exercising the power of patronage and the politician exploiting the power of party, each seeking to influence the deliberation of the two Houses of Parliament. It is the purpose of this essay to examine that contest in order to discover the locus of power in later Stuart England. It is an essay about power, not administration, about those contests that arise when push comes to shove, not those manifold decisions that monarchs, lord treasurers, lord chancellors, and secretaries of state make in the daily conduct of government. More particularly, it is an essay that seeks to discover how great was the king's influence in Parliament? Could he drive through Parliament those measures he favored and could he find in Parliament support for ministers of his own choice?

There exists, of course, an extensive literature on this subject. It falls roughly into two schools. On the one hand, there are those like Macaulay, Trevelyan, Mark Thompson, and David Ogg who say little about patronage, much about party, and who date the beginnings of the supremacy of Parliament with the revolution.[1] It could be called the Whig school. On the other hand, there are those like Betty Kemp, Robert Walcott, J. P. Kenyon, and Archibald Foord who emphasize the king's influence, play down the importance of party, and argue that the revolution created a balance of government, with the king's power very little diminished.[2] This could be called the Namier school. And the question that this essay seeks to answer might well be phrased in this manner: which model, the Whig or the Namier, more closely fits the facts of political life in later Stuart England?

But before I turn to this question, I should like to say a word about the origin of the patronage system and the beginnings of party. Despite the fulminations of Joel Hurstfield against Thomas Cromwell for setting aside an election at Canterbury,[3] I do not believe that the Tudor monarchs sought to pack Parliaments with their servants. They sought to bring a few privy councillors into the House, as Sir John Neale has observed, the better to manage it, but they did not seek systematically to pack it; that is, they did not until the 1590s, when Robert Cecil, alarmed by the challenge posed by the Earl of Essex, sent letters to numerous boroughs promoting the election of his friends.[4] In 1604, with Essex gone, Cecil neglected to do so, but he and James saw the error of their ways and intervened actively in the ninety-five by-elections that followed. In one-third of them the crown secured the return of a royal official or a person closely connected with the government.[5] In 1612 Sir Francis Bacon gave formal expression to the tactics that Cecil had stumbled upon. He advised James to use the power of patronage both to influence elections and to win members over to the court. How, he asked, might the Cinque Ports and the duchy be used to bring in the well-affected? How might the lawyers be won or bridled? He rejoiced that Yelverton has won, Neville has hopes, Crew and Hyde stand to be serjeants, Martin has money. In Bacon's world men were to be won, owned, frightened, bridled, silenced, and seduced.[6] Yet James I was too lazy and Charles I too proud to follow Bacon's advice, for which Menna Prestwich, in her life of Cranfield, chides them. She defends the practicability of Bacon's advice by listing a dozen patriots won to the court by place, though she neglects to mention that not one of them was ever again useful in the management of Parliament.[7]

What is certain is that the Court party nearly disappeared by

the autumn of 1640, for in that year only 49 officials and courtiers sat in the Commons, whereas in 1614 there had been 160.[8] By
the year 1664 it was all very different. In that year the Earl of
Clarendon drew up a list of 167 members of Parliament who were
either officeholders or recipients of favors from the court. Clarendon, as J. R. Jones observes, was "the first minister effectively to
undertake political organization with the object of obtaining a
controlling interest over parliamentary proceedings."[9]

Not only the patronage system but the party system too came of
age at the Restoration. No doubt its roots stretched back into the
early seventeenth century. One can read of the Patriots, the
Country party, the Puritan faction, the Root and Branch party,
and the Middle group; but these groups were loosely knit and
short-lived. Their leaders produced nothing like the elaborate list
of Presbyterian members which Philip Wharton drew up in 1660
and 1661.[10] It is surely no accident that the earliest list of a Court
party and the earliest list of an opposition party date from the
1660s. Before the Restoration, more particularly before 1646, the
leaders of the House of Commons sought to win a consensus
there; they spoke for a nation, not a party. But after 1645, as
Mark Kishlansky has recently shown, parties came into the open
and their leaders sought to win a majority, not a consensus.[11] By
1660, therefore, both parties and the patronage system had come
into existence. The question then became, how strong was each?

In 1675 Sir William Coventry, the most esteemed politician in
Restoration England, declared that the forty placemen of 1661
had become the 200 placemen of 1675, and that Parliament
threatened to become merely a body to register the king's decrees,
like the Parlement of Paris.[12] Sir William could find support for
his alarm in a list drawn up in 1673 of 177 M.P.'s who had received offices or favors from the court. A similar list, drawn up in
1677, names 215 such M.P.'s.[13] But these lists should be taken
with a grain of salt, for they include anyone remotely connected
with the court. The earl of Danby, who in 1675 undertook the
systematic application of the power of patronage to the management of Parliament, drew up lists with fewer names. He listed 92
court dependents in 1671, 108 in 1675, and 100 in 1677.[14] Danby
also won men to the Court party by granting them pensions on
the Excise, the number of such pensioners reaching 40 by 1678.[15]
Placemen plus pensioners thus numbered about 130. But these

numbers tell us little about the actual effectiveness of the power
of patronage in the management of Parliament. With parliamentary management, as with much else, the proof of the pudding
lies in the eating. What could Danby accomplish with his Court
party?

In the spring of 1675 he could accomplish very little, with the
result that he doubled the number of Excise pensioners that summer and prepared more carefully for the autumn session. But he
was again unsuccessful, failing by a vote of 151 to 124 to secure
the money needed to build twenty ships for the Navy.[16] In 1677,
however, the Danbean system came closer to success than ever.
Parliament voted enough money to build thirty ships and renewed the Additional Excise on Beer, votes that were gained,
asserts Sir John Reresby, more by purchase than affection.[17] The
spring session of 1678 proved to be the true testing time for the
power of patronage, with the courtiers carrying some motions by
four or five votes, losing others by the same margin. In May the
courtiers failed to prevent a censure against Lauderdale, causing
an angry Charles to take prompt action to discipline the Court
party. He banished Henry Savile from court and dismissed William Lowther from the customs for supporting Lauderdale's censure, and he threatened a like action against any other servant
who failed in his duty.[18] His minatory actions led to a softening of
the address against Lauderdale, but they could not save the earl
of Danby himself the next autumn, when the hysteria unleashed
by the Popish Plot swept all before it. The Commons, by 179 to
116, voted to impeach Danby of high treason, and among the 179
were numerous placemen.[19] When the chips were down, the
power of place and pension proved no match for the dictates of
passion and principle.

On the surface, Danby with his 130 placemen and pensioners
should have carried most measures through the House of Commons, for the total number of votes cast on both sides in an average division was only about 240.[20] But there were serious limitations to the power of patronage, at least five of them. In the first
place, there were not enough places to satisfy all those who hun-
gered for them. Samuel Pepys believed that Charles forebore
removing Clarendon's sons from office because, though he could
gratify some House of Commons' men with their places, he would
anger all those not provided for.[21] Second, many members held

offices for life or in the gift of someone other than the king. Sir Robert Howard could attack Danby with impunity, for he held the office of auditor of the exchequer for life and Gilbert Burnet was secure as preacher at the Rolls Chapel, because his patron was the master of the Rolls.[22] Third, those detached from the opposition by the offer of place soon fell into disrepute. In 1672, Sir Richard Temple, long a tribune of the people, accepted a place at the customs and immediately became the worst-heard member of the House.[23] Fourth, the grant of place to win men over from the opposition encouraged others to oppose until they, too, were favored. As the French ambassador observed, "Where five or six are won over, many others join the opposition."[24]

But the most serious limitation on the power of patronage was the defection of placemen and pensioners whenever the court embarked on policies which they believed harmful or dangerous. Sir William Temple, the diplomat, summed it up in this law of Restoration politics: when the court falls into the true interest of the nation, it can, through corruption, carry the House; when it does not, it cannot.[25]

The failure of the Danbean system in 1678 led Charles to dissolve Parliament in 1679. This presented a new problem: could the power of patronage succeed in electoral management where it had failed in parliamentary management? Danby estimated that through the lord lieutenants in the counties he could influence nearly 350 elections, while the eight lord lieutenants hostile to him could influence only 82.[26] But he had not allowed for the earl of Shaftesbury, who in 1675 set out to organize a Country party that could resist Danby's Court party. Shaftesbury now opposed to Danby's dispensation of court patronage his own dissemination of Whig propaganda. In the ensuing contest, party won out over patronage. Shaftesbury's Worthy Men won 302 seats in the new Parliament, the Court party only 158.[27] And when Charles prorogued and then dissolved Parliament in order to prevent it from passing the Exclusion Bill, 80 percent of those who voted for Exclusion secured reelection, while only 55 percent of those who opposed Exclusion won reelection.[28] In March 1681 Charles ordered all his servants to vote for expedients, not exclusion, but the House defeated the proposed expedients.[29] Only by proroguing Parliament and not meeting it again, could he preserve his brother's right to succeed to the throne.

J. H. Plumb has suggested that Danby's skillful management, combined with the royal prerogative, helped Charles to stumble through his reign.[30] This considerably exaggerates Danby's skill at management, for Danby's parliamentary and electoral management proved no match for Shaftesbury's. W. C. Abbott is nearer the truth when he writes that "the Court majority was annihilated in Danby's administration."[31] It was not the power of patronage that allowed Charles to defeat Exclusion, but the power of the purse, a power that permitted him to govern without Parliament.

Even for the early years of Charles's reign the suggestion is misleading, for Charles's greatest parliamentary triumphs, those of 1670 and 1671, when Parliament voted him additional revenues, were won when the system of patronage was rudimentary and the king's alliance with the Church party close. By 1673 the Declaration of Indulgence had shattered the Church party beyond repair. Not until 1675 did Danby's Court party replace it, but the Court party never enjoyed the success that the Church party had in 1670 and 1671. When the Court party in 1678 sought to gain the king an additional revenue, it met defeat by 202 to 145. W. C. Abbott finds it a paradox that a House that became corrupted simultaneously became more independent. The solution to the paradox is simple: the king could manage Parliament more effectively by allying with the prevailing party there than by employing the power of patronage.[32]

Danby was second to no man in his appreciation of the need for a close alliance with the Church party. And he used the patronage at his disposal to strengthen that alliance. As Andrew Browning has written, "They were bribed to be diligent in their business rather than false in their convictions."[33] And herein one can see the true importance of patronage in Restoration England. It could not seduce more than a few men from their principles. It could not withstand the gusts of popular opinion. But it could act as a cement holding together the Church party in Parliament. Danby's tragedy lay in his inability to keep Charles closely allied to the Church party and its Protestant policies.

James II governed through standing armies, not Parliaments, so little can be said of party and patronage in his reign, though it might be observed that the earl of Sunderland, whose cynicism rivaled Bacon's, advised James in 1686 to meet Parliament once again, and to govern it through the two hundred royal servants he believed sat there. And though James rejected this advice, he did closet himself with many royal servants, only to discover that they preferred dismissal to casting a vote for the repeal of the penal laws.[34] James's attempts at electoral management in 1687 proved equally ineffectual, for men would not engage to elect persons who would repeal the penal laws. Charles's and James's juggling with borough charters had proved of no avail.[35]

William III had no choice but to govern through Parliaments, since the financial settlement at the revolution and the outbreak of war in 1689 reduced him to a financial dependence on Parliament. Yet the war also, as J. H. Plumb has reminded us, greatly increased the size of the executive, an executive that became "inextricably entwined in the legislature."[36] Yet not all of the increase in the size of the executive was reflected in an increase in placemen, as Henry Horwitz has lately shown us. He found that the number of placemen in the House of Commons rose from 101 in 1689 to 131 in 1693, then fell to 120 in 1695, rose again to 132 in 1698, and dropped to 124 in 1701. In short, placemen, as they did in nearly every Stuart Parliament, made up from one-fifth to one-fourth of the House of Commons. In the House of Lords they made up a much larger proportion. The number of placemen in Parliament was certainly sufficient to delight Court managers like Henry Guy and Sir John Trevor and to alarm Country patriots like Sir Edward Hussey, who introduced a bill into Parliament to banish placemen from it, and John Toland, who wrote on *The Danger of Mercenary Parliaments*.[37]

Though the number of placemen was substantial, the limitations on their effectiveness were as real as ever. To begin with, there were too few places. As Sir Miles Cooke, a courtier, observed: "the loaves and fishes were on our side," but "without a miracle four or five baskets full of preferments will hardly be able to feed 500 persons."[38] And many places were held for life or good behavior, particularly places in the law and subordinate places in the exchequer. Furthermore, favor at court brought disrepute in the house. "All the young men that have places," wrote James Lowther, "meet with the greatest discouragement, so that hardly any venture to speak."[39] And the grant of office to buy off mutineers like Sir Edward Seymour infuriated those whose loyal services went unrequited.[40] But the chief limitation was still the defection of those placemen who allowed country prejudices or party loyalty to wean them from their duty. In 1692, for example, the court was unable to carry an Abjuration Bill because the Tory placemen deserted, and unable to defeat a Place Bill because the Whig placemen deserted.[41] In 1694, fifty placemen deserted the court to vote for a Triennial Bill and during the 1697 session, thirty Tory placemen voted repeatedly against the court.[42] When the disbanding of the army came before the House, Whig placemen openly opposed the court's efforts to keep 15,000 men afoot.[43] Tory placemen in December 1701 defeated the court's nominee for Speaker.[44] Although the number of placemen in the House ranged around 120, the number of dependable placemen ranged around 60.[45]

But the court and the party allied with it made good use of these 60 or so dependable placemen. Placemen helped the Tories remove the Sacheverell clause from the Corporation Bill in 1690, raise 65,000 men for the war in 1691, defeat a new Treason Bill in 1692, and elect Harley Speaker in 1701.[46] And when the Whigs in turn allied with the court, they used placemen to establish the bank, to lower the price of guineas, to pass Fenwick's attainder, and to prevent the revival of the impeachments of the Whig lords.[47] But though the courtiers could help in these ways, they could not withstand the tide of popular opinion. Placemen could not prevent the House of Commons from appropriating supplies, from establishing Commissions of Accounts, from passing Triennial and Place Bills, from seizing forfeited lands in Ireland, from reducing the army to 7,000, and from taking the Dutch Guard from William. One hundred twenty placemen allegedly opposed the disbanding of the Dutch Guard and the reduction of the army to 7,000 men, but the king lost both measures.[48]

The placemen were manifestly not numerous enough to carry unpopular measures for the king. Were they numerous enough to allow him to maintain in office ministers of his own choice? At heart, William was a trimmer, who sought in 1689 to govern through a mixed ministry, but the rage of parties in 1690 forced him to give up his attempts to govern through a mixed ministry.[49] He therefore chose to govern through a coalition of Tories and placemen. The earl of Danby, now the marquis of Carmarthen, organized the placemen with the help of Sir John Trevor, William Jephson, and Henry Guy, but these practitioners of the Carmarthen art (as the corruption of men by place and pension came to be called) were unable to sustain the new ministry for long, even though the number of placemen rose to 130, and even though William bought off Sir Edward Seymour with a place.[50] By the spring of 1693 military defeats abroad had thoroughly discredited the ministry. To rescue William from this impasse the earl of Sunderland, who had crept back to England in 1690, advised him to make a greater use of the power of patronage: make Mulgrave a marquis, give Brandon a regiment, fix men with money; but, he added, do nothing to alter the balance between Whig and Tory or to injure the prerogative.[51] It was advice consonant with his advice to James II to rely upon his two hundred servants in Parliament, and it was advice whose wisdom J. P. Kenyon has praised.[52] But Kenyon fails to see that the destruction of the English Straits Fleet in July 1693 transformed a plan to save the ministry by the power of patronage into a plan to save it by the power of party, the Whig party.[53] The marquisate promised Mulgrave and the regiment promised Brandon counted for little in the politics of 1693, but the dismissal of Nottingham and the appointment of Russell and Montagu, both Whigs, counted for nearly everything. William did not wish to dismiss Nottingham, but he had to, for the placemen in the House could not, and the Whigs could, secure him the £5 million he needed to carry on the war.[54]

Having secured a foothold in the ministry in 1693, the Whigs went on to secure a near monopoly of the ministry by 1697. They also went on to seize the power of patronage itself. Over Godolphin's objections they brought Whigs into the excise and customs commissions.[55] Over Henry Guy's objections, they brought Littleton, not Duncombe, into the treasury.[56] Lord Somers demanded the right to recommend men to offices of law.[57] And when the earl of Sunderland smuggled Vernon into a secretaryship, the Whigs connived at the earl's downfall.[58] By 1697 there were some seventy-five Whig placemen in the House of Commons.[59] When the Tories, in turn, gained power, they also proved more eager to capture than to destroy the power of patronage. Robert Harley himself, the great enemy of placemen, chastised William for not commanding his servants to support a motion to apply Mary of Modena's jointure to public uses.[60] There are few phenomena in English history which historians have so egregiously ignored, so totally overlooked, as the capture of patronage by party.

The Whigs, and the Tories after them, were able to force the closet and to capture the power of patronage, because they governed in the House of Commons; and they were able to govern in the House of Commons because of the force of party. Henry Horwitz, I. F. Burton, P. W. J. Riley, and Ted Rowlands, in two cogent articles, have thoroughly documented the fact of party and have shown how it influenced the votes of members of Parliament.[61] But they have overlooked one important emanation of party spirit: the willingness of men to resign from, or refuse to accept, office if those of another party were employed. In *The Growth of Political Stability,* J. H. Plumb writes: "Men in politics in this period obeyed their monarch's command to serve. If offered an office they accepted it, and stayed until dismissed."[62] The facts of William's reign suggest otherwise. Shrewsbury resigned in 1690 because William turned to the Tories. Edward Russell resigned as admiral in 1693 rather than take orders from Nottingham. Lord Cornwallis and Sir Richard Onslow resigned from the Admiralty Board because the command of the fleet was entrusted to Tory admirals. Sir John Lowther resigned as vice-chamberlain in 1694 because William turned to the Whigs. Sir William Trumbull resigned in 1697 because he had no say in patronage matters. In 1699 Edward Russell, now Lord Orford, resigned because Admiral Rooke continued at the Admiralty Board. And Godolphin in 1701 resigned from the treasury the moment William announced his decision to dissolve Parliament.[63] Nothing circumscribed William's free choice of ministers more than the refusal of members of one party to serve with those of the other. "Trimming between parties is beneath you," Thomas Wharton told William; and Carmarthen declared it to be "the most destructive method your Majesty can take."[64]

William could not, therefore, by parliamentary management maintain in power ministers of his own choice. Could he, however, by electoral management secure them a majority in a new House of Commons? Betty Kemp has written that electoral defeat for the king's ministers was impossible before the decline of patronage after 1784, and G. N. Clark has asserted that in a general election it was the invariable fact "that the government automatically got a majority."[65] These assertions do not accord with the facts of political life during William's reign. In the first place, William declined to intervene actively in election campaigns. In 1690, for example, he waited until after the election before he

named a new treasury commission and altered the London lieutenancy. In 1695 he altered no commissions of peace to help the
Whigs win a victory, though once they had consolidated their
power in 1696 he allowed them to restore Tories to the commissions of peace.[66] In the second place, William's intervention was
not decisive when it did occur. William brought the Tories into
office in the autumn of 1700, but the Tories then failed to achieve
the sweeping victory they had anticipated. In the autumn of 1701
William turned to the Whigs, but his halfhearted support for
them proved ineffective. In truth, it was not royal influence but
private patronage and party loyalties that determined the results
of elections. Toward the end of the reign, royal intervention
might even have been harmful. A placard in Buckinghamshire in
1698 read, "No Courtier, No Pensioner, No Judas."[67]

The pattern of politics that emerged in the reign of King William continued in the reign of Queen Anne.[68] From 120 to 140
placemen regularly sat in the House of Commons, about one-fifth
to one-fourth of the House. The proportion in the Lords was
larger, about 40 percent. But many placemen held offices for
life; many others allowed their loyalty to party to triumph over
their duty to the court. Defections were numerous. Over the handling of the Scottish Plot, Somerset, the master of the horse,
attacked Nottingham, his fellow councillor. Seymour, comptroller of the household, joined the opposition to a proposed grant to
Marlborough, captain-general of the Forces. In 1705 twenty Tory
placemen refused to vote for the court nominee for Speaker. In
1708 the solicitor general declined to defend the government's
Spanish policy. And in 1711 twenty-one Whig placemen voted
against the policy of abandoning Spain. In effect, the court could
only count on the support of fifty or sixty of the queen's servants.[69]

These fifty or sixty servants did, on occasion, prove useful. In
1704 the queen's servants, well drilled by Godolphin, ensured the
defeat of the Tack.[70] Without the votes of twenty-seven Tory
placemen, Smith could not have defeated Bromley for the Speakership in 1705.[71] Yet there were other times when the placemen
were too few or too rebellious to be effective. In 1704 they failed,
though it was within their power, to prevent the condemnation of
a "Peace without Spain."[72] It is a striking advertisement of the
weakness of patronage and the strength of party that Robert Harley could carry the peace in the Commons, where the placemen

were few and the Tories many, but not in the Lords, where the placemen were many and the Tories few. Only after the queen had created twelve new Tory peers could she win in the Lords. On the whole, the placemen in Parliament could only carry those measures that divided men into two nearly equal camps.

Men mattered as much as measures in the reign of Queen Anne, which posed the problem: could the queen name ministers of her own choice and, through the power of patronage, find them support in Parliament? The queen and her immediate ministers, her managers, certainly believed that it was her rightful prerogative to choose her own ministers. Their favorite expedient for accomplishing this purpose was government by mixed ministries, that is, by ministries composed of moderate Tories, moderate Whigs, and courtiers. The queen's managers made three attempts during her reign to govern by mixed ministries, in 1702, in 1705, and in 1710. They all failed.

In the spring of 1702, Godolphin and Marlborough hoped to govern with a ministry that was mutually acceptable to both parties, but the importunate demands of the Tories and a Tory victory at the polls (giving them a majority of 133) wrecked their scheme.[73] It soon became obvious that a "moderating scheme" could only succeed if the two parties were evenly balanced, which is exactly what happened in the general election of 1705. The voters returned 205 Tories, 160 Whigs, and 85 placemen. John Eyles promptly wrote that "the Whig and Tories are equal, so that the placemen will turn the balance," and Robert Harley rejoiced that no party could carry it without the queen's servants joining them.[74] But Harley's hopes that the moderate Tories would join with the court and the Whigs to support the government were soon dashed. Only about two dozen moderate Tories supported the court nominee for Speaker, and during the ensuing session the Tories repeatedly attacked the government, thus forcing Godolphin and Marlborough to fall back upon the Whigs.[75]

Robert Harley's opportunity came in 1710, when he won the queen's favor and supplanted Godolphin and Marlborough as the queen's manager. He now promised Queen Anne that he would, by creating a mixed ministry, rescue her from the tyranny of party. The new creed was that persons and parties should come to the queen, not the queen to them.[76] In pursuance of this scheme, Harley offered places on the Treasury Board to two Whigs, Richard Hampden and Jack Smith. They refused.[77] A month later, in September, Harley implored Lord Cowper and Henry Boyle to remain in office. They also refused. Harley brought intense pressure on Cowper, but Cowper answered that "things were plainly put into Tory hands, a Whig game, either in whole or in part, impracticable; that to keep in, when all my friends were out, would be infamous."[78] The next day Lords Wharton and Orford resigned. When he presented his resignation to the queen, Lord Wharton declared that he could not serve with honor in the company of men who were taking measures contrary to those he had always pursued. Lord Halifax put it more graphically: to mix Tories and Whigs was to mix oil and vinegar.[79]

The passions of party, allied to the practice of resigning, had destroyed Harley's dream of a mixed ministry. He was forced to go upon a Tory bottom, though he did not give up dreaming. He wrote to Newcastle in September: "As soon as the Queen has shewn strength and ability to give the law to both sides, then will moderation be truly shewn in the exercise of power without regard to parties only."[80] But Harley lived in a dream world, for just eight months later the House of Commons formally condemned those ministers who "framed to themselves wild and unwarrantable schemes of balancing parties."[81]

In his British Politics in the Age of Anne, Geoffrey Holmes recognizes the impracticability of mixed ministries, but he goes on to argue that the managers, drawing on the reserves of power which still remained in the crown, constructed and managed the queen's ministries, not as servants of party, but as servants of the queen. By organizing the court interest in Parliament and by forming a partnership with that party whose policies more closely corresponded to royal policy, they were able to harness the power of party to the purposes of the crown. In this way they provided the crown with the most effective means of managing Parliament that it had possessed since 1603. The managers were the key figures; the party leaders were the junior partners. Under no circumstances should the party leaders be allowed to force themselves on the sovereign by exploiting their parliamentary strength.[82] It is worth asking how much truth there is in this picture.

In the reign of Queen Anne there were three instances of such a partnership between the court interest and a party interest. The first occurred between the years 1702 and 1704, when Godolphin and Marlborough allied with the Tory party. But it collapsed when Rochester and Nottingham discovered that Godolphin did not intend to purge the remaining Whigs from government or to promote a Bill against Occasional Conformity. They were unwilling to be junior partners in the firm. Rochester resigned in 1703 when the queen ordered him to take up his duties in Ireland.[83] Nottingham resigned in 1704 when the queen refused his demand that she remove Devonshire and Somerset, two Whig peers, from the cabinet.[84] The managers were forced to rely upon the Whigs, who, indeed, were far readier to vote supplies for the war in France than were the High Tories. After the fierce contest between Smith and Bromley for the Speakership in November 1705, the Whigs became the junior partners in the alliance between court and party.[85] The court was now in a stronger position than ever, for the placemen, some sixty strong, held the balance. It was clearly the power of patronage that gave Godolphin and Marlborough the option to choose to ally with the Whigs rather than with the Tories, for the Whigs could never have carried it alone in a house that had about twenty-one more Tories than Whigs.[86]

In the next three years, however, Whig strength steadily grew as a result of their astonishing unity (and some disputed election returns). Geoffrey Holmes has shown that throughout Queen Anne's reign only ten Whigs in the Commons ever (according to extant division lists) voted against their party and only three Whig peers ever left a proxy with a Tory peer.[87] The Whigs met at Bolton House, dined at the Kit-Kat, and employed court whips to secure the attendance of their members at Parliament. "Though they hate one another," wrote Robert Harley of the Whigs, "yet they unite together to carry on their designs."[88] Their designs were not to alter the policies of the government, for here they were at one with the managers in desiring a vigorous prosecution of the war.[89] Their designs, rather, were to gain high office and to capture the power of patronage. The queen resisted these designs with a vehemence and stubbornness that Geoffrey Holmes has fully illuminated, but it must be recorded that in every case the power of party prevailed over the influence of the crown. In 1705 the Queen named Cowper lord keeper, though she wished to name a moderate Tory.[90] In 1706 she named Sunderland secretary of state, though she swore it would make her a prisoner of party.[91] In 1708 she named Somers and Wharton to the cabinet, though she declared it would be her "utter destruction."[92] And in 1709 she reluctantly agreed that Orford should go to the admiralty.

Nor was it merely high office that the Whigs sought. They also sought to capture the power of patronage. Cowper agreed to serve as lord keeper only because of the extensive clerical patronage that it brought, and Lord Orford demanded the right to purge the admiralty of all officials whom he thought insufficient.[93] When Queen Anne, in the summer of 1707, named two Tory clergymen to bishoprics, the Whigs protested long and loudly and opposed the government that winter in both the Lords and Commons.[94] The parliamentary session of 1707-08 was one of the most tumultuous of Queen Anne's reign, largely because the Whigs played a cat-and-mouse game with the government. They would join with the Tories to censure the government, then rally behind the government to defend it. By showing their power to do both good and ill, they persuaded the managers that they must rely upon the Whigs. Queen Anne even promised the Whigs that in the future she would heed their wishes in making clerical appointments.[95] The results of the general election of 1708 guaranteed the dependence of the managers on the Whigs. The Whigs won a majority of sixty-nine and the placemen ceased to hold the balance. By 1709 the junior partners had taken over the firm.

The same story repeated itself when Robert Harley in September 1710 entered into a partnership with the Tories. It was his declared purpose to pursue moderation, to continue Whigs in office, to retain control of patronage, and to free the queen from the tyranny of party. But he found it impossible to manage Parliament without yielding to the High Tories, who in the winter of 1711 formed the October Club. In early February the club had 70 members, by March, 100, by April, 150. They met weekly at the Bell Tavern; they agreed to act as one body in the Commons; they demanded the purge of all Whigs from office.[96] Robert Harley had declared it to be his creed that parties were to come in to the queen, not the queen in to parties. Sir Arthur Kaye, a member of the October Club, now announced the opposite creed: the purpose of the October Club, he declared, was "to make the ministry in a great measure come in to us."[97] Or as Bromley wrote Harley in 1711: "our Constitution in Church and State" can only be protected "by putting power in the hands of our friends."[98] To prove their point the Tories were even willing to oppose putting an excise on leather.[99]

As a result, Harley, now the earl of Oxford, retreated. He brought Nottingham's nephew, son-in-law, and cousin into office, thus showing how patronage might be used to cement a party. By September 1711 the cabinet was wholly Tory. By January 1712 all the commissioners of the customs were Tory. In June 1712 five more Tories were brought into office.[100] These changes caused the October Club to dwindle in size, but the Hanoverian Tories, some seventy strong, led by Sir Thomas Hanmer, took their place. In 1713 they defeated the Treaty of Commerce with France by joining with the Whigs in voting against it. Edward Harley, Robert's brother, declared that this vote showed the folly of depending on any party, but William Bishop concluded quite otherwise. "You see," he wrote Dr. Charlett, "what comes of Trimming it betwixt two parties; neither cares for you."[101] William Bishop was nearer the mark than Edward Harley, for the Hanoverian Tories openly confessed that they had opposed the treaty because Oxford had not purged the commissions of peace, the excisemen, and the collectors of the customs of Whigs, as he had promised to do twenty times over.[102] That summer Oxford brought yet more Tories into office and that autumn the Tories won a landslide at the polls, securing 363 seats to the Whig 150. Oxford once again removed more Whigs from office. A scheme of administration which had begun as a scheme to rescue the queen from party had become a scheme to bind her to a party. During these four years she did not, to my knowledge, name a single Whig to office. When it was rumored in 1711 that she might name Cowper and Somers to the cabinet, the Tories erupted in anger and the queen desisted. The Tory party had captured the power of patronage.[103]

There remains the question: could the queen—as Kemp and Walcott and Foord assert—name ministers of her own choice and then secure them a majority in the next election?[104] Jonathan Swift thought she could, writing in 1711 that the queen might, after a dissolution, obtain any kind of majority she liked. Lord Cowper told George I that it was wholly within his power, by showing his favor to one or the other party to give them a clear majority.[105] But their remarks only show how mistaken contemporaries can be about their own age. To begin with, the number of members returned from government boroughs was not as large as Robert Walcott has estimated. He found twenty-four such boroughs, returning forty-eight members. Yet in the year 1717, the year of the greatest court and Tory triumph of the reign, twenty Whigs were returned from these twenty-four boroughs.[106] Nor can the rigging of commissions of peace and lieutenancies explain the great swings in voting which occurred during these years. The Tories purged the commissions in 1704, *after* their electoral victory in 1702; and the Whigs altered them in 1708, *after* their victory that year.[107] The inactivity of the government was proverbial. The Tories in 1702 and the Whigs in 1705 complained of the little help given them by the government. In 1708 Sir John Cropley, a Whig, wrote that the ministers would not venture to be concerned in any elections.[108] Robert Harley in 1710 gave little support to the Tories, since a House of Commons dominated by a Tory majority would be unmanageable.[109]

The true explanation for the election results of these years lies, as W. A. Speck has shown, in an electorate divided along party lines, in the existence of a substantial floating vote, and in campaigns waged on controversial issues. The pull of party can best be seen in those constituencies where four candidates stood, two on the Tory interest and two on the Whig interest. In such constituencies the votes were solidly cast in appropriate pairs. It was the floating vote, of course, which accounted for the swings in the results, swings as high as 24 percent. These floating voters responded to the issues of the day. The queen's accession in 1702, the Tack in 1705, the abortive Jacobite invasion in 1708, and the Sachevell impeachment in 1710 swayed the voters of England to turn to the Tories, then to the Whigs, then to the Tories again.[110]

The general election of 1705 provides a test case. The court used its influence to defeat the Tackers and return moderate Tories. The court's Whig allies were content to brand all Tories whatever as Tackers. The result was the return of ninety Tackers and many other Tories who followed their lead—thus driving the government to rely on the Whigs. "So far from Government policy dictating the outcome of a General Election," writes W. A. Speck, "the result of the 1705 election dictated government policy."[111]

During the past fifteen years Henry Horwitz, I. F. Burton, P. W. J. Riley, Ted Rowlands, W. A. Speck, Geoffrey Holmes, and J. H. Plumb have demolished Robert Walcott's picture of connections and cousinhoods, and have demonstrated the reality, the ubiquity, and the vehemence of party. But these historians, particularly Geoffrey Holmes and J. H. Plumb, have been reluctant to admit that the rage of party lessened the power of the crown. They have chronicled the growth of parties but have not described the consequences of that growth. Geoffrey Holmes speaks of "the great reserves of power latent in the Crown," and of "the Queen's jealous care for her prerogative." He declares, "It remained the Queen's undoubted prerogative to appoint, retain, and dismiss ministers at her own pleasure, and not at the whim of whichever party the triennial seesaw had temporarily placed in the ascendant." To prove this assertion he cites the dismissal of Nottingham, Jersey, and Seymour in 1704, at a time when they controlled Parliament, and the dismissal of Godolphin and the Whigs in 1710, at a time when they had a substantial majority in the Commons.[112] But Holmes overlooks the fact that the High Tories lost control of the Commons in November 1704 and that the Whigs lost their majority in October 1711. The political crisis of 1710 is crucial to Holmes's argument. He maintains that Godolphin and the Whigs fell from power then because, though they had a majority in the Commons, they had lost the countenance of the queen, a loss which spelled death to the political ambitions of any minister.[113] This reading of the crisis, however, overlooks the fact that the Whigs were so frightened by the prospect of a dissolution of Parliament and defeat at the polls that they did not offer their collective resignation, as they had in 1708. In 1708 Robert Harley enjoyed the countenance of the queen to the fullest, but had insufficient support in the Commons and in the nation. He therefore met defeat.[114] In 1710, because of war weariness and anger at Sacheverell's impeachment, he enjoyed both the nation's and the queen's support. Every political observer that summer concluded that a new ministry meant a new Parliament.[115] Harley himself finally saw this truth and advised the queen to dissolve Parliament, whereupon the Whig Lord Wharton said to the Tory Lord Dartmouth, "If you have the majority, we are undone, if we have the majority, you are broke."[116]

J. H. Plumb's account of these years is less misleading than

Holmes's only because it is more enigmatic. In *The Growth of Political Stability* he repeatedly speaks of the executive gaining control over the legislature, but he leaves it unclear whether he means by "the executive" the crown or the ministry. On the whole, I think one must assume he means the crown or court, as when he writes: "Over the long term the control of Parliament could be achieved in three ways: by building up a Court party powerful enough to dominate the Commons among those elected; by making certain of obtaining a Court-tied majority through electoral management; or by a mixture of both."[117] Now, the curious fact is that though he devotes many pages to a discussion of place bills, though he asserts that it was only through the spoils system that Harley achieved and maintained power, and though he declares that the growth of the executive allowed William and Anne to begin to win back the initiative in the House of Commons, he offers almost no evidence to prove these assertions.[118] Similarly, though he writes about the remodeling of corporation charters and though he implies that court patronage secured a Whig Parliament in 1715, he offers no evidence that the court, and not party, carried this and other elections.[119]

The strangest fact about *The Growth of Political Stability* is that in it Plumb speaks often about the rage of party, yet never entertains the idea that party could capture patronage, could seize the executive, could make the monarch a prisoner of party. He rightly sees that single-party government brought political stability to England, but he does not see that it severely checked the monarch's liberty to choose his or her own servants.[120] But though Plumb does not see this, William III and Queen Anne did. William struggled his entire reign to trim between parties and to escape servitude to any one party.[121] And Queen Anne knew better than many modern historians how destructive to her power was the rage of parties. To give the seals to Cowper, she declared, would be to put her insensibly in the power of the Whigs. To name Sunderland secretary would be to put herself "in the power of one set of men." To employ Somers would be her "utter destruction." She prayed for liberation from "the merciless men of both parties."[122] But Cowper received the seals, Sunderland became secretary, and Somers entered the cabinet.

The conclusions that emerge from this essay are five in number. First, the power of patronage in later Stuart England was feeble, a frail reed, certainly too feeble to carry unpopular measures in Parliament or to support unpopular ministers there. Though there were some 120 placemen in most Parliaments, the court could depend upon only about 60 of them. Second, the power of patronage nevertheless did have its uses. It could carry measures through a divided House and it could support ministers when there was a balance of parties. Above all, it was a cement holding together the party with whom the court allied, be it the Church party or the Tory party or the Whig party. Third, in later Stuart England the power of party overwhelmed the power of patronage. It did so not only in the consistent voting of members of Parliament but in the practice of party leaders resigning from, or refusing to accept, office because the monarch employed men of another party. The practice of resigning or refusing to serve deeply eroded the monarch's liberty to govern through mixed ministries. Fourth, the use of the power of patronage in electoral management proved no more effectual than in parliamentary management. Party loyalties, local ties, and controversial issues determined the outcome of elections in these years, not the intervention of the court. And last, during these years political parties went far toward capturing the power of patronage itself. This did not mean that the monarch could no longer name men to office, but it did mean that the monarch could do so only within limits set down by party.

The passions of party, the practice of reigning, and the capture of patronage severely checked the power of the crown in these years. The crown continued to exercise a vast discretionary power in the field of daily administration, but once a decision or a policy caught the attention of Parliament, the crown could oppose to the passions of party only the frail power of patronage. In this sphere, and for these years, the old-fashioned Whig model undoubtedly fits the facts more closely than the newfangled Namier model.

NOTES

1. William Babington Macaulay, *The History of England* (London, 1849-61); George Macaulay Trevelyan, *England Under the Stuarts* (London, 1904); Mark A. Thomson, *A Constitutional History of England 1642 to 1801* (London, 1938); David Ogg, *England in the Reigns of James II and William III* (Oxford, 1955).

2. Betty Kemp, *King and Commons 1660-1832* (London, 1957); Robert Walcott, *English Politics in the Early Eighteenth Century* (Cambridge, Mass., 1956); J. P. Kenyon, *Robert Spencer Earl of Sunderland 1641-1702* (London, 1958); Archibald S. Foord, *His Majesty's Opposition 1714-1830* (Oxford, 1964). G. R. Elton has summarized the Namierite view in a chapter on "Parliament" in his *Studies in Tudor and Stuart Politics and Government* (Cambridge, 1974), II, 161-162. He writes: "It is not true that 1688 produced a system in which the Crown was controlled by the Commons and the Commons were controlled by a majority party elected by the nation (however that last term may be qualified); no respectable historian would nowadays suppose so, though the interpretative scheme still in use depended on the notion. All the work of the last thirty-five years, stemming largely from Namier's original researches, has tended to show us a very different picture by stressing how very unlike those parties of the seventeenth and eighteenth centuries were to what developed after 1800. But the consequences of what by now is a commonplace still do not seem to have been drawn. We know that after 1688 the king continued to be in control of 'the Executive,' continued to govern in person or through ministers whom he chose. We know that he required reasonably regular support in the Commons and endeavoured to obtain it through the use of a Crown interest in the House round which temporary government 'parties' was intermittent and inconsistent, and that the bulk of those not connected with government behaved according to the name of independents on which they prided themselves. In other words, after 1688 (and in great measure also between 1660 and 1688) constitutional peace and the carrying on of the king's government depended on the reasonable cooperation, in Parliament, of kings, Lords and Commons, and this cooperation was achieved by the management of opinion and business provided by the government."

3. Joel Hurstfield, "Was There a Tudor Despotism After All," *Transactions of the Royal Historical Society*, 5th Series, XVII (1967), 101 (hereafter cited as *Tr. Royal Hist. Soc.*).

4. J. E. Neale, *The Elizabethan House of Commons* (London, 1949), pp. 270-288.

5. J. E. Neale, *Elizabeth and Her Parliaments*, II, 243, 370-371; David Willson, *The Privy Councillors in the House of Commons* (Minneapolis, 1940), pp. 104-105, 117, 119-120.

6. James Spedding, *The Life and Letters of Francis Bacon* (London, 1857-1874), IV, 279-280, 365-368, 370, 381.

7. Menna Prestwich, *Cranfield* (Oxford, 1966), pp. 136-146, 287-289, 432-436, 483.

8. Thomas Moir (*The Addled Parliament of 1614* [Oxford, 1958], pp. 56-57) states that there were 160 officials and courtiers in the House. Of these 60 were officials, 65 courtiers or ceremonial officials, and 31 relatives or clients of officials. Mary Frear Keeler (*The Long Parliament* [Philadelphia, 1954], p. 21) found 27 officials and 22 courtiers in the Long Parliament.

9. J. R. Jones, "Court Dependents in 1664," *Bulletin of the Institute of Historical Research* 34, 81-83 (hereafter cited as *BIHR*).

10. During the Convention Parliament Philip Wharton drew up a list of 23 staunch Presbyterian members, who were to manage 121 other Presbyterian members; he also listed 9 members who were to manage 90 members (some to manage 7 or 8; Wharton himself to manage 29). See G. F. Trevallyn Jones, "The Composition and Leadership of the Presbyterian Party in the Convention," *The English Historical Review* LXXIX (1964), 312, 318-320 (hereafter cited as *EHR*).

11. Mark Kishlansky, "The Emergence of Adversary Politics in the Long Parliament," *The Journal of Modern History* 49 (1977), 628-640.

12. Anchitell Grey, *Debates of the House of Commons from the Year 1667 to the Year 1694* (London, 1769), III, 53-58.

13. Both lists are published in E. S. de Beer, "Members of the Court Party in the House of Commons, 1670-1678," *BIHR* XI (1933-34), 1-23.

14. Ibid.

15. Andrew Browning, "Parties and Party Organization in the Reign of Charles II," *Tr. Royal Hist. Soc.*, 4th series, XXX (1948), 34; K. H. D. Haley, *The First Earl of Shaftesbury* (London, 1968), p. 27. David Ogg points out (*England in the Reign of Charles II* [Oxford, 1934], I, 589-590) that some of these excise pensioners were merely previous farmers of the excise who were bought out in 1675.

16. *Commons' Journal* IX, 373-374. Kenneth Haley observes (*Shaftesbury*, p. 398): "Danby's pensions had not, after all, been sufficient to sway the 'Pensionary Parliament.'"

17. Andrew Browning, ed., *The Memoirs of Sir John Reresby* (Glasgow, 1936), pp. 114-115.

18. Osmund Airy, ed., *The Lauderdale Papers* (Camden Society, 1885), III, 131, 133.

19. Barillon to Louis XIV, French Transcripts, Public Record Office, 23 December 1678/2 January 1679; Robert Southwell to the Duke of Ormond, Bodleian Library, Carte MSS 38, f. 682v.

20. Wilbur Curtis Abbott, "The Long Parliament of Charles II," *EHR* XXI (1906), 273-275.

21. *The Diary of Samuel Pepys*, edited by Robert Latham and William Matthews (Berkeley, Los Angeles, London, 1970-1975), IX, 9-10.

22. Browning, "Parties and Party Organization," *Tr. Royal Hist. Soc.*, 4th ser., XXX, 27.

23. Sir William Temple, a distant cousin, wrote in October 1673 that the court's only unofficial spokesmen in the House were Sir Robert Carr and Sir Richard Temple, "who are the worst heard that can be in the House, especially the last." See *Essex Papers*, ed. Osmond Airy (London: Camden Society, 1890), I, 132.

24. Colbert de Croissy to Louis XIV, French Transcripts, Public Record Office, 7/17 June 1669.

25. *The Works of Sir William Temple, Bart.* (Edinburgh, 1754), II, 429.

26. Browning, "Parties and Party Organization," *Tr. Royal Hist. Soc.,* 4th ser., XXX, 33.

27. J. R. Jones, "Shaftesbury's Worthy Men," *BIHR* XXX (1957), 233.

28. Andrew Browning and Doreen Milne, "An Exclusion Bill Division List," *BIHR* XXIII (1950), 207.

29. Ogg, *Reign of Charles II,* II, 483.

30. J. H. Plumb, *The Growth of Political Stability in England 1675-1725* (London, 1967), p. 34.

31. Abbott, "The Long Parliament of Charles II," *EHR* XXI, 281.

32. Ibid., pp. 262, 278, 281. For Charles's success in 1670 and 1671 see Denis Witcomb, *The Cavalier House of Commons* (Manchester, 1966), pp. 98-103.

33. Browning, "Parties and Party Organization," *Tr. Royal Hist. Soc.,* 4th ser., XXX, 26.

34. Kenyon, *Sunderland,* pp. 146-147; Henry Horwitz, *Parliament, Policy and Politics in the Reign of William III* (Manchester: Manchester University Press, 1977), p. 4.

35. J. R. Western, *Monarchy and Revolution* (Totowa, N.J., 1972), pp. 221-224. Betty Kemp (*King and Commons,* p. 21), Mark Thomson (*Constitutional History,* p. 63), and David Ogg (*Reign of Charles II,* p. 476) concur that the remodeling of the boroughs did little to strengthen the local influence of the crown, and may have strengthened the local influence of the nobility.

36. Plumb, *Growth of Political Stability,* pp. xv-xvi.

37. Horwitz, *Parliament, Policy and Politics,* pp. 102 n. 66, 109, 124, 237, 313, 359.

38. *Calendar of State Papers Domestic, 1698,* p. 376.

39. James Lowther to Sir John Lowther, 6 January 1699, Lonsdale MSS, Cumberland Record Office, Kendal.

40. Horwitz, *Parliament, Policy and Politics,* p. 99.

41. Ibid., 109; Robert Yard to Sir William Colt, December 16, 1692, B.L. Add. MSS 34,096, f. 39v; Leopold von Ranke, *History of England* (Oxford, 1875), VI, 198.

42. Denis Rubini, *Court and Country 1688-1702* (London, 1967), pp. 111-112; Horwitz, *Parliament, Policy and Politics,* p. 217.

43. Historical Manuscript Commission Reports, *Portland MSS,* III, 595 (hereafter cited as H.M.C.); G. P. R. James, ed., *Letters Illustrative of the Reign of William III from 1696 to 1708 Addressed to the Duke of Shrewsbury by James Vernon, Esq. Secretary of State* (London, 1841), I, 461.

44. James Lowther to Sir John Lowther, 30 December 1701, Lonsdale MSS., Cumberland Record Office, Kendal.

45. Rubini (*Court and Country,* p. 267) calculates that in the last session of the 1690-1695 Parliament 42 percent of the placemen were in opposition (50 out of 117).

46. Horwitz, *Parliament, Policy and Politics,* pp. 42, 72, 74, 281. Of

the vote to grant the king 54,562 soldiers in 1692, Robert Harley wrote (3 December 1692, B.L. Loan 29/186, f. 223): "The weight of the debate on one side [the country] lay upon seven or eight at the most against all the place men on the other side. Though they have gained this point I hope we have done the parts of honest men. . . . They did not pretend to answer, but carryd all by their perchased votes."

47. Horwitz, *Parliament, Policy and Politics,* pp. 129-132, 177, 186, 301-302.

48. Robert Price to the Duke of Beaufort, 19 January 1698/9, Bodleian, Carte MSS. 130, f. 397.

49. To Halifax William declared, I must "absolutely go upon the bottom of the trimmers, that is the good foot." See Helen Foxcroft, *Halifax* (London, 1898), II, 230. For examples of William's balancing between parties see Stephen Baxter, *William III* (London, 1966), pp. 269-270, 278, 296, 309, 377, 394-395.

50. Andrew Browning, *Thomas Osborne, Earl of Danby and Duke Leeds* (Glasgow, 1944-1951), III, 178-179.

51. Sunderland to Portland, 20 June 1693, Japikse, *Correspondentie van Willem III en van Hans Willem Bentinck* (Hague, 1928), II, 38-39; Sunderland to Portland 19 July 1693, Portland Papers PwA 1222, University of Nottingham.

52. J. P. Kenyon, "The Earl of Sunderland and the King's Administration, 1693-5," *EHR* LXXI (1956), 577-588.

53. Kenyon suggests (ibid., pp. 580, 584) that even before the Straits Fleet was destroyed Sunderland had urged William to employ the Whigs and dismiss Nottingham. I can find no evidence for this.

54. William to Heinsius, 3 November 1693, B.L. Add MSS. 34,504, f. 130; Queen Mary wrote (R. Doebner, *Memoirs of Mary, Queen of England* [Leipzig, 1886], p. 61), the King was forced to "part with Lord Nottingham to please a party who[m] he cannot trust."

55. *Calendar of State Papers Domestic,* 1694-5, pp. 179-186; Narcissus Luttrell, *Brief Relations* (Oxford, 1857), III, 353.

56. Guy to Portland, 31 May 1695, Portland Papers, PwA 502, University of Nottingham; Luttrell, *Brief Relations,* III, 467, 469.

57. Philip Yorke, Earl of Hardwicke, *Miscellaneous State Papers* (London, 1778), II, 426-428.

58. *Vernon Correspondence,* I, 446, 448.

59. Horwitz, *Parliament, Policy and Politics,* p. 210.

60. Harley Memoirs, B.L. Add. Mss 34,515, fols. 10-11v.

61. Henry Horwitz, "Parties, Connections, and Parliamentary Politics, 1689-1714: Review and Revisions," *Journal of British Studies* VI (1967), 45-67; I. F. Burton, P. W. J. Riley, and E. Rowlands, "Political Parties in the Reigns of William III and Anne: the Evidence of the Division Lists," *BIHR,* Special Supplement No. 7, November 1968.

62. Plumb, *Growth of Political Stability,* p. 154.

63. Horwitz, *Parliament, Policy and Politics,* pp. 59, 109, 128, 257, 297; Kenyon, *Sunderland,* pp. 295-296.

64. Sir John Dalrymple, *Memoirs of Great Britain and Ireland* (London, 1790), II, App. 195-196; Horwitz, *Parliament, Policy and Politics,* p. 66.

65. Kemp, *King and Commons,* p. 114; G. N. Clark, *The Later Stuarts* (Oxford, 1934), p. 175.

66. Horwitz, *Parliament, Policy and Politics,* pp. 50-52, 179, 294, 312.

67. Ibid., pp. 238, 280, 313, 315.

68. Geoffrey Holmes, *British Politics in the Reign of Anne* (London, 1967), pp. 353-354, 364-366, 387, 415.

69. Ibid., pp. 347-348, 354-355.

70. Henry Snyder, "The Defeat of the Occasional Conformity Bill and the Tack: a Study in the Technique of Parliamentary Management in the Reign of Queen Anne," *BIHR* XLI (1968), 181-185.

71. W. A. Speck, "The Choice of a Speaker in 1705," *BIHR* XXXVII, no. 95 (1964), 33.

72. Holmes, *British Politics,* pp. 387, 390, 395.

73. W. A. Speck, *Tory and Whig* (London, 1970), p. 113; Holmes, *British Politics,* p. 367.

74. H.M.C., *Portland,* IV, 291; Mr. Eyles to the Earl of Portland, 27 July 1705, Portland Papers, PwA 410, University of Nottingham; Speck, "Choice of a Speaker," *BIHR,* XXXVIII, 34-35.

75. Speck, *Tory and Whig,* pp. 108-109. Godolphin wrote Marlborough that he would have been uneasy at the large number of Tackers had he not known the Queen could depend on the Whigs (ibid.).

76. Lowther to Gilpin, 10 August 1710, Lonsdale MSS., Cumberland Record Office, Kendal; James J. Cartwright, ed., *The Wentworth Papers 1705-1739* (London, 1883), p. 31.

77. Ibid.

78. *The Private Diary of William First Earl Cowper, Lord Chancellor of England* (Eton, 1833), pp. 43-44.

79. Walter Graham, ed., *The Letters of Joseph Addison* (Oxford, 1941), p. 240; Cowper, *Diary,* pp. 11-12.

80. H.M.C., *Portland,* II, 219.

81. *Commons Journal,* XVI, 684.

82. Holmes, *British Politics,* pp. 367-374, 414-416.

83. Gilbert Burnet, *History of His Own Time* (Oxford, 1823), V, 58.

84. Henry Horwitz, *Revolution Politicks* (Cambridge, 1968), pp. 190-198.

85. As W. A. Speck has written ("The Choice of a Speaker," *BIHR,* XXXVII, 35), "Consequently the promotion of Smith for the Chair signified more than a readjustment of groups; it marked a decisive shift in the government's parliamentary policy from a Tory to a Whig scheme."

86. Speck, *Tory and Whig,* p. 113.

87. Holmes, *British Politics,* pp. 34, 45. The three Whig proxies were left with Godolphin at a time when the Whigs were supporting the court.

88. Quoted in Holmes, *British Politics,* p. 248.

89. The Imperial Ambassador wrote in December 1707 (Onno Klopp, *Der Fall Des Hauses Stuart* [Wien, 1875-1888], XIII, 63), "Lord Sunderland and the whole Whig party believe that they have not only won for themselves a great part of the Ministry, but the upper hand in it. In many respects this is not to be doubted. However in what concerns troops and money, if once voted, Marlborough and Godolphin do what they please with it."

90. Winston Churchill, *Marlborough* (London, 1947), II, 29.

91. Ibid., pp. 203-205; Beatrice Brown, ed., *The Letters and Diplomatic Instructions of Queen Anne* (London, 1935), pp. 196-197, 199-200.

92. Brown, *Letters,* p. 246.

93. Cowper, *Diary,* p. 12; Holmes, *British Politics,* p. 112. In Ireland Lord Wharton quarreled furiously with Godolphin over the control of patronage, a quarrel that can be followed in *The Marlborough-Godolphin Correspondence,* edited by Henry Snyder (Oxford, 1975), III, 1248, 1251, 1289, 1299.

94. G. V. Bennett, "Robert Harley, the Godolphin Ministry and the Bishopric Crisis of 1707," *EHR* LXXXII, 730-732.

95. Ibid., pp. 745-746; Cropley to Shaftesbury, 15 December 1707, P.R.O. 30/24/20, 136.

96. Holmes, *British Politics,* pp. 342-343.

97. Cited in Horwitz, *Revolution Politicks,* pp. 226-227.

98. H.M.C., *Portland,* V, 116.

99. *Wentworth Papers,* pp. 189-190; Luttrell, *Brief Relations,* VI, 707.

100. Abel Boyer, *The History of the Reign of Queen Anne Digested into Annals* (London, 1703-1715), X, 225-227; XI, 121; Brydges Papers 57 (Huntington Library), vol. 5, f. 134; H.M.C., *Portland,* III, 417-418, IV, 683-684. These changes led the Earl of Strafford to comment (James Macpherson, *Original Papers* [London, 1775], II, 350), "The Queen saw that reigning by one party was but being a slave to the heads of that party; and therefore when she first made her change, it was positively resolved not to stick to parties, but to those who served her best. However, the other party's opposition and violence may have made her change her mind, for the mere necessity, at this conjecture."

101. Harley Memoirs, B.L. Add. MSS 34,515, f. 162; Ballard MSS (Bodleian Library) 31, f. 104v.

102. Macpherson, *Original Papers,* II, 419-420; George Harris Healey, ed., *The Letters of Daniel Defoe* (Oxford, 1955), pp. 418-419.

103. Holmes, *British Politics,* p. 49.

104. Kemp, *King and Commons,* 42, 76, 113-114, 143-144; Walcott, *English Politics,* pp. 85, 88, 193-194; Foord, *His Majesty's Opposition,* p. 19.

105. Jonathan Swift, *Journal to Stella* (Oxford, 1948), II, 435; Speck, *Tory and Whig,* p. 79.

106. Speck, *Tory and Whig,* p. 73. Party could capture electoral patronage as well as parliamentary. The Tory ministry in 1702 used its interest in the Cinque Ports on behalf of Tories. When the Earl of Westmorland, a Whig, became Deputy Warden, he used the government's influence to return Whigs (ibid., p. 72).

107. Ibid., p. 81.

108. Holmes, *British Politics,* p. 351.

109. Sir John Cropley to Shaftesbury, PRO 30/24/21, f. 52.

110. Speck, *Tory and Whig,* pp. 22, 31, 61, 76-77, 85-87.

111. Ibid., pp. 98-110.

112. Holmes, *British Politics,* pp. 208-209, 346, 414.

113. Ibid., pp. 208-210, 415.

114. W. A. Speck and Geoffrey Holmes, "The Fall of Harley in 1708 Reconsidered," *EHR* LXXX, 673-698; Harry Snyder, "Godolphin and Harley," *The Huntington Library Quarterly,* XXX, 241-271.

115. Such as Peter Wentworth (B.L. Add. MSS 31, 143, f. 486v.), Hoffmann, the Imperial Envoy (Klopp, *Der Fall Des Hauses Stuart,* XIII, 432), Sir Thomas Hanmer (H.M.C., *Bath,* III, 437), Sir John Cropley (17 June 1710, Stanhope MSS. 24/16 at the Kent Record Office), Sir James Brydges (Godfrey Davies and Clara Buck, "Letters on Godolphin's Dismissal in 1710," *The Huntington Library Quarterly* III, 230-231), and Abel Boyer (*Annals,* IX, 235).

116. H.M.C., *Portland,* II, 219.

117. Plumb, *Growth of Political Stability,* p. 33.

118. Ibid., pp. 14, 48-49, 96, 144-151.

119. Ibid., pp. 29, 33-34, 161.

120. Ibid., pp. 126, 148, 152-158, 176.

121. Horwitz, *Parliament, Policy and Politics,* pp. 35, 41, 43, 50, 77, 99, 139, 178, 192, 217, 256-257, 260, 270, 294, 312, 315.

122. Churchill, *Marlborough,* II, 29, 31, 203-205; Beatrice Brown, ed., *The Letters and Diplomatic Instructions of Queen Anne* (London, 1935), pp. 199-200, 246.

VII

NEW LIGHT ON GEORGE I
OF GREAT BRITAIN

Ragnhild M. Hatton

The picture of George I which seems possibly indeliby etched on the minds of English and American students alike is oversimplified to the point of caricature. The lines are few but bold. He was fifty-four years old when he came to the throne, set in his ways, and unable as well as unwilling to adapt to British ways and traditions. He was uninterested in Britain, had not wanted to take on the succession, and spent most of his reign escaping to Hanover, his beloved electorate, for the benefit of which he was prepared to sacrifice the welfare of his kingdom. He knew nothing of the English language, laws, and constitution, and was too old to learn. The only good service he did Britain was, to quote the still current assumption, that owing to his lack of knowledge of English and his general indifference, he contributed, however unwittingly, to the development of the modern cabinet system: since he absented himself from the cabinet, it is argued, he helped along modern constitutional practice. This service was brought about, so goes another version of the story, by his hatred of his son and heir, George Augustus, who did know some English: George I did not wish to rely on his son as interpreter at cabinet meetings and therefore stopped his own attendance. This hatred of the son

213

and heir is thought of as something typically Hanoverian imported into England by George and bequeathed as a tradition for future generations: in his case it went so far as attempts to rob his son of the succession in Great Britain.[1] For the rest, his personality was dull (the "honest blockhead" of Lady Mary Wortley Montagu's characterization is still the favorite summing up);[2] he was lazy; he was content to leave affairs of state to ministers, Bernstorff and Görtz for the electorate, and Stanhope, Sunderland, Townshend, and Walpole for the kingdom. He had no intellectual or artistic interests whatsoever. "Painting, which at this time particularly depended on court patronage, suffered most from the indifference of the first two Georges, but none of the other arts gained from royal attention. Not even music, which both George I and George II enjoyed, could stir them into sympathetic action": so runs a verdict of the 1970s.[3] His personal life was held to be lurid. Had he not had his wife's lover, Count Königsmarck, murdered and the erring spouse, Sophia Dorothea, imprisoned for life in Germany? To England, it was averred, he had brought two favorite mistresses (the thin Maypole or Giraffe, [Ehrengard] Melusine von der Schulenburg, and the fat Sophia Charlotte von Kielmansegg) and had left behind a younger—said to be his favorite—mistress, because she was a Catholic and therefore not acceptable in his Anglican kingdom. One of his reasons for going to Hanover was, it was surmised, to be periodically reunited with her.[4] Quite apart from this little harem, it seemed highly suspicious that George had brought two Turks (Mehemet and Mustafa) with him to England: were they not sinister, there to pander to the king's "depraved tastes" or at best "to cater for his strenuous sex-life"? Even worse, the whole of his Hanoverian retinue, and the king himself, were thought of as greedy and unscrupulous: they sucked England dry and did not mind what means they used to enrich themselves at the cost of Great Britain.[5] In short, there was nothing much to be said for George, except that he was better than the alternative: a Catholic Stuart king brought up in France, who had refused to convert to Anglicanism and was thought more than likely to have absorbed the absolutist ideas of Louis XIV, the host first to his father, the late exiled James II, and then, after 1701, to himself.

Scholars have, at least to some extent, realized in recent years that the caricature picture does not quite fit. Professor J. H.

Plumb has concluded, from his own researches into the career of Robert Walpole and his investigation into the growth of political stability in Engliand between 1675 and 1725, that George had a complex and by no means commonplace mind; and that he was determined and perspicacious enough to prevent the factions inside the cabinet, which had been so typical of the reigns of William III and Queen Anne, from taking control.[6] Plumb's pupil, Professor Beattie, was the first to demonstrate the political aims of George I between 1718 and 1720 from so unlikely a source as the accounts of the royal household.[7] The researches of Professor George Schnath, who has now completed three volumes of his *Geschichte Hannovers* — a fourth is still to come — for the period 1674 to 1714 has by his thorough knowledge of Hanoverian and European archives demonstrated, in this work as well as in his other researches, the political aspects of the divorce of George and Sophia Dorothea in 1694 and has given us new insight not only into George's years as electoral prince but also into his reign as elector up to 1714. Pupils of Professor Schnath, and scholars indebted to him, have also undertaken research that — though not directly focused on George — has been extremely useful.[8] Among my own pupils, Edward C. Gregg, in his study of the Protestant succession in international politics, 1710-1716, and in his published articles, has given definitive proof of George's strong interest in the English succession before 1714;[9] and — in part following my own publications as a prelude to the biography of George I as elector and king — there are now intimations in reviews and general histories that a reevaluation of the reign and the king is expected.[10]

The problem all along, it seems to me, has been the dearth of material that would bring certainty or near certainty in assessing George as a ruler, or, to be more precise, the difficulty of finding the right kind of material to illuminate George's role in government and the decision-making process in general, particularly for the years 1717-1720 when Charles Townshend and Robert Walpole were in opposition. For their periods of office before 1717 and after 1720, the publications of Archdeacon Coxe, printing many letters in full and others in extract, have provided a great deal of significant material. Indeed, the experience of later scholars, when they have gained access to the same private collections, has invariably been that on the whole Coxe had "creamed the field" and had only rarely been too discreet in suppressing embarrassing evidence.[11] But even Coxe was often content in his text to repeat what amounts to gossip, written down long after the events; particularly that which came from the pen and tongue of the youngest son of Robert Walpole, Horace, in his old age. What Horace Walpole has to say from firsthand experience, as, for example, when he as a boy of ten was presented to George and Melusine rings true and can indeed be confirmed from other evidence;[12] but the stories he retells at secondhand have proved highly unreliable.[13] The memoirs of Hervey have been the subject of a critical study by Gerik, and though they have a good deal of factual information derived from his own experience that can be shown to be correct, it would be unwise to trust him on persons and personalities without corroboration.[14] On the whole, it would seem that early sensationalism easily conquers the drabber, if more reliable, evidence that later becomes available. A tendency to make the punishment fit the crime, at a kind of folklore level, also seems to operate: how else can one explain the repetition in English books of recent years of the hoary tale that George's death in June 1727 on his way to Hanover was due to the shock of receiving a letter, on Dutch soil, written by his late divorced wife (who had died in November 1726) in which she prophesied that George would die within a year of her own death?[15]

A similar problem for later writers has been caused by contemporary Jacobite propaganda, which had less effect at the time (and which was of course counteracted by government propaganda) than it has had recently. This Jacobite propaganda concentrated on two themes: George as usurper of the throne and George as a failure and a coward when a military commander. That both contentions made their late mark is shown by several modern books accepting the Jacobite contention that George refrained from touching for the king's evil — a ceremony William III had abandoned and Queen Anne had revived, but which George chose to discontinue — because he himself had doubts about his rights to the throne.[16] At least one military historian has assumed that George lost a battle (that of Rumersheim) at which he was not even present, though I hasten to add that the historian in question does not repeat the Jacobite slur that George and his army ran away.[17] I do not wish to be too hard on those who uncritically perpetuate Jacobite propaganda, contemporary superficial gossip, and late reminiscences. Government propaganda had a harder time of it, as it was on the defensive and could easily be dismissed as panegyrics, then as now. In a period when Britain was war weary after the Nine Years War and the War of the Spanish Succession, there was little point in stressing George's own long military career between 1675 and 1710, both on the western fronts against France and the eastern fronts against Turkey. Moreover there was, of course, a kernel of truth, however twisted, in every one of the accusations or assessments I have mentioned. Königsmarck was murdered, though George was far away and knew nothing about it; there was a divorce in 1694, though at Sophia Dorothea's express desire; there was a quarrel in the royal family between 1717 and 1720 though the French contemporary phrase, *désunion* and the German one, *Verwirrung,* are more accurate as I hope to show; George did have a mistress, Melusine von der Schulenburg, of long standing (whom the family regarded as his morganatic wife, though I incline to the opinion that they were not legally married) and had with her three daughters and a happy family life. The "harem" seems, however, to have been a pure invention; and though the fact (long since known) that Sophia Charlotte von Kielmansegg was George's half sister would not in itself prove that she was not his mistress, we have ample evidence that renders this highly unlikely.[18] Until professional historians can get across to the general reader, the student, and the writer of textbooks the results of their own researches, it would, all the same, be silly and even unfair to complain of such misconceptions and distortions.

The obstacles in the way of serious research on George both as a personality and as a ruler are many. The House of Hanover was only too conscious, after the Prinzenstreit (that terrible struggle of the 1680s and 1690s which tore the family asunder over the question of primogeniture and isolated George from all but one of his brothers, the youngest), the Sophia Dorothea-Königsmarck scandal, and the Electress Sophia's outspoken acceptance that James Edward Stuart was not a supposititious child, of the damage that private letters, when divulged, could cause. After his mother's death, George asked his cousin, Elisabeth Charlotte, duchess of Orleans, to burn those of the late electress' letters that touched on family affairs. After George's own death, his daughter, the queen of Prussia, asked her brother (now George II) to

destroy—after perusal—the letters she had written to her father
and which she knew he had kept in a special box in his closet.[19]
Luckily, some thirty letters that George wrote to his mother and
those he wrote to his daughter after 1714 have survived and tell us
a good deal about him as a person.[20] There proved, on investigation, to be a variety of material—including George's private
accounts between 1698 and 1726—which further helped to illuminate the personality.[21] Less promising for solving the puzzle of
George as a ruler was the fact that his British ministers, and their
relatives, had been nearly as sensitive as the House of Hanover in
respect to keeping diaries and correspondence written in times of
crisis. One example is that of the Cowpers. The diary of William
Cowper, lord chancellor from 1714 to 1718, is not extant after
his appointment;[22] while that of his wife shows a long gap during the estrangement between the Old and the Young Court, and
is known to have suffered destruction for all entries after 1720.
Neither have the surviving portions been published in their entirety.[23] For the period of the quarrel between George I and his
son, however, sufficient letters in the correspondence section of
the Panshanger Papers can be found to demonstrate the efforts at
reconciliation by the Cowpers, Bernstorff, Melusine von der
Schulenburg, and the Gräfin zu Schaumburg-Lippe, a lady in the
confidence of both courts.[24] It is noticeable that little material,
compared with the riches for the earlier part of the archives, has
survived for Sunderland and Stanhope at Blenheim and Chevening. What has been kept at Chevening was for me of great importance, giving evidence of George's direct orders to Stanhope on
issues of foreign policy when the two were prevented by circumstances from daily consultations.[25] The same comparative dearth
of material for given periods can be seen in the Cholmondeley
(Houghton) Papers now deposited at Cambridge University
Library. I well remember my disappointment when I hastened to
search through them, in the expectation of finding proof that
Horatio Walpole, Robert's younger diplomat brother, influenced, or at least gave advice to his more illustratious elder on
issues of foreign policy. He may well have done, but I could not
demonstrate it for George I's reign, since the box that contained
communications from Horatio Walpole before 1727 related to
sentiment, and not high policy: the scrap of paper on which
Horatio, when a student, had written his "I Owe You" for money

lent him by Robert; pleas from Paris by the now middle-aged Horatio that Robert might ride over to Wolterton to see how Horatio's *allée* of trees was getting on and report back to a diplomat abroad homesick for his Norfolk estate. Yet as my search progressed, I picked up some interesting bits and pieces connected with George, and letters from the king's Hanoverian entourage. Bits and pieces is the right phrase: not for Robert Walpole the grand bound volumes of many lesser personages familiar to us from the British Museum but here we have bundles, odd sheets, and brief notes, now sorted into boxes and files.[26] The manuscript collections of the British Museum (or Library as we must now get used to calling it, at least in our footnotes) proved another happy hunting ground for miscellaneous information, once I made up my mind not only to go through the well-known series of papers (though they yielded solid information)[27] but to investigate also the autograph and other, at first sight unpromising, volumes. I was well rewarded. Among the plums was a letter from George on his "non-engagement" to Princess Anne in 1681, and his private will of 1726 in favor of Melusine. Similarly, the Public Record Office, apart from the much-used volumes for the reign, provided a great deal of information that was new. I was astonished, when rereading the State Papers Domestic, Regencies series, that is, the volumes that cover incoming correspondence from Hanover when George was on his five visits to the electorate (in 1716, 1719, 1720, 1723, and 1725) and letters sent to Hanover from Whitehall, what I had missed when I had read them in earlier years with purely foreign policy matters in mind. One of the plums here was brought to my attention by Professor Stephen Baxter, who, with great generosity, when we were discussing "the king's English" in London, gave me the reference to a sentence of George I's written in English at the bottom of a memorandum, in English, by Townshend.[28] I had already come to the conclusion that George understood a good deal and spoke some English, and read it with increasing ease, so that his personal accounts were entered in English, and French copies were no longer necessary even in diplomatic dispatches dealing with complicated problems. But I had not myself—and have not since—found a longish sentence in his own hand written in English.[29] The second great gain was that the correspondence between Hanover and Whitehall, particularly the letters of British undersecretaries and clerks to their opposite numbers serving at home, gave a great deal of information—as did at times the letters of the secretary of state (or secretaries of state; there were two in 1723)—about the king's daily routine, both in respect to work and to his leisure pursuits. So far from George being tight with money, they marveled at his great expenses for hospitality at Göhrde, his hunting palace, and expressed their relief that these vast sums, used in the interests of Britain as well as of Hanover, were defrayed from the king's patrimonial estate.[30] It was also in the Regencies volumes that I came upon convincing proof that George held cabinet meetings, which he himself attended, throughout his reign. To evidence from the 1717-1720 period, from a collection I will turn to in a moment, on regular cabinets (confirmed by a letter in the Panshanger Papers from Cowper to his wife of October 1717 informing her that Sunderland has called him, on the king's order, to a cabinet meeting at Hampton Court),[31] I could now add a letter from Carteret of 1723 which referred to a certain decision George had made previously in the cabinet.[32] It would take too long to refer to other insights from the Public Record Office archives; but I can't forbear mentioning that a study of the wills or copies of wills in the probate section for a number of George's extended family (i.e., Melusine and two of their daughters), ministers, and officials influenced my conclusion on the emotive question whether the Hanoverians "sucked England dry."[33]

With all the material I had collected, I might still not have been able to convince my fellow historians that George had a foreign policy or was interested in British constitutional and economic issues. These historians, whose judgment I respect, saw even the foreign policy as dictated to him by his ministers. There is a remark in a letter of 17 December 1726 to the Emperor Charles VI, printed already in Coxe's *Memoirs of Robert Walpole,* by the Austrian diplomat Palm which possibly lies at the bottom of this assumption, to the effect that George I was "captured and besieged by his English ministers"; though of course the British ministers themselves, and especially Townshend and Walpole after 1723, used to boast, more or less discreetly, that this was so.[34] It should be noted, however, that in Palm's case there is a strong element of self-justification at a time of tense relations between Whitehall and the Hofburg, when he could make little or no headway in his negotiations and needed an ex-

cuse for his failure. Also, his main contact in London was Bothmer, George's chief Hanoverian minister after Bernstorff's retirement, who was at one and the same time anxious to mollify Palm
to improve Austro-Hanoverian relations (and thus facilitate
investitures for Bremen and Verden). Bothmer was annoyed, at
least momentarily, that George's British ministers discussed the
affairs of the empire with Palm and that the king, though he did
not exclude his Hanoverian advisers, permitted this encroach-
ment on what Bothmer thought the field of the *Deutsche Kanzlei*.[35] Indeed, this was probably more than a passing annoyance,
for we find Bothmer in his private correspondence with Bernstorff
gloomily prophesying in another letter of 1724 that Hanover
would soon, like Ireland, become a mere province of Great Britain.[36] Mentioning the Bernstorff correspondence reminds me
that it is soon time for me to turn to the German archives and
their significance for a study of George as king of Great Britain. I
will try to persuade you that without some of the collections in the
Hanover Staatsarchiv, without the Bernstorff papers at Gartow,
and without the Görtz papers (now deposited in the Darmstadt
archives), no definitive study of George I as a British ruler would
have been possible. But before I do so, I want to conclude the section on my search for material in Britain by stressing what a
pleasant surprise I had in the Royal Archives at Windsor where —
contrary to received tradition that "there was nothing really on
George I" — all kinds of marvelous items turned up: evidence that
George was not at all sensible in money affairs and did not make
a killing in the South Sea speculation (on the contrary he lost
heavily);[37] a hugh volume of wardrobe accounts which had the
most exquisite colored design for Vanbrugh's tabard as Claren-
ceux king of arms, the first tabard to show the Saxon horse,[38] but
which also, by the issues for canopy, state Bible, and so on showed
the genuineness (which has been doubted) of important diplomatic missions planned but postponed;[39] detailed information
about George as a fond grandfather in the letters of Caroline,
princess of Wales to her lady-in-waiting Mrs. Clayton, an intrigu-
ing bundle of letters (significant also for the quarrel in the royal
family, the peerage bill, and other political matters), in which
hardly a single letter is dated and all are difficult to read. This is
not so because the princess' French spelling is any odder than that
of most contemporaries, but because of her open, flowing hand.

The recipient complained frequently that she could not decipher the sentences, a complaint that Caroline repeated to her husband, who implied that he was not surprised. "You write like a cat," was the prince's comment, which the princess passed on to Mrs. Clayton.[40]

Finally, a volume must be mentioned, returned to the royal family in 1771 because it was felt to contain documents "unfit to be in the library of a private subject," which amplified what we already knew, from the researches of the late Dr. Drögereit, of George I's political testament envisaging the ending of the dynastic union between the electorate and the kingdom,[41] a topic I shall pick up later on.

Now let us turn to the German archives. The Hanover Hauptstaatsarchiv suffered considerable damage during World War II,[42] and British historians have tended to believe that there is hardly anything of value for the Georges. While not wishing to belittle the damage done, and while wanting to praise highly the restoration work achieved on water-damaged archival material, I wish to stress that the Staatsarchiv is indispensable for anyone who wishes to work on British foreign policy in the eighteenth century, and essential for those interested in the personality of at least the two first Georges. Since I am here limiting myself to George I as ruler of Great Britian, I will only mention in passing the material most illuminating for his personality and his pre-1714 reign as elector. The letters to his mother, to which reference has already been made, were written mainly in French but with some in German—his hand, by the way, is good and clear both in the German *Schrift* and in French, though at times his French spelling is odd (the slip of *chiens* for *gens* comes to mind);[43] and the section in the *Kriegssachen* papers which contains letters received by George during his campaigns, especially that of the War of the Spanish Succession, and the correspondence between the *Hofmarschall* who accompanied him and the Hanoverian ministers who stayed at home. These are significant both for his policies and his opinions and have not been systematically studied.[44] There is a huge series in the Calenberg Brief Archiv which covers Hanover's foreign relations. The section (*Designation*) *England* is particularly important for George's attitude to the British succession. Next in importance, both for the pre- and post-1714 period, is the section on *Österreich;* but all sections had to be consulted, since taken together they correspond to the combined volumes of Correspondence and Entry Books in the State Papers Foreign of the Public Record Office, containing copies of instructions sent as well as the originals of incoming letters. One series that was destroyed dealt with the deliberations of the Hanoverian ministers in the electorate after 1714, though for important issues that gap can largely be filled from the papers of the *Londoner Kanzlei* (the name by which, naturally enough, the *Deutsche Kanzlei* in London was known in the electorate). Both these series are quite well known and have been much used by scholars of the period. For me one of the most fascinating series, which had been little used, was a vast collection of drafts, memorandums, plans, projects, incoming letters in originals or copies (including memorandums addressed to British ministers), arranged according to area or topics such as the Great Northern War, Affairs of the *Reich,* the Quadruple Alliance, Italian fiefs' problems, the Bremen and Verden investitures, and so on.[45] Here I could study motives and trace discussions, in short, the early stages of the decision-making process for which the end result only is available in diplomatic instructions. Here I could see the *état de question* in the sense of being able to view contemporary problems as they appeared to George and his British and Hanoverian advisers at the time when they were attempting to cope with them. It should also be noted that the private papers of the House of Hanover, the so-called Haus and Hof Archiv, belonging to Prince Ernst August of Hanover, have been deposited on loan in the Staatsarchiv and can be consulted by permission of His Royal Highness, never refused to genuine scholars.[46] Among these papers are the private accounts of George, mentioned earlier, which tell us what books he bought, the benefit performances to which he contributed, the size of his expenditure over the years on clothes and wigs, on coffee and toilet water, on presents to relatives and on New Year gifts to musicians and other members of his household, on sums given to the poor and spent during progresses in England (I recall how astounded I was to find how large were the customary gratuities for the bellringers who celebrated the king's passing their church).[47] There are in this private archive also masses of material connected with the Hanoverian court, on positions, salaries, names of actors and singers, records of performances, and so on. Some of this has recently been used for a valuable study by Dr. Wallbrecht on the theater in Hanover and Celle in the baroque period.[48]

I also had the good fortune to be given access by the present Graf Andreas Gottlieb von Bernstorff to the papers of his ancestor, the Freiherr whose Christian names have descended in the family to the eldest son. These papers are still kept at Gartow, the palace George I's minister built and where he spent his retirement: he was already seventy-four years of age in 1723 when he gave up his position as an active Hanoverian minister. He had served George's uncle, Duke Georg Wilhelm of Celle before the union (the so-called *Kombination*) of Celle and Hanover on the Duke's death in 1705. Those who have shared my experience of being let loose in a private archive that you know will contain important material can imagine my excitement, in 1971 on my first brief visit, and the joy of my second, longer, visit to Gartow in 1973.[49]

Bernstorff was an expert on foreign affairs and had long corresponded with foreign statesmen and diplomats as well as with those who served the two branches of the House of Brunswick-Lüneburg abroad. His papers are fuller for the pre-1705 period than for the post-1705 years; probably because George, on Bernstorff's death, asked his heirs that "official papers" should be returned.[50] Even so, there was nearly an embarrassment of riches. I shall here only be able to mention a few examples of the way in which the Bernstorff papers gave definitive proof for conclusions I had half formed from other evidence, or where they provided unexpected material that forced me to rethink and rewrite. Of the latter kind were some letters of the Electress Sophia to her brother-in-law, Georg Wilhelm, at the time of George's engagement to Sophia Dorothea, which necessitated a reevaluation of the concept of a purely "political" marriage;[51] of the former, an extended series of letters and drafts or copies of answers which demonstrated George's control of a secret negotiation with a Saxon minister relating to peacemaking in the Great Northern War in 1717 and 1718.[52] These complemented the evidence from Chevening, already mentioned, which showed George I in control of the negotiations connected with the peace plan of the south. There was of course much more, from fresh information about the repercussions of the South Sea Bubble on British public opinion[53] to outspoken criticism by Hanoverian ministers that George was becoming increasingly more British in his policies, looking at European affairs from the point of view of London rather than from that of Hanover.[54]

The third archive was something of a windfall, in that the papers of George's Hesse-born Hanoverian minister, Friedrich Wilhelm von Schlitz, called von Görtz, who influenced Hanoverian domestic affairs and was the virtual regent in Hanover during George's absences,[55] became available to scholars through their deposition in the Darmstadt archives. I was permitted to use them in the autumn of 1973, when the first draft of my book on George I was already completed, and I had expected to start the polishing of my text during a term's sabbatical leave. What I found, however, made me, if not tear up, at least drastically revise much of what I had written about the period 1717 to 1720, and especially the section about the quarrel in the royal family. There is surely an element of luck involved in research, though I like of course to think that the luck is not entirely undeserved. The Görtz archive is a large one with a great many interesting series of correspondences, and includes more of the drafts (or copies) of answers from Görtz than does the Bernstorff archive. Görtz's handwriting, incidentally, is not as excruciatingly difficult to decipher as that of Bernstorff, which consists of a series of vague wavy lines with the occasional dot for the i. I started in Darmstadt with the folders for the letter S, hoping to find either something from or to Stanhope, and possibly also letters from Johann Matthias von der Schulenburg, the Venetian field marshal.[56] But there was also a large bundle of letters from another Schulenburg, in very good French with the occasional German or Latin tag, in a clear hand, easy to read.[57] He was another Friedrich Wilhelm, and though I guessed that he might be one of the half siblings of Johann Matthias and Melusine from their father's second marriage, I had at first no clear idea how he fitted in. The letters addressed to Görtz were mainly from London, and written most postdays between February 1717 until an abrupt break in December 1719. They were so riveting that I could hardly bear to stop reading long enough to search for him in the Schulenburg family history. He proved to be the half brother of Johann Matthias and Melusine. George I had taken an interest in his education and he had been entrusted with minor diplomatic missions until he was made a *Kammerherr* to George. He was, of course, in a privileged position, always at court, except when he had to leave to visit his mother in the summer of 1718 (when George had to stay in England because of the delicate state of the Quadruple Alliance negotiations). He had to leave for the same purpose during at least part of George's stay in Hanover in 1719. He was regularly in attendance at the king's supper, habitually taken in Melusine's apartments. He regarded Görtz as his patron: there was at this time a distinct tension between those who were of the Bernstorff connection and those who sided with Görtz, though the rivalry between these two abated as they both became older and were challenged by younger men among the Hanoverian ministers. He therefore kept Görtz informed of the state of Bernstorff's influence and worked on Görtz's behalf with George. He reported on the king's health—we learn of a great concern for George's health in the summer of 1717 when a fistula operation was debated[58]—and on the topics of conversation at the supper table, retelling not only the stories which the king most enjoyed or told himself but also George's opinions, views, and reactions to events, particularly to the prolonged ministerial and parliamentary crises between 1717 and 1720. Young Schulenburg was interested in British politics and had introductions to men of a moderate Tory opinion known to Görtz from the time he had spent in London after George's accession. Of the Whigs he admired Robert Walpole most and was cast down on his resignation in 1717: "Voila, ce parlement perdu pour le Roy."[59] His attitude to the king was devoted but not sycophantic. Though he was genuinely concerned for the king's peace of mind at the time of the quarrel in the royal family, he makes shrewd and somewhat ironic comments, wondering how the king is going to get out of this or that difficult situation, accusing George, if with a smile, of trying to curry favor with his British subjects by praising with equal enthusiasm the different brews of beer presented to him.[60] Quite apart from the importance of the Schulenburg letters for the biographer of George, they give us a unique view of British politics from the near ringside, providing us with information that cannot be obtained from other sources; for this reason I hope that they can be published in full.[61] We learn, to give you but a few examples, that Stanhope, admittedly an unsuccessful House of Commons man, threatened—in the politest terms—to resign his ministerial

post unless he could be rid of the burden of leading the government in the lower house, and that he successfully withstood
George and Sunderland's pleas to "soldier on just for one more
year." We also hear that, after Stanhope's elevation to the peerage, the fairly obscure Boscawen was asked to shoulder the task,
only to refuse (in spite of the promise of a large monetary compensation), since ministerial office to give him "weight" was not
included in the offer.[62] When the drama of the family quarrel
was at its height, we are informed that 523 members (the "largest
number ever") turned up in the House of Commons, including
more than fifty who had not attended a single sitting since George
I's accession.[63] Schulenburg admired the English, but he subscribed to the general European view of their changeability and
noted their adoption of masquerades in George's reign as one
example of this.[64] He was much struck by their party spirit, their
competitive drive, and their desire for revenge on party or personal foes. I quote only one of his aphorisms: "Il est très difficile
de tenir trois Anglois unis long temps ensemble aussitôt qu'Ils
aspirent chaqu'un de son côté à la Faveur du Maître."[65] There is
a strong streak of independence in young Schulenburg. Like
others, he at times worried about his letters being opened by the
post office, but this made him discreet only on Hanoverian personal "intrigues" (which he saved "for when I shall meet you and
inform you by word of mouth").[66] Where English affairs are concerned he took courage, declaring that it might do the ministers
good to read his honest opinion of them and their measures.[67]

Now, what did the Schulenburg letters contribute to my knowledge of George I? First, the letters strongly reinforced the evidence that I had already gathered from the Chevening and Bernstorff papers of George I as a decision maker in foreign policy.
They proved that the memoirs of the young Fabrice, a Hanoverian subject, though in Holstein-Gottorp service as a diplomat
until he in 1719 became a *Kammerherr* to George I as elector, in
constant attendance on him both in England and during his visits
to Hanover, are not exaggerated. Such a conclusion might seem
tempting for the historian who reads the boastful accounts of
Fabrice's amorous adventures in Germany, Turkey, and England,
and who notes that he wrote down his memoirs in the 1730s,
though based on contemporary jottings. But in the Schulenburg
letters we find detailed and independent confirmation of Fa-

brice's visits to Hampton Court and London in 1717, with firm dates, and of Fabrice's spending long hours alone with George I discussing the peace negotiations with Sweden.[68]

In respect to southern Europe we again find independent corroboration of George's leadership in the peace plan. This plan, by historians usually labeled the Quadruple Alliance,[69] was intended to solve Italian problems in particular and Mediterranean problems in general, since Emperor Charles VI and King Philip V of Spain were still technically at war and sought to achieve a balance of "mutual advantages and mutual sacrifices."[70] Stanhope, whose share in the southern peace plans should not be diminished,[71] is ill with a fever, and it is George I who works with Dubois, the French coarchitect of the peace plan, and Pentenrriedter, the Imperial diplomat, both of them lodged at Hampton Court (respectively in the apartments of Stanhope and Addison, the two secretaries of state) to be near the king.[72] Schulenburg and Melusine are to some extent drawn into the negotiations in the sense that Dubois cultivates them and enlarges on the French situation in the hope of counteracting the emperor's influence at court, which he fears excessive.[73]

The king remains in control of the southern peace plan even after Stanhope's recovery: when the secretary of state is sent on missions abroad (to Paris, to Madrid, and again back to Paris), George stays at the center at home, all the threads in his own hands, unable to contemplate a visit to Hanover until success is assured.[74] George was familiar, from his knowledge of late seventeenth-century Hanoverian policies, with the ideas of exchanges and equivalents that figure so largely in the northern and southern peace plans; and also of the barrier concept both in the sense of buffer states and of its further development, that of neutral garrisons to keep such a buffer zone viable.[75] In this, as in much else, George was a ruler imbued with Early Enlightenment rational ideas, not tied by the shibboleth of dynastic claims or claims of conquest but willing to promote radical solutions backed by force. Here, I think, is the secret of his relative success. He was a practical, experienced ruler, versed both in diplomacy and warfare, and though essentially sensible and shrewd, he had a fairly ruthless streak in his makeup. He did not conceive his plans as paper plans only; nor the congress system that he, with French cooperation, inaugurated as the ineffective adjunct to European diplomacy which it has usually been judged.[76]

Historians of my kind are not given to speculation, but I must confess to having wondered more than once whether Anglo-Spanish relations in the eighteenth century would have proceeded more smoothly if George and Stanhope had been able to carry the British with them in their suggested sacrifice of Gibraltar (both argued that Minorca was a naval base sufficient to safeguard Britain's position in the Mediterranean) as part of Britain's contribution to the reciprocal renunciations of the southern peace plan. But here, though George never gave up his hope that the conjunctures would permit him to restore Gibraltar to Spain, he met with the determined opposition not only of Parliament but of most of his British ministers: Gibraltar was too symbolic a reward for the expenses in money and men during the War of the Spanish Succession. "Tho' his Majesty were ever so much disposed to part with it [Gibraltar]," wrote an English minister, "it may be doubted whether he would have it in his powers to do so."[77]

I bring in this quotation to show within what restraints George had to work; he certainly did not have total freedom of action. Nor was he exempt from the vicissitudes of fate. Though his Hanoverian advisers and courtiers deemed him "lucky" (a phrase that recurs several times in Schulenburg's letters),[78] circumstances at times robbed him of the fruits of long years of work. The wardrobe accounts I mentioned earlier give proof that George did intend to send Stanhope to the proposed Congress of Cambrai already in the autumn of 1720: all preparations were made, the ambassadorial accouterments had been requisitioned, and Stanhope had, endearingly enough, asked that since he was in Hanover with the king during the summer, the advice of his wife should be asked on the issue of the ambassadorial plate.[79] And then what happened? The bursting of the South Sea bubble in the summer of 1720 brought about a domestic crisis of such dimensions (revolution raised its dreaded specter, ran the reports from London to Hanover) that the congress had to be postponed.[80] Even more decisive (since the Congress of Cambrai did meet in 1722) was the effect of the South Sea crash—combined with the outbreak of plague in France, which spread ever more menacingly from Marseilles[81] toward the capital—on the northern peace plan. George and the regent of France (Philippe II, duc d'Orléans, the son of George's cousin Elisabeth Charlotte, second wife of Philippe I, Monsieur, the brother of Louis XIV), with whom he had cooperated ever since 1716, were paralyzed at a vital period in their attempts to impose the northern peace plan on Tsar Peter to create a sensible balance of power in the north.[82] At the time, contemporaries were impressed with George's successes both in the south and in the north; but in retrospect it is clear that the initiative in the autumn of 1720 passed to Russia. George could only advise Sweden to make the best terms it could with Peter, and the Peace of Nystad of 1721 left far more of the east Baltic coast to Russia than the northern peace plan had envisaged.[83]

Though the Schulenburg letters play their part, as do the Bernstorff papers, in clarifying the decision-making process in both peace plans, it is perhaps in his revelations about the so-called quarrel in the royal family that we are most indebted to young Schulenburg. This quarrel can now be seen as inextricably interwoven with what I might call the English situation in the early modern period: the presence of a parliamentary opposition which, whenever there was an heir apparent or presumptive of grown age, courted that heir and flattered him or her that they could topple the ruler's ministry and give power to the heir via Parliament even before he or she succeeded to the throne. The heir is less important than the desire for power and influence of those who either want to use the heir while the ruler is alive, or oust from power ministers they feel stand in their way both in a personal and political sense, or build for the future when a grateful heir is expected to reward them on his or her accession. We can see this in the reign of James II when there was an alternative heir in the future William III, on whose ambitions as well as on whose principles and objectives the opposition could work. We can see it in Queen Anne's reign when there were two possible heirs, James Edward Stuart and the Electress Sophia, though the worst effects were then prevented by George once he was a naturalized British subject and took increasing control of his mother's succession policy.[84] In the Schulenburg letters we can follow this "English situation" day by day after George I's return from his first Hanover visit of the reign. During the king's absence, as can be seen already in letters printed by Coxe (and amplified by Schulenburg's letters), the Prince had been flattered by men who persuaded him that they would bring him greater influence on policy and independence from the control of his father. The crisis with George's ministry that had developed during the summer of

1716 over policies (the pursuit of Hanoverian objectives in the Great Northern War, the timing of the alliance with France) played into the prince's hands. With the cohesion of George's cabinet gone, by Townshend and Robert Walpole's alienation from Stanhope and Sunderland, the prince of Wales on his father's return absented himself from attendance at the cabinet and worked against the king in Parliament through his *gens,* the members of his household and others who were in some dependence on him, or through those who, in some sense, tried to manipulate the prince for their own purposes. (Those wretched Tories, who are wanting to use us, is the substance of an undated letter by Princess Caroline to Lady Mary Cowper at one stage of the *désunion* in the royal family).[85]

George I was fully aware of the dangers inherent in the situation. There was clearly a challenge to the king's authority by the prince of Wales, and efforts to bring him back into the cabinet and to cooperation with his father's ministry began immediately, with visits to the prince and princess by Stanhope and Bernstorff. These were not expected to bear fruit, however, until the ministerial crisis had been resolved by a reconciliation between Stanhope and Sunderland on the one hand and Townshend and Walpole on the other.[86] Here George took a direct part; he liked and respected both men, and though Townshend was less indispensable than earlier now Stanhope had shown his aptitude for diplomatic negotiations, the king was conscious of Robert Walpole's power in the House of Commons and did not wish to let either of the brothers-in-law go.[87] He made much of both, virtually apologizing to Townshend for his own share in the "misunderstandings" of the summer and promising him a speedy restoration to a more central post than that of viceroy of Ireland, the demotion which the events of the autumn of 1716 had brought. Both grew daily, according to Schulenburg, in the king's credit.

Success seemed within George's grasp when Townshend suddenly overplayed his hand, refusing to remain a member of a ministry that included Sunderland.[88] Of the four ministers, Sunderland was the one George liked and trusted the least,[89] but he would not let Townshend dictate the composition of his ministry and therefore dismissed him. The resignation of Robert Walpole and of others who had taken Townshend's side followed. These men, and particularly Townshend and Walpole, now gave their strength to the prince's party, the term that is used in the list which Schulenburg drew up for Görtz's information of the king's party, the prince's party, and those who were neutral.[90] To some extent, Townshend and Walpole used the prince, but he also used them; yet whatever balance existed between them at any one time, the effect on George I's plans for the coming session was drastic. Bills for relief to dissenters and university reform had to be postponed; and though attempts at reconciliation with the young court continued, success was only partial.

There was great relief among the king's party when George Augustus and Caroline joined the king at Hampton Court in August 1717; but it soon became apparent that the prince of Wales persisted in his opposition and boasted openly of his certainty that he could bring his father's ministry down as soon as Parliament met again.[91] Sunderland, supported by Stanhope, began to argue that as the gentle methods (*la voye de douceur*) of the king had failed, stronger measures must be taken to break the prince. It was suggested that he should be sent away from the royal palaces.[92] This, please note, was a month or more before the birth of the king's grandson, George William, in October 1717, whose christening is generally held to have provoked the king's anger and the prince's expulsion from St. James's and Kensington. We must now conclude that the much publicized christening row (over Newcastle's godfathership) was the occasion that made George accept ministerial advice rather than the cause of the break. Again, the king tried reconciliation, though memories of the *Prinzenstreit* of the 1680s and 1690s added bitterness to his "how dare you challenge my authority and interfere with parliament" (or words to that effect), while the prince's proud defense of his right "as an Englishman" to choose the godparents for his children brought a specific British element to the quarrel.[93]

Reconciliation except on the king's terms was not to be had and these the prince refused: he denied the king control over the appointment of his *gens*, which would have been the only means to weaken the prince's party in Parliament; and he tried, if unsuccessfully, to obtain legal custody of his children.[94] George — contrary to what is generally believed — did all he could to soften the estrangement by permitting Caroline secret or semisecret access to her children; and contact, again semisecret, with those of her ladies-in-waiting whose husbands were adherents of the Old Court.[95]

The long-drawn-out tension began to tell on George. He had been ill in the summer of 1717 (the fistula scare mentioned above). Even then he had kept in good humor, worked hard, visited noblemen's houses, entertained with splendor; but when in the first half of 1718 the young prince died as the *Verwirrung* in the royal family escalated, the king became depressed and sick-looking enough to worry his courtiers. I wonder if Kneller's sketch of the long, thin, sad face of George (the drawing often reproduced from the Windsor Castle royal collection) dates from this period? I have seen, at Marienburg castle, a three-quarter-length painting by Kneller (not exhibited, as it is in need of restoration), which is arresting in the impression it conveys of unhappiness and pain. When the princess of Hanover took me to see it, I could not help but connect it with the Schulenburg phrase that the king in 1718 was "not himself," due to the *facheuses* family affair.[96] Basically tough, George rallied as the absorbing and demanding work of the southern peace plan and the negotiations to end the Great Northern War absorbed all his energies from the early summer of 1718 onward: there was no time to think of a visit to Hanover for that year, even if Schulenburg thought of this as the best cure. The king remained in good health for the rest of his life. His "fainting-fit" at the Prussian court in 1723 caused only minor concern, seeing that it occurred after a long day's drive when George, according to his habit, had not stopped for rest or meals. Anyhow, he recovered quickly.[97] The letters of the secretaries of state, undersecretaries, and clerks on duty in Hanover in 1719, 1720, 1723, and 1725 marveled at the amount of exercise the king took and the work he got through. His long walks at Pyrmont and Kensington were proverbial. In 1726 Melusine's brother, Johann Matthias, thought he could not long support the king's three-hour tours around Kensington Gardens.[98] But this was after the reconciliation of 1720, a reconciliation which Schulenburg was not there to report.

Quite apart from the hitherto unknown or unused archival sources that I have concentrated on here, there are, of course, large amounts of relevant information for an assessment of George I available in published correspondence and diaries; in specialist literature like that dealing with Handle, Voltaire, and William Kent; in studies of constitutional and economic, naval and military, artistic and intellectual life, both on the continent of Europe and in the British Isles; and in virtually every thesis or monograph dealing with relations between European states in the north, south, east, and west for the nearly thirteen years of George's reign. I have said something about the historiography of the period in an article published in 1975[99] and will confine myself here to stressing that, without the work of other scholars, my own would not have been possible.

Now, in summing up, what new light can I shed on George I? First, he was as tenderhearted as his mother always maintained, without, as foreign diplomats guessed, wishing to wear his heart upon his sleeve.[100] He was much in love with Sophia Dorothea of Celle and deeply hurt by her growing indifference to him. Yet he was able to rebuild his emotional life, and was indeed luckier than Sophia Dorothea, who had to be confined to a small court of her own, first for the sake of the Hanoverian electorate (whose enemies had hoped to make use of her in opposing the new dignity), and after 1714 because the Jacobites attempted to exploit her position to damage George.[101]

Second, he was not as intellectually limited as is usually assumed. He loved good conversation, and though he at times waxed indignant at Leibniz's slowness with the *Historia Domus* ("this invisible book" he called it), he missed his intelligent talk when Leibniz went on his journeys.[102] He deeply mourned the Raugraf Karl Moritz (who died in 1702), just because the latter was well read and entertaining. He supported the French anti-absolutist writer Bucquoy who came to Hanover in 1711, received a pension for life, and long outlived George. He encouraged with presents and money Voltaire and other writers.[103] Books were dedicated to him—the German translation of Pufendorf's *Of the Duty of Man and Citizen,* de la Motraye's *Travels,* and Leone's edition of *Palladio,* among others.[104] He read books sent to him, as correspondence in the Görtz archive proves[105] and retained throughout his life an interest in manuscripts and publications dealing with the art of war, diplomacy, the history of the interests of European states, and descriptions of non-European countries.[106] Nor was he unfamiliar with French literature and drama. The books he bought are known to us, and from the letters of his youngest brother, and his own to his mother, we get evidence of his familiarity with the works of Corneille, Racine, and Molière.[107]

He writes to Sophia apropos a pump invented by an English engineer (which he hoped will benefit not only the Herrenhausen fountains but also the mines of Harz) in terms of the battle between the ancients and moderns: "you can deduce from my enthusiasm for this new invention that I am of those who believe the world is getting better every day."[108] His conversation had a slightly ironic turn reminiscent of that of his mother. The king said "a world of sprightly things," Lady Mary Cowper noted in her diary early in the reign;[109] and Schulenburg's letters report both witty remarks and stories well told.[110] His love of the theater and of music is well attested. Schulenburg marvels that at the moment of high political crisis in 1717, while an important vote was being taken in Parliament, the king insisted on going to the theater for the benefit performance of an old actor, a *Whig outré* (meaning a republican), at that.[111] George's historical patronage of Handel is well known, though the misconception that Handel "deserted" Hanover to George's great annoyance is still with us. Handel went to England with George's permission, drawing his usual salary, to widen his experience at a time when there was no opera in Hanover.

The War of the Spanish Succession had demanded economies and — as Professor Schnath has recently reminded us — George could not, as his father Ernst August had done, pay the expenses of the Hanover opera from his income as prince-bishop of Osnabrück.[112] So there was no need for the reconciliation that is supposed to have taken place in 1717 with the performance of the Water Music.[113] From 1714 onward, Handel was active at court, as music teacher not only to the daughters of the Prince and Princess of Wales but to George's two younger daughters with Melusine.[114] And it was George who gave vital support, financial and moral, to the Academy of Music established in 1718. It is possibly symptomatic that it did not long survive his reign.[115]

George's love of building and of landscape gardening is equally well documented. The hunting Schloss at Göhrde, built to replace the modest lodge he inherited from his uncle in 1705, was very much his own palace with theater, fine stables, and experiments, not always successful, in tree planting.[116] The transformation of the Herrenhausen Gardens, from the original Dutch model to that of the French, took place by his initiative,[117] though the total rebuilding of the palace planned in his father's reign and partly carried out was not completed.[118] First the War of the

Spanish Succession put a stop to the project; then the move to England made it unnecessary. But his embellishment of the *Galerigebäude* and his continued work on the gardens, including the planting of the great allée of linden trees connecting the Herrenhausen palace with the capital, are enduring monuments to his involvement.[119]

In England, when he had leisure and money to build, he resisted grandiose plans for a new Whitehall palace. Instead he extended Kensington Palace with a new set of state rooms and several new courts, and replanned its gardens. His patronage of Kent, especially for decorations of the new apartments between 1722 and 1725, made Kent "fashionable" and gave the architect and designer further opportunities, as at Houghton Hall.[120] We are lucky enough to know, from the unpublished journals of Sir John Evelyn (deposited in Christ Church College, Oxford) details of George's rehanging of pictures in the Long Gallery at Kensington.[121] George's indifference to paintings can no longer be maintained; particularly after Prüser's research, which has stressed the close interest George took in the family portraits he had copied for Göhrde.[122] He clearly appreciated good paintings and his choice of painters—La Fontaine and Mercier—whom he called to England to paint his grandchildren was good; the former also painted between 1725 and 1726 a particularly fine portrait of the king.[123]

Generally speaking, George was a product of the Early Enlightenment, who took reason as his guide. I have already mentioned that he thought touching for the king's evil superstitious (though he permitted a woman who regretted the loss of the old ceremony an audience on condition that she accepted the fact that he did not claim to cure scrofula). He had sensible ideas on medical matters and did much to encourage inoculation against smallpox.[124] He strongly favored religious toleration; but the plans, to which he gave his support, to reunite the Calvinists and the Lutherans met with opposition.[125] He had a keen sense of the ridiculous as well as of political realities. When an Irish bill was presented to him which proposed castration for Irish Catholic priests caught proselytizing, he refused his consent, explaining (though he did not hide his private mirth) that there was little sense in giving offense to European Catholic monarchs, who would be quick to accuse the British of barbarism and bigotry.[126]

His introduction of the regius professorships at Oxford and Cambridge is another mark of his realistic assessment: new skills were needed — knowledge of history and languages — to train officials and diplomats in an age when Britain was closely linked to Europe.[127]

This brings me to my third point. George was, by his upbringing and experience, particularly well qualified to heal the temporary break in Britain's friendship with those European powers that had been its allies in the Nine Years War and in the War of the Spanish Succession, but had strongly resented the Anglo-French separate peace of 1710-11 when the phrase "perfidious Albion" (coined by the French Bishop Bossuet) came into general usage.[128] Not only had George protested against the Tory separate peace but he had kept his own troops in the fight till the emperor and the empire made peace with Louis XIV. As soon as he became king of England, he took care to repair the damage done by fresh alliances with the Dutch republic, the chief guarantor of the Protestant succession, and with the emperor. He went further and made a significant departure in post-1688 English foreign policy: close cooperation with France.

His family relationship with the regent for Louis XV contributed something to this cooperation; but shared interests and, above all, George's conscious efforts to win the confidence of Philippe, once he was reasonably sure that the regent would not back the cause of the pretender, counted more. Original letters from George to the French regent are found at Windsor Castle and elsewhere.[129] Original letters from Philippe to George, with copies of royal letters, addressed to the regent, in the Chevening papers also testify to the close cooperation that developed after the Anglo-French alliance of 1716.[130] It is thanks to this cooperation that the first experiment in an eighteenth-century congress system took place. Its central idea was that, based on interlocking guarantees to uphold treaties embodying reciprocal advantages and reciprocal sacrifices by all interested parties, congresses should be held in peacetime to diffuse tension when problems connected with putting treaty clauses into effect arose, to provide opportunities for the ventilation of contested issues, and to gain time.[131]

We have already mentioned the Congress of Cambrai, but we should also note that in the very last year of George's reign the gathering storm clouds (which had tempted many to predict war as the only outcome) were dispersed by the skillful diplomacy of Cardinal Fleury, Anglo-French cooperation having survived the deaths of Dubois, the regent's chief diplomatic adviser, and the regent himself. Preliminaries for the settlement of the several problems involved were signed before George's death (though not ratified till October 1727), and the meeting place for the new congress fixed at Aix-la-Chapelle (later changed to Soissons). In 1726-27 George could not act as openly in arranging the preliminaries and the congress as in the case of Cambrai, since Great Britain was embroiled both with the emperor and with the king of Spain. But it should be stressed that it was George, in the 1716 to 1720 period, who played the leading role and contributed a certain ruthlessness, as typical of him as his shrewdness and relative caution, once he knew the die was cast. His strong position in England made him a more determined and active proponent than the regent of the need to, in some measure, impose solutions on those deemed unreasonable in their ambitions or expectations. I need only remind you of the way in which the British fleet was used off Cape Passaro, before the short-lived war with Spain, to force Philip V to accept the terms of the Quadruple Alliance.[132] This service of George to the experiment of solving European problems with minimum recourse to war was highly valued by contemporaries. The king took risks, Schulenburg admitted, but he gained *gloire* in securing the peace.[133] Writers like Voltaire in his ode to George particularly praised his successful efforts to spare Europe large-scale war.[134]

In this work, George from the very beginning of his reign began the natural progression of becoming a British ruler who put the kingdom first, the electorate second. The process was not complete until he had fulfilled what he regarded as his electoral duty in securing Bremen and Verden for Hanover. In the first years of his reign he made shrewd and skillful use of the potential and actual power of the British navy to ensure this success, while officially upholding British commercial interests alone. The debate whether he "sacrificed" British interests for those of Hanover is to some extent unreal, since British trade was protected and Britain received commercial advantages at the time of the peacemaking in 1719.[135] In the post-1718 years, George's Hanoverian advisers often felt that the interests of the electorate could have been pursued more vigorously: why did not George court Emperor Charles VI to obtain for Bremen and Verden the imperial investitures, the hallowed seal on their acquisition, instead of squabbling with the *Hofburg* over British issues such as the challenge to British trade by the Ostend Company of the Austrian Netherlands? Indeed, as Graham Gibbs has shown, there is a sense in which the electorate was at risk between 1725 and 1727,[136] though George himself remained calm: he felt certain he could hold on to Bremen and Verden come what might.[137] It will not do, however, to overemphasize the divergent interests of Hanover and Britain. In trade matters, for instance, George's encouragement of Hanoverian canal building and extension of the port of Harburg was praised in England,[138] as was his concern for British commercial and financial advancement. Townshend, back in the influential position as secretary of state, implored Robert Walpole to think out such schemes: nothing, he argued, would fix them so securely in the king's favor as the submission of such projects.[139]

Perhaps the strongest proof of how enmeshed Hanoverian and British interests had become is the British opposition to George's plan to separate the succession of the electorate from that of the kingdom. This plan, embodied in a will which George framed as early as 1716 and to which codicils were added in 1720, was imbued both with George's practical enlightened ideas and with his well-known concern for justice. He did not wish to rob anyone living, either his son or his grandson, of their birthright. But he laid down that if his grandson Frederick had more than one son, the elder should inherit the kingdom (note that the kingdom came first in George's mind; just as he had coveted the English succession for himself, so he wished to keep it in the House of Hanover) and the second son the electorate. If Frederick had only one son, then—failing other heirs from the Brunswick-Lüneburg branch—the electorate would go to the Brunswick-Wolfenbüttel branch. George immediately began negotiations with the emperor to gain support for such a solution (which did not break the imperial constitution: the Golden Bull decreed that an elector could not be robbed of his dignity, but he could renounce it). Good progress was made, and before George died, he had obtained a promise that the electoral dignity could be extended to include the Brunswick-Wolfenbüttel line, in any case more senior than the Brunswick-Lüneburg branch. Copies of George's will were deposited with the archbishop of Canterbury, the emperor, and the duke of Brunswick-Wolfenbüttel.[140] He also spoke to his grandson Frederick and won him for the idea of a separation of kingdom and electorate when the time came. Separation would have many advantages; it would secure the independence of the electorate; it would put an end to Jacobite agitation in Britain; it would, in the Pufendorfian sense, ensure the maximum happiness for the subjects of both states.[141]

George's plans, however, met with resistance in England. His legal advisers told him that he might succeed in his absolute preference for males above females in the succession (a separate problem which he had submitted to them), but that the English fears of "an interregnum" were such that his will would jeopardize the succession both in Britain and in Hanover. What security could there be that the elder son who renounced the electorate to gain the British crown would not afterward try to force his brother out of Hanover? What could prevent a younger son, however solemn his renunciation of his right to the crown, from challenging the son of his elder brother on the death of the king, becoming a new pretender, attempting invasion of the kingdom if he received support from other powers? And how could the necessary renunciations be carried out without an interregnum, however short, that would offend against the proper principle of the British succession, whereby the heir is king from the moment of his predecessor's death, as implied in the age-old "The King is dead, Long Live the King"?[142] This setback George accepted, but it did not prevent him, as we have seen, from preparing for the future as best he could, along the lines of his will. Whether he held that reasons of state permitted interference in the fundamental law of succession (in which the king cannot be a testator) we do not know for certain; but renunciations to prevent absorption of one state into another were, after all, part and parcel of the rational ideas of the early eighteenth century.[143]

We have seen that George wanted the British succession, that he was not ignorant either of its language or its constitution, and that he continued the system of presiding in the cabinet, while, as was the custom, leaving his ministers to prepare matters in their separate meetings as lords of the committee. He was energetic and hardworking himself, and saw ministers individually or in groups in his "closet."[144] Indeed, "closet-government" is a phrase that needs to be borne in mind for George I's reign, since his control of the cabinet would not have been possible without it. This control was never total. George was at times under strong pressure from individual ministers; and at other times, as Boscawen once informed Schulenburg, his ministers kept him in ignorance of the true state of affairs.[145] Nor was he always wise himself. The peerage bill fiasco was one for which he must take part of the blame; and in the de Vrillière affair, which forced him to sacrifice Carteret, a secretary of state he liked and respected, his own responsibility was larger.[146]

But on the whole he did well by Great Britain, guiding the country calmly and responsibly through the difficult postwar years and repeated invasions or threatened invasions.[147] He had meant to govern without reference to "parties," but adapted to the situation when this became inevitable. He respected the law, and we have only two instances when he is said to have asked members of the House of Commons to abstain "for his sake" in a vote.[148] He liked efficiency and expertise, and had long experience of running an orderly state. His mother wrote of him that he had no need to read the works of Davenant to become *"un bon roi et bon econome"*: he had the necessary training already.[149] He cared for the quality of his ministers and his officers, army and naval, and the strength of the navy in fast ships grew during his reign. He kept a sharp eye on appointments in the administration and was—everyone admitted—admirably just, and even generous, to those who served him in whatever office or court position. He showed political vision and ability in the way in which he used British power in Europe. What he achieved there was subject to the erosion of time, changed circumstances, and new men in charge; but the congresses called to solve problems before they escalated into war set an example which has not yet been lost. All in all, the founder of the dynasty deserves, in my judgment, more than a caricature portrait in our history books.

NOTES

1. For the assumption on George and the cabinet, see, e.g., Dorothy Marshall, *Eighteenth Century England* (London, 1962), p. 127; for George's wish to rob his son of the English succession, see, e.g., Charles

Grant Robertson, *The Hanoverians,* 13th ed. (London, 1944), p. 56. For the general picture, see, e.g., A Redman, *The House of Hanover* (London, 1960); Elizabeth Burton, *The Georgians at Home* (London, 1967); Joyce Marlow, *The Life and Times of George I* (London, 1973); and Charles Chenevix Trench, *George II* (London, 1973).

2. *Letters and Works of Lady Mary Wortley Montagu,* I, 126. For the dating of her "Account of the Court of George I at His Accession" see my "In Search of an Elusive Ruler, Source Material for a Biography of George I as Elector and King" in *Fürst, Bürger, Mensch, Untersuchungen zu politischen und soziokulturellen Wandlungsprozessen im vorrevolutionären Europa,* ed. Friedrich Engel-Janosi, Grete Klingenstein, Heinrich Lutz (Vienna, 1975), p. 33 n. 86.

3. Michael Foss, *The Age of Patronage: The Arts in Society 1660-1750* (London, 1971), p. 111; cf. John Steegman, *The Rule of Taste from George I to George IV* (London, 1968), p. 110: "George I and George II, admittedly, were almost devoid of interest [in the Arts] or taste."

4. This lady, Sophie Charlotte (born von Offeln) had in 1697 married Ernst August *Graf* von Platen, the brother of Sophia Charlotte von Kielmansegg. For the contemporary belief that she was George's mistress see Lady Mary Wortley Montagu's "Account" (pp. 128-129), cited in n. 2 above; for its acceptance by modern historians, see, e.g., J. H. Plumb, *Sir Robert Walpole,* Vol. II: *The King's Minister* (London, 1960), p. 56. For another view of her relationship to the king, see my *George I: Elector and King* (London, 1978), pp. 135, 157, 275.

5. For the Turks, see the libel noted by John Percival in his diary for 26 January 1715 (British Library [hereafter B.L.], Add. MSS 47028) that "the King keeps two Turks for abominable uses," and for the quote on their duties, see Philip Howard, *The Royal Palaces* (London, 1971), p. 155. For the Hanoverian greed, see, e.g., Sir George Young, *Poor Fred, the People's Prince* (London, 1967), p. 18; and Burton, *The Georgians at Home,* p. 2.

6. See J. H. Plumb, *Sir Robert Walpole,* Vol. I: *The Making of a Statesman* (London, 1956), p. 201 for the assessment of George's personality; idem, *The Growth of Political Stability 1675-1725* (London, 1967), pp. 103-107 for George I and the cabinet.

7. John M. Beattie, *The English Court in the Reign of George I* (Cambridge, 1967), especially chap. 8.

8. Schnath's so-called Sophia Dorothea trilogy is indispensable: three important articles (one of them new, and two reprinted), most easily accessible in his *Ausgewählte Beitrage zur Landesgeschichte Niedersachsens* [hereafter A.B.] (Hildesheim, 1968), namely, chap. 6: "Der Fall Königsmarck: Leben, Ende und Nachlass des Grafen Philipp Christoph von Konigsmarck im Licht neuer Funde" (from *Hannoversche Geschichtsblätter* 1953); chap. 7: "Eleonore v.d. Knesebeck, die Gefangene von Scharzfels" (from *Niedersächsisches Jahrbuch für Landesgeschichte* 1955); and chap. 8: "Die Prinzessin in Ahlden: Sophie Doro-

theas Gefangenschaft 1694-1726." Cf. his *Geschichte Hannovers,* Vol. II (Hildesheim, 1976), chap. 3. Vol. III of the *Geschichte Hannovers,* covering the period 1698-1714 (but reserving the issue of the Protestant succession for a fourth volume), was published early in 1978, in time for me to refer to a significant discovery of his in n. 32 below. Of the work of his pupils and scholars indebted to him, see the studies by Brauer, Colshorn, Fricke, Junge, Knoop, Lampe, and Prüser listed in my *George,* bibliography section III.

9. "The Protestant succession in international politics, 1710-16" (Ph.D. diss., London, University, 1972). See his articles: "Was Queen Anne a Jacobite?" *History* (1972); and "Marlborough in Exile, 1712-1714," *Historical Journal* (1972).

10. See, e.g., the review by T. Blanning in *History* (1977), p. 140, of the 1975 article mentioned in n. 2; and the comment by W. Speck, *Stability and Strife* (Cambridge, Mass., 1977), p. 284, based on my brief essay, "George I as an English and a European Figure" in Vol. II of the "Publications of the McMaster University Association for 18th Century Studies," ed. Paul Fritz and David Williams (Toronto, 1972), for the full title of which see n. 11 below.

11. See Mark A. Thomson, *Some Developments in English Historiography During the Eighteenth Century* (London, 1957), pp. 15 ff.; and Paul Fritz, "Archdeacon William Coxe as Political Biographer," passim, in *The Triumph of Culture: 18th Century Perspectives,* ed. Paul Fritz and David Williams (Toronto, 1972).

12. The details about how George I looked and was dressed on the occasion when Horace Walpole was presented to him are confirmed by the La Fontaine portrait (now at Buckingham Palace) of George done in 1726-1727: illustration no. 40, though alas in black and white, in my *George.*

13. For Schnath's examination of Walpole's story of "Königsmarck buried under the floorboards at the Leineschloss" see his *A.B.,* p. 88 n. 69; for the unreliable stories connected with Sophia Charlotte von Kielmansegg, see Erich Graf Kielmansegg, *Briefe des Herzogs Ernst August zu Braunschweig-Lüneburg an Johann Franz Diedrich von Wendt aus den Jahren 1703 bis 1726* (Hanover/Leipzig, 1902), ed. note covering the major part of pp. 59-68.

14. H. Gerik, *Die Memoiren des Lord Hervey als historische Quelle* (Freiburg, 1936), pp. 105 ff.

15. Ruth Jordan, *Sophia Dorothea* (London, 1971), pp. 267, 271-273; and Trench, *George II,* p. 127. Other authors have been influenced by William Coxe, *Memoirs of Sir Robert Walpole* (London, 1798), I, 266, who assumes that George I died from a surfeit of melons, though they vary as to the cause of the trouble and even as to the place of the death; see, e.g., Young, *Poor Fred,* p. 26, for misinformation on a number of counts: "George I had a happy end on his return to Herrenhausen and Madame von Platen, as a result of his first repast of gherkins and pickled herring."

16. See, e.g., Trench, *George II*, p. 52.

17. David Chandler, *Marlborough as a Military Commander* (London, 1973), p. 25; for the Jacobite propaganda, see my *George*, p. 173 and n. 10.

18. This evidence is printed in Eric Graf von Kielmansegg, *Familien-Chronik der Herren, Freiherren and Grafen von Kielmansegg*, 2d ed. (Vienna, 1910), Appendix III, 17; additional evidence is given in the correspondence of the electress Sophia, who stressed that Sophia Charlotte was never one of George's ladies who accompanied him on his visits to hunting lodges: these were Melusine; her sister Sophia Juliane, married to Rabe Christoph von Oeyenhausen, George's *Oberforstmeister*, the "official" mother of George's youngest daughter with Melusine; and Maria Katharine von der Weyhe (married, after the death of her first husband, Johann von dem Bussche, to general Christian Friedrich von Weyhe), the aunt of Sophia Charlotte on her mother's side. See my article of 1972, mentioned in n. 10 above, pp. 196-197. For George's relationship to Melusine and his daughters with her, see my article of 1975, mentioned in n. 2 above, pp. 17-19, and my *George*, pp. 49 ff., 135 ff.

19. For George's request to Elisabeth Charlotte see *Letters from Liselotte*, translated and edited by Maria Kroll (London, 1970), p. 166; for Sophia Dorothea's request to her brother, see Public Record Office, State Papers Foreign, vol. 22, letter from du Borgay to Townshend of 17/28 June 1727, with a note that its cyphered portions had been read to George II on 27 June O.S.

20. Thirty-one letters from George to his mother, written between 1681 and 1704, are in the Hanover Hauptstaatsarchiv [hereafter Hann.] 91: *Kurfürstin Sophie*, 19a, and were first studied as a whole for my 1972 article (see p. 195) and have since been edited in an exemplary fashion by Professor Schnath for the *Niedersächsisches Jahrbuch für Landesgeschichte* 1976; extracts from George's letters to Sophia Dorothea have been published from the Brandenburg-Preussisches Hausarchiv as early as 1937 by R. L. Arkell, "George I's letters to his Daughter," *English Historical Review*, 52, 492-499.

21. These accounts in 27 boxes from the *Haus und Hofsachen* are deposited in the Hanover Hauptstaatsarchiv and are classified as *König George Archiv* [hereafter K.G.], now listed as Dep. 84, Cal. Br. 22 XIII Anhang no. 3, and are referred to either as the *Schatullrechungsbeläge* or as the *Hofhaltsquittungen*, or more briefly as the *Quittungen*. J. Beattie, *The English Court*, used some of them for his study of George I's English court; and they have been used in their entirety for my biography of George as elector and king.

22. See *The Private Diary of William First Lord Cowper, Lord Chancellor of England*, ed. Edward Craven Hawtrey (Eton, 1833).

23. See *The Diary of Mary, Countess Cowper 1714-1720*, ed. Hon. C. S. Spencer (London, 1864). Entries from the end of October 1716 to April 1720 were destroyed by the diarist in 1722, and the editor softened some expressions out of delicacy and left out some entries, presumably

because he regarded them as uninteresting. The original is in the Panshanger MSS., now deposited in the Hertford County Record Office; it has been used by J. H. Plumb to good effect and also by myself for *George*.

24. For this correspondence, see my *George,* Bibliography section II.

25. Chevening MSS (now deposited in the Kent Record Office, and consulted by kind permission of H.R.H. the Prince of Wales) 84/11: George I's orders to Stanhope conveyed by Robethon, 3 and 4 January 1720 (on the affairs of the North and on Italian problems).

26. Cholmondeley (Houghton) Papers, deposited in the Cambridge University Library and consulted by kind permission of the Marquess of Cholmondeley. Most useful for me were Robert Walpole's incoming letters; and his notes, with copies of George I's own papers, in respect to the king's South Sea Company investments.

27. The most significant papers from the well-known series in B.L. were those of Carteret, Coxe, Hardwicke, Newcastle, Stanhope, Stepney, Townshend, Vernon, and Whitworth. Also useful were the King's MSS, the Egmont Papers, letters to William Wake, archbishop of Canterbury, papers connected with the Utrecht Peace, Letters of Princes of Germany (Add. MSS 1559-1802), and the Craggs, Hanover, and Robethon copies in the Stowe MSS. For the letters to Mrs. Hughes of 1682, see my *George,* pp. 39-40, and for the private will, ibid., p. 154.

28. Public Record Office, State Papers Domestic Regencies [hereafter Regencies] 43, vol. 5: the memorandum is undated, but placed with letters of 10 and 11 December N.S. 1723.

29. See my *George,* pp. 128-132, section entitled "The King's English."

30. See, e.g., Regencies 43, vol. 3, letters between 2 May and 16 November 1720 and vol. 5, Tilson to Delafaye, 30 November/11 December 1723; for fuller details, see my *George,* n. 14 to chap. IX.

31. Panshanger MSS: Correspondence between Cowper and his wife (no day of the month given). I am most grateful for permission to use these papers.

32. Regencies 43, vol. 4, Carteret to Stanyan, 16/27 July 1723. Since my lecture was given, Professor Schnath has made the discovery (see his *Geschichte Hannovers,* III, 14-15) that George as elector, in contrast to his father who did not attend meetings of his ministers, met with his ministers in what in England would have been called cabinet council (as did most of the German ruling princes), as well as seeing them in his closet (*Kabinett* in German): half of the notes, and other mention of these meetings found, date from the period 1711-1714, the first from 1699. Whether this change was due to his knowledge of the system as it operated in the kingdom to which he expected to succeed is not known; but in my judgment it is at least probable. In any case George's presence at such meetings would have prepared him for the English cabinet meetings.

33. The wills I found, apart from those of Melusine (1743), the

Gräfin von Delitz (1723), and the dowager countess of Chesterfield (1778), were those of Bothmer (1723 with codicil of 1728) and Robethon (1722); for my use of these, see *George,* pp. 151-155.

34. For Palm's letter of 17 December 1726, see William Coxe, *Memoirs of Robert Walpole,* II, 205; for the delight of Stanhope in 1719 to have got the better of Bernstorff, see his letter to Newcastle of 27 October 1719 (B.L., Add MSS 32686); for more confident crowing of Townshend in 1723, see Regencies 43, vol. 5, letter to Robert Walpole of 7/18 October 1723.

35. Bernstorff papers: AG 29, vol. iv, Bothmer's letter to Bernstorff of 14/25 April 1724.

36. Ibid., Bothmer's letter of 17/27 April 1724.

37. Windsor Castle, Royal Archives [hereafter R.A.] (consulted by gracious permission of Her Majesty the Queen): 52837-52848, John Aislabie papers sent to George II by his son William Aislabie in 1742; for the result of my study of them, see the article of 1975, pp. 24-25, and my *George,* pp. 251-253.

38. Windsor Castle, R.A.: Geo 57581-57582: Wardrobe Account volume for 1714 to 1727.

39. Particularly important is the evidence this volume gives of the completeness of preparation for Stanhope's presence at the Congress of Cambrai, the opening of which was planned for the autumn of 1720.

40. Windsor Castle, R.A.: Geo Add. MSS 28, letters from Caroline, princess of Wales, in French (with contemporary transcripts and translations into English by the recipient, Mrs. Clayton, one of her ladies-in-waiting); the comment of the prince of Wales in letter (they are nearly all undated) now numbered 52.

41. Ibid., 53017, a volume of legal opinions sent to the royal family in 1771 by Thomas Astle; for which see my *George I,* Bibliography section I.

42. For this damage, see Professor Schnath's article in *Studia Leibnitiana* (1972), pp. 263-267.

43. Hanover Hauptstaatsarchiv: Hann. 91 Kurfürstin Sophie 19a. This particular slip might have been "psychological"; usually his slips are in the nature of an intrusive *s* in words beginning with *ch,* e.g., *schasser.*

44. Ibid., Cal. Br. 16: Kriegssachen und Kriegsereignisse.

45. Ibid., Cal. Br. 11 E I: files between numbers 99 and 284.

46. I gratefully acknowledge permission to use these Haus und Hof papers and also the many kindnesses I have received from the prince and princess, whose interest in historical and pictorial research for the House of Hanover has been an inspiration to scholars.

47. K.G., Schatullrechnungen: passim, between 1714 and 1726.

48. R. E. Wallbrecht, *Das Theater des Barockzeitalters an den welfischen Höfen Hannover und Celle* (Hildesheim, 1974).

49. Between my first and second visits, Professor Schnath worked at Gartow and made a useful catalog of the papers of Freiherr Andreas

Gottlieb von Bernstorff. A copy of this typewritten catalog is now at the Hauptstaatsarchiv and I have adopted its classification in my published work since 1973. A descriptive catalog of material of especial interest for English history has been compiled by me, with the help of Dr. Derek McKay and Robert Bergh, and can be consulted on request.

50. We know of this request from Aage Friis, *Bernstorffene og Danmark,* (Copenhagen, 1903), I, 7; since the papers of the Hanoverian *Geheime Rat* were destroyed during World War II, we have no means of ascertaining the fate of letters (if any) returned.

51. Bernstorff Archive: AG 24, Sophia to George Wilhelm, three letters, one undated; the two others of 4/14 and 13/23 September 1682.

52. Ibid., AG 62, letters from Jacob Heinrich, Graf von Flemming, with draft answers or copies of answers. Corroboration for George's control of the negotiations with Flemming is found in a letter of George's, dated Hanover 7 November 1719, to the French regent when the king recounts his secret negotiations with Flemming in the electorate: Stair, *Annals and Correspondence of the Viscount and the First and Second Earl of Stair,* ed. John Murray Graham (London, 1875), II, 397-398. This file also contains copies of other papers relevant to northern affairs: e.g., a copy of a letter to George I from Tsar Peter of 5 January 1718 declining the king's invitation to a congress to solve the problems of the north: the tsar refuses to enter into any negotiations "dans un Congres Publique."

53. Bernstorff Archive: AG 70, letters to Bernstorff from his London banker, and from Bothmer and Plessen, from the time of George's departure for Hanover in the summer of 1720. They continue after the king's return, since Bernstorff stayed on the Continent, it was at first thought just for a few months; but eventually he decided not to go back to England, though he remained an active minister of George as an elector until 1723.

54. Ibid., AG 29, vol. iv, Bothmer's letters of 14/24 and 17/28 April 1724. This is not surprising; for a comparison between William III and George I in this respect, see my "The Beggarly Electorate" in no. 65 of the Purnell part edition of Winston Churchill, *History of the English Speaking Peoples* (London, 1971), pp. 294 ff. See my article of 1972, pp. 205 ff.

55. George's youngest brother Ernst August was the official regent, but in 1715 he became prince-bishop of Osnabrück in accordance with the alternating Catholic and Protestant (the latter in the House of Brunswick-Lüneburg) succession laid down by the 1648 settlement; he was installed in 1716.

56. Those to Stanhope show that Görtz took his part in the quarrel with Townshend, and those to and from the field marshal give information, not otherwise available, about Melusine and her South Sea Company investments.

57. Görtz Archive: 121/6.

58. The information Schulenburg gives us of the king's illness (see my

George, pp. 205-206) is unique; though it should be noted that the Jacobite court learned that George was "not in good health" at this time: Historical Manuscript Commission, *Stuart MSS,* V, 44.

59. Görtz Archive: 121/6, P.S. to Schulenburg's letter of 20 April 1717.

60. Ibid., letters of 20 April and 27 July (re the king's difficult position); 16 July 1717 (beer). For implied criticism of the king, see letters of 27 July and 9 November 1717: in Schulenburg's opinion George should not listen to his minister but be more accommodating to Tories, like Harcourt, who could be useful to him in Parliament.

61. They amount to 233 pages in typescript.

62. Görtz Archive: 121/6, Schulenburg's letters of 23 and 27 July 1717.

63. Ibid., letter of 28 January 1718.

64. Ibid., letter of 4 March 1718.

65. Ibid., letter of 7 February 1719.

66. Ibid., e.g., letter of 23 April 1717.

67. Ibid., letter of 11 May 1717.

68. Ibid., e.g., letters of 24 and 27 August 1712, 12 and 19 November, and 3 December 1717 compared with *Die Memoiren des Kammerherrn Friedrich Ernst von Fabrice, 1683-1750,* ed. R. Grieser (Hildesheim, 1956), pp. 117-121. Note that Fabrice wrote his memoirs in French but that the editor translated them into German to make them more generally accessible in Germany.

69. The alliance is often thought to have been called after the assumed first four signatories, Great Britain, France, Austria, and the Dutch Republic; however, it should be noted that the Dutch never signed, though they were willing to do so by 1719: see my *Great Britain and the Dutch Republic 1714-1721* (London, 1950), pp. 64-74, 176-205. Victor Amadeus II of Savoy did sign in 1718 as a fourth member; and when Philip V signed in 1720, the Quadruple Alliance was complete as originally envisaged in its main signatories.

70. This phrase indicates one of the main tenets of the peace plan and was frequently used in diplomatic correspondence, as was the term "reciprocal advantages, reciprocal sacrifices" found in the English translation of the treatise by François Callières, *The Art of Negotiating with Princes* (London, 1716), for which see my *War and Peace 1680-1720* (Inaugural lecture, London, 1969), pp. 23-24.

71. It would be wrong to minimize, as a reaction to the assumption that Stanhope was the only begetter of the peace plan, the minister's share: contemporaries like Schulenburg who were fully aware of George's part, rated Stanhope's share highly: Görtz Archive: 121/6, Schulenburg's letter of 26 April 1718.

72. Ibid., letters of 26 October and 5 November 1717 and 22 March 1718.

73. Ibid., letter of 22 February 1718.

74. See my *George,* pp. 231-235. It is clear from Schulenburg's letters

throughout the first half of 1718 that the courtiers pressed strongly, on the ground of the king's health, for a visit to Hanover.

75. Ibid., pp. 80-81, 86, 101-102, 124-125 and authorities there cited.

76. The streak of ruthlessness in the execution of his European policies has been stressed both in my *Charles XII of Sweden* (London and New York, 1968), pp. 370, 403, 416, and in my *George,* pp. 183 ff., 233 ff., and 294. For a positive evaluation of the congresses of Cambrai and Soissons, see J. H. Plumb, "In Defence of Diplomacy," *The Spectator,* 1 April 1969; my *War and Peace,* p. 22; and my *Europe in the Age of Louis XIV* (London and New York, 1969), p. 209.

77. Craggs to Stair, 18 February 1720: *Annals and Correspondence,* II, 413-416. My quotation is from the private letter in English of that date, not from the one in French meant to be shown to the regent.

78. Görtz Archive: 121/6, e.g., Schulenburg's letters of 2 July 1717 and 18 January 1718.

79. Windsor, R.A., Wardrobe Account volume for issue, 29 September 1720, of ambassadorial appurtenances; for Stanhope wanting his wife's advice, see my *George,* chap. 9, n. 35.

80. Bernstorff Archive: AG 70, Bothmer's letter of 4/15 October 1720: "Nous ne serons pas loin d'une révolte. Croyez moy que je n'exagere rien, on parle deja de son [George I's] absence avec une extreme liberté."

81. For recent research that demonstrates the northward spread of the plague, see the article by Claude Sturgill, "La Municipalité de Mende et la peste de 1721-1722," *Bulletin du centre d'études et de recherches litteraires et scientifiques de Mende* (1974), pp. 12-15.

82. See my *George,* p. 24, and authorities there cited.

83. *British Diplomatic Instructions,* Vol. I: *Sweden 1689-1729,* ed. J. F. Chance (London, 1922), pp. 146-150; for the peace of Nystad, see (from the Swedish point of view) Jerker Rosén, *Svensk Historia,* I, 610 ff., and the authorities cited in my *Charles XII,* nn. 4, 10, and 16 to the "Epilogue"; also (though it is mainly concerned with the effect of domestic strife on the peacemaking) the study by Göran Wensheim, *Freden i Nystad* (Lund, 1973); for the Russian side, see L. A. Nikoforov, *Vneshniaia politika Rossii v poslednie gody Severnoj voiny: Nistadskii mir* (Moscow, 1959), and G. A. Nekrasov, *Russkoshvedskie otnosheniia i politika 1721-26* (Moscow, 1964).

84. See the section "Struggle over the English Succession between George and his Mother" in my *George,* pp. 76-78, and authorities there cited.

85. Panshanger MSS, letter (undated) from the princess of Wales to Lady Mary Cowper, entered in Family Letter Books, vol. 4, 323; she writes of *Les Diables de Tories* who threaten the prince of Wales that, unless he votes with them in Parliament, they will join with the court and attack him.

86. Görtz Archive: 121/6, Schulenburg's letters of 6 and 20 April 1717.

87. Townshend had married Robert Walpole's sister Dorothy. She was a help to him in his career, both because her looks were admired ("as fine a face I think as ever I saw" is the verdict of the young Dudley Ryder: *The Diary of Dudley Ryder 1715-16,* ed. W. Matthews [London, 1939], p. 77) and because she was willing to accompany him abroad (for her presence in Hanover in 1723, see my *George,* p. 287).

88. Görtz Archive: 121/6, Schulenburg's letters between 12 February and 20 April 1717.

89. See my *George,* pp. 122, 210.

90. Görtz Archive: 121/6, Schulenburg's party list, on a loose piece of paper, but enclosed with letter of 12 February 1717. Changes in this list, as circumstances changed, are noted in the correspondence, passim.

91. Ibid., Schulenburg's letters between 2 April and 13 August 1717.

92. Ibid., letters of 3 and 28 September 1717.

93. George's actual phrase (from a copy of his letter to the prince of Wales printed in *The Diary of Mary, Countess of Cowper,* pp. 191-192) runs "Je voudrais sçavoir quel Droit vous avez de faire messages à la Chambre contre mon Intention"; the prince's words, to emissaries sent by his father, are printed in my *George,* p. 215, in the asterisk footnote from the Chevening MSS 84/10: written report dated 3 December 1717 by the dukes of Kent, Kingston, and Roxburghe.

94. Windsor Castle, R.A.: Geo Add. MSS. 28; see Görtz Archive: 121/6, Schulenburg's letter of 28 January 1718. The fullest report of the legal tussle over the upbringing of George's grandchildren is in Windsor Castle, R.A., 53017; see also Görtz Archive: 121/6, Schulenburg's letters of 8 and 11 February 1718.

95. For proof of this from the Schulenburg letters, correspondence in the Panshanger Papers and Windsor Castle R.A., see my *George,* nn. 83, 84, 87 to chap. VIII; see also *Briefe der Gräfin Johanne Sophie zu Schaumburg-Lippe an die Familie von Münchhausen zu Remeringhausen 1699-1734,* ed. Friedrich-Wilhelm Schaer (Rinteln, 1968), letters between 24 January 1718 and 13 January 1719.

96. Görtz Archive: 121/6, Schulenburg's letters of 8 March and 5 April 1718; see also my *George,* pp. 208-209.

97. Regencies 43, vol. 5, Townshend's letter of 28 September/9 October 1723.

98. *Leben und Denkwürdigkeiten Johann Matthias Reichsgrafen von der Schulenburg* (Leipzig, 1885), II, 256, for the Kensington walks; for those at Pyrmont (which amounted to five hours a day) see, e.g., Regencies 43, vol. 6, Tilson's letter to Delafaye of 9/20 July 1725.

99. "In Search of an Elusive Ruler"; for work which has appeared since that article was sent to the press, see my *George,* Bibliography section III; of particular importance are the study by Hans Bagger (in Danish) of 1974 on Russia's foreign policy after 1721; G. V. Bennet's, *The Tory Crisis in Church and State, 1688-1730; the Career of Francis Atterbury, Bishop of Rochester* (Oxford, 1975); the essays by Bennet and by Quentin Skinner in *Historical Perspectives: Studies in English*

Thought and Social History in Honour of J. H. Plumb, ed. N. McKendrick (London, 1974); J. Bossy, *The English Catholic Community 1570-1850* (Cambridge, 1975); Reed Browning, *The Duke of Newcastle* (New Haven, 1975); G. W. Chalkin, *The Provincial Towns of Georgian England* (London, 1974); David Chandler, *The Art of Warfare in the Age of Marlborough* (London, 1976); Linda J. Colley, "The Tory Party 1727-1760," doctoral thesis, Cambridge, 1976; H. T. Dickinson, *Politics and Literature in the Eighteenth Century* (London, 1974), and the same author's "The Eighteenth Century Debate on the Sovereignty of Parliament," *Transactions of the Royal Historical Society* 1976; Paul S. Fritz, *The English Ministers and Jacobitism between the Rebellions of 1715 and 1745* (Toronto, 1975); Ray A. Kelch, *Newcastle: A Duke Without Money: Thomas Pelham Holles 1693-1768* (London, 1974); William Marshall, *George Hooper, Bishop of Bath and Wells, 1640-1727* (London, 1976); Miguel Martin, "The Secret Clause, Britain and Spanish Ambitions in Italy 1712-31," *European Studies Review* (1976); Paul-Emile Schazmann, *The Bentincks: The History of a European Family* (English translation, London, 1976); George Schnath, "Die Uberwaltigung Braunschweig-Wolfenbüttels durch Hannover und Celle zu Beginn des Spanischen Erbfolgekrieges Marz 1702," *Braunschweigisches Jahrbuch* 1975; and the theater study by R. E. Wallbrecht, *Das Theatres des Barockzeitalters.*

100. See, e.g., Sophia's letter to her granddaughter Sophia Dorothea of 16 December 1706 printed in *Briefwechsel der Kürfurstin Sophie von Hannover mit dem Preussischen Königshaus,* ed. G. Schnath (Berlin/Leipzig, 1927), p. 105; for the French diplomat d'Arcy Martel noting that George was in love with his wife, "quoyque sans démonstration extérieure," see the report of his Hanover mission printed as an appendix (pp. 711-730) to Schnath, *Geschichte Hannovers,* I (Hildesheim, 1938), quotation from 726.

101. The only well-researched and -argued treatment of Sophia Dorothea after 1694 is the one by Schnath, *Geschichte Hannovers,* Vol. II.

102. Sophia's letter to her granddaughter Sophia Dorothea of 7 March 1711, printed in the *Briefwechsel* cited in n. 100, p. 207.

103. See my *George,* pp. 90-91, 291, and nn. 40 and 44 to chap. 10.

104. Ibid., pp. 165, 291, and n. 39 to chap. 10.

105. See, e.g., Weber's correspondence in Görtz Archive: 126/2.

106. For his purchases (some of which are listed in my *George,* p. 291), see the K.G., Schatullrechnungen; for his interest in the war against the Turks and Prince Eugene's campaigns, see Görtz Archive: 121/6, e.g., Schulenburg's letters of 3 and 10 August 1717. Aubrey de la Motraye tells us that when he met George (on his way to Hanover) in the Dutch republic in June 1727, the king discussed his travels with him and also asked whether he had profited from the newly published French edition of his *Travels:* see preface to the 2d English edition of 1732.

107. See the Ernst August letters to Wendt (for which the title is given in n. 13) and George's letters to his mother in Hann. 91 Kurfürstin Sophie 19a, for quotes and other proof of his familiarity with French plays.

108. Hann. 91 Kurfürstin Sophie 19a, George's letter to his mother of 15 November [1704].

109. Spencer, ed., *Diary*, p. 12. The ironic element could at times be bitter: see the quotation in my *George*, p. 57, from a letter to his wife of 23 June 1693.

110. Görtz Archive: 121/6, e.g., Schulenburg's letters of 12 February and 24 September 1717.

111. Ibid., Schulenburg's P.S. to letter of 6 April 1717.

112. Schnath, *Geschichte Hannovers*, II (Hindesheim, 1976), 392. There seems to have been a very temporary period of uncertainty in 1713, for which see Schnath, *Geschichte Hannovers*, III (Hildesheim, 1978), 510-511; but from Professor Baxter's recent find in a letter book of Sophia's (Huntington Library, HM 44710, fols. 57-58, C. F. Kreienberg to Robethon, London, 3/14 July 1713), it is clear that the Hanoverian resident was now "bien aise de ce que Vous m'ecrivés sur le sujet de Mr. Handel," that he had let Handel know that he was "nullenment en disgrace auprés de S.A.E.," so that he "ne pourra pas manquer d'estre fort bien *quand Mgr l'Electeur sera icy.*" The cyphered portion of this letter (here italicized) goes on to refer to the information Handel was supplying from London: "*Il continuera a me dire tout ce qu'il scaura.*" It can be deduced from Schnath, III, 511, quoting an extract of Onno Klopp's from the now lost Robethon papers, that this information principally derived from one of Queen Anne's royal physicians. That this *Leibartz* can be identified as David Hamilton is clear from my *George I,* p. 108, and n. 38 (his conversation with Queen Anne and his information sent to Johann Matthias von der Schulenburg via Steingens the Palatinate diplomat). I am most grateful to Professor Baxter for putting his Huntington find at my disposal: that Handel gave regular information to Kreienberg has not been known before.

113. Görtz Archive: 121/6, Schulenburg's letter of 27 July 1717 adds something (though nothing material) to the accounts we have of this treat, arranged for George by Sophia Charlotte and her husband. For Johann Adolf von Kielmansegg's sponsorship of Handel, see Erich Graf Kielmansegg *Familien-Chronik*, p. 447.

114. O. R. Deutsch, *Handel, A Documentary Biography* (London, 1955) is especially useful for the relations between Handel and the Court. Schazmann, *The Bentincks,* in the alphabetical list in n. 99, has a charming illustration of Handel at the harpsicord with George's granddaughters, their governess, the dowager countess of Portland, and other members of their suite.

115. For the Academy of Music see my *George*, pp. 265 ff. and authorities there cited.

116. See Jürgen Prüser, *Die Göhrde: Ein Beitrag zur Geschichte des*

Jagd-und Forstwesens in Niedersachsen (Hildesheim, 1969), with good plans and other illustrations.

117. For Herrenhausen see U. von Alvensleben, *Herrenhausen, die Sommerresidenz der Welfen* (Hanover, 1929), with a new edition revised by Hans Reuther, published in 1966; and K. H. Meyer, *Königliche Gärten: Dreihundert Jahre Herrenhausen* (Hanover, 1966).

118. For this see Herbert Westermann's study of the architect "Brand Westermann" in *Hannoversche Geschichtsblätter* (1974); Schnath, *Geschichte Hannovers*, II (Hildesheim, 1976), 396 ff. and III (Hildesheim, 1978), 521 ff.

119. The larger part of the marble busts of Roman emperors bought by George still decorate the interior of the Galerigebäude. The original colors of the ceiling pattern have recently been in part uncovered. If total restoration of the early coloring can take place, the somewhat "heavy" look of the ceiling (I hasten to say that this judgment is a personal one) will vanish and the fine, large "gallery" will be seen to have started out even finer.

120. For Kensington Palace, see the recent works by J. Hayes, *Kensington Palace* (London, 1971) and Olwen Hedley, *Royal Palaces* (London, 1972), as well as my *George,* pp. 262 ff. and authorities there cited; particularly useful for Kent's work has been Margaret Jourdain, *The Work of William Kent* (London, 1949) and the three articles by Christopher Hussey in *Country Life* for 1928 on Kensington Palace.

121. I am grateful for permission to use these journals, which extend over the whole of George's reign (with information also from entries in George II's reign for that of George I), though with gaps for parts of the years 1716-1717 and 1723-1724. For information about the paintings at Kensington Palace see the entries for 8 May and 3 September 1721, and (for rehanging) entry for 11 October 1729.

122. See Prüser, *Die Göhrde,* pp. 60 ff. and authorities there cited.

123. For the portrait (from the royal collection at Buckingham Palace) of George I by La Fontaine see my *George,* illustration no. 40. La Fontaine painted also George's two grandsons by his youngest daughter with Melusine. From evidence in the letters of the Gräfin zu Schaumburg-Lippe (for which see note above), and with the kind help of Prince Philipp Ernst of Schaumburg-Lippe, I traced these paintings to one of the buildings of Bückeburg castle: they are reproduced in illustrations nos. 33 and 34 in my biography of George I.

124. It was George who arranged for the inoculation of two of his granddaughters by the prince and princess of Wales (the third in his care had already had smallpox, though lightly). He also proposed that Frederick (their elder brother) should make the decision whether he wished to be inoculated or not, sent a doctor over to carry out the inoculation once Frederick had consented, and rewarded the doctor royally. There is evidence in his letters to his daughter Sophia Dorothea as well as in the letters of Caroline, princess of Wales, that George was against bloodletting for children and warned both not to listen too much to

medical advice: see my *George,* p. 290, asterisk fn. and n. 11, chap. 10.

125. For these plans see Norman Sykes, *William Wake Archbishop of Canterbury 1657-1737* (Cambridge, 1975), II, 70 ff.

126. See my *George,* asterisk fn. p. 290.

127. Ibid., p. 290 and n. 37 to chap. 10.

128. For the resentment of the emperor and empire, see Petronella Fransen, *Leibniz und die Friedenschlusse von Utrecht and Rastatt-Baden* (Purmerend, 1933); for that of the Dutch, see my "John Drummond in the War of the Spanish Succession: A Merchant turned Diplomatic Agent," in Ragnhild Hatton and M. S. Anderson, eds., *Studies in Diplomatic History: Essays in Memory of David Bayne Horn* (London, 1970), pp. 69 ff. and authorities there cited.

129. One of the letters from Windsor Castle, R.A.: Geo Add. MSS I/25, has been used as illustration no. 31 in my *George,* as a sample of his handwriting and also as an illustration of his control of affairs.

130. Chevening MSS.: 83/17, letters exchanged between 1716 and 1719.

131. Good work on the Austrian side of the Congress of Cambrai has been published by Anneliese Drodtloff in her biography of *Johann Christoph Penterriedter, Freiherr von Adelshausen* (Vienna, 1964); but much work remains to be done both on Cambrai and Soissons. Luckily, research is in progress, by Peter Barber on the Congress of Cambrai, and by Paul Hilton Jones on the Italian problems which loomed so large in both congresses. See n. 76.

132. See my *George,* pp. 232-233, and authorities there cited.

133. Görtz Archive: 121/6, Schulenburg's letter of 11 August 1718.

134. This ode is printed in Archibald Ballantyne, *Voltaire's Visit to England 1726-1729* (London, 1893).

135. For his debate, see my *Charles XII of Sweden* (1968), pp. 402 ff. and nn. 23-40 of Book VI. See my article of 1972, pp. 205-206 and my *George,* pp. 184-190, 285, and authorities there cited.

136. Graham Gibbs, "Britain and the Alliance of Hanover, April 1725-February 1726," *English Historical Review,* vol. 73 (1968).

137. See my *George,* p. 147 and n. 106 to chap. 8, based on Hanoverian archive material.

138. Ibid., pp. 247 and 292-293, and authorities there cited.

139. Regencies 43, vol. 4, Townshend's letters of 28 July and 8 September 1723.

140. Wolfgang Michael, the author of *Englische Geschichte im 18. Jahrhundert,* 5 vols. (Berlin/Basel and Berlin/Leipzig, 1896-1955), was aware that George had made a will favoring separation of the kingdom and the electorate and wrote briefly on this theme. It remained the only treatment until the pioneer work in the archives of Dr. R. Drögereit, which resulted in his article, "Das Testament König Georgs I und die Frage der Personalunion zwischen England und Hannover," *Niedersächsisches Jahrbuch für Landesgeschichte,* 1937. Thanks to Dr. Drögereit's work we now have George's political testament, with its codicils,

in print as well as an authoritative account of George's negotiations in Vienna on the subject matter of the will. See also my *George*, pp. 167 ff., based on new material, for the British attitude to the will.

141. For Pufendorf's maxim "the general good is the highest law" permeating the will, see Drögereit, "Das Testament König Georgs I," pp. 107-126.

142. Windsor Castle, R.A.: 53017 (the volume sent to Queen Victoria in 1771 by Thomas Astle from his late father-in-law's library).

143. See my *Europe in the Age of Louis XIV*, pp. 102-103 and 108-109. The subject of "renunciations" is worth investigating further, and I hope to be able to do so.

144. The custom in George's reign was that cabinet ministers had free access to the closet; others were called to the closet, though certain individuals, e.g., Cadogan at given periods, had free access.

145. For Boscawen's comment to Schulenburg see Görtz Archive: 121/6, letter of 27 July 1717; cf. letter of 2 November 1717 for Schulenburg's suspecting Sunderland of misinforming the king on the situation. Evidence for pressure being put on George during the period of the peerage bill comes from the English ministers themselves and is, to some extent at least, confirmed by the Schulenburg letters.

146. For this, see my *George*, pp. 137-138 and 275, and authorities there given.

147. There were only two invasions (in 1715-1716 and in 1719-1720) but other invasions were at times expected; see my *George*, pp. 256-257 and 296.

148. The information about this, involving Joseph Jekyll and Robert Molesworth, is based on unpublished Stuart Papers; but, given the circumstances, it seems fairly reliable: see my *George*, pp. 255-256 and n. 37 to chap. 9.

149. This comment of the Electress Sophia (from 1702) is in *Briefe der Königin Sophie Charlotte und der Kurfürstin Sophie von Hannover an Hannoversche Diplomaten*, ed. R. Doebner (Leipzig, 1905), p. 218.

VIII

THE EXCISE AFFAIR REVISITED: THE ADMINISTRATIVE AND COLONIAL DIMENSIONS OF A PARLIAMENTARY CRISIS

Jacob M. Price

It is a commonplace that eighteenth-century politics were the politics of management. It was the function of a prime minister (under whatever style) to use the influence of the crown and his own political and personal support in the House of Commons to make the three parts of the constitution — King, Lords, and Commons — work together harmoniously. They were like the three interconnected gears of a mighty machine: properly meshed and properly driven, they worked together beautifully, and the machine achieved wonders of production. But let them be ill made or ill fitted and the machine could be brought to an immediate stop or reduced to disappointing levels of output. The great political machinist of the eighteenth century was, of course, Sir Robert Walpole. He is commonly held to be the very prototype of the prime minister as political manager in the eighteenth century. Under his sharp eye and gifted hand, the machine of state purred on for twenty-one years. It is ironic, therefore, that two of the great breakdowns of eighteenth-century machine politics occurred during his administration. He has the distinction of

257

being the only chief minister between the revolution and 1830 to be forced to resign because of an ill-managed election. He is also perhaps the only head of the treasury in the century who was obliged to withdraw a major piece of fiscal legislation because of popular and parliamentary resistance. This was the famous Excise Bill of 1733, whose bursting and fading so startled and even bewildered contemporaries. A technical piece of fiscal legislation to place tobacco and wine taxation under excise instead of customs, it led to a major parliamentary crisis and the great man's only important legislative defeat.

The recent appearance of Paul Langford's excellent new book on the political history of the excise affair[1] provides a useful point of departure for an investigation of just what this crisis was and what historians have made of it. The first serious scholarly account of the affair by a historian was that by Archdeacon Coxe in the 1790s.[2] Coxe had access to Walpole's papers but made very limited use of them for the excise chapter.[3] His talents were basically those of a diplomatic historian and he does not appear to have had much interest in financial history. His account of the excise affair is based primarily on reports of parliamentary debates. For him the affair itself was basically something that began and ended in Parliament. Coxe also made one significant error. He transposed the parliamentary investigation that followed the excise affair in 1733 to 1732 and thus created an erroneous history of extensive preparations which really never took place. Other historians down to the present have followed Coxe in this error.[4]

Since Lecky virtually ignored the affair, the standard nineteenth-century account must be Lord Mahon's.[5] His briefer account is based largely on Coxe but gives proportionately more attention to the popular agitation against the excise proposal. Even so, like Coxe, Mahon saw the excise affair as essentially an incident in parliamentary history. Mahon's intelligence and judiciousness make his something like the standard account, the model for textbook writers for a century or more. Later nineteenth-century writers on Walpole tended to follow either Coxe (e.g., Ewald) or Mahon (e.g., Morley).[6]

In the twentieth century, professional historians have tended to give rather more attention to opposition groups and their methods. Two American writers applied this focus usefully to the excise affair. Turner examined some of the pamphlets that were published for and against the scheme, while Laprade analyzed the activities of the opposition press, particularly the *Craftsman*.[7] Other twentieth-century scholars such as Vaucher and Brisco added something to our knowledge of details or context but essentially remained within the traditional parliamentary focus.[8] Popular accounts of this century had little to add to Coxe and Mahon. Several had so little sense of the real interests involved in the dispute that they did not so much as mention the fact that perhaps the leading place among the parliamentary debaters opposing Walpole and the scheme was taken by Micajah Perry, M.P. for London and a leading tobacco merchant.[9] We have been carried much further in recent years by the publication of Volume II of J. H. Plumb's study of Walpole and of Langford's monograph on the excise crisis.[10] Both are based on heavy but not exhaustive use of Walpole's surviving papers. Both are rich in detail, and Langford is much more successful than previous writers in placing the crisis in the context of the financial problems facing Walpole, ca. 1732. His book will probably long remain the standard account of the excise crisis as a political event. He is particularly good in analyzing the defection of Walpole's supporters in the House of Commons and the abortive court cabal against him, as well as the resulting election of 1734. However, both Plumb and Langford, even while recognizing that there was an American angle, still see the crisis as almost exclusively an event in parliamentary history.

Two neglected American historians have attempted to show that it may have been something more. In 1906, St. George Leakin Sioussat published an article on "Virginia and the English Commercial System, 1730-1733," in which he tried to suggest some relationship between the excise crisis, the Colonial Debts Act of 1732, and the Virginia Tobacco Inspection Act of 1730.[11] Sioussat's article, though highly suggestive, does not quite come off. Because he relied heavily on public rather than private records, Sioussat did not really prove the interconnectedness of these measures as well as he might have, and the reader is rather left with the impression that their relationship may have been more chronological than organic. A half century later, John Hemphill submitted an as yet unpublished thesis with almost the same title as Sioussat's article, in which he depicted with great detail and force the depressed condition of the Virginia tobacco economy in the years immediately preceding the excise crisis. Though not concerned with the crisis for its own sake, Hemphill's work does suggest a much broader context in which to place that political excitement.[12]

In this essay I shall attempt to pursue further some of the lines of investigation suggested by Sioussat, Hemphill, and my own previous work[13] in this same area and to suggest ways of looking at the excise crisis not simply as an event in British political history but as something also strikingly revelatory of longer term developments in administrative and colonial history. In this sense the excise crisis is simply one link in a chain of developments that began with the advent of much higher taxation on tobacco and wine in 1685 and reached their ultimate denouement in the American Revolution and the financial reforms of the younger Pitt. Insofar as tobacco and wine are still very heavily taxed commodities in Britain today, in the longest-run sense the story is far from over.

Although much noise was made by Walpole's opponents about the threat of "general excise," the scheme actually announced by Sir Robert called for excises only on wine and tobacco. In any event, only the tobacco bill was introduced. When it was abandoned, the wine scheme died with it. The tobacco trade produced in the General Assembly of Virginia the only important extraparliamentary body lobbying for the excise. Great attention was given in parliamentary speeches, pamphlets, newspapers, and the subsequent report of the House of Commons select committee to problems of the tobacco trade and revenue. Though it will not be possible within the scope of this paper to pursue every possible line of political, journalistic, and literary history opened up by the crisis, a considerably expanded view of the affair can be obtained by viewing it as an event in the fiscal and commercial history of tobacco.

AN ADMINISTRATIVE PROBLEM

Walpole's excise proposals were rather simple in outline: (1) all tobacco and wine imported were to be placed in the king's warehouse until all duties had been paid; (2) the existing customs duties on those two products would for the most part be replaced by excise duties payable when tobacco or wine was removed for home consumption. These two proposals reinforced each other but were not inseparably connected. It would be quite possible, as we shall see, to have a warehouse scheme without necessarily transferring responsibility for collection of duties from customs to excise.

During the 1660s and 1670s there had been considerable debate in Parliament, and even in the press, about the relative advantages of customs and excise. Much of this debate touched upon proposals for additional duties on tobacco.[14] Because excise on foreign commodities was generally paid by the first domestic purchaser and not the importer, one could argue that excise was less of a burden on foreign trade than was customs. Because the excise service reached every parish in the realm, it could also be claimed that it was more efficient and less easy to defraud than customs. On the other side, others argued that this very all-pervasiveness made excise, so alien in its origins and spirit, a danger to the liberty of the subject, particularly because the excise administration had extraordinary search and judicial authority. By the late 1670s, however, this debate had died, and the general consensus in the political nation seemed to be that those items placed under excise in 1660 should be left so, but that few new excise duties should be established. When the war in the 1690s forced some extension of the excise, a few pamphleteers tried to reopen the broader question — rarely with reference to tobacco — but proposals for a general substitution of excise for customs never received any serious attention in the treasury or Parliament.[15]

Warehouse proposals were another matter. Tobacco and wine were not arbitrarily joined by the projectors of the excise proposal of 1733. They had long been associated in the minds of treasury and customs technicians because they were both subject to very heavy duties, and importers of both were granted the privilege of "bonding" part of those duties, that is, of giving security for future payment rather than paying the duties in cash at the time of importation. The amounts of bonds outstanding in both trades reached into the hundreds of thousands of pounds by the 1690s, though bonding was relatively more important for the tobacco trade than for the wine trade. All the duties on tobacco were bondable except the Old Subsidy (first penny per pound) of

1660.[16] Many of the duties on wine, however, had to be paid in cash at importation; only the Additional Duty of 1660 and the Impost on Wine of 1685 were bondable.[17] Succeeding governments had been more liberal to tobacco than to wine because most wine (about 97 percent) imported was intended for domestic consumption,[18] while at least two-thirds of the tobacco imported was, by the beginning of the eighteenth century, intended for reexportation (73.6 percent by 1727-1731). There seemed little point in forcing merchants to pay in cash duties of several hundred percent that in all likelihood would be drawn back a few weeks or months later.

The mixed cash and bonding system used for both wine and tobacco duties produced several important difficulties. From the standpoint of the government, the most important was that merchants might not pay their bonded debt in time or might go bankrupt and never pay; if their securities also went bankrupt, the government might lose substantial sums. From the standpoint of the merchants, there were also difficulties:

1. They might not have cash on hand to pay the part of the duties that had to be paid down—a very real danger in wartime, when a fleet of one hundred vessels might come in from the Chesapeake at one time. (This consideration tended to keep new men with inadequate capital out of the tobacco and wine trades.)

2. They might have difficulty finding other traders or affluent persons to sign their bonds as sureties. (This also kept newcomers and outsiders out of the trade.) If another merchant signed one's bonds, one would be obliged to sign his in return and might thereby assume ruinous commitments.

3. Those bonds which were for relatively short periods might become due before one had a chance to reexport the tobacco intended for a foreign market. If one delayed payment, knowing that exportation was intended, customs might try to collect interest.

The government of Charles II in 1662 had tried to help those merchants who could not find the necessary ready money by providing that merchants so circumstanced could deposit their tobacco temporarily in the king's warehouse until they could make the proper entry and pay down the Old Subsidy. In 1672 this privilege was limited to one-fourth of the tobacco imported and was little used thereafter. By contrast, the problem of unpaid bonds became progressively more serious after duties on wine and tobacco were substantially raised in 1685, and attracted much treasury attention during 1699-1715. Again and again the government was forced to concede that anyone who paid his overdue bonds within a stipulated number of months would be forgiven interest. The bonding problem in both commodities, and the cash problem in tobacco, reached crisis proportions during 1708-1712, years of unprecedentedly heavy tobacco imports. In 1711, a wave of bankruptcies hit the tobacco trade—the most disastrous of the seventeenth or eighteenth century. The practice of merchants signing each other's bonds meant that one merchant's failure could bring down others, whose failures in turn undermined still others. With credit badly shaken and foreign markets unable in wartime to absorb quickly the heavier than usual imports, even solvent merchants found it impossible to satisfy old bonds or pay the portions of duties that had to be paid in cash. Thousands of hogsheads of tobacco were stored for a year and longer in dozens of ships on the Thames because the merchants to whom they were consigned could not find the cash to pay the Old Subsidy.

In this conjuncture, the tobacco merchants joined with their old allies the wine merchants to petition the government for legislative relief. A bill affecting both trades was passed by the House of Commons in 1713 but thrown out by the Lords because it contained "jobs"—clauses designed to help individual merchants, particularly the great wine merchants, Sir John Lambert and Samuel Shepherd. A more carefully drafted bill, limited to the tobacco trade, was passed in 1714. Its principal clause extended to a uniform eighteen months the duration of all bonds on tobacco duties—replacing the older system in which some had been due in three or nine months. (The House of Lords in this and the next reign prevented any relief for interest on older bonds.)[19]

The great arrears in bonds and the great losses to the crown from the failures of 1711 encouraged serious thought in high places about the whole bonding system. As early as 1695 an anonymous merchant had published a pamphlet advocating the "foreign" warehouse system: merchants importing tobacco would be required to place it duty-free in a royal warehouse for up to a year. They would pay duty in full when they removed the tobacco for domestic consumption. The author felt that the existing system worked unfairly to the advantage of the richest merchants, who could get generous discounts for the early payment of duty, and penalized the small trader who had difficulty finding cash or securities.[20] No attention was paid to the proposal at the time, but in 1711, the year of so many failures, essentially the same proposal for tobacco and other commodities was publicized by Defoe in his *Review*.[21] As this was a sponsored publication, its appearance there can only mean that Oxford or the customs commissioners were thinking of such changes. In fact, in May 1713, the customs board proposed just such a scheme to the committee of the House of Commons considering the tobacco bill.[22] This proposal was violently attacked by the tobacco merchants of London, who insisted on their need to have access to their tobacco for inspection and sales as well as for grading, sorting, and even manufacture before export. This opposition proved effective.[23] The unsuccessful tobacco bill of 1713, as well as the bill eventually passed in 1714, both contained provision only for an optional, and not a compulsory, warehouse facility.[24]

When word of the abortive warehouse scheme of 1713 reached Virginia, both Governor Spotswood and the council wrote separately to the Board of Trade expressing their enthusiasm for such an arrangement, which they thought would benefit consigning planters significantly. A warehouse scheme should greatly reduce the pressure on the merchant to sell and thus enable him to hold out longer for prices beneficial to the planter.[25] Thus, we see, twenty years before Walpole's excise proposal, Parliament debated many of its essentials in the warehouse project of 1713, and the sides of 1733 were already very clearly drawn—the revenue and the planters against the tobacco merchants. Some in 1733 were to remember 1713.[26]

Walpole was not uninformed about the tobacco trade and the revenue when he approved the excise proposals. Quite apart from what he may have remembered from Queen Anne's time, his own treasury board had had to give considerable attention to that revenue during 1721-1723. The day after he became first lord in 1721, the merchants of Bristol, Liverpool, and Whitehaven began a concerted attack upon the growing Scottish presence in the tobacco trade—a presence which they ascribed, not without some reason, to customs frauds substantial enough to give the

Scots an unfair advantage. Various corrective proposals were made, including one — from Whitehaven — that would have ended the union as far as the tobacco trade was concerned and required tobacco moving from Scotland to England to draw back the duty paid in Scotland and pay the duty afresh in England. Walpole quickly saw that any attack upon the principles of the union would be extremely dangerous and must at all costs be avoided. He played for time by ordering various reports and investigations which tended to go against the Scots. When the matter could not be prevented from coming before the House of Commons in 1723, Walpole temporarily lost control of the situation when the House accepted a motion by the Tory M.P. Archibald Hutcheson that the Scottish and English customs boards be replaced by a single British board. Walpole quickly regained control of the situation but had to make major concessions to the tobacco merchants to deflect them from their anti-Scots vendetta. The single customs board was conceded pro forma but was in fact divided into separate sections sitting in London and Edinburgh. More seriously, the level of duties was significantly reduced by increasing the automatic "allowances" or deductions made from the nominal duty and by giving up as drawback on exportation the last halfpenny per pound of the Old Subsidy, which since 1660 had been retained by the crown when the other duties were refunded at export. This concession alone cost about £55,000 per annum at the time and was to cost much more as the tobacco trade burgeoned in succeeding decades. Walpole appears to have made these revenue concessions primarily for political reasons. However, the removal of retained duty on reexported tobacco was a great commercial success. Reexports, particularly to France, were extremely buoyant in the next twenty years. A halfpenny per pound did make a difference on an average peacetime purchase price for the French monopoly of about 2d. ¼ per pound, and it might have been very difficult politically for the French monopoly to have bought as much in Britain as they did, if the British government had taxed tobacco exports to France.[27]

Within the year of the passage of the Tobacco Act of 1723, a significant change took place in Walpole's treasury. William Lowndes died and in January 1724 was replaced as secretary to the treasury by John Scrope, hitherto a baron of the exchequer in

Scotland. Lowndes's great work had been in war finance, and this had required close cooperation with the leading figures of the city. This habit of consultation extended into other treasury matters as well. Almost everything concerning the tobacco trade in Lowndes's time seems to have been settled by consultation with the relevant interests. A great exception would be the commercial treaty of Utrecht, but this did not originate in the treasury. Scrope seems to have brought to the treasury a keen if humorless sense of duty, a narrow fiscal outlook, and an air of secretiveness. These presumably were qualities which Walpole appreciated.

One of the finest manifestations of this new and more narrowly fiscal outlook was the legislation of 1724 altering the duties on coffee, tea, chocolate, and coconuts. Most — but not all — of the existing customs duties on those commodities were lifted and replaced by an "inland duty" or tax on domestic consumption. On importation, the four commodities were to be placed in the king's warehouse and kept there until exportation or until the "inland duty" had been paid, upon which they could be removed for home consumption. Although often described as an "excise," the new "inland duty" of 1724 was in fact a hybrid. The warehouses were under the jurisdiction of customs, to whom the new duty was payable. However, once the coffee, tea, and the like, had paid the "inland duty" and left the warehouse, they passed under the jurisdiction of excise, with whom all dealers and retailers had to register, and who had inspection powers and the usual summary excise trial jurisdiction (with no removal to other courts by writ of certiorari). Though the warehouse part was similar to the arrangement suggested for tobacco in 1713, the excise police jurisdiction was quite new for a customable commodity. Even so, the new scheme went through both houses without any trouble at all, probably because it was really in the interest of the East India Company, the big importer of tea and coffee. It proved a success fiscally, with the revenue from those commodities rising by £120,000 per annum, and the reexport trade in tea and coffee reportedly much helped.[28]

This peculiar combination of a customs-administered warehouse scheme with an excise police responsibility provided a model that might be very attractive for the tobacco revenue. A warehouse scheme was designed to solve structural problems (capital, credit, cash flow) of firms in the trade, as well as to assure the government a greater security in its revenue than that provided by bonds; an excise, by contrast, was almost entirely fiscal in its rationale. Customs officers tended to be concentrated in the large ports where most of their business was. Patrols along the coasts by customs sloops or land guards tended to be rather thin, except in the vicinity of major ports (e.g., along the coasts of Essex, Kent, and Sussex). Excise, however, with its responsibility for beer and malt taxation, had some sort of presence in every parish in the land and itinerant officers almost anywhere. Thus, a commodity like tobacco, which could be legally exported to Holland and then *relanded* from thence on the thinly populated coasts of northern Scotland, might be more readily detected by the omnipresent officers of excise than by the more concentrated officers of customs. If all dealers were registered and the officers given a broad right of search, then serious evasion of excise should be even more difficult.

There were intelligent people in London who could perceive that the passage of the Inland Duty Act of 1724 marked a shift in the goals and methods of public fiscal policy. One of these was John Crookshanks, then a retired rentier living at Twickenham. Crookshanks, of English or Irish origin, had been appointed comptroller-general of customs in Scotland in 1707. He prepared the first book of instructions sent out by the new Scottish customs establishment. Godolphin was allegedly quite pleased with his work and wanted to make him accountant general of customs in England (as a check on both the receiver general and comptroller general), but this was blocked by Lord Chief Justice Holt, brother of the then comptroller general Rowland Holt. After Sir John Holt's death in 1710, Godolphin apparently decided to make Crookshanks comptroller general in England, but fell from office before this could be effected. Harley refused to confirm the change, but consulted Crookshanks on matters concerning Scotland, as did Halifax, Aislabie, and Sunderland (particularly on the Equivalent). About 1717, however, Crookshanks got into a quarrel with Smith and Scrope, barons of the exchequer in Scotland, who insisted on changing the accounting system used in the comptroller-general's office. This weakened Crookshanks's position, and Aislabie procured his dismissal in 1719. Though Stanhope and Sunderland—according to Crookshanks—wanted to give him a pension or another job in England, he got nothing from them, nor did he do any better when Walpole first arrived in power. He had, however, inherited some property in Ireland and did not starve. Eventually, in 1730, Walpole made him secretary to the "commissaries" appointed under the Treaty of Seville to settle the claims of British subjects arising from alleged Spanish depredations. Crookshanks kept this rather well-paying post at Seville till his death in 1738.[29]

In advising both Oxford and Walpole, Crookshanks tended toward more extreme proposals than ministers were ready for. In 1721, as the anti-Scots agitation was beginning, Crookshanks sent to Walpole some accounts relating to the tobacco revenue in Scotland, together with a suggestion that a simple penny per pound duty on tobacco, not refundable at export, would produce more than the current 6d.1/3 with all its allowances and export drawbacks.[30] This fiscalist argument did not impress Walpole, who at that stage was seeking to encourage exports; in fact, in the 1723 Tobacco Act, Walpole did exactly the opposite of what Crookshanks recommended—he increased drawbacks and allowances. By 1724, however, Walpole and Scrope appear to have swung around to a more fiscalist stance that was more congenial to Crookshanks. In July 1724 three months after the new tendency realized statutory form in the Inland Duty Act of that year, Crookshanks sent a letter and memoir to Walpole via Scrope, whom he had known well in his Edinburgh days. Crookshanks argued that the existing multiplicity of duties was too complicated for merchant and customs officer and was not really working properly for either *wine or tobacco!* He recommended going all the way and taking those two commodities out of customs and putting them under a warehouse scheme with *excise* duty: 12d. per pound for tobacco and £15 per ton for wine. Smuggling would be discouraged and the revenue in England alone would increase by £100,000 per annum for wine and £200,000 per annum for tobacco; at least £40,000 more per annum should be obtained from Scotland.[31] In other words, John Crookshanks, going through Scrope, proposed in 1724 an excise scheme on wine and tobacco identical in all essentials (except the level of duties) to the scheme later put forward by Walpole in 1733.

Crookshanks was in Spain when the actual excise scheme was introduced in 1733 and thus can in no way be considered its immediate father. (He did write excitedly from Seville then, offering his advice and literary services.)[32] But his scheme of 1724 was more than a crank's proposal. Walpole may well have given it some serious consideration then. In the next few months he obtained accounts of the tobacco revenue in both England and Scotland.[33] At the time, however, he did not act.

A more limited warehouse scheme for tobacco only, analogous to the "Inland Duty" of 1724, was proposed to Walpole a few years later by Robert Dinwiddie, the future governor of Virginia. Dinwiddie was a Glaswegian, the son and brother of Glasgow tobacco merchants. He himself had started out in trade there but by 1721 had settled in Bermuda as a merchant and admiralty agent. In 1727, he was made collector of customs there (though continuing as a merchant) and in 1738 was promoted to be surveyor general of customs in the southern district of North America, with his residence in Virginia.[34] In early 1730, Dinwiddie was in London soliciting for a position on the Bermuda council. To help this ultimately successful application, he submitted varying "observations on American trade" to the Board of Trade and to Robert Walpole. The two schemes had many recommendations in common, but the one sent to Walpole differed from that sent to the Board of Trade by the inclusion of a warehouse scheme for tobacco. Dinwiddie proposed to Walpole that merchants importing tobacco should pay down the first penny of the Old Subsidy in cash on entry but be required to put their tobacco in the king's warehouse until the remaining duties (to be reduced to 4d.) could be paid in cash or the tobacco be exported. On exportation, the merchants would get a drawback of only 20s. per hogshead (of at least 500 pounds) instead of 43s. 9d. on a 700-pound hogshead (net) under existing practices. The merchant would also be obliged to pay warehouse rent and to give bond to remove his tobacco within eighteen months. "By this Scheme. . . the Revenue cannot come short of what it now is: for the Drawback being considerably lessen'd, it will do more than answer the Deficiency of the Duty on the Consumption; Moreover . . . the Merchants will avoid the Risque of being bound for one another and the Revenue will not suffer by the Losses that so Frequently happen in giving so large a Credit to the Merchant."[35]

Dinwiddie wanted to make a good impression, and he clearly knew what was within the realm of possibility. His schemes contained a recommendation for permitting the export of rice from

South Carolina to Spain and Portugal, a proposal enacted that very year.[36] Although he said nothing about excise, his tobacco proposals may have had some influence. They foretold at least the reduction of the nominal level of duty embodied in Walpole's ultimate scheme.

Dinwiddie may have got the idea for his warehouse scheme from talks at the time with London tobacco merchants. For several years tobacco prices had been falling, causing cash-flow and credit problems for planters and merchants alike. In 1729, the London merchant, Edward Randolph, a Virginian by origin, received a shipload of tobacco and apparently had trouble finding other merchants to stand surety for him on the bondable duties. (He eventually failed.) He applied to the customs for permission to warehouse his tobacco as provided by the Tobacco Act of 1714. Since that act's optional warehousing provision had fallen into disuse, customs consulted the attorney general, Philip Yorke (the future Lord Hardwicke), who advised that the 1714 provision was inoperative since it had not been reenacted by the Tobacco Act of 1723.[37] Randolph tried to remedy this by getting a clause for warehousing inserted into a bill going through Parliament in the spring of 1730, but was unsuccessful. Other London merchants, also weakened by the great drop in tobacco prices, then appealed to the treasury for official support for such reenactment. The customs board reported on 19 February 1730/31 that they considered that such a clause would "be a Security to the Revenue as well as an ease to the Merchant Importer."[38] Nothing, however, was done about the matter in the parliamentary session of 1731, and the merchants again petitioned unsuccessfully in March 1732.[39] One can only conclude that the treasury did nothing for the London merchants in 1732-1733 because they had a more ambitious project in mind.

It is likely that both Crookshanks's scheme of 1724 and Dinwiddie's of 1730 helped shape Walpole's excise scheme of 1733, while the more limited warehouse proposal of the London tobacco merchants may have had a lot to do with its timing. Yet the excise scheme was more than just an administrative reform. Like its 1713 predecessor, it was also a proposal to alter significantly some key features of the existing commercial organization of British-Chesapeake trade. Such proposals were intensely controversial both in 1713 and 1733. Therefore, to understand the fuller impli-

cations of the excise controversy of 1733, we must also look at
it from an American perspective.

THE COMMERCIAL AND COLONIAL DIMENSION

The tobacco trade between Britain and the Chesapeake had in
the late 1720s become subject to great stresses and was under-
going significant structural change. The trade had grown very
rapidly in the seventeenth century, though the rate of growth
slowed down in the last quarter. By contrast, there was complete
stagnation in the first quarter of the eighteenth century, with
English and Scottish imports combined for 1721-1725 averaging
less per annum (33.7 million pounds) than English imports alone
during 1699-1702 (34.6 million pounds).[40] This stagnation was
associated with the wartime depredations of French privateers,
with an interruption in the recruitment of labor and with the loss
of many time-expired indentured servants to nearby colonies
whose economies were less adversely affected by the wars. The
continuation of some of these conditions into the peace meant
relatively high prices for tobacco, about 1713-1725, and put in
the hands of the planters the wherewithal to purchase African
slaves and thus ultimately break the labor bottleneck.[41] Market
pressures could also affect institutional structure. During the
period of relatively short crops, 1713-1725, the consignment merchants of London and Bristol (in particular) were at a disadvan-
tage vis-à-vis those competitors (particularly the Scots) who purchased their tobacco directly in the Chesapeake. The latter could
give their agents and supercargoes wide latitude to pay what was
necessary to fill their ships. The consignment merchants could
only send out vessels and hope for consignments — and planters
often preferred not to consign but to sell in the country when
prices were high. Thus the consignment merchants in these years
often saw their ships return half empty, with very great losses.

These tendencies reached a turning point about 1725. A poor
crop in 1723[42] and a very bad crop in 1724 meant a drop in imports in the ensuing marketing years, 1724-1725. In fact 1725 saw
the lowest imports (except for 1715) and almost the highest prices
of any peacetime year in the eighteenth century.[43] However, these
very high prices — following so closely on the equally high prices
of 1713-1718 — encouraged an expansion of the area of cultiva-

tion, made possible by the improved slave labor supply. Larger crops were achieved, starting with that of 1725, marketed in 1726, so that British tobacco imports of 1726-1730 (44.8 million lbs. per annum) were 33 percent higher than those of 1721-1725. Even with increased French buying, the market could not support these greatly increased supplies, and prices dropped precipitately. Good price data for the 1720s are lacking, but we know that the Amsterdam price-currents annual average price for Virginia tobacco declined from .325 guilders per pound in 1725 to .18 (one of the lowest prices of the century) in 1729-1731.[44] What this might mean for an average planter can be seen in some surviving accounts of Richard Bond and his widow Sarah. Without any returns for the peak year 1725—when London prices reportedly reached 5d. per pound—we yet see that ordinary tobacco consigned by the Bonds to the London merchant William Dawkins and sold by him to Peter Cavalier, the then French buying agent, obtained 2 7/8-3d. in 1726 and only 1 3/4-2d. in 1729, so that the hogsheads consigned netted on an average £4 13s. each in 1726, but only £3 1s. in 1729.[45]

The lower tobacco prices of the late 1720s proved to be the beginning of a secular trend that lasted until the American Revolution and beyond. Institutionally, these lower prices in Europe at first severely hurt those merchants who bought their tobacco in America, so that the Scots trade in particular stagnated until 1740.[46] The London and Bristol commission merchants, however, benefited because bigger crops made it easier to fill their ships and their enhanced earnings from freight and commissions were only minimally influenced by price. The planters were the chief sufferers, and they were not at all pleased to see the merchant's freight and other charges and commissions remain relatively constant while their prices and net earnings plummeted.

Inevitably the attention of the planters was directed to state policy or political action. In 1728 the Virginia legislature for the last time passed a law restricting production, on this occasion to ten thousand plants for planters without slaves and six thousand plants per laborer for those with slaves. Despite the objections of some London merchants, the Board of Trade let this law stand.[47] The Virginians were less successful with their effort of 1728 to limit the labor supply (and thus production) by taxing the importation of slaves; after protests from the slave traders of London,

Liverpool, and Bristol, this was disallowed by the privy council, as was a 1726 law to exclude North Carolina tobacco from the Virginia market.[48] Walpole's Tobacco Act of 1723 had contained a clause (put in by the outport and Scottish merchants over the objections of the Londoners) banning the importation of "stemmed" tobacco. (Some greater planters used their excess labor during the relatively idle winter months to cut out the petiole and midrib from the tobacco leaf; this reduced freight and improved quality, since only the cheapest snuff was made from these "stalks and stems.") The only justification for banning this practice was to increase the king's gross revenue by increasing the weight of imported tobacco. The consigning planters were particularly anxious to reduce freight charges after the fall in prices and in 1728 sent over to London the local lawyer John Randolph to solicit for the removal of the ban on stemmed tobacco. He obtained this from Parliament in 1729.[49]

The Virginians went far beyond this on their own. Their new governor, William Gooch, studied the matter and agreed with the Virginians that they could only raise prices by restricting production. Since the crown would not let them do this by taxing the importation of slaves, he had other ways to seek. In 1729 he sent home to the secretary of state, the duke of Newcastle, a scheme to control quality and indirectly limit quantity, which the Virginia assembly adopted in 1730. By this "inspection law," no hogshead of tobacco could be sold in or exported from Virginia until it had first been taken to a public warehouse, opened, inspected for quality, passed, and marked. Inferior tobacco was to be burned without compensation. It took great political skill for Gooch to get this act through and prevent it from being repealed the next year. In the long run, the scheme was accepted by the Virginians as beneficial and was retained till well after the Revolution. Gooch thought that the merchants of London would give him a piece of silver plate in thanks for the law, but he heard afterward that some of them, particularly Alderman Micajah Perry, M.P., did not like it, and prejudiced the customs commissioners against it. Gooch's disappointment was symptomatic of the suspicion between the Virginia planters and London merchants in these years of economic stress.[50]

How much did Walpole know or care about the problems of the tobacco trade? We can find one or two relevant memoirs in his papers, but they do not answer the question. Correctly, a colonial lieutenant governor corresponded with the secretary of state for the southern department and the Board of Trade, and not with the treasury. However, there were other lines of communication besides the "correct" ones. Gooch himself was East Anglian; his brother Thomas (1674-1754) was master of Caius College, Cambridge (1714-1754) and later bishop of Bristol (1737-1738), Norwich (1738-1748), and Ely (1748-1754).[51] Although Governor Gooch's own papers have not survived, we do have his letters to his brother. They show him to have been fairly close to Bishops Edmund Gibson of London (with whom he corresponded), and Thomas Sherlock of Bangor (whom he regarded as a protector).[52] Even more suggestive of lines of additional communication was Governor Gooch's agent in London, Peter Leheup.

Peter Leheup was one of those almost invisible behind-the-scenes personalities whose exposure reveals so much about the character of eighteenth-century society and administration. His father, Thomas Le Heup (1668-1736), was a Huguenot émigré from Normandy, who came to London after the revocation of the Edict of Nantes. He was active in London as a merchant and financier, appearing as an original subscriber to the Bank of England and the South Sea Company. It is likely that he profited by the South Sea Bubble, for the family suddenly appear vastly wealthy in the 1720s, when Thomas's sons purchased considerable real estate in Norfolk and Suffolk.[53] His eldest son, Isaac Leheup (c. 1686-1747), of Gunthorpe, Norfolk, in 1720 married Elizabeth, daughter and coheiress of Peter Lombard of Burnham Thorpe, Norfolk, also a Huguenot refugee, sometime diamond merchant of London and purveyor to Queen Anne. Lombard's other daughter and heiress, Mary Magdalen, had a few weeks before married Horatio Walpole, brother of Sir Robert, and thus created a most useful political connection for the Leheup family. Isaac Leheup was an M.P., 1722-1741, and a commissioner of customs, 1741-1742. He was dismissed from that post on the fall of Robert Walpole, despite the personal intercession of his brother-in-law, Horatio Walpole. He had had a brief diplomatic career in 1726-1727 in Germany and Sweden, but was recalled from Stockholm after he insulted Frederick, prince of Wales in a particularly arrogant way.[54] The second son, Michael Leheup (c. 1697-1749), secretary of the presentations to the lord chancellor, purchased the manor of Hessett in Suffolk and other lands in Suffolk, Norfolk, and Warwickshire.[55] The third son, Peter Leheup (1699-1777), of Steeple Morden, Surrey, also owned extensive lands in Norfolk. In 1721 the year Robert and Horatio Walpole returned to the treasury, he became an underclerk there; the next year he established his own family influence in that department by marrying Clara, daughter of William Lowndes, secretary to the treasury.[56]

Peter Leheup was underclerk at the treasury from 1721 to 1752 and then chief clerk, 1752-1755.[57] That was, however, only the beginning of his activity and income. Very early, his father-in-law William Lowndes made him a comptroller of exchequer bills.[58] In addition, he served for decades (c. 1721-1742) as deputy to Horatio Walpole in his capacity as Auditor-General of Plantation Revenues.[59] He was on several occasions employed by the government to dispose of large sums (£7000 at a time) from the Virginia quitrents and other funds "without accompt," that is, as special or secret service expenditures.[60] In addition he was employed as trustee for the payment of the dowries of George II's daughters, the princesses of Orange and Hesse.[61] Finally, he was frequently named a manager or director of government lotteries.[62] This proved his undoing, for in 1754 a House of Commons committee uncovered irregularities in the sale of tickets in a lottery for the British Museum and blamed Peter Leheup. He was tried in King's Bench in 1755, fined £1000, and dismissed as chief clerk of the treasury. He lost most of his other positions then, too,[63] but was allowed to continue as comptroller of exchequer bills until the "slaughter of the Pelhamite innocents" in 1762. He tried to rejoin the gravy train when the Rockinghams came back in 1765 but, despite his many friends, was unsuccessful.[64]

In addition to all these other positions, Peter Leheup was also a colonial agent: for New Jersey, 1723-1727; for New York, 1724-1730; for Barbados, 1730-1736; and, particularly, for Virginia, 1722-1754.[65] The £100 or £150 a year—plus expenses—Leheup got from each of these agencies, when added to the £350 a year he received as comptroller of exchequer bills, his £50-100 as a treasury underclerk, with his substantial fees there, and whatever Horatio Walpole allowed him as deputy auditor-general must have added up to a nice competence.[66] Leheup obviously knew how to operate along the corridors and backstairs of power. He cleared the government's £26,000 donation for the infant colony of Georgia through the treasury without the deduction of the usual (£700) fees.[67] In 1729 he was given a special commission by New York to obtain an act permitting the direct importation of salt from Europe. Though his name appears nowhere in the official record, Parliament did pass such a law in 1730. For this, he had the assistance of Alderman Micajah Perry, who acted as *rapporteur* for the House of Commons committee on the bill.[68] The next year he was equally successful fighting Micajah Perry, tobacco merchant as well as M.P., over the Virginia Tobacco Inspection Law of 1730. Perry had gone behind his back and obtained an unfavorable report on the measure from the customs commissioners. Leheup, however, interceded with the Board of Trade (and perhaps others), and the law was not disallowed.[69]

Neither the papers of Governor Gooch nor those of Peter Leheup, his agent, are known to have survived. Without them, we shall never know the full story of the Virginia side of the excise crisis. It is clear, though, from fragments that do survive that Virginia was much closer to Leheup's treasury than one might at first suspect. The treasury, for example, intruded into colonial appointments outside its formal area of responsibility. Gooch was very suspicious of Micajah Perry, who wanted to control Virginia's patronage as an aid to his business, and who was resentful of the governor's independent line. In 1732, Gooch learned from a man-of-war captain with friends in the treasury that:

[Perry] goes one morning into the Treasury, fell into discourse with Mr. Leheup about the appointment of a Councillor for Virginia, and finding it was not like to be as he would have had it, flew into a great Passion, said you [Governor Gooch] had deceived him in the recommendation . . . and that he would have you out of your Government upon which Leheup, Mr. [Christopher] Lowe and the rest of the Clerks in the office, sett up an Horse laugh at him, telling him it was not in his Power, so away he went.[70]

Sometimes Gooch's policies made him fear the resentment of a much larger circle of merchants. In 1730, he wrote to his brother of his doubts about the reception of his plans for what became that year's Tobacco Inspection Act:

I hope . . . to have an answer to the scheme that I sent Home for improving our Trade. The Ministry will find that . . . I have the King's Interest much at Heart, but in the City I am apt to think by what I have heard, that I have disturbed an hornet's nest, the Merchants from high to low being concerned in running of Tobacco, which my Scheme is calculated to prevent, and to raise the Revenue, which such Frauds is [has] reduced to £150,000 per annum, to upwards of £400,000.[71]

Gooch had tried to make his Tobacco Inspection Act palatable to the treasury in London by including in it clauses requiring that the new inspectors mark on each hogshead its weight at inspection and that the naval officer of each port send home a duplicate manifest of each ship's cargo specifying the original weight of each tobacco hogshead.[72] Such information would make almost impossible the great weighing frauds of which the Scots were accused in 1721-1722. We can be sure that there had been substantial correspondence between Gooch and Leheup before these carefully drafted clauses were incorporated into the Virginia act. By choosing in 1731 to fight Gooch's bill against the adroit and well-armed Leheup, the London tobacco merchants only helped reopen in the minds of those higher up the whole question of customs fraud in tobacco.

The peace years between the Treaty of Seville (1729) and the start of the War of the Polish Succession (1733) provided a pause in which parliamentary time could be found for a variety of colonial questions pushed by one interest or another. In 1730, there was the act permitting the direct export of rice from Carolina to southern Europe, as well as the law for the direct importation of European salt into New York.[73] In 1731 there was an act for the importation of nonenumerated plantation goods into Ireland.[74] In 1732 there was "an act for the encouragement of the growth of coffee in America" and "an act for the more easy recovery of debts in his Majesty's plantations"; and in 1733 the famous Molasses Act.[75] A lot of attention was being given to colonial matters in these years, as even the French informants in London reported.[76]

Both Isham Randolph (brother of John and Edward Randolph), Virginia's special agent then in London, and the London Virginia merchants petitioned against the molasses bill when it was considered in 1732.[77] By contrast, the debt act of that year set Isham Randolph and the merchants at opposite poles. It was the culmination of five years of bickering between the Virginians and their British mercantile correspondents, bickering made all the more bitter by the decline in tobacco prices in the late 1720s which hurt both sides. When Gooch went out to Virginia as gov-

ernor in 1727, he carried with him standard instructions to ask
the legislature for a law "whereby the creditors of persons becoming bankrupts in Great Britain and having estates in our . . . provinces of [Virginia]" may collect the debts owing to the bankrupt
in Virginia.[78] The Virginians thought such a law unnecessary,
but when Gooch tried to explain their reasoning to the Board of
Trade, he was reprimanded.[79] As a slight concession, the Virginians passed a law in 1728 weakening previous legislation declaring slaves to be real property and unavailable to satisfy certain
classes of debts.[80] The merchants, led by Micajah Perry, then
took the initiative and complained to the Board of Trade against
a Virginia act of 1705 that provided time limits within which suits
could be brought for sums owing on judgment, bond, note, bill,
or an open account (book debts). The Board of Trade's legal
adviser recommended disallowing the 1705 act on the grounds
that it was contrary to an act of 21 James I, by which rights
created by judgment or bond were unlimited in time. On the recommendation of the board, the 1705 act was disallowed by the
crown in 1731. This created some problems, for there were other
noncontroversial clauses in that act which were thereby disallowed too, including one establishing a procedure whereby a
British merchant having sums owing him in Virginia could prove
the same in Virginia courts by sending over a certificate sworn
before two magistrates in the place of his residence.[81] Gooch,
forewarned, suggested that the Virginia legislature in 1730
reenact some of these noncontroversial clauses, but the resulting
legislation did not contain the clause for the proving of debts by
creditors not residents in Virginia.[82]

Angered and threatened by this very pointed retaliation, the
Virginia merchants of London joined with their colleagues trading to Jamaica, and with similar merchants in Bristol, to petition
the king. The petition was referred to the Board of Trade, which,
after receiving counterarguments from the governor and council
of Virginia, reported in early 1732 in a sense generally favorable
to the merchant petitioners. The board recommended that governors of colonies henceforth be instructed to consent to no laws
that discriminated against residents of Great Britain. However,
the existing rights of British debtors would require legislative protection by Parliament.[83] The battle was thus transferred to Westminster, where it was pursued by merchant delegations from

London, Bristol, and Liverpool. Although the resulting bill affected all the colonies in North America and the West Indies, only Virginia and Jamaica appear to have been discussed in Parliament and only Virginia petitioned against it. Forewarned — most likely by Leheup — the House of Burgesses sent Isham Randolph over specifically for this purpose. Despite his best efforts — which included testimony before the House of Lords — the bill, essentially a government measure, passed in 1732. The resulting Colonial Debts Act followed the recommendations of the Board of Trade: (1) British litigants in colonial courts in suits for debts henceforth could prove their accounts by taking an oath before any "chief magistrate" (mayor or provost) in Great Britain; and (2) the lands, houses, chattels, and slaves of debtors in the American colonies became liable for the satisfaction of debts "in the like Manner as Real Estates are by the Law of *England* liable to the Satisfaction of Debts due by Bond or other Specialty."[84] The first of these clauses caused little stir; it could not have disturbed the Virginians for it simply reenacted a provision present in their law from 1705 to 1731. The second clause, however, was deeply offensive to those slave colonies, particularly Virginia, where planter legislators had over the years sought to protect their real estate and slaves from seizure for any debts except those secured by mortgage.[85] The Virginians did not have to look for an object at whom to direct their rage. Alderman Micajah Perry, M.P. had been one of the prime movers in the original petition to the king and he and John Scrope were charged by the House of Commons with the preparation of the bill. The anger of the Virginia legislators on the debt question was, we shall see, to be the catalyst that converted them into ardent advocates of the excise proposal, now an instrument of revenge against the merchants.

WALPOLE'S PRIORITIES

Ultimately, all possible aspects of the excise proposal had to be weighed in Walpole's mind, for it was his decision that sent the proposal forward and ultimately called it back. What were his priorities? Modern historians keep reminding us that his primary objective was to win the loyalty of the country gentry to the dynasty and Revolution Settlement. This is so obvious as to be unchallengeable; it is also too obvious to be useful — for a consideration true of every action a statesman takes does not go far to explain any one of them.

Contemporaries were more earthbound in their explanations. Hervey, who knew more than he understood, reported that Walpole needed a £500,000 increase in tax yields in 1733 and that the salt duty which he had just reestablished would only produce one-third that; hence the excise scheme. Without new levies, it would by administrative reorganization produce the other two-thirds.[86] Hervey can be taken as an accurate reporter of what was being said around court at the time, but his circle of well-placed gossipers did not extend into the lowly worlds of commerce and administration. Nevertheless, we must ask ourselves what was behind his £500,000 figure.

In general, the two decades between the South Sea Bubble of 1720 and the start of the Spanish War in 1739 were years of economic stagnation. However, this stagnation was uneven. External trade in these years was growing at a rate of around one percent per annum, while the value of agricultural output stagnated or declined.[87] This last phenomenon was caused by a combination of static population, abundant harvests, and resulting very low prices. Wheat prices, for example, relatively high during 1725-1729, started downward in 1730 and were at their lowest levels for any peacetime year in the eighteenth century during 1732-1733 — particularly the last quarter of 1732 and first quarter of 1733 — when the decisions about the excise scheme had to be made.[88] Great harvests and low prices have different economic consequences for different sectors of society. For the poor generally, they meant low bread prices and money for other things (including imported things and excisable things). For farmers and landlords, however, they meant sharply diminished incomes and arrears of rents. Despite or perhaps because of the post-bubble depression, Walpole at first followed the most conservative fiscal policy. Except when prevented by the little war with Spain, 1726-1729, he strove not only for a balanced budget but also for a surplus that would honor the spirit of the sinking fund and permit some of the national debt to be paid off. In fact, the national debt was reduced from £54.9 million in 1721 to £46.9 million in 1739.[89] However, he had always to be conscious that in the eighteenth century the land tax was regarded as an emergency tax for wartime and had to be reduced with the return to peace. Thus, following the Treaty of Seville with Spain in 1729, he was able not only to cut military expenditures, but also to reduce the land tax from 4s. (1727) and 3s. (1728) to 2s. (1730) in the pound.[90] He did this not because he was more than normally sensitive to the political importance of the landed gentry, but because all heads of the treasury in the eighteenth century were expected to do as much on the return of peace. In addition, he acceded to back-bench pressure that year when Parliament abolished the salt tax. However in 1732, amid much controversy, Walpole brought back the salt tax, in order to reduce the land tax to 1s.[91] This was prob-ably more than a ploy for the political support of the landed gentry; it can also be viewed as a practical farmer's recognition that exceptionally low prices gave the agricultural sector a legiti-mate claim to tax relief.

Despite these reductions in taxes, Walpole had a comfortable budgetary surplus down through 1733. Only in the fiscal year Michaelmas 1733-Michaelmas 1734 did he go into deficit. This deficit was caused partly by his reduction of the land tax, but more seriously by a very substantial increase in expenditures for the armed forces. The start in 1733 of the War of the Polish Suc-cession (involving France, Spain, the Austrian Hapsburgs, and Russia, as well as Poland) found Britain not for the only time with a radically reduced defense establishment needing immedi-ate restocking, even though Britain never entered the war. These expenditures were met by raiding the sinking fund and going into deficit beyond that. This is good Keynesian countercyclical pol-icy. But Walpole was not a Keynesian fighting a depression; he was a conventional eighteenth-century financier borrowing in time of war or threat of war. Balanced budgets and the sinking fund were pieties for peacetime only. Too many economic his-torians forget about things like the War of the Polish Succession.

For students of the excise affair, the significance of the data in table 8.1 is this: Walpole had a deficit by the end of 1733. He did not, however, have a deficit in 1731 and 1732, when the crucial decisions about the excise reform were made. It was thus much more likely that these decisions were initially governed more by administrative and colonial considerations than by budgetary necessity. Furthermore, neither Walpole nor any other statesman of the eighteenth century could ever have known how much addi-tional revenue an administrative change would produce. One

TABLE 8.1

BUDGETARY SITUATION, 1728-1734[92]

(IN THOUSANDS OF POUNDS STERLING)

	Government income				Surplus of income over expenditure	Expenditure on defense
	Customs	Excise	Land tax	Total net		
1728	1,833	2,626	1,977	6,741	+237	3,118
1729	1,669	2,649	1,644	6,294	+584	2,383
1730	1,601	2,810	1,558	6,265	+691	2,359
1731	1,525	2,786	1,217	6,080	+733	2,308
1732	1,689	2,712	1,129	5,803	+829	1,824
1733	1,521	3,028	721	5,522	+927	1,494
1734	1,560	2,918	710	5,448	-913	3,249

could only try and see. However, the fact that commerce was relatively prosperous at a time when agriculture was in great distress made it both equitable and politically attractive to consider administrative reforms that might shift part of the burden of taxes from agriculture to trade. That Walpole could not bring this off tells us something about the limits of the self-perception, if not the power, of the agricultural interest in eighteenth-century England.

CHRONOLOGY

The precise interrelationship of budgetary, political, administrative, and colonial-commercial considerations may become somewhat clearer if we try to reconstruct the chronology of the two years preceding the introduction of the excise scheme in Parliament in March 1733.

The key ideas of the excise scheme had been recommended to Walpole by Crookshanks in 1724 and by Dinwiddie in 1730, but there were no pressing reasons for Walpole to take them up then. In 1731, three relatively minor occurrences forced the treasury to think about the tobacco trade and revenue. One was the request of the merchants of London for a *voluntary* or optional warehouse scheme analogous to that provided for in the Tobacco Act of 1714, but inoperative since 1723. The second was the attempt of some of the same London tobacco merchants to obtain a royal disallowance or veto of Gooch's Virginia Tobacco Inspection Law of 1730. This effort was supported by the customs board but resisted by the Virginia agent, the treasury clerk Peter Leheup. The third was a report, received in September, of extensive frauds in the port of Dumfries involving, among other officers, the surveyor-general of tobacco in that area, Duncan Lamond. This raised the whole specter of Scottish frauds that had so excited the merchants and Parliament in 1721-1723. The government's response to all three was on the surface rather minimal. The Inspection Law was allowed to stand for a trial period, though without formal royal approbation. The Scottish charges were referred to the Edinburgh customs commissioners for careful investigation.[93] The London request for warehousing elicited no visible response at all. However, Walpole's surviving papers show that about this time — 1731 — warehouse schemes for tobacco were under consideration. Estimates were obtained as to costs, and a merchant was consulted about some of the problems to be faced, not from the optional warehouse scheme asked for by the merchants, but from a compulsory warehouse scheme.[94]

Sometime no later than October 1731—that is, only a few weeks after the Scottish charges were received—a decision was made to proceed not just with a compulsory warehouse scheme but with a full-blown excise scheme such as that suggested by Crookshanks in 1724. The decision to add the excise feature was radical and, in the end, fateful for the scheme. Walpole obviously made the decision, but who was then its crucial advocate? It was later alleged by a mercantile opponent of the scheme that it was "in great measure cooked up by their [the Virginians'] standing Agent here [P. Leheup], and sent to Virginia to get the Sanction of the Council and Assembly to it."[95] Leheup knew what the Virginians and the treasury were thinking and was uniquely placed to help concoct a scheme that would be attractive to both. Leheup could be effective, however, only if the thinking of Scrope and Walpole was moving in a direction congenial to the interests of Virginia. Whoever was the key advocate of excise in 1731, there was some solid evidence giving his arguments credence. Table 8.1 shows a steady decline in the yields of customs between 1727 and 1733 (17 percent aggregate), while excise yields increased 15.3 percent in the same years. These trends should have been evident by 1731 through routine departmental reporting, without the treasury's having to request special reports.

One point is certain: Walpole and his confidants reached at least a tentative decision in 1731 to proceed toward an excise on tobacco—nothing was said then about wine—without requesting any special statistical or other reports from customs. Despite what some historians have suggested about lengthy preparations, it was a decision reached on the basis of a few vague proposals and an emerging judgment (or hunch) that excise was really more efficient than customs.

Although a decision was made in 1731 to proceed with an excise-warehouse scheme on tobacco, it was not deemed pressing enough to bring forward in the coming parliamentary session of 1732. The budgetary situation was not then acute and Walpole presumably had already made the decision to use that session to bring back the salt tax and reduce the land tax another shilling in the pound. Instead, the idea for a tobacco excise was secretly sent out to Virginia for the opinion of the governor and council there. Since it was not sent out through the orthodox channels (the secretary of state and the Board of Trade), it could only have gone out through Leheup, as was charged at the time.[96]

The decision to go ahead was apparently reached early in October 1731, about the time the treasury lords returned to London from the country. Leheup presumably then conveyed the idea to Governor Gooch in Virginia, who received it early in December. The minutes of the Virginia council for 15 December 1731 (with only seven of the twelve councillors present) show that:

The Gov[erno]r Communicated to the Council a Scheme projected in Great Britain for putting the Tob[acc]o under an Excise instead of the present method of paying the Duties thereof & desir'd their Opinion thereon, Whereupon the Board are of Opinion that the Scheme proposed would be greatly for the Interest of his Majesty in securing his Customs[,] prevent the running of Tob[acc]o prove very beneficial to the Inhabitants of this Country But forasmuch as this Matter is of very great Moment & divers of the Members of this Board being Absent the Council are of Opinion that if the Weather will permit a full Council be called to meet hereon the 23d instant or Otherwise that the Gov[erno]r will be pleas'd to send Copies of the Scheme af[ore]s[ai]d to the several absent Members & receive their Sentiments thereon & accordingly transmit his answer to the person [Leheup] from whom he rec[eive]d the said project.[97]

Gooch apparently decided not to call that special meeting of the council. Presumably, he uncovered no opposition from the other members and so informed Leheup.

One of the absent council members was Robert Carter, president of the council, and a regular correspondent of Micajah Perry. Although nothing on the scheme appears in the surviving letterbooks of Carter, we must assume it inevitable that Carter or another member of the council would let the secret out and that it would soon reach London. In fact, by March 1732, Sir James Lowther, M.P., principal landlord and patron of the tobacco port of Whitehaven, had obtained an interesting view of Walpole's plans:

There is a huge clamor ag[ain]st S[r] Rob[t] about this Salt Duty w[hi]ch he designs to make perpetual next year, also to have an excise both upon

Tobacco & Wines instead of the Customs in order to make every pound & every Qu[ar]t pay the full & to have no Land tax the next year, but the Year after when he has gott more Excises then to have the Land Tax also, & to make every County in England pay the full Land tax by w[hi]ch he proposes to raise as much by [one] s[hillin]g land tax as at present by two [;] if this can be effected it will entirely ruin the poor remote Countys from London w[hi]ch has gott almost all the mony. This with the Companys & Joinstocks will soon gett all the mony of the Kingdom into the hands of Royal Family, the ministry & Dir[ecto]rs of Companys, but some think there will be publick disturbances before he can effect it.[98]

This letter is interesting for a variety of reasons. First, it shows that an independent Whig M.P. knew about the tobacco and wine excise almost a year before it was introduced[99] and had also learned that "there will be publick disturbances before he can effect it." If Lowther knew this much, it is clear that the Virginia merchants and other elements in society who might wish to oppose the excise scheme had a full year to concoct their plans and knew fairly well what their tactics would be. Secondly, his letter shows that at least some landed proprietors were suspicious of Walpole's schemes for reducing and perhaps eliminating the land tax, lest its abolition one year simply be the prelude to its reintroduction the next year with a new and more equitable assessment that might hurt hitherto undertaxed counties such as Cumberland.

Although the tobacco and wine excise scheme seemed to be firm in early 1732, the treasury, busy with the salt tax that year, proceeded at a very unhurried pace. After hearing of the Virginia council's approval, word must have been sent back to Gooch through Leheup that some sort of petition or memorial from Virginia would be helpful. When the Virginia assembly met in late May 1732, the excise scheme was brought forward. Between 8 and 30 June, first the council and then the House of Burgesses worked on the matter and finally agreed, virtually unanimously, to send an address to the king, a petition to the House of Commons, and a letter to the lords of the treasury complaining about the distressed state of the tobacco trade and asking "to put Tobacco under an Excise" to prevent frauds and relieve the planter. It was further agreed to send John Randolph back to London to solicit the affair with a subvention of £2200. The size of this honorarium shows that the Virginians took the matter very seriously and were not simply acting as cat's-paws of the ministers in London.[100]

Why did the Virginians react so positively to the excise proposal? Their enthusiasm was both impetuous and calculating. As President Robert Carter explained to Micajah Perry, the assembly had only been sitting a short time when news arrived of the passage of the Colonial Debts Act. If the act had only concerned the proving of merchants' accounts, "it would not have alarm'd us in the manner it has done but with that . . . [and the section making planters' realty and slaves liable to nonmortgage debts] it has raisd so general a fury in the Assembly" that they rushed into the excise scheme; "the torrent [was] so strong there was no stemming the tide." But Carter also made it clear that it was more than revenge. The planters viewed the excise as a rational device to protect them from mercantile bankruptcies and abuses.[101] The planters, however, were not simply concerned with bankruptcies and frauds; they were also concerned with normal mercantile practices. As hinted in 1713, they calculated that an excise would save them commission. As already noted, approximately 70 percent of the tobacco sent to England about 1732 was reexported. Because the merchant had to pay or secure the duty on this while it was in England, even though all the duty was drawn back at exportation, he charged his 2½ percent commission not just on the export price but on the value of the customs as well. This more than trebled the commission. An 800-pound hogshead of ordinary tobacco, sold to the French at 2d. ¼ per pound, would bring in £7 10s. gross, but the duty paid and bonded, and ultimately refunded, was £17 12s. Including the duty thus raised the 2½ percent commission from 3s. 9d. for the hogshead to 12s. 6d. Commissions of this magnitude seemed an injustice when the net yield of a hogshead dropped to £3 or £4. If tobacco were warehoused under an excise scheme, no duty would have to be paid or secured on the 70 percent of the crop reexported, and the planters could well imagine that they would thereby save more than two-thirds on their commissions. Thus, for planter and merchant, the question of excise was a question of narrow interest and class struggle. Indeed, it could be argued that, far from being cat's-paws of the ministry in London, the planter-legislators of Virginia were using the interest of the ministry to obtain a most concrete advantage for themselves. As far as the planters were concerned, all the talk of fraud and smuggling was by the way. Whether or not the crown gained a penny by the excise scheme, planter consigners stood to gain many thousands of pounds in savings on commissions.[102]

Not everyone in the Chesapeake, however, was prepared to express his frustration by as orderly an exercise as a petition for an excise. The very low tobacco prices of the past five or so years were borne heavily by the smallest planters, a far from orderly lot. In Maryland, where there was no inspection law, there were very serious plant-cutting riots (a primitive form of crop control) by the smaller planters in 1731. These were serious enough to force Lord Baltimore to make a trip to his proprietorship in 1732 — a very rare occurrence.[103] The riots spread from Maryland to the northern neck of Virginia where they were rather directed against Gooch's new tobacco inspection law — inspired, the governor felt, by false rumors spread by merchants hostile to the law.[104] These riots must have made some stir in England, for a French informant reported to Paris:

On est actuellement fort occupé au Bureau du Commerce et des Plantations à chercher les moyens les plus propres d'Empecher la Destruction entiere des Colonies angloises de Tabac que les habitans mêmes ont resolu entre eux de detruire, faute, disent-ils, d'Encouragement raisonable de la part de la G.B.; Tous les vaisseaux qui sont depuis peu arrivé de ces païs là en raportent des Relations, par lesquelles Il paroit que plus de la moitié des Plantages des Toutte la Province de Mary Land, et à l'exemple de celle cy de la Virginie y est detruite et que sans un prompt rémedie tout le reste poura avoir le même sort.[105]

Such "information" was, of course, also available to the treasury. How much weight it had there we can only guess. However, at just about the time the French informant was writing — early summer 1732 — at what was probably the prorogation meeting of the full cabinet, the ministry discussed the excise proposal and apparently decided collectively to proceed with it.[106]

Such was the situation when the ministers reassembled in London toward the end of September 1732 after their summer holidays in the country. Although some sort of decision had been made to proceed with the excise proposal, and signals had been sent to Virginia inviting a petition, next to nothing had been done at the treasury to prepare a concrete excise proposal. It was probably not too late to draw back. However, at this juncture, new charges were received at the treasury of serious frauds in the tobacco revenue at Glasgow. This was a very sensitive matter, coming as it did after like charges about Dumfries a year before. Similar allegations in 1721-1723 by the merchants of London, Bristol, Liverpool, and Whitehaven, acting in concert, had led to a strong parliamentary attack upon the Scots and serious suggestions in Parliament that the Act of Union should be abrogated as far as the tobacco trade was concerned. Walpole deflected this attack in 1723 by merging—at least nominally—the English and Scots customs boards and making significant reductions in the level of taxation on tobacco. These concessions cost the crown about £55,000-£75,000 per annum at the time, and more as the trade expanded.[107] Walpole could not want such an uncontrollable situation to develop again.

On 3 October 1732 a paper was read at the treasury board "containing an Acco[un]t of many Notorious frauds Comited with respect to the Customes at Port Glasgow and more particularly in relacon to Tobacco exported and the Debentures obtained for the same." The treasury lords took these charges very seriously and ordered Gwynn Vaughan, one of the Edinburgh customs commissioners, to make a personal survey of the tobacco ports and get to the bottom of the matter. They cited a previous successful survey made by Humphrey Brent, another customs commissioner, in 1722.[108] The Scottish board recognized the seriousness of the matter, and Vaughan, accompanied by the collector of Leith, left almost immediately on his survey. He completed his inspection and report by Christmas, a remarkably swift operation by eighteenth-century standards.

In his report of 18 December 1732, Gwynn Vaughan gave details of irregularities in the tobacco trade at most of the ports of southwestern Scotland. The great fraud of 1721-1722—bribing the weighing porters and officers to underweigh the tobacco at importation—had been corrected. Now the great irregularities were in the export trade: (1) Tobacco legally exported with drawback of duties was subsequently surreptitiously relanded. (2) Because the officers did not weight every hogshead, exporters were given an opportunity to put peat and stones in some hogsheads or to grossly overenter the weights of hogsheads not weighed. When the board in 1732 ordered the officers at Irvine to strip and weigh each hogshead, average weights at exportation dropped by one-third. (3) There also were numerous attendant irregularities in record keeping and oath taking. A hogshead could be sent over-land to the east coast and shipped to England. Subsequently what purported to be the same hogshead could be exported from the west coast of Scotland and draw back full duty, since the west-coast officers had no knowledge of the eastern coastal business. In a subsequent private letter to John Scrope, Vaughan blamed the incompetence of the Scottish patent officers and the influence of the great men who got them their positions and protected them.[109]

Vaughan ordered the Edinburgh comptroller-general's office to prepare accounts of the tobacco revenue in Scotland for trans-mittal to London. When we compare these data with similar accounts for England received at about the same time (table 8.2), we see how dreary the Scottish picture really was. In England, the revenue concessions of the 1723 legislation had been in great part balanced out by revenue improvements (particularly the burning of damaged tobacco), so that average "net yields" for tobacco had declined from £218,477 in 1717-1722 to only £196,899 in 1723-1727 and then recovered to £223,364 in 1728-1732. (Sums paid into the exchequer also mirror the recovery.) In Scotland, however, payments to the receiver general had declined from £7,619 in 1719-1722 to £6,810 in 1723-1727 and only £2,953 in 1728-1732. Though the English yield was disappointing, that in Scotland was shocking, with North Britain's share of British receipts falling from 3.9 percent in 1723-1727 to only 1.8 percent in 1728-1732. Vaughan thought Scottish net receipts should be at least £28,000 per annum, or roughly ten times what they were.

The remarkable thing is that the government made very little use of this Scottish information in the subsequent excise debate. For this reticence they may have had both political and practical reasons. The attack on Scottish customs irregularities in Parlia-ment in 1721-1723 challenged the whole spirit of the union. The government could not want to open that Pandora's box again. Practically, too, Scotland was not very important for the revenue. Even if payments on tobacco in Scotland increased five- or ten-fold, the sums received still would not be very large. To justify a change to excise, Walpole would have to persuade Parliament that there were great improvements in the revenue to be realized

TABLE 8.2

ANNUAL YIELDS OF TAXES ON WINE AND TOBACCO, 1717-1732

| | England | | Scotland |
	Wine[110] (net yield)	Tobacco[111] (net yield)	Tobacco[112] (paid into exchequer)	Tobacco[113] (paid into receiver-general)
1717-22	£552,215	£218,477	—	£7,619*
1723-27	478,441	196,899	£153,006 (96.1%)	6,180 (3.9%)
1728-32	515,807	223,364**	163,572 (98.2%)	2,953 (1.8%)

*1719-22
**1728-31

in England, improvements that could produce results in six figures. The government's reticence on Scotland does not mean that Scotland was not on the mind of some at the treasury—particularly John Scrope, with his long experience north of the border. The Scottish revelations at the end of 1732 may well have been the final blow that sent the government lurching forward with its excise burden.

Although rumors of an excise scheme had been around all through 1732, although the well-informed could report that it was definite in October[114]—the month when the opposition press opened its attack on "General Excise,"[115] although John Randolph arrived with the Virginia petitions early in November,[116] the treasury did not begin to make any concrete plans until December 1732. The years of preparation some historians have imagined were largely psychological. On 5 December 1732, Scrope, apparently on his own authority, wrote to the customs board in Edinburgh for accounts of the gross and net proceeds of the duty on tobacco and wine for seven years. On 12 December, he was ordered by the treasury board to get rather fuller accounts from the English and Scottish commissioners. That order of 12 December is the first formal indication that anything approaching an excise scheme was discussed at the treasury board.[117] Only after the receipt of those accounts at the end of the month and in January could Walpole and Scrope begin detailed work on the scheme. Scrope was noted as the great legislative draftsman of his day and probably wrote the bill. Walpole's working papers of this time are rather those of one drafting a speech or pamphlet on a controversial subject.[118] The papers also show that Walpole consulted a few outsiders who advised him against the excise scheme —including an anonymous merchant[119] and Sir Richard Lane, former Bristol merchant and proministerial M.P. for Worcester, who liked the warehouse scheme but thought that excise administration "seems unnecessary and impracticable" and "Will certainly disoblige—so that we shall lose our Elections."[120]

The long delays between the leaking of the excise proposal in early 1732 and the actual introduction of the scheme in March 1733 gave its enemies more than enough time to concert their attacks. Sir James Lowther was spreading a hostile word in the northwest in March 1732, and the first of Pulteney's hostile pamphlets came out in June. However, the concerned journalistic attack only started in November, with a flood of pamphlets following in the new year.[121] For both the political and economic historian, a most interesting feature of the opposition was the flood of letters, memorials, etc. received by M.P.'s from their constituents, asking them to oppose the excise scheme. Paul Langford has published a list of fifty-four constituencies sending such instructions to their members, and perhaps five more can be added to his list.[122] Langford adds, "The instructions against the Jew Bill of 1753, the petitions and instructions following the loss of Minorca in 1756, the petitions and addresses associated with the Wilkes and reform agitations of the sixties and seventies were scarcely on this scale." However, Langford's comparisons are all with political questions important in London, but not matters that would affect ordinary shopkeeper voters the way an excise might. If we want an apter comparison, we have only to look back a few years in the journals of the House of Commons: between 18 February and 24 April 1730, petitions were presented to the house from shopkeepers in 79 different communities protesting against the unfair competition of hawkers and peddlers; a further 25 were presented in 1731 and two more in 1732. About half the places petitioning against excise had earlier petitioned against peddling, but petitions against peddling were received from sixty-two communities that did not petition against excise. The sixty-two were for the most part small places, but they included Berwick-on-Tweed, Cambridge, Derby, Durham, Halifax, Hereford, Hertford, Leeds, Lincoln, Plymouth, Preston, Salisbury, and Wakefield.[123] This antipeddler agitation shows that there was already in existence in the mercantile community a network of communication that could be utilized for political action. (There was a lot of petitioning to the Commons on other subjects ca. 1730-1732, but none on the scale of the antipeddler agitation.) The list of places that petitioned on peddling, but not on excise, also suggests that the antiexcise hysteria in the country was not as frenetic as the London publicists tried to make it. Whether indifference, proministerial sentiment, or local controlling political influences kept those sixty-two places quiet, the shopkeepers of the interior were *not* as a class totally swept into the antiexcise furor.

In the larger port towns, particularly those connected with the wine and tobacco trades, there was more frenzy and unanimity.

London, of course, took the lead, but the other important tobacco ports—Bristol, Liverpool, and Whitehaven, in particular—joined in. Only Scotland was strangely, perhaps guiltily, silent.[124] In the English ports, economic motives were mixed with political. The Walpole regime was not popular in the large port towns, as became all too evident a few years later in the Jenkins' Ear agitation and riots. As the French minister in London reported to the minister of foreign affairs, ". . . si l'on en Excepte les Directeurs de la Compagnie de Commerce, toute la Cité de Londres est generalement Indisposée, pour ne pas dire plus, contre la Cour et contre Son Gouvernement."[125] Lord Stair made this much more explicit when he warned the queen about the unwisdom of the excise: "he [Walpole] is hated by the city of London, because he never did anything for the trading part of it, nor aimed at any interest of theirs but a corrupt influence over the directors and governors of the great moneyed companies."[126] In the intense hostility of the larger ports to the excise scheme, we must see both this political antipathy of an alienated urban population and the calculations of merchants and shopkeepers who knew when their interest was affected.

At Bristol, the mayor was Lyonel Lyde, a prominent Virginia merchant. When news was received in early January of the impending excise scheme, both the Society of Merchant Venturers and the Common Council of the town adopted resolutions against it and sent these to the two members for the town. One of these was John Scrope, the secretary to the treasury, from whom they could expect little, but the other was Sir Abraham Elton, the younger, who had a long family association with the tobacco trade, and who was much more sympathetic. On the eve of the introduction of the bill in March, the council and the Merchant Venturers shared the costs of a delegation sent to London to lobby against it.[127] At Liverpool, the merchants met in January and not only adopted resolutions against excise but also "have written to most of the Towns in that County desiring their Friends to make early Application to every Member of Parliament they have the least Pretension to ask a Favour from, to oppose every Attempt of any . . . Extension of the Excise Laws." In February, the Liverpool town council wrote to their members to this effect.[128]

At Whitehaven, the situation was more complex, because the

town was not a parliamentary borough. Its principal landlord, Sir James Lowther, was member for the county. He, it will be remembered, had written in alarm about the scheme a year in advance and feared that Walpole only wanted to abolish the existing land tax in order to institute a new and reformed one, in which the northern counties would pay a higher assessment. Even while opposing the scheme, he was not above publicizing his interpretation of it, in hopes that both together would depress land values so that he could buy more cheaply.[129] When the concerted opposition became intense in January, Lowther (who was also corresponding with Liverpool) sent his agent Spedding a letter to be shown to the justices at the next quarter sessions and suggested that a delegation of Whitehaven merchants lobby at the sessions. He also sent printed ballads and suggested that the Whitehaven merchants go en masse to Cockermouth (nearby parliamentary borough) and join the burgesses there in letters to the members and the duke of Somerset. Spedding attended the sessions and managed things well, for letters against the excise were eventually sent by the justices and other gentlemen of the county, as well as by the burgesses of Cockermouth and the merchants of Whitehaven.[130]

The chief burden of opposition, however, fell on the Londoners. Toward the end of November the tobacco merchants met and resolved to organize to fight the excise. On 8 December, the wine importers met and resolved to do the same, and agreed to levy a contribution of 6d. per pipe on all wine imported after 1 January for their lobbying expenses.[131] To maximize their effectiveness, however, a broader appeal was needed. On 22 December 300-400 "merchants, traders and citizens" of London, Whig and Tory, Anglican, Dissenter, and Papist, attended a meeting at the Swan Tavern in Cornhill and chose a committee of twenty-five to solicit the members for the city and other places against the excise. This committee appears a most interesting group, even though all its members cannot be identified. There was a strong representation of wine importers: Sir William Chapman, baronet, who presided; Alderman George Champion, Alderman Robert Godschall, Robert Willimot, Daniel Lambert, Samuel Wilson, William Cleaver, and George Stanford. The tobacco trade was less strongly represented by three importers (Samuel Hyde, Samuel Haswell, and Thomas Hyam) and three manufacturers (John Bosworth, Benjamin [?] Bradley, and Joseph Dash). There was a strong element of prominent city Tories: Godschall, Willimot, Lambert, Marshall, and Lockwood, all of whom were future M.P.'s and all but the last future lord mayors of London.[132] That there were not more prominent names from the tobacco importers suggests that some elements in the trade (noticeably the Scots and the Quakers) had doubts about being too conspicuous followers of Perry and Hyde in what was bound to be most distasteful to their correspondents in America. Nevertheless, early in January, the tobacco merchants met and raised £130 in subscriptions and agreed to use for the antiexcise cause the proceeds of their long-standing 3d. per hogshead "political fund."[133] At a similar meeting on 5 (?) January, the tobacconists joined the fray, appointing a committee of their own.[134]

All through January and February, the tension mounted, with the press and newsletter writers reporting a constant stream of remonstrances from the country and delegations of London and Southwark merchants in long rows of coaches waiting on the speaker or this or that M.P. While pamphlets poured from the press and rumors chased rumors that the excise scheme was dropped or that tobacco would come forward without wine,[135] Walpole, Scrope, and their unknown aides worked at their own pace drafting the bill. Gradually, everyone perceived that the battle would have to be fought out in the House of Commons.

There were at this time only five M.P.'s who had any sort of personal involvement in the tobacco trade: Micajah Perry, M.P. for London, a great Virginia merchant; Edward Tucker, M.P. for Weymouth and Melcombe Regis, a smaller Virginia merchant; Daniel Campbell of Shawfield, M.P. for Glasgow, a former Virginia merchant; Sir Abraham Elton the younger, M.P. for Bristol, an occasional tobacco merchant; and Robert Bristow, Clerk of the Green Cloth, M.P. for Winchelsea, grandson of a Virginia merchant from whom he had inherited an estate there.[136] Tucker, who was a local political ally of Bubb Dodington, a junior treasury lord, was characteristically absent from the excise debates and voting in March, but eventually voted against excise in April. Campbell and Bristow were inveterate supporters of government and voted for the scheme.[137] That left only Elton and Perry to fight against it in Parliament, and Elton's ineffectiveness let the chief burden fall on Perry. He was the head of the greatest Virginia house in London, founded by his grandfather in the reign of Charles II. Almost from the time he succeeded his father and grandfather in 1720-1721, he was recognized as a leading figure in the Virginia trade, being elected virtually perpetual treasurer (head) of the committee of Virginia and Maryland merchants.[138] Unlike his father and grandfather, he was attracted to the public life of the city and in 1727 was elected M.P. for London in the government interest. By 1729 he had drifted into opposition along with John Barnard and the other London popular antiministerialists. He was an exceptionally active M.P., speaking on almost every issue affecting America and serving on numerous select committees. His opposition to the excise bill was both the zenith of his political career and the beginning of his commercial downfall.

Next to nothing was said about the excise from the government side when Parliament convened in January, though Barnard and other opposition figures used the occasion of the debate on the address to attack the idea of excise. On 6 February, the government began the process of having the house call for accounts on tobacco, wine, coffee, tea, and the like, a necessary first step in the legislative process. These accounts started coming in on 25 February. Not till 7 March was the government ready to move that on 14 March the House should "resolve itself into a Committee of the whole House, to consider of the most proper Methods for the better Security and Improvement of the Duties and Revenues already charged upon... Tobacco and Wines."[139]

When the matter finally came up for discussion in the committee of the whole on the fourteenth, Walpole in his very long speech concentrated heavily upon the colonial and administrative aspects of the problem. He discussed the distress of the planters and the degree to which they had suffered at the hand of their mercantile correspondents in England "who from being their servants, are become their tyrants." He then went on to discuss ways in which the crown was cheated by frauds at weighing inward and outward and by exporting stalks and scraps as good tobacco. The principal reply was made by Micajah Perry who defended the honor of the tobacco merchants, particularly the commission merchants. If the planters knew distress, "the hardships the factors [commission merchants] labor under, are by much the most numerous and most grievous." If the scheme were adopted, the commission merchants would have to give up trade and then the planters would be truly distressed with so few ships to take away their tobacco. After a long and not very enlightening debate, the customs commissioners were called in and, through John Hill, Walpole's manager on the board, answered factual questions. Late that night, the government's excise resolutions for tobacco were accepted by the committee of the whole, 265-204. Two days later, when the committee's report was presented to the house, a motion to bring in a tobacco bill as recommended by the committee passed 249-189. A separate bill for wine was to come later, but in the event never appeared.

The existing duties nominally totaled 6.33d. per pound but with automatic allowances and discounts came to only 5.28d. when bonded and 4.75d. when paid in cash. The resolutions accepted by the House on 16 March called for removing all the customs duties on tobacco except the subsidy of 1697 (a penny per pound nominally, but with 25 percent discount when paid in cash). The 1697 subsidy duty, alone of the various duties on tobacco, was payable to the king's civil list and, by leaving it as it was, the ministry hoped to avoid the charge of attempting to fatten the civil list. The remaining duties nominally totalling 5.33d. —but actually only 4.43d. when bonded and 4d. when paid in cash—were to be replaced by an "inland duty" of 4d. per pound. Tobacco would be warehoused on entry without paying anything but the 1697 subsidy, but could not be removed from the king's warehouse until the "inland duty" had been paid in full. All this appeared to be similar to what had been adopted for coffee, chocolate, and tea in 1724 and what Dinwiddie (but not Crookshanks) had recommended in 1730. Though nothing explicit was said about excise,[140] no one was fooled.

When the bill was introduced on 4 April, it was a rather full-blooded excise measure. On entry, tobacco was to pay down the 1697 subsidy (reduced from a nominal penny per pound to three farthings because now paid in cash) and then be warehoused. The tobacco could be removed from the warehouse for export and draw back the subsidy; but it could be removed for domestic consumption only after paying the full inland duty of 4d. per pound. (Special arrangements, however, could be made to remove tobacco intended for manufacture and export without paying the inland duty.) A radical provision provided that all

exported tobacco must give bond against relanding, such bonds
to be discharged only upon return of sworn evidence that the
tobacco had been landed abroad. This proposal had been advocated for generations but had previously only been adopted for
Ireland. Unlike the 1724 Inland Duty Act for coffee, tea, and so
forth, which left the warehouses and duty collection in the hands
of customs, the new bill provided that those powers be vested in
the commissioners to be named by his majesty for the new inland
duty, that is, the excise commissioners. Their officers were given
the universal powers of search common to excise officers. No one
could trade in tobacco without registering with those officers and
reporting to them in advance all intended movements of tobacco.
As in other excise legislation, the commissioners in London were
given extensive judicial powers; however, in the provinces such
powers were in the first instance given to J.P.'s and not to excise
officers (as in earlier legislation), a change designed to make the
scheme seem more constitutional. From the excise commissioners
or the J.P.'s, appeals could be carried only to special commissioners of appeal named from the judges of the high courts of Westminster and the judges of assize.[141] The final version was thus
much closer to Crookshanks's full excise model than to Dinwiddie's more moderate scheme.

A long and spirited debate accompanied the introduction of
the bill. A leading part was taken by Micajah Perry who, like
others in opposition, put very low (£20,000 in his case) the
amount that the government could possibly gain by the scheme.
Against that were to be weighed the harassment to retailer and
merchant. He thought he should have to give up the trade if the
bill passed. Walpole in reply gave his personal estimate that the
excise on tobacco and wine would bring in a further £300,000 to
the crown (Crookshanks's figure). However, he insisted, even if it
only brought £100,000, that was a sum worthy of their serious
consideration. A motion by the opposition that the bill was out of
order was easily defeated by the government, 232-176, a majority
of 56 compared with 60 in March; a later motion to adjourn was
defeated 237-199 (majority of 38), while the key motion that the
bill should have a second reading passed 236-200, a majority of
36. The next day, the opposition forced a division on a motion to
print the bill. This was contrary to precedent, for printing would
invite petitions which were not received on money bills. Neverthe-

less, the government turned back the opposition by only 128-112, a majority of only 16. Walpole then announced a further delay in bringing in the wine bill. He admitted that he wanted to see what happened to tobacco first.[142]

The City of London then took the initiative. Despite the established precedent that the House did not accept petitions against money bills (confirmed that very March on a petition from Rhode Island against the Sugar Bill),[143] the Common Council decided to sponsor a petition against the excise. This was carried to the House of Commons on the tenth, the day before the second reading, in a great procession of at least 80 coaches—a deliberate manifestation of the wealth of the City. A bitter debate ensued and the government was able to carry the rejection of the petition by a vote of only 214-197, a majority of just 17. Walpole had already decided that he must drop the scheme. The next day, when the bill came up for a second reading, he moved a postponement until 12 June, which effectively killed the measure. The wine bill was never introduced.[144] Illuminations, bell ringings, and some rioting greeted the news all over England.[145]

It is not the purpose of this essay to analyze the inner parliamentary history of the excise bill. Paul Langford has done an excellent job of that.[146] He emphasizes the significance of the developing opposition to Walpole in court circles, led by Lord Chesterfield. This manifested itself to only a limited degree in March by the defection of some Scots, particularly the Dalrymple kin of Lord Stair and the "dependents" of the Duke of Montrose and the Earls of Marchmont and Haddington.[147] Most of the defections in March, however, were of independent Whigs on whom the government could never count for sure. By contrast, on 10 April, a large number of normal government supporters abstained. Langford prints a list of seventy "Absent Members."[148] This list may not be absolutely representative of any given division, but it does indicate that many normal government supporters lost heart and simply stayed away in April. Quite the contrary happened to the opposition. Another list, which Langford apparently did not use, contains the names of twenty-seven or twenty-eight members who did not vote against the bill in March but did so later.[149] This list indicates that there were only seven "Whigs" who voted for the bill in March and against it in April.[150] The other twenty-one had not been present in March but showed up to vote "no" in April. They included two new Tory members of the House,[151] nine previously absent Tories,[152] six absent antiministerial Whigs[153] and four absent otherwise pro-ministerial Whigs.[154] In other words, while the discipline of Walpole's forces broke, the opposition was able to bring in the most lethargic country gentlemen and vote something close to their full strength.

The opposition was not able to sustain this effort and make very much out of their victory over Walple. Langford analyzes masterfully their failure to use the excise issue in the election of 1734.[155] This inability to capitalize on Walpole's excise retreat was immediately manifest when on 20 April Sir John Barnard attempted to present a petition from the coffee, tea, and choco-late dealers asking to be relieved of the excise supervision estab-lished in 1724; the government was able to have the petition rejected, 250-150. When the opposition moved for a select com-mittee to investigate frauds in the customs, the government could not resist, but succeeded in packing the committee with their own nominees.[156] The resulting report presented by Sir John Cope on 7 June is one of the most informative committee reports of the eighteenth century on a financial or commercial question. While very factual, it gave essentially the government's view of the prob-lem, paying particular attention to the testimony of Sir John Ran-dolph, the Virginia agent, and the various frauds that the gov-ernment had turned up in recent years.[157]

If the victory proved Pyrrhic for the political opponents of Walpole, it proved a quite substantial victory for the wine and tobacco dealers. Not till the time of the younger Pitt were they to be subjected to really tight controls. Who had used whom?

For one tobacco dealer, the victory was rather bittersweet. Although Micajah Perry, who had borne the heaviest load against excise in the debates, was triumphantly reelected to Par-liament for London in 1734 and was chosen Lord Mayor in 1738-1739, all was not well for him. In the debates, he had frequently insisted that the Virginia memorials had been obtained by false pretenses and that the majority of the planters were really opposed to excise. But, as Stephen Bordley of Maryland wrote to a merchant in Britain: "Notwithstanding the pains that You Mer-chants take to spread your Scurrilous libels amongst us against the Excise, I Can assure You we are Generally for it here . . . & that . . . strenuously."[158] In fact, the legislature of Virginia was so distraught by the news of the withdrawal of the excise bill that they sent an address of loyalty and thanks to the king with very sharp remarks about those who had blocked the king's good intentions towards them on the excise. Peter Leheup, their agent, thought the language too strong and after consulting the duke of Newcastle, secretary of state, suppressed the memorial.[159]

Perry became the chief object of these resentments. For three generations, his family had acted as financial and occasional political agents for Virginia and he still retained the former function in 1733. This involved handling fairly large sums, for Virginia's export duties were payable in sterling bills of exchange.[160] But, as Governor Gooch explained to his brother in 1735, "No wonder the Alderman [Perry] is silent, he has lost sufficiently by opening his mouth too wide, Mr. [John] Grymes [receiver-general] having taken the public money out of his hands and put it into [Robert] Cary's." Gooch himself moved his own business to Cary.[161] Walpole was even more vengeful. His private papers contain numerous reports on the weights of hogsheads imported and exported by Perry.[162] After the election of 1734, suit against Perry was begun in the Court of Exchequer alleging relanding of tobacco sold by Perry for export. Although there is no evidence that Perry had to pay anything, the suit went on for years and must have cost him much in legal fees.[163]

The average planter was less obviously but just as effectively vengeful. He simply reduced his tobacco shipments to Perry. Year after year, ship after ship of Perry's returned to London with less than full cargo—a most serious loss to a commission merchant who owned or chartered a vessel. Perry is reported to have lost more than £10,000 on shipping alone. (He also lost his seat in Parliament to a Tory in 1741.) In the mid-1740s he was forced to wind up his business under conditions of great distress. When he resigned his aldermancy in 1746, the corporation of the city gave him a pension of £200-£400 to save him from distress. After eighty years, the name of Perry disappeared from the trade.[164]

THE SUBSTANTIVE ISSUES

After all the excitement and passion of 1732-1734 had died down, what remained? What was the excise crisis really about? What were the real issues? Who had gained and who had lost?

For the political opponents of Walpole, the substantive issues were unimportant. What was important for them was the chance to embarrass Walpole and perhaps bring him down. They surely succeeded in embarrassing him, but they failed in their broader objective of bringing him down in 1733 or at the next general election in 1734. Even so, something had been gained, for, as Lord Percival noted in his diary on the very day of Walpole's retreat, "it may be foretold that Sir Robert Walpole's influence in the House will never be again so great as it has been."[165]

For those on the other side there were, by contrast, a number of quite solid substantive issues which they hoped to convey to the House and to the nation—not, it has been seen, with very much success. These substantive issues were both commercial-colonial and administrative-financial. The older historians tended to neglect them, perhaps because they depended too much on the somewhat skimpy reports of parliamentary debates. There is a limit to what can be conveyed by even a two- or three-page summary of a long speech, and a limit to what a minister can convey of a technical subject in even the longest speech. In addition to the reports of debates, there were, of course, the pamphlets issued by the dozens during the excitement. In general they were neglected by historians till their usefulness was pointed out by Turner in 1927.[166] But even Turner was rather undiscriminating in his use of the pamphlets. Nine out of ten of them were written by politicians or hired hacks who had no personal knowledge of either the colonial or the administrative dimensions of the problems being discussed. There were, however, a small handful of pamphlets written by people with personal knowledge of the issues in dispute. Attention to these few is an economical way of coming to grips with the interests at stake.

The support of Virginia for the excise scheme was very clearly stated in a document prepared in June 1732 by committees of both houses of the Virginia assembly, including the very literate William Byrd II. After John Randolph's arrival in London, this document was issued early in 1733 as a pamphlet entitled *The Case of the Planters of Tobacco in Virginia as Represented by Themselves, Signed by the President of the Council and Speaker of the House of Burgesses.* After the legitimacy and validity of this document were attacked by the tobacco merchants of London and the opposition press, John Randolph issued a rather detailed sixty-nine-page pamphlet containing both the *Case* and a *Vindication of the said Representation,* of which he was the assumed author. The principal replies of the merchants to these very informed charges came in three pamphlets: (1) *Considerations Relating to the Tobacco Trade at London, so Far as it Relates to the Merchants who are Factors, issued in* mid-March 1733;[167] (2) *Observations on the Cast of the Planters of Virginia In a Letter to* [Sir John Randolph], dated 3 April 1733;[168] and (3) *A Reply to the Vindication of the Representation of the Case of the Planters of Tobacco in Virginia, In a Letter to Sir J[ohn] R[andolph] from the Merchants or Factors of London.*

In their publications, the Virginians made five principal points: (1) the tobacco trade was in an unprecedented depression; (2) the consigning planter was in these difficult times particularly exploited by the commissions and charges of the commission merchant which seemed to rise as prices fell; he was also exploited by the standard deductions from the weights (*draught* or turn of the scale and sample) and by the London deduction of *tret* and *clough* on perishable goods; (3) the consigning planter was also defrauded by the mysterious shrinkage in the weights of his consigned tobacco, whether it was owing to pilferage by sailors and porters or to frauds at the scale on importation; (4) the consigning planter was further injured by the bankruptcies of the merchants to whom he had consigned his tobacco or the manufacturers to whom it had been sold; and (5) grievances 2-4 would be considerably alleviated, if not cured, by an excise scheme.

In their replies, the merchants attempted to answer every point of the planters' complaint: (1) they denied that the trade was in an unprecedented depression, citing earlier years when prices of tobacco had been even lower *in America* (presumably wartime); (2) they denied that miscellaneous charges had risen in recent years; such charges varied only because actual expenses varied; samples were needed for sale to manufacturers and retailers; the commissions charged were quite reasonable when one considered that the merchant was out of funds for months at a time for sums paid down for the duty and for freight and did not charge the planter interest on this; (3) since more than the tobacco imported was on the account of merchants and not planters, the merchants were as aggrieved as the planters by pilfering and all forms of smuggling; if Midford and one or two other merchants had been caught in fraud, the whole community of merchants ought not to be condemned; (4) there had been very few bankruptcies in the trade in recent years, and the only big ones were inexperienced Virginians who had attempted to set up as merchants in London and were trusted too uncritically by their friends in the Chesapeake — an allusion to Edward Randolph, the merchant brother of Sir John and Isham Randolph, who at that very moment was in debtor's prison owing the crown over £10,000;[169] and (5) adopting an excise scheme would solve nothing.

Although there were many political slurs and even falsehoods in the merchants' replies — particularly the claim that Sir John Randolph had been instructed by Virginia to oppose and not support an excise scheme — the economic part of their reply was not unreasonable. Underlying it all was a sense of the capital needs and "cash-flow" problems of the trade that was absent in the planters' complaint. Whether or not a merchant supplied goods to a planter on credit, he started to spend money as soon as he began to load a vessel for the Chesapeake. When the vessel returned, he had to find cash quickly for part of the duties (the Old Subsidy) and for freight and handling charges. While his tobacco was waiting months for sale, all these funds were tied up and if the tobacco was reexported, customs could be very slow in paying the drawback of duties. One important thing that alleviated the cash-flow problems of the trade was the long credit on the duties allowed by the government. Supported by such credit from the crown, "the Merchant . . . generally sells on Credit to a Wholesale Dealer; who likewise sells on Credit to the Country Dealer, and to the Shopkeeper in Town; the Shopkeeper retails it out, and often credits the Consumer."[170] If the crown credit were withdrawn, entry into the trade at every level would be limited to the more affluent, a development likely to reduce competition and lower prices. The excise scheme thus might help the reexport trade but would hurt the domestic trade which took the best and highest-priced Virginia tobaccos. To the extent that they could not see this, the planters of Virginia, it was implied, did not know their own best interests.

When we try to reconstruct the substantive issues as they may have existed in the mind of Walpole, we are severely circumscribed. No relevant confidential letters or reports of confidential conversations survive. Instead we must rely, as did the earlier historians, on his speeches, plus the pamphlets ascribed to him and his now available working papers.[171] Although his pamphlets and his speeches show some courteous concern about the suffering of the planters and the desirability of improving other revenues so that the land tax can be lightened, most of their space is devoted to the narrow administrative problems of the tobacco revenue. This impression is supported by his working papers at Cambridge. In other words, Walpole appears to have seen the excise scheme as not very different from the countless other technical reform measures concerning taxation that the treasury brought in almost every year. A branch of the revenue was discovered to be producing less than it should; some change would have to be made in its mode of collection. Several such measures passed in almost every session of Parliament, for the most part without debate or a record division. (One such measure affecting tobacco was passed about every second year, ca. 1689-1727.) That this one did not slip through in the usual way was due to a variety of factors to which different historians may honestly ascribe different weights: the long delay between the leaking of the government's intention and the introduction of the scheme, which enabled both parliamentary and mercantile opposition to perfect their plans; the inherent suspiciousness of the English in matters of public money and personal liberties; the exceptional propagandistic effort in the provinces; the defection of the court grandees, which may have accounted for much of the demoralization among Walpole's normal supporters; and, finally, that conjuncture of economic depression, epidemics with high mortality (in the late 1720s) and political boredom uniting to create a kind of social and political malaise that could easily convert a minor proposal into a political grand explosion.

But all the bonfires and bell ringings that hailed the retreat of Walpole did not alter the objective circumstances that had made both Virginia planters and Whitehall bureaucrats interested in the excise scheme. The Virginia and Maryland planters in the future expressed their distrust of the consignment system by selling their tobacco in the country rather than consigning it—to the advantage of the merchants of Glasgow and Whitehaven in particular, who bought directly and did not wait for consignments. By the time of the American Revolution, it is doubtful if much more than a quarter of the tobacco coming to Britain was still coming on consignment. The bureaucrats and technicians of the treasury also bided their time. In 1751, Henry Pelham's Tobacco Act (24 Geo. II c. 41) adopted much of the record keeping, paper controls, and searches of the excise scheme without using that horrible word. In 1789 the younger Pitt's Tobacco Act (29 Geo. III c. 68) finally brought in the compulsory warehouse and most of the remaining excise controls, while dividing the duties between customs and excise. Only when customs and excise were merged in the next century did the problem of names finally disappear.

Was this all then just a tempest in a teapot, or a storm in a snuffbox? Yes and no. The cutting edge of the early modern state was its ability to tax. Only as the state expanded both its legal and its effective powers of taxation could it expand its more general pretensions and its ability to act in broader spheres externally and internally. The enemies of the state knew this, whether one is talking about the obstreperous *Parlements* of Louis XV or the House of Commons of Charles I, or the Stamp Act Congress. In England, so many of the great constitutional questions from the Bates Case to the Boston Tea Party started, of course, as questions of taxation. Thus, currants and tobacco and wine and tea, like stamps and ship money, can, in the context of taxation, acquire a historical significance that has nothing to do with their intrinsic importance. In a parliamentary regime, the shrewder experienced bureaucrats and technicians must realize that "you win a few and you lose a few," but the problem remains. The defeat of Walpole's excise scheme did not stop for long the process of the growth of taxation and state apparatus in Great Britain.

NOTES

1. Paul Langford, *The Excise Crisis: Society and Politics in the Age of Walpole* (Oxford, 1975).

2. William Coxe, *Memoirs of the Life and Administration of Sir Robert Walpole, Earl of Orford,* 3 vols. (London, 1978) I, 366-407; III, 129-137. An earlier account by a hostile contemporary, but with the same parliamentary focus, is [James Ralph], *A Critical History of the Administration of Sir Robert Walpole, now Earl of Orford* (London, 1743), pp. 256-279.

3. Coxe, *Robert Walpole,* I, 379-380.

4. One historian who noted Coxe's error was Edward Raymond Turner, "The Excise Scheme of 1733," *English Historical Review* XLII (1927), 47.

5. Philip Henry Stanhope, 5th Earl Stanhope (styled Lord Mahon when history published), *History of England from the Peace of Utrecht...,* 7 vols. (London, 1836-1854), II, 241-257.

6. Alexander Charles Ewald, *Sir Robert Walpole: a Political Biography 1676-1745* (London, 1878), pp. 228-242; John Morley, *Walpole* ("Twelve English Statesmen" ser.) (London, 1889), pp. 169-182.

7. Turner, "The Excise Scheme of 1733," pp. 34-57; William Thomas Laprade, *Public Opinion and Politics in Eighteenth Century England to the Fall of Walpole* (New York, 1936), especially pp. 337-342. See also Robert Emmet Carson, "Journalistic Opposition to Sir Robert Walpole...1727-1742" (Ph.D. diss., University of Michigan, 1944).

8. Paul Vacher, *La Crise du Ministère Walpole en 1733-1734* (Paris, 1924); Norris Arthur Brisco, "The Economic Policy of Robert Walpole" (Ph.D. diss., Columbia University, 1907).

9. E.g., Frederick Scott Oliver, *The Endless Adventure,* 3 vols. (London, 1930-35), II, 234-277; George Robert Stirling Taylor, *Robert Walpole and His Age* (London, 1931), pp. 275-284. Other authors who fail to mention Perry include Laprade, Mahon, Morley, etc.

10. See n. 1; J. H. Plumb, *Sir Robert Walpole: the King's Minister* (London, 1960), pp. 248-271.

11. American Historical Association, *Annual Report, 1905* (Washington, D.C., 1906), I, 71-97.

12. John M. Hemphill II, "Virginia and the English Commercial System, 1689-1733" (Ph.D. diss., Princeton, 1964).

13. Particularly Jacob M. Price, "The Tobacco Trade and the Treasury, 1685-1733: British Mercantilism in its Fiscal Aspects" (Ph.D. diss., Harvard University, 1954).

14. Ibid., chap. I, pp. 9-23.

15. Some of the early literature on excise is reviewed by E. R. Turner, "Early Opinion about English Excise," *American Historical Review* XXI (1916), 314-318. An able example is the anonymous *Considerations Touching the Excise of Native and Foreign Commodities* of ca. 1661. A well-known work not mentioned by Turner that advocated an excise for tobacco was John Cary, *An Essay on the State of England* (Bristol, 1695). Cary, a Bristol merchant, wanted to tax the export of unmanufactured tobacco to create employment at home.

16. Price, "Tobacco Trade," chap. X, pp. 812-861.

17. Henry Saxby, *The British Customs* (London, 1757), pp. 13, 25.

18. Account of wine imported and exported, 1710-1765, in W. L. Clements Library, Ann Arbor, C. Townshend MSS 8/22A/34. Tobacco data in U.S. Bureau of the Census, *Historical Statistics of the United States* (Washington, D.C., 1975), II, 1189-1191.

19. Price, "Tobacco Trade," chap. X, pp. 883-887. The unsuccessful

tobacco bill of 1713 is in *House of Lords MSS,* n.s., X, 211-222, with the tobacco clause on p. 213.

20. *A Discourse of the Duties on Merchandize* ([London], 1695); Price, "Tobacco Trade," chap. X, pp. 867-868.

21. 6 September 1711; 12 February 1711/12. Defoe's ideas were elaborated upon in an anonymous pamphlet, possibly by him: *Plunder and Bribery Further Discover'd in a Memorial. . . to the British Parliament* (London, 1712); Price, "Tobacco Trade," chap. X, pp. 868-890.

22. Public Record Office (hereafter PRO) T.1/161/19B ff. 66-67; *Commons Journals* XVII, 369; Price, "Tobacco Trade," chap. X, p. 891.

23. *Commons Journals* XVII, 368-372; Leo Francis Stock, ed., *Proceedings and Debates of the British Parliaments Respecting North America,* 5 vols. (Washington, D.C., 1924-1941), III, 324n.

24. 13 Annae c. 8 s. 5, 6 (*Statutes of the Realm,* IX, 918); *House of Lords MSS.,* n.s., X, 213; Stock, *Proceedings,* III, 336-337; see pp. 330-335. For the infrequent use of the optional warehouse, see Price, "Tobacco Trade," chap. X, pp. 896-897.

25. *Calendar of State Papers Colonial, America and West Indies* (hereafter *Cal.S.P.Col.AWI*), *1712-1714,* nos. 356, 473, i, ii, 647; *Journal of the Commissioners of Trade and Plantations, 1709-1715,* pp. 527-528.

26. The 1733 House of Commons committee on customs frauds reprinted part of the Representation of the Council of Virginia to the Board of Trade, 11 September 1713. *The Report with the Appendix, from the Committee of the House of Commons Appointed to Enquire into the Frauds and Abuses in the Customs. . .* (London, 1733), p. 86, reproduced in Sheila Lambert, ed., *House of Commons Sessional Papers of the Eighteenth Century* (Wilmington, Del., 1975), XII, 323-345.

27. Based on a forthcoming paper on "Scotland and the Customs Legislation of 1723." The main events are also covered in Patrick W. J. Riley, *The English Ministers and Scotland 1707-1727* (London, 1964), pp. 276-280; T. C. Barker, "Smuggling in the Eighteenth Century: the Evidence of the Scottish Tobacco Trade," *Virginia Magazine of History and Biography* LXII (1954), 387-399.

28. 10 Geo. I c. 10 (*Statutes at Large,* Pickering ed., XV, 132-159); Stock, *Proceedings,* III, 472-474. Cf. Plumb, *The King's Minister,* pp. 233-237; Brisco, "Economic Policy," pp. 95-96; Coxe, *Robert Walpole,* I, 377; and Samuel Baldwin, *A Survey of the British Customs* (London, 1770), II, 119.

29. On Crookshanks, see Riley, *English Ministers,* passim; Calendar of Treasury Books, XXI, 258-259, 401; XXIV, 597; XXVI, 106; XXIX, 222, 270, 275, 342, 549; XXX, 427, 548; XXXI, 108; XXXII, 73, 76, 82-83, 105, 562, 593; *Calendar of Treasury Papers, 1702-1707,* 527; *1708-1714,* 14, 77, 82; *1714-1719,* 88, 121, 132, 266; *Calendar of Treasury Books and Papers,* I, 377, 567, 598; II, 214 and passim; III,

passim; IV, 148, 176; Cambridge University Library (hereafter CUL) Cholmondeley (Houghton) MSS, Correspondence, no. 1415 Crookshanks to Walpole, 5 January 1726/27 with enclosed "Case and Petition" and appendices. Crookshanks' publication was *Instructions for the Collectors and Other Officers Employ'd in Her Majesties Customs, &c. in the North-Part of Great-Britain* . . . (Edinburgh, 1707).

30. CUL Cholmondeley (Houghton) MSS., correspondence no. 923 Crookshanks to Walpole, 21 October 1721.

31. Ibid., nos. 1150, 1151, 1162 Crookshanks to Walpole, 24, 26 July, 25 August 1724; and ms. 29/6.

32. Ibid., correspondence no. 1944 Crookshanks to Walpole, Seville, 1 January 1732/33.

33. Robert Paul, assistant comptroller general in England, sent Walpole on 1 October 1724 an intelligent explanation of the current tobacco duties and their disappointing yield: only about £120-£130,000 per annum in England net. Ibid., 29/5. The next summer, the treasury received detailed accounts of the Scottish tobacco trade, 1722-1725. PRO T.36/13.

34. On Dinwiddie, see *Dictionary of American Biography* and Louis Knott Koonz, *Robert Dinwiddie* (Glendale, Calif., 1941), pp. 33, 35; and see. *Journal of the Commissioners of Trade and Plantations, 1718-1722,* pp. 386-387.

35. CUL Cholmondeley (Houghton) MSS 86/124; *Cal.S.P.Col.A WI, 1730,* nos. 82, 119, 121, 195.

36. 3 Geo. II c. 28 (*Statutes at Large,* Ruffhead ed., VI, 35). There were substantial interests pushing for the rice liberalization bill. If Dinwiddie did not "cause" it, he was at least alert to the real possibilities of his time.

37. PRO T.1/272/27.

38. PRO T.1/276/21 ff. 104-111.

39. PRO Ind. 4624 (Treasury Reference Book, IX), p. 457.

40. *Historical Statistics of the United States,* II, 1190.

41. The best account of the Virginia tobacco economy at this time is John M. Hemphill, "Virginia and the English Commercial System." For the Maryland side, see the articles by Russell E. Menard, Gloria L. Main, and Paul G. E. Clemens in Aubrey C. Land et al., *Law, Society and Politics in Early Maryland* (Baltimore, 1977).

42. University of Virginia, Carter letter book, I, 16, 34; Virginia Historical Society, Carter letter book, I, 28.

43. See n. 40. In 1725, the price of ordinary tobacco for export reached 5d. per lb. in London, a price not reached again till the American Revolution. Cf. CUL Cholmondeley (Houghton) MSS 29/7.

44. Jacob M. Price, *The Tobacco Adventure to Russia* (Transactions of the American Philosophical Society, n.s., LI, pt. 1) (Philadelphia, 1961), 103.

45. North Carolina State Archives, Raleigh, Treasurer's and Comptroller's Papers, Port Roanoke, vol. 13 ff. 48-57.

46. For Glasgow losses in the period of low prices, ca. 1728, see Robert Wodrow, *Analecta* (Maitland Club, 60) (Edinburgh, 1842-43), IV, 1-2, 10, 84, 162-163; University of Virginia, Carter letter book, I, p. 12; Virginia Historical Society, Carter letter book, I, p. 25.

47. *Cal.S.P.Col.AWI, 1728-1729,* no. 351; 1 Geo. II c. 4 (Hening, ed., *Statutes at Large of Virginia,* 197); PRO C.O.5/1321/R.90 (transcripts of C.O.5 in LC).

48. *Cal.S.P.Col.AWI, 1728-1729,* nos. 241, 402, 416, 510, 740, 742, 879; 1 Geo. II c. 1 (Hening, *Statutes at Large of Virginia,* 182); PRO C.O.5/1321/R.76, 87, 88, 89, 106; C.O.5/1322 ff. 27-28 (pp. 53-56). For the 1726 act against North Carolina, see Hening, 175-177 and *Cal.S.P.Col.AWI, 1728-1729,* nos. 184, 372; *1731,* nos. 323, 382, 515, 516; PRO C.O.5/1321/R.95; C.O.5/1323/S.2.

49. 2 Geo. II c. 9 (*Statutes at Large,* Ruffhead ed., V, 680) repealed the objectionable clause in 9 Geo. I c. 21 (Ruffhead, V, 456-459). Cf. Stock, Proceedings, IV, 12-13, 25-28; *The Case of the Planters of Virginia and the Merchants Trading Thither* (London, 1729); and University of Virginia, R. Carter letter-book, I, 18-20, *Cal.S.P.Col.AWI, 1728-1729,* nos. 241, 262, 562, 611, 641; PRO C.O.5/1321/R.76, 99, 107-108; C.O.5/1337 ff. 42-43, 92-93 (old nos. 69-71).

50. *Cal.S.P.Col.AWI, 1728-1729,* nos. 796, 797, 897; *1730,* nos. 159, 264, 289, 348, 350, 538, 577, 580, 591, 635; *1731,* nos. 62, 74, 85, 86, 164, 187, 199, 289, 363; PRO C.O.5/1322 pp. 47-50 and R.127, R.133-136, R.141-142, R.144, R.147, R.151, R.160, R.163, R.170; C.O.5/1337/72, 75, 80; Colonial Williamsburg Foundation (hereafter CWF), transcripts of letters from Gov. Gooch to brother, 28 June 1729, 7 January 1729/30, 9 April, 28 May, 24 July 1730, 12 June 1731, 28 July 1732; Library of Congress, transcripts from archives of Bishop of London, formerly at Fulham Palace, Commissary Blair to Bishop, 14 May 1731, Francis Peart to Geo. Gibson, 15 April 1732.

51. On Bishops Sir Thomas Gooch, bart. and Thomas Sherlock, see *Dictionary of National Biography.* The former had married the latter's sister. See also L. P. Curtis, *Chichester Towers* (New Haven, 1966), pp. 13-27, for their roles in the politics of Chichester cathedral chapter.

52. CWF, Gooch transcripts, 9 April 1730, 28 July 1732.

53. There are two genealogies of the Le Heup or Heheup family, one in the Wagner genealogies, Library of the Huguenot Society of London, formerly at Horsham, now at University College, London; the other in Gery Milner-Gibson-Cullum, *Pedigree of Wittewronge of Ghent in Flanders... together with... Le Heup and Cullum* (London, 1905), pp. 23-28. Both err in describing Peter jr. rather than Peter sr. as the treasury clerk. See also Bank of England Record Office, subscription book (1694) and P. G. M. Dickson, *The Financial Revolution in England* (London, 1967), pp. 449, 495.

54. On Isaac, see Romney Sedgwick, *The History of Parliament: the House of Commons 1715-1754,* 2 vols. (Oxford, 1970), II, 208; Nottingham University Library, Newcastle deposit: Henry Pelham MSS, box 1,

H. Walpole to Pelham, 9 August 1742; J. F. Chance, *List of English Diplomatic Representatives in Denmark, Sweden and Russia* (Oxford, 1913), p. 26; D. B. Horn, *British Diplomatic Representatives 1689-1789,* Camden Third Series, XLVI (London, 1932), 41, 142.

55. On him, see n. 53 and *Gentleman's Magazine,* XIX (1749), 332. There was a fourth brother, Thomas (baptized 1705) who had died by 1744.

56. See n. 53.

57. J. C. Sainty, *Office-Holders in Modern Britain I: Treasury Officials 1660-1870* (London, 1972), pp. 6, 35, 37, 98, 136. Peters son Thomas Leheup was briefly assistant solicitor of the Treasury (1746-1747) but died in 1747, aet. 21.

58. According to Dickson, *Financial Revolution,* p. 381, the office was not established till 1725. Peter, however, wrote that he had held that post since its establishment by his father-in-law Lowndes. BM Add. MS 32,869 fol. 100, P. Leheup to Newcastle, 19 July 1765; *Cal. T. Papers, 1720-1728,* p. 234; *Cal. T.B.&P. 1735-1738,* p. 231.

59. Dora Mae Clark, *The Rise of the British Treasury: Colonial Administration in the Eighteenth Century* (New Haven, Conn., 1960), pp. 63, 102; *Cal. T. Papers, 1720-1728,* pp. 535-536; *Cal. T.B.&P., 1729-1730,* pp. 120, 122, 215, *1735-1738,* p. 356; *1739-1741,* p. 489.

60. *Cal. T.B.&P., 1731-1734,* p. 166; *1735-1738,* pp. 265, 337, 432; *1739-1741,* 153, 364; *1742-1745,* 187, 604, 800.

61. Ibid., *1735-1738,* pp. 253, 296; *1739-1741,* pp. 461, 495; *1742-1745,* pp. 19, 45, 232.

62. Ibid., *1742-1745,* pp. 238, 252, 579, 644, 648, 663, 688.

63. *Commons Journals* XXVI, 861, 870, 872, 873, 879, 975, 979, 987-1001; *Gentleman's Magazine,* XXV (1755), 184, 2330 Clark, *British Treasury,* p. 86; Edward P. Lilly, "The Colonial Agents of New York and New Jersey" (Ph.D. diss., Catholic University of America, 1936), 61n; Henry Roseveare, *The Treasury: the Evolution of a British Institution* (London, 1969), pp. 105-106. Most of the charges against Leheup were procedural, but Newcastle was determined during his first months in office to give an appearance of utmost rigor. (He dismissed most of the customs officers at Bristol at the same time.) For Leheup's side, see BM Add. MS 32,735 f. 320, Add. MS 32,855 ff. 385, 467-469, Add. MS 32,856 f. 1, Add. MS 32,871 f. 178, Leheup to Newcastle, 23 May 1754, to [James West?]; 7 June 1755; to Newcastle, 11, 16 June 1755, 30, May 1757. The last alleges that during the "Forty-Five," Leheup had a special commission from Henry Pelham to wait on all the rich men in London and ask them to advance money on the security of the land tax. (I am indebted to Dr. Daniel Hirshberg for copies of the Leheup correspondence.)

64. BM Add. MS 32,869 f. 100, Leheup to Newcastle, 19 July 1765.

65. Lilly, *Colonial Agents,* pp. 61-62, 68-71, 84-85, 99, 161, 225; Lillian M. Penson, *The Colonial Agents of the British West Indies* (London, 1924), pp. 167-168, 250; Ella Lonn, *The Colonial Agents of the Southern Colonies* (Chapel Hill, N.C., 1945), pp. 60-61, 290, 295. Pen-

son limits his service for Barbados to 1735-36, but Lilly (61n) dates his service there from 1730. Leheup was still in touch with New York in 1736. E. B. O'Callaghan, ed., *Documents Relative to the Colonial History of the State of New York*, 14 vols. (Albany, 1856-1883), VI, 78.

66. On his income, see Lilly, *Colonial Agents*, pp. 68-71; Lonn, *Colonial Agents*, pp. 304, 313; Dickson, *Financial Revolution*, p. 381 [mistakenly calling him Thomas]; Sainty, *The Treasury*, p. 6. According to Roseveare, *The Treasury*, p. 104, underclerks received from £30 to £350 per annum in fees, depending on seniority, while chief clerks were getting £700 per annum by the 1750s.

67. *MSS of the Earl of Egmont: Diary of... Viscount Perceval* (Historical Manuscripts Commission, 63), 3 vols. (London, 1920-1923), II, 183; see also II, 73, 123.

68. Lilly, *Colonial Agents*, pp. 205-206; 3 Geo. II c. 12 (*Statutes at Large*, Ruffhead ed., VI, 5); Stock, *Proceedings*, IV, 56, 58-60, 62, 75.

69. Lonn, *Colonial Agents*, pp. 239-240; 3 & 4 Geo. II c. 3 (*Virginia Statutes at Large*, Hening ed., IV, 247-271); *Cal.S.P.Col.AWI*, as in n. 50.

70. CWF, Gooch transcripts, Gov. Gooch to Dr. Thomas Gooch, 28 July 1732.

71. Ibid., 7 January 1729/30.

72. 3 & 4 Geo. II c. 3 s. 10, 31, 32 (*Virginia Statutes at Large*, Hening ed., IV, 247-271). S. 3 also prohibited the exportation of loose or "bulk" tobacco whose importation was already prohibited in Britain to check smuggling.

73. 3 Geo. II c. 12, 28 (*Statutes at Large*, Ruffhead ed., VI, 5, 35).

74. 4 Geo. II c. 15 (*Statutes at Large*, Ruffhead ed., VI, 59).

75. 5 Geo. II c. 7, 24; 6 Geo. II c. 13 (*Statutes at Large*, Ruffhead ed., VI, 74-75, 116-119).

76. Cf. Archives des Affaires Étrangères, Paris, Correspondence politique: Angleterre, v. 378 ff. 26-27, 86-88.

77. Stock, *Proceedings*, IV, 115, 128, 165.

78. Leonard Woods Labaree, ed., *Royal Instructions to British Colonial Governors 1670-1776* (New York, 1935, 1967), I, 338. The clause appeared in the instructions to governors of the thirteen colonies repeatedly between 1689 and 1754 (Virginia, 1702-1738).

79. *Cal.S.P.Col.AWI*, *1728-1729*, nos. 45, 190, 351; PRO C.O.5/1321/R.70, 90.

80. *Cal.S.P.Col.AWI*, *1728-1729*, no. 241 (pp. 117-118); PRO C.O.5/1321/R.76; 1 Geo. II c. 11 (*Virginia Statutes at Large*, Hening ed., IV, 222-228).

81. *Cal.S.P.Col.AWI*, *1728-1729*, nos. 593, 606, 614, 637, 722, 730-731. The 1705 act complained against was 4 Annae c. 34 (*Virginia Statutes at Large*, ed. Hening, III, 377-381).

82. *Cal.S.P.Col.AWI*, *1730*, no. 289; *1731*, no. 434, iii; PRO C.O.5/1337/75. The unsatisfactory law was 3 & 4 Geo. II c. 5 (*Virginia Statutes at Large*, ed. Hening, IV, 273-275).

83. Bristol, Merchants Hall Archives, Minutes of Proceedings, V, 23

February 1730/31; *Cal.S.P.Col.AWI, 1731*, nos. 367, 401, 406, 434, 473; *1732*, nos. 22, 24 [same as previous 473], 32, 36, 55, 176, 196, 197; PRO C.O.5/1322 ff. 187-191v, 194-199v, 216-217v.

84. 5 Geo. II c. 7 (*Statutes at Large*, Ruffhead ed., VI, 74-75); Stock, *Proceedings*, IV, 128, 130, 145, 150, 153-155, 160. The House of Lords Record Office (transcripts in LC) contains a copy of the Board of Trade report of 21 January 1731/32 and I. Randolph's petition to be heard. See also *Cal.S.P.Col.AWI, 1732*, no. 136; and Bristol, Merchants Hall Archives, Minutes of Proceedings, 14 December 1731.

85. The resentment of the Virginians against the merchants is very clearly expressed in *Cal.S.P.Col.AWI, 1731*, no. 473; *1732*, no. 24, PRO C.O.5/1322/R.169 (the council's remonstrance) and in the hand-bill prepared by I. Randolph: *The Case of the Tobacco Planters in His Majesty's Colony of Virginia, as to the Bill now Depending in the House of Lords, for the More Easy Recovery of Debts in His Majesty's Planta-tions and Colonies Abroad* ([London, 1732]); imprint in John Carter Brown Library, but MS version in BL Add. MS 22,265 ff. 102-104.

86. John, Baron Hervey, *Memoirs of the Reign of George the Second from His Accession to the Death of Queen Caroline*, ed. John Wilson Croker, 2 vols. (London, 1848), I, 160-161; ed. Romney Sedgwick, 3 vols. (London, 1931), I, 132-133.

87. Phyllis Deane and W. A. Cole, *British Economic Growth 1688-1959* (University of Cambridge, Department of Applied Economics, Monographs, 8) (Cambridge, 1962), pp. 29, 48, 65, 78, 80.

88. T. S. Ashton, *Economic Fluctuations in England 1700-1800* (Oxford, 1959), 181; Sir William Beveridge, *Prices and Wages in England from the Twelfth to the Nineteenth Century, Vol. I . . . Mer-cantile Era* (London, 1939), p. 82. The price of wheat (Winchester Col-lege) in the last quarter of 1732 and first quarter of 1733 was 21s. 9d. per quarter, lower than the price at any time since 1670, except for the latter half of 1705, when it was a few pence lower. It was to be still lower in 1742-1744, but those were years of war when access to foreign mar-kets could be restricted.

89. B. R. Mitchell and Phyllis Deane, *Abstract of British Historical Statistics* (Cambridge, 1962), p. 401.

90. Langford, *The Excise Crisis*, p. 33; Brisco, *Fiscal Policy*, p. 85.

91. Brisco, *Economic Policy*, p. 100; Plumb, *The King's Minister*, pp. 239-244; Edward Hughes, *Studies in Administration and Finance* (Manchester, 1934), pp. 291-307.

92. B. R. Mitchell and Phyllis Deane, *Abstract of British Historical Statistics* (Cambridge, 1962), pp. 387, 389; T. S. Ashton, *Economic Fluctuations in England, 1700-1800* (Oxford, 1959), p. 186; "Net In-come and Expenditure of Great Britain and Ireland since 1688," *British Parliamentary Papers* (1868-1869), XXXV (*Accounts and Papers*, 2), II, 280-281 (762-763).

93. PRO T.17/10 p. 158, Scrope to Edinburgh board, 28 September 1731.

94. PRO T.1/283 ff. 105-117, contains drafts of a warehouse scheme without an excise connection, plans for bonds on export (similar to 1724 "inland duty" act on coffee and tea), with notes on the number of warehousekeepers to be needed. These documents are undated but have been bound in the volume for May-August 1733. However, since they contain no mention of *excise*, they cannot be later than mid-1731. Similar models can be found in CUL Cholmondeley (Houghton) MSS 29/25-26. Among Walpole's own papers are a warehouse-only scheme (perhaps from Arthur Dobbs) ibid., 41/51 and a merchant's comment on a warehouse scheme (ibid., 29/4/2). Both called for limiting the number of ports open to tobacco, a proposal not pursued by Walpole.

95. *Observations on the Case of the Planters of Virginia, In a Letter to* [John Randolph] (London, 1733), p. 2. This was probably written by Micajah Perry. Another person who has been mentioned as a possible source of Walpole's ideas was Arthur Dobbs, Irish M.P. and later governor of North Carolina. Dobbs was particularly interested in the problem of smuggling and relanding from the Isle of Man and had interviews with Walpole on visits to London in 1730 and 1732. After the latter, he sent Walpole a scheme for acquiring the suzerainty of the Isle of Man from Lord Derby and for a *general excise*, in place of customs duties on highly taxed imports. Dobbs, however, may have picked up this idea from the London press in late 1732; there is no firm evidence that he advocated it at his earlier interview with Walpole in 1730. C. R. Fay, "Arthur Dobbs, Adam Smith and Walpole's Excise Scheme," *Historical Journal* IV (1961), 203-207; Desmond Clarke, *Arthur Dobbs Esquire 1689-1765* (London, 1958), pp. 29-42. Dobbs was named engineer and surveyor-general of Ireland in 1733. Among the anonymous schemes received by Walpole showing special concern for Ireland are those in CUL Cholmondeley (Houghton) MSS 29/25 and 41/51.

96. Langford (*The Excise Crisis*, p. 30) suggests that the scheme may have been sent out by Horatio Walpole, auditor-general of the plantation revenues. However, there is nothing in Gooch's surviving correspondence to suggest that he was in correspondence with Horatio. All the work of the auditor general's office appears to have been done by the deputy Leheup!

97. *Executive Journals of the Council of Colonial Virginia, vol. IV, 1721-1739*, ed. H. R. McIlwaine (Richmond, Va., 1930), pp. 258-259.

98. Cumbria Record Office, Carlisle, Lonsdale MSS., 2nd dep., correspondence, bdle. 50, no. 97, Lowther to Spedding, London, 21 March 1731/32. Cf. also no. 35, same to same, 17 June 1732.

99. Lowther knew his way around Whitehall, and his acquaintance included John Hill, Walpole's manager on the customs board.

100. *Legislative Journals of the Council of Colonial Virginia*, ed. H. R. McIlwaine, 3 vols. (Richmond, Va., 1918), II, 796, 798, 808-813; *Journals of the House of Burgesses of Virginia, 1727-1740*, ed. H. R. McIlwaine (Richmond, Va., 1910), pp. 152, 159-161, 164, 167. The letter of introduction for Randolph to the treasury (1 July 1732) is in

PRO T.1/279/20 ff. 92-93; the more circumspect letter of introduction from Gooch (16 July 1732) is in T.1/279/23 ff. 98-99.

101. University of Virginia, R. Carter letter book, IV, 68, to M. Perry, 10 July 1732.

102. Price, "Tobacco Trade and Treasury," pp. 894-895.

103. Vertrees Judson Wyckoff, *Tobacco Regulation in Colonial Maryland* (Johns Hopkins University Studies in Historical and Political Science, Extra Volumes, n.s., 22) (Baltimore, Md., 1936), p. 154; Archives des Affaires Étrangères, Paris, Correspondance politique: Angleterre v. 378 ff. 86-88 (7 September 1732); *Read's Weekly Journal,* no. 382 (15 July 1732).

104. *Cal.S.P.Col.A WI,* 1732, pp. 97-99 (no. 149); PRO C.O.5/ 1323/S.6; Archives of the Bishop of London formerly at Fulham Palace: Virginia, I, no. 137, Gooch to Bishop, 12 August 1732 (LC transcript).

105. Archives des Affaires Étrangères, Paris, Correspondance politique: Angleterre v. 378 ff. 26-27.

106. The holding of such a full cabinet meeting is inferred from a report by Lord Perceval that Horatio Walpole told him in April 1733 that Lord Scarborough "was the very man who last summer pressed the resolution of this Excise, because it would be the most grateful thing that could be to the nation." *Perceval Diary* (H.M.C. 63), I, 359. The second Earl of Scarborough, a privy councillor and Master of the Horse, would only have been consulted at a full cabinet meeting. Such meetings of the full or "outer" cabinet took place normally only at the beginning and end of a parliamentary session.

107. Riley, *The English Ministers and Scotland,* pp. 270-289.

108. PRO T.29/27, p. 158; T. 17/10, p. 303, Scrope to Edinburgh board, 6 October 1732.

109. PRO T.36/13 Report of 18 December 1732, covering letter of 21 December 1732 and accompanying documents. See also National Library of Scotland, SB 19 Vaughan to Milton, Ayr, 15 November 1732.

110. W. L. Clements Library, Ann Arbor, C. Townshend MSS, old no. 8/22A/34.

111. Price, "Tobacco Trade and Treasury," I, 107-111; CUL Cholmondeley (Houghton) MSS 29/20; PRO T.1/281/12, T.1/278/30, PRO 30/8/81.

112. Ibid.

113. PRO T.36/13 Accounts of 5 March 1728/29 and 15 December 1732 signed A. Norman.

114. E.g., BL Add. MS 33,085 G. Longueville to T. Pelham, 21 October 1732.

115. Laprade, *Public Opinion and Politics,* pp. 337-338. Pulteney had earlier raised the cry of "general excise" in *The Case of the Removal of the Salt Duty,* published around 1 June 1732 and answered in the *Daily Courant* of 24 June. Such charges had some effect, for John Spedding wrote to James Lowther on 14 June 1732 from Whitehaven, "The

Country begins to be mightily allarm'd w[i]th the designs that are on foot for introducing a Generall Excise." Cumbria RO, Carlisle, Lonsdale MSS, J. Spedding letterbook [25]. The first leading article on excise appeared in the *Craftsman* of 4 November.

116. *American Weekly Mercury*, no. 684 (30 January-6 February 1732/33), p. 2, story dated London, 11 November 1732. Randolph was knighted on the occasion of his presentation of the address to the King.

117. The English accounts were not received till after 16 January. PRO T.29/27 (Minute Book), pp. 173, 181; T. 17/10, pp. 339, 344, 368, 373, 389; T.27/25, pp. 131, 139, 148, 149. The Treasury Board met less frequently than usual during January-May 1733.

118. In particular, CUL Cholmondeley (Houghton) MSS 29/27, 29, 31, 33; 43/1-11. Walpole's own rough notes show excise and Scottish material suggestively mixed.

119. Ibid., 29/32.

120. Ibid., 29/29a, notes of an interview with Lane.

121. See n. 115. The principal pamphlet literature is analyzed in Turner, "The Excise Scheme of 1733," *The English Historical Review* XLII (1927), 34-57.

122. Langford, *Excise Scheme*, pp. 47, 172. There are two collections of these letters, etc.: (1) *A Collection of Letters from Several Counties, Cities and Boroughs, Containing Instructions to their Representatives in Parliament to Oppose any Extensions of the Excise Laws* (London, 1733), p. 27, and (2) *Excise: Being a Collection of Letters, &c. Containing the Sentiments and Instructions of the Merchants, Traders, Gentry . . . to their Representatives in Parliament, against . . . any Extension of Excise Laws . . .* (London, 1739), p. 39. From the latter, pp. 8, 22, 34-35, we can probably add Bedwin (Wilts), King's Lynn (Norfolk!) and Sudbury (Suffolk). Birmingham and Oxford apparently should be added too. BL Add. MS 47,085 (1 February 1732/33); M. G. Hobson, ed., *Oxford Council Acts 1701-1752* (Oxford Historical Society, n.s., X) (Oxford, 1954).

123. *Commons Journals* XXI, 447-448, 451-452, 457, 459, 462, 466-467, 470, 472, 476, 479, 482, 484, 489, 495, 498, 502, 506, 510, 534, 544, 546, 558, 641-643, 645, 647, 650, 663, 676, 698, 701, 793, 830. The grievances involved are expressed in two contemporary publications: *A Brief State of the Inland or Home Trade . . .* (London, 1730) and *The Case of the Shopkeepers, Manufacturers, and Fair Traders . . .* (S.l. [ca. 1730]). Both try to link the peddlers with smuggling and are thus part of the psychological prehistory of the excise affair.

124. I have noted only two Scottish pamphlets touching on the excise affair: *An Enquiry into Some Things that Concern Scotland . . .* (Edinburgh, 1734). On pp. 13-14, the antiministerial author blames the remittance of the malt and other taxes for impoverising Scotland; excise would have taken another £30,000 per annum. This was in answer to a proexcise pamphlet, *Some Considerations for Continuing the Present Parliament*.

125. Archives des Affaires Étrangères, Correspondance politique: Angleterre, v. 376 ff. 158v-160 [Chauvigny?] to [Chauvelin].

126. Hervey, *Memoirs,* ed. R. Sedgwick, p. 138.

127. John Latimer, *The Annals of Bristol in the Eighteenth Century* (s.l, 1893), pp. 183-185; *The History of the Society of Merchant Venturers of the City of Bristol* (Bristol, 1903), p. 189; Merchants House, Bristol, Book of Proceedings, V, 9 January, 12 March 1732/1733; Latimer's calendar, 318.

128. Sir James Allanson Picton, ed., *City of Liverpool: Municipal Archives and Records from A.D. 1700...* (Liverpool, 1886), p. 149; *Excise, being a collection of letters,* 22; *Craftsman,* 6, 20 January 1732/33.

129. See n. 115 and Cumbria RO, Lonsdale MSS, 2d dep., correspondence, bdle. 50, Lowther to Spedding, 18 November, 12 December 1732.

130. Ibid., bdle. 50 Lowther to Spedding, 4, 6, 11, 18, 20 January, 10 February 1732/33; John Spedding's letter book [25], 1732-33, to Lowther, 12, 17 January, 4 February 1732/33. The Whitehaven merchants received other letters from London to the same effect.

131. BL Add. MSS 47,074 newsletters of 2, 9 December 1732.

132. *Daily Journal,* no. 3736 (23 December 1732); *Excise, being a Collection,* 19-20; BL Add. MS 47,084, newsletter, 23, 30 December 1732.

133. BL Add. MS 47,085 newsletter, 9 January 1732/33. On the continuity of this threepenny levy, see Archives des Affaires Étrangères, Mem. et doc.: France, v. 2008 ff. 344v-345; Price, "France and the Chesapeake," 651.

134. *Read's Weekly Journal,* no. 408 (13 January 1733).

135. BL Add. MS 47,085 newsletters, 4, 6, 9, 11, 13, 18, 23, 27, 30 January; 1, 6, 8, 15, 17, 20, 24 February; 3, 6, 8, 13 March 1732/33; Add MS 27,732 ff. 95, 99, 123-126, 131-132. On 15 February, the Lord Mayor, Aldermen and Common Council of London adopted a formal representation to the city's M.P.'s asking them to vote against the excise. See also *Perceval Diary* (H.M.C. 63), I, 306-308, 311-312, 329, 330, 338, 340; *MSS of the Earl of Carlisle at Castle Howard, Yorkshire* (H.M.C. 42: *XVth Report,* part 6), pp. 97-103; Cumbria RO, Lonsdale MSS 2d dep, correspondence, bdle. 50, Lowther to Spedding, 20 February 1732/33; William Maitland, *The History and Survey of London,* 3d ed., 2 vols. (London, 1760), II, 546-548; *American Weekly Mercury,* no. 697 (3-10 May 1733).

136. See their biographies in Sedgwick, *House of Commons.*

137. Campbell's son John was a commissioner of customs at £1000 per annum, while his second son was Inspector of Tobacco at £350 per annum. National Library of Scotland MS SB 19 Milton to Islay, 3 April 1733. Three others, cousins or factors of D. Campbell, were also in the Scottish customs, for another £450 per annum.

138. See nn. 133, 136. Perry at first was not only consulted about Vir-

ginia patronage, but was allowed to nominate a surveyor of houses in Lancashire. PRO T.29/26, p. 158.

139. *Commons Journals* XXII, 26-27, 58, 77, 79, 89. (Some of the accounts presented were originally prepared when the House considered the anti-Scottish complaints in 1721-1723.)

140. Stock, *Proceedings,* IV, 197-201; *Commons Journals* XXII, 89-91; [John Almon], *An History of the Parliament of Great Britain, from the Death of Queen Anne to the Death of King George II* (London, 1764), pp. 226-239; Maitland, *London,* II, 548-562; *Carlisle MSS.* (H.M.C. 42), pp. 103-105; *Perceval Diary* (H.M.C. 63), I, 342-343; BL Add. MS 27, 372 ff. 137-140, 143-144 Delafaye to Essex, 15, 22 March 1732/33; Add MS 47,085 newsletters 15, 17 March 1732/33. Sir James Lowther reported that Walpole "has bin forc't to alter his first Scheme, & there may be further alterations made . . . so as he may not be so fond of it." Cumbria RO, Lonsdale MSS, 2d dep., correspondence, bdle. 50, Lowther to Spedding, 20, 31 March 1732/33. In addition to the division list for 14 March given in Langford, *The Excise Crisis,* pp. 173-174, there are at least four further examples: (1) *The List,* a four-page broadside in BL Egerton MSS 2543 ff. 409-410 and Houghton Library, Harvard, with a p.s. listing 27 members (including Tucker) who "voted afterwards against the Excise." This list is significant, because Langford tells us that there are no division lists after 14/16 March. (2) *The Lords Protest in the Late Session of Parliament . . . with an Alphabetical List of all the Members who Voted For and Against the Excise-Bill. . .* (London, 1733) in BL, etc.; (3) *An Exact and Compleat List of the House of Commons* (s.l. [1733]) in Houghton Library, Harvard; and (4) in the W. L. Clements Library, Ann Arbor, a list appended to the version of the excise bill published by A. Moore (see next note).

141. Though the House never authorized the printing of the excise bill, there were several private unauthorized printings. I have used that printed in London by A. Moore (*The Excise Bill for Repealing Several Subsidies and an Impost on Tobacco. . .* [1733]), which also contains a division list. Another version is in *The Most Important Transactions of the Sixth Session of the First Parliament of. . . King George II A.D. 1733* (London, [1733]).

142. Stock, *Proceedings,* IV, 204-206; *Perceval Diary* (H.M.C. 63), I, 347-356; BL Add. MS 47,085 newsletter, 5 April 1733; Add. MS. 27,232 ff. 147-148 Delafaye to Essex, 5 April 1733; Cumbria RO, Lonsdale MSS, 2d dep., correspondence, bdle. 50, Lowther to Spedding, 5 April 1733; *Weekly Register,* no. 156 (7 April 1733).

143. Stock, *Proceedings,* IV, 189-194.

144. Ibid., IV, 209; BL Add. MS 27,732 ff. 152-153 Delafaye to Essex, 12 April 1733; Add. MS 47,085 newsletters 7, 10, 12, 14 April 1733; *Perceval Diary* (H.M.C. 63), I, 356-361; *Carlisle MSS.* (H.M.C. 42), 107-111; Cumbria RO, Lonsdale MSS, 2d dep., correspondence, bdle. 51, Lowther to Spedding, 10 April 1733.

145. BL Add. MS 47,085 newsletter, 12, 14, 21 April 1733; Cumbria

RO, Lonsdale MSS, 2d dep., correspondence, bdle. 51, Lowther to Spedding, 12, 14 April 1733, cf. also 8 May; *Read's Weekly Journal,* 14, 21 April 1733; *Remarks and Collections of Thomas Hearne,* XI:*1731- 1735,* ed. H. E. Salter (Oxford, 1921), 185; *American Weekly Mercury,* nos. 705, 709 (28 June-5 July, 26 July-3 August 1733); Latimer, *Bristol in 18th Century,* pp. 183-185. After the withdrawal, quiet people in the country began to wonder whether it might not have been desirable. See *The Autobiography of William Stout of Lancaster 1665-1752* (Manchester, 1967), p. 212. Sir James Lowther was disturbed at the spread of such ideas in Cumberland. Cumbria RO, Lonsdale MSS, 2d dep., correspondence, bdle. 51 to Spedding, 8, 10, 15, 22 May 1733.

146. Langford, *Excise Crisis,* chaps. 6-7.

147. There are some interesting comments on the Scottish side in National Library of Scotland, SB 20 Islay to Milton, 17, 24 March, 14 April 1733.

148. Langford, *Excise Crisis,* pp. 80-83, 175-176.

149. *The List,* 4 (as in n. 140). There is confusion over one name, "Sir William Ellis"; there was no such person in Commons then. I have assumed that this was a typographical error merging two names: Sir William Lowther and Richard Ellys.

150. Lord Charles Cavendish (Westminster), Lord James Cavendish (Derby), Sir Thomas Clarke (Hertford), Sir William Lowther (Pontefract, Yorks.), Lord Tyrconnel (Grantham, Lincs.) and John Yorke (Richmond, Yorks.). Sir Thomas Prendergast (Chichester) had not yet returned when the resolutions were carried in committee but was present two days later to vote *for* the excise on the report.

151. Sir Charles Bunbury, bt. (Tory, Chester), Sir Edward Dering, bt. (Tory, Kent).

152. Sir George Beaumont, bt. (Leicester), George Clarke (Oxford University), Sir John Coryton, bt. (Callington, Cornwall), Lord Coleraine (Boston), Sir Edward des Bouverie, bt. (Shaftesbury, Dorset), John H. Gifford (Westbury, Wilts), Thomas Horner (Somerset), Francis Knollys (Oxford), Edmund Mortimer Pleydell (Dorset).

153. Thomas Bootle (Liverpool), Richard Ellys (Boston), William Noel (Stamford, Lincs.), Edward Rudge (Aylesbury, Bucks.), John Rudge (Evesham, Worcs.), John Weaver (Bridgnorth, Salop).

154. Sir Cecil Bishop, bt. (Penryn, Cornwall), Ralph Jenison (Northumberland), Benjamin Haskin Stiles (Devizes, Wilts), and Edward Tucker (Weymouth, Dorset).

155. Langford, *Excise Crisis,* chap. viii.

156. Carlisle MSS (H.M.C. 42) 111-114; BL Add. MS 27,732 ff. 154- 155, 162-163 Delafaye to Essex, 19, 26 April 1733.

157. Stock, *Proceedings,* IV, 220-224; published separately as in n. 26. The report from the customs board to the committee is in CUL Cholmondeley (Houghton) MSS 29/35.

158. Maryland Historical Society, S. Bordley letterbook, I, 82-84, to Samuel White, 25 September 1733.

159. PRO C.O.5/1337 ff. 170-172, Leheup to Couraud (secretary to Newcastle), 8 January 1734/35, with enclosed address, endorsed "it was thought improper to print this Address."

160. Lonn, *Colonial Agents*, 283. Perry was also agent for Pennsylvania. For the work of financial agents, see Jacob M. Price, "The Maryland Bank Stock Case," in Aubrey C. Land et al., *Law, Society and Politics in Early Maryland* (Baltimore, Md., 1977), pp. 3-8; Percy Scott Flippin, *The Financial Administration of the Colony of Virginia* (Johns Hopkins University Studies in Historical and Political Science, ser. XXXIII, no. 2) (Baltimore, 1915), pp. 59-60.

161. CWF, Gooch transcripts, 35-36, 41-42, 45-46 to brother, 20 July 1733, 8 March 1734/35, 5 July 1735.

162. CUL Cholmondeley (Houghton) MSS 29/2, 3; 44/42.

163. *The Political State*, XLIX (January 1735), 22-24; LI (January 1736), 31-32; LII (August 1736), 131.

164. Sir William Purdie Treloar, bt., *A Lord Mayor's Diary 1906-7 to which is added the Official Diary of Micajah Perry 1738-9* (London, 1920), pp. viii-x, xv-xx; *Felix Farley's Bristol Journal*, no. 130 (10 January 1746/47); LC Jones Papers, V, ff. 687-688, W. King to T. Jones, 6 December 1743, Custis Family Papers, J. Hanbury to J. Custis, 7 March 1745/46.

165. *Perceval Diary* (H.M.C. 63), I, 361.

166. Turner, "The Excise Crisis."

167. There is a copy in the Kress Library, Harvard. The pamphlet is mentioned in a newsletter of 20 March 1732-1733 in BL Add. MS 47,085.

168. Similarities to points made in the speeches of Micajah Perry suggest that he is the author.

169. An account (9 April 1733) in PRO T.38/364 shows that Edward Randolph was then "in Goal & the Sureties insolvent." He originally owed the government £18,397 but this had been reduced to £10,123. The possessor of another famous Virginia name, Arthur Lee, had failed some years before and the £9,613 he still owed the Crown was considered lost. Arthur Lee was the son of Francis Lee (d. 1714), merchant of London, son of Richard Lee (I) of Virginia. The only other big loss since 1720 was John Midford, who had died insolvent owing the Crown £17,134, which had since been reduced to about £6000.

170. *Considerations Relating to the Tobacco Trade*, p. 2.

171. Including: *A Letter from a Member of Parliament to His Friends in the Country, Concerning the Duties on Wine and Tobacco* (London, 1733); *Some General Considerations Concerning the Alteration and Improvement of the Public Revenuws* (London, 1733); and *A Vindication of the Conduct of the Ministry in the Scheme of the Excise of Wine and Tobacco* (London, 1734).

IX

THE CONDUCT OF THE
SEVEN YEARS WAR

Stephen B. Baxter

When students enquire at the Algemeen Rijksarchief in The Hague about the surviving diplomatic materials, they are warned that the Dutch records are like an onion. The outermost layer consists of dispatches that were to be read by all the members of the States General. Peel that away, and there was a second layer of dispatches that were to be read by people who had a certain nuisance value, men who must be beguiled into thinking that they were "in the secret." Beneath that second layer is a third, or in rare cases a fourth, with the real news.

A similar onion faces the student of Hanoverian political history, and many of those who start out reading in the period leave it in tears. The outermost layer in this field consists of the *Memoirs* of Hervey and Walpole and Dodington, the *Letters* of Walpole and Chesterfield and Frederick the Great.[1] All these works portray George II as a buffoon. All, as it happens, are acts of revenge, written after the author had been beaten by George II in a struggle for money or influence. Unfortunately for the student, such writings are on the whole vindictive nonsense. Yet they are so well done that they are studied for their own sake as literature. I have no objection to that, so long as we remember to define the word *literature* as *fiction*. George II was not an easy man to live with, and he did not begin to be appreciated at his true worth until people had had some experience with his successor. Contemporary memoirs and letters can only be used occasionally in the study of the administrative history of this period, and then only with great caution.

When we discard the outermost layer of this onion, the next thing to greet us is the work of the scholars of the generation that ended in, say, 1920. The work of Basil Williams, Julian Corbett, and their contemporaries is much more sophisticated than that of Hervey and Walpole. Ostensibly, at least, it was based on original sources, and it was certainly cloaked in a pompous and magisterial prose style. Writers of that generation were given far more generous word limits than you and I get from our publishers today, so that the very weight of these books made them impressive. These people were in fact just as interested in what they wrote as Hervey and Walpole had been. A good many of them were Liberals; even those who were not could not escape the drama of the long struggle to mend or end the House of Lords. This was a generation that put up a statue of Oliver Cromwell, that dictator, outside the House of Commons without recognizing any incongruity. Why? Because Oliver had been also an enemy of the hereditary principle. He must therefore have been a friend of the people. Morley, a Liberal cabinet minister, wrote a *Life* of Cromwell as well as one of Gladstone. Rosebery, a Liberal prime minister, wrote a *Life* of the younger Pitt. And it is never safe to forget that Basil Williams, whose dead hand lay so heavy for so long on Hanoverian England, came out of Milner's Kindergarten. We may, and I think we do, owe that generation of scholars a great deal, but we must never make the mistake of taking their work at face value.[2]

A third layer of the onion consists of the writings of Sir Lewis Namier, Romney Sedgwick, and their epigones.[3] For many years criticism of this group of scholars was unthinkable, and even today it remains an important school. But it is, I think, fair comment to point out that *The Structure of Politics* appeared in 1929 and *England in the Age of the American Revolution* in 1930, that is, half a century ago. Namier was Polish, and it has been remarked often enough that he thought in terms of the aristocratic Polish republic of the eighteenth century, one in which a king had very little authority and—most of the time—even less wisdom. Both Namier and Sedgwick seem to have entertained a personal dislike of George III, who did sometimes veer away from strict truthfulness in his conversation; and they seem to have been shocked by one of his early letters to Lord Bute in which the young man called his Groom of the Stole "My dearest."[4] Now this was a generation obsessed by vice, which was not indeed entirely unknown in Bloomsbury, and it was all too easy to picture the prince of Wales as a young Alexander with Lord Bute as his Hephaestion, or at least his Fruity Metcalfe. Unfortunately for Namier's memory, it now appears that he knew very little about English history outside the twenty years—precisely the period 1760 to 1780—of which he made himself a master. It is perfectly reasonable to assume that the prince wrote in a hurry and dropped the third word from the ordinary "My dearest Lord" or "My dearest friend," which were standard forms of address in the first half of the century, forms entirely lacking any sexual overtones.

Perhaps we may even, through our tears, discern something like a fourth layer of the onion lurking beneath the work of Namier and Sedgwick. This would be the increasing emphasis on collective biography and on social history which has overtaken the profession in the years since World War II. Namier contributed to this himself, of course, with his History of Parliament Trust, but there is also a political element to be considered. A school that traces its origins to Tolstoi's *War and Peace* with its hatred of the hero and its exaltation of "necessity," and which has been reinforced by E. H. Carr's dislike of King Alexander's monkey, does not care for the older forms of historical writing. You recall perhaps that in the year 1920 his pet monkey bit King Alexander of Greece, who died of it. There ensued a civil war, and Winston Churchill chose to say that the monkey had caused a quarter of a million deaths. E. H. Carr, in *What is History?*, was not having any of that. Such accidents occur; they may well have significant consequences, but it is impossible to derive a rational scheme of history from them. Such an attitude takes care of individual biographies and also of the older forms of historical writing —political, diplomatic, constitutional—in favor of work on crime, children, rural bastardy rates, and so on. Even those reactionary souls who venture into biography, such as J. H. Plumb and Reed Browning, though they are willing to illustrate the operations of a ruling class, are not willing to penetrate into the harem and tell us what the sultan was up to. Both of them write history with the king left out, and some of the results are pretty extraordinary. But few present-day scholars are willing to go nearly so far as Plumb or Browning.

Perhaps, when we have peeled all these layers from the onion, there will remain only a void. We may hope, however, to find an updated version of Ranke's *Geschichte wie es ist eigentlich gewesen,* and to have an opportunity to see how the system actually worked. It is all most undemocratic, but it does happen to be the case that the Seven Years War stopped for five days on one occasion when the duchess of Newcastle was ill and her husband stayed by her bedside.[5] I am rather afraid that in western history, at least until the time of the French Revolution, the digestive problems of a duchess of Newcastle are of greater significance to the short-term conduct of affairs than Tolstoi or E. H. Carr would admit. In their own Russian field, the conduct of the Seven Years War depended, as it happens, on the equally fascinating question of the health of the Empress Elizabeth. England was willing to go to war in 1755 and 1756, to a curious extent, on the basis of a gamble that the tsaritsa was about to die. A present of ten thousand pounds to the Grand Duchess Catherine was thought likely to square the next Russian court. And it was a matter of real dismay to the Western powers that the Empress Elizabeth survived until January of 1762, while their friend Ferdinand VI of Spain died in August of 1759. Those who feel that the role of accident in history is not worth studying might ponder on what would have happened had Elizabeth died in 1759 and Ferdinand in 1762, or what would have happened had both of them lived on into the mid-sixties.

Those particular might-have-beens do not concern us here. I would like to point out, however, that the current interest in collective biography and in social history gives us a skewed picture of the way in which political and diplomatic England really worked in the eighteenth century. Five hundred fifty-eight men in the House of Commons did not read the foreign dispatches nor did the 180-odd members of the House of Lords. At the very top there were between three and six people who were "in the circulation," with larger meetings of sixteen, at most, in moments of crisis, and when one is dealing with groups this small, questions of health and other accidental factors do come into play. Contemporaries certainly did not think in terms of the History of Parliament Trust. They thought in terms of courts, through which one manipulated blocs that would otherwise have been of unmanageable size. No one had time to negotiate with seven hundred individuals, and then with others outside the two houses of Parliament.

"All countries have their *Pits,* & their *Fox's,* but with proper resolution, & management, that can be withstood every where."[6] As late as 1755, neither Pitt nor Fox was "in the circulation," and George II retained a modified freedom of action through the operation of what I have ventured to call the departmental system and what Ragnhild Hatton calls closet government. Its operation can be seen most clearly when the king was in Germany, for then the component parts were separated and the functions of each can be observed in isolation. In 1750, for example, the French ambassador asked permission to attend George II in Hanover during the coming holidays. When permission was denied, the ambassador asked for and received permission to take a vacation in France.[7] Clearly, then, the government of England was not in London during the summer of 1750. But on that occasion, Newcastle was minister in attendance, and one is still left to ask whether the "government of England" is Newcastle or whether it is George II. A better example, perhaps, is the summer of 1755, when the cipher Holdernesse was minister in attendance and Newcastle remained in London.

The basic decision for war had been taken in the previous year. Braddock's secret instructions made war inevitable, and although they were approved by the cabinet, they were also approved by the king. George II not only retained the right to assign or withhold business from the cabinet, but also retained the right to say which ministers should attend individual meetings, and at least on occasion the right to change his mind on matters after a cabinet minute had been sent him. Both military and diplomatic correspondence were handled outside the cabinet, and so too were the more delicate political maneuvers. When he was in a bad mood George II could argue that there was no such thing as a first minister in the English system.[8] This was of course not true, and we may perhaps agree with those observers who argued that Newcastle was first minister during his brother's lifetime and that he remained first minister on the death of Henry Pelham in March of 1754.[9] But even Newcastle had very little influence over the military department, which was in the hands of the king's son the duke of Cumberland, and he could not prevent the king from being enthusiastic for the war to begin. Nor could he prevent the Hanover voyage of 1755, though it came at a particularly awkward moment for the English ministers.

The trip to Germany was to be the king's last, as it happened, and he made the most of it. By forbidding outsiders to come, George could achieve a much less formal etiquette than the one that surrounded him in England. There he had his coin collection and his stud, his *Gartentheater* with its flats composed of rows of trees punctuated by gilded marble busts. The latest French plays were sent him in the diplomatic pouch, so that they could be performed in this delightful outdoor setting at Herrenhausen. When he went indoors, it was to permit the six leading courtiers to sit at table with him every day at one o'clock when he dined with the countess of Yarmouth. Although he was nearly seventy-two, the king "eats with a better appetite than any of us and is, thank God, as well as ever I saw him. The only change I can perceive is, that I think he does not hear quite so well." He refused to be bothered by Braddock's failures in America. Braddock had certainly neglected the common rules of war, George felt, but that was not his responsibility: "he wash'd his hands of it as he did not choose him, for that his son had recommended him, and he owned he had been surprised at it, at the time."[10]

Such an interpretation of the departmental system may well seem extravagant, even for a man who loved to delegate, even for a very old man. And in 1755 George II was a very old man for a king, the oldest living sovereign since the Norman Conquest. Deafness was not quite his only problem. He was beginning to have trouble with his eyesight, and later that autumn he would ask all his servants to use darker ink when they wrote to him. From this point on we might easily be confused about what constituted the royal diet of letters. For there exist in all collections documents written in a large round hand, with very black ink, and one might well conclude that these were the only papers the king read after the autumn of 1755. In fact he continued to read everything: the ostensibles, the ordinary letters, the secrets, the most secrets or *entre-nous,* the little notes that ended with the command, "Burn this letter" and which no one, for that very reason, ever dared to burn. When he was tired, his secretaries or Lady Yarmouth could read to him, but the quantity of material the king processed by himself amazed his physicians. On one day in 1758 when he was in bed with fever and eye trouble, he had to go through nine dispatch boxes full of papers, and the doctors complained rightly enough that this did his eyes no good at all.[11]

The daily work load of George II was so heavy that some kind of organization was essential. Fortunately, this king was very much more businesslike than his father had been. Until June of 1727, Lord Townshend could get away with some very sloppy filing of important state papers. From then on, presumably at the command of the new king, the state papers are much better kept, and they survive in much better order — even though Townshend was still minister. George II set a rigid schedule for himself as well as for others, and it was commonly said that you could set your watch by him. We probably all remember accounts of his daily calls on his mistress Lady Suffolk, which took place precisely at 7:00 P.M. If by any chance he came a few minutes early, the king would pace up and down outside the door of her apartment, his own watch in his hand. It is a ridiculous picture, and both Lady Suffolk and the rest of the court were bored by it all, but the rigid schedule was the key to the king's life. And it may help us to take a look at a few aspects of it here.

Hanoverian England moved at a slower pace than we do now. Normally speaking, the continental mails came in twice a week, although there were of course expresses when something important was going on. These were read by the king, and some of them were handed on to the ministers who were in the circulation. Not all of them, ever; George II knew how to keep his own secret. Hanoverian matters were handled by the German chancery, but papers that might affect England were normally passed to a secretary of state. The efficient cabinet would think up a reply which the secretary would draft and then read to the king. After this was approved, the text might still be amended in the copying stage, and this of course gave opportunities for an unscrupulous secretary to try to change policy. Thus, in 1758 and 1759 the king and the duke of Newcastle were afraid that Denmark might enter the war and perhaps even get the Dutch to join them, because of the misconduct of the English privateers and the even worse misconduct of the English Admiralty Courts. Both king and duke wanted the Dutch to be treated kindly, and they were able to get cabinet support for their attitude. Yet Holdernesse, who would draft the relevant dispatch, was a hardliner whose letter turned out to be at variance with the agreed policy.[12] That particular gaffe could be corrected because the king maintained a secret channel of communication with his ambassador at The Hague, as he maintained another secret channel of communication with Frederick the Great. His grandson was not so experienced, and in 1761 the needless rudeness of one of Secretary Egremont's dispatches to Madrid was thought to have been the immediate cause of the outbreak of war with Spain. Again, Egremont's dispatch seems to have been sent off without proper consultation. A young king could not control the errors of a young secretary, but not too much damage was done. There would have been a Spanish war sooner or later, in any case.

English court etiquette did not permit George II to dine with his servants when he was in England, at least not "upstairs" in his own part of his palaces. It was also the rule that ministers went to court on a fixed schedule. Going on an unscheduled day could cause alarm, for it meant that something was wrong. The king liked to go to Richmond on Saturdays and on one day—either Wednesday or Thursday—in midweek. His minister, the duke of Newcastle, left London for his villa at Claremont on Friday afternoons and refused to return for the king's Sunday working sessions. Thus, the Seven Years War was perhaps the only war in English history to have been fought on the basis of a four-day week. Normally, cabinets met on Monday evening at seven, or later in the war on Tuesday evenings, but several members of the efficient cabinet were old, and some were ill. A good deal of work therefore had to be done in writing, and it is to this that we owe our knowledge of how the system operated.

If it happened to be a minister's day, he went upstairs to the king's closet, his office, which was on the *piano nobile* of St. James's, or Kensington, or Hampton Court. There he apparently stood while the king transacted what business the king chose to transact. George II was an impatient man who loathed long speeches or ceremonies. If a preacher dared to go over the fifteen-

minute limit with his sermon, there was sure to be a complaint
sent to the archbishop of Canterbury. If Hardwicke wrote a long
speech from the throne, the king would insist that it be cut before
he would deliver it. But he does seem to have enjoyed reading the
triple sets of dispatches that were sent to him from foreign courts
and, when he was at Hanover, from London as well. These correspond to the layers of the Dutch onion, and the system may well
have been derived from the Dutch example. The ostensibles
could be shown to the outer cabinet or, when the king was
abroad, to the regency; the regular letters were intended for, or
written by, what Sir Lewis Namier called the "efficient cabinet,"
a group of four to six men, depending on the administration of
the moment. The most secret layer of the correspondence was to
be read only by Newcastle and by Chancellor Hardwicke, if by
anyone in England. In May of 1755 the Hanoverian government
was not transmitting its secret intelligence to Newcastle, while
Newcastle was not transmitting his in-letters to the duke of Cumberland.[13]

Cumberland was not only the king's son but also the head of
the army. During this summer the regency often met in his apartments at St. James's. But it would not have been proper for such
an exalted person to attend meetings of the efficient cabinet,
even had Newcastle liked him; and the two men happened to disagree on many of the issues of the day. Newcastle took the position that Cumberland had the military power, and that he would
become a threat to the constitution if he held the civil power with
it. For Newcastle thought in terms of patronage, and to him
places *were* power. If he could make Barrington secretary at war
without telling Cumberland, much less asking his advice, then
Newcastle's position as *the* minister would be evident. If he failed
to get his own man appoined dean of Gloucester he was ready to
resign, because it was a public demonstration that he was out of
favor with the closet.[14]

Ministers needed such public demonstrations of support. Unfortunately, the closet was often in a bad humor or took things
the wrong way when new business was first mentioned. This posed
problems, and there were also occasions when George II did not
wish a minister to speak on some topic outside his particular
department. It was a contravention of etiquette, furthermore, to
mention the same topic twice in a single audience. For what we

call extended remarks and the English call supplementaries, it would be necessary for a minister to go downstairs at the end of the audience and explain the matter to Lady Yarmouth. It was better to do so anyway, even when the king was in a good humour, because what took place in the Closet was binding on King and minister alike, even though it was oral. Repetition of a discussion with the king to Lady Yarmouth made it safer for the minister concerned, even though George II had a truly royal memory. When he happened to be in a bad mood, or took things the wrong way, then recourse to Lady Yarmouth could often bring about a change of view. Amelie de Walmoden was also very good at hinting what the king was too polite to say for himself, and she had, as it happens, her own correspondence with her relatives, who occupied important positions on the Continent. Her influence on society may have been deleterious: an increase in divorce and in more or less irregular domestic arrangements is to be noted at the highest levels of society after her arrival in England in 1737. Her influence on the course of government was immense and it was almost entirely benign.

Another essential person in government was P. A. Baron von Münchhausen, the Hanoverian minister. On occasion he would sit in on meetings of the English efficient cabinet, as Newcastle or Holdernesse would sit in on meetings of the Hanover cabinet when they were in Germany. Usually the two governments were in precise agreement, that is, in general the Hanover ministry danced to the English tune. This was not the case in 1755 or later, and even when the two governments did have a single policy, the king had greater freedom of action in Germany than he did when he was in England. He was also easier to get at.

Thus, Frederick II of Prussia chose the Hanover holiday of 1755 as the moment to try to make friends with his uncle. For fifteen years he had been trying in vain to make an alliance, or even to obtain an interview. Now his chance had come. Through his sister the duchess of Brunswick, he suggested the possibility of a marriage between a Brunswick princess and the prince of Wales.[15] It was one of those delightful anachronisms that were known to captivate George II. A dynastic marriage in which the bride would bring a Prussian alliance for her dowry would titillate the old king. Whatever we may think of the royal power in 1755, it is a matter of observation that Frederick II had been trying to get an English alliance ever since 1740, and that much of the English political world had been trying to get a Prussian alliance for an even longer time, with absolutely no success. George II would not hear of one, on any reasonable terms. Only when he was approached by the Brunswicks with the offer of their daughter did his heart soften. The alliance would be made in January of 1756; and it is worth remembering, perhaps, that the Diplomatic Revolution was first delayed and then worked out by George II as a personal act, this time without Newcastle. The role of the English government was limited. All concerned may very well have been playing games so as to humor the old gentleman; but unless George II was humored, there would be no Diplomatic Revolution. It is fair to say, putting it at its lowest, that he retained a veto on the formulation of foreign and military policy.

The coming of war made it possible for various politicians to exercise vetoes of their own, for they knew that the king would need them. Thus Speaker Onslow, among others, had a veto over the government's tax proposals which he exercised from time to time.[16] Whoever was the king's minister for the House of Commons would have such a veto, if he dared to use it, by refusing to bring in proposals with which he disagreed. Even Henry Bilson Legge, the chancellor of the exchequer, refused in August to sign the warrants needed to implement a Hessian subsidy treaty that had been negotiated by Holdernesse at Hanover.[17] As it happens, the king had played fair; he had not told either the Hanoverian or the Hessian government the price that as king he was willing to pay for the Hessians, and therefore Holdernesse had been able to make a good bargain. But it was not good enough for Legge or for William Pitt, and both men opposed the subsidy treaty.

The king's weakness became greater at the time of the French attack on Minorca in the spring of 1756. The London government knew of the possibility of an attack before the end of January, and even the languid administration of the island itself knew enough to start a council of war on February 5.[18] Unfortunately, very little could be done for Minorca, for the mother country was also threatened with a possible invasion. *Just* enough help was in fact sent off, in time, with orders to pick up additional men at Gibraltar. But Governor Fowke at Gibraltar would not lend the needed regiments, Byng certainly did not show much vigor against Galisonnière, and Minorca was lost in a particularly humiliating fashion.

I get into trouble with my friends in London when I suggest

that, for the aristocracy, the Enlightenment signified a period of glorious disobedience, an era in which they did not perform the tasks for which they were paid. But that is exactly what was happening. In the military arena, George II was in a position to resent such disobedience. Fowke was cashiered for not lending the Gibraltar regiments. Byng was shot for his pains, and I think we must agree with Newcastle that his execution was another personal act of the king. At much the same time, a young captain who ran his ship into port without orders to refit, Lord Harry Paulet, lost the king's favor and never held another command.[19] In the short run, ruining Paulet cost the king three votes in Parliament, and in time Lord Harry became sixth duke of Bolton. But he never held another command once George II convinced himself that Paulet might be a coward. In the political world the king had no such authority even before the loss of Minorca, and after it he was in serious difficulties. In October, Henry Fox resigned as secretary, in the hope of ruining Newcastle and weakening the king's military authority. Newcastle was clever enough to resign himself, the first and perhaps the only prime minister to resign with a majority of 150. He was replaced by his friend the fourth duke of Devonshire, with William Pitt as secretary of state.

Devonshire, the proprietor of one of England's great fortunes, had a private spy ring operating inside France; but he was clearly not the man of the hour, nor was Pitt. At this time the minister of the day was expected to give a levée at least twice a week so that the hungry might have an opportunity to ask for the loaves and the fishes. During the Devonshire ministry the levée was held at Lady Yarmouth's apartments, for no one knew where else to go. If Mrs. Thatcher looks into the matter, she may find that she is only the second female prime minister. Technically the job was Devonshire's; but he did not want it, or like it, and he saw to it that Newcastle, unlike Pitt, was kept informed of the thread of affairs, so that he could resume office without awkwardness.[20] This ministry was so weak that foreign ambassadors were told that England's foreign policy was still being conducted by Newcastle, even though he was out of office.[21] His return was merely a matter of timing. Newcastle wanted the supplies voted for the year, and the investigation into the Minorca disaster out of the way, before he would come back. And he would not come back at all without the support of both the king and the prince of Wales.

Only if the two courts were united behind him could he act with authority.[22] When the king became impatient and precipitated a crisis in April, Newcastle still refused to move, and it was not until the middle of June that all the details were ironed out. Then he returned to office as first lord of the treasury and as prime minister and held those places until the end of the reign, supported, if needed, by the prince of Wales and by Lady Yarmouth.

One of Newcastle's demands had been that Pitt resume office as secretary of state, rather than Henry Fox. The king would have preferred Fox and warned with a sneer that in any combined administration Newcastle would be nothing more than Mr. Pitt's clerk. Certainly Pitt tried to claim all the credit for himself, and too many scholars have taken his blustering at face value. Pitt was not in charge of the war as a whole. As secretary for the Southern Department he was in charge of the American theater, and it was also his duty to issue the orders to fleet commanders as well. The orders went out over his signature. But they had been hammered out in cabinet, and they represented the joint wisdom of the combined administration. A good many of the better ideas came from Hardwicke. Pitt excelled as an administrator, that is, in getting the orders of the cabinet carried out. He excelled also, at least at times, in the design of particular operations such as the assault on Martinique and Guadeloupe, which he devised working together with Mr. Cleveland of the admiralty.[23] But their plan had to obtain cabinet approval before it could be put into effect, and neither Pitt nor Mr. Cleveland was ever prime minister in this reign. The administration continued to operate on the departmental system, and, much to everyone's surprise, it was Newcastle rather than Pitt who had the ear of Lord Bute. When in 1758 a breach occurred between Leicester House and the ministry, it was a break with Pitt and not with Newcastle. And toward the end it is clear that Newcastle was losing favor with George II as he held his own at Leicester House. I am sure he knew what he was doing. It did not take the regular warnings of Chesterfield to remind him that the prince of Wales was fifty-five years younger than his grandfather.

In 1755 Newcastle had not forced the prince of Wales to marry his princess of Brunswick in order to cement the Prussian alliance. When he found that the young lady would be personally distasteful to Prince George, Newcastle dropped her and by so doing gained the favor of the prince and of the dowager princess as well. Then Newcastle persuaded the king to give the prince £40,000 a year as an eighteenth birthday present. This was handsome enough, since Prince Frederick had only been given £24,000 a year when he started out. But George announced that, grateful as he was for the £40,000, he would really prefer to continue to live at home with his mother; and he would like to have Bute appointed his groom of the stole. The king rejected both requests and was at first prepared to be firm. But the loss of Minorca so weakened the king's position that by September of 1756 the prince of Wales had his money and his mother and his groom of the stole.[24] If Pitt is considered to be the favorite of Leicester House, that is true as against Fox; but not as against the duke of Newcastle, who was thought to be an old crook but was admittedly an indispensable old crook, at least during the lifetime of George II. What did surprise Bute and the prince was being told in December of 1758, not that Newcastle was currently prime minister—that they knew—but being told by Pitt that it would be a good idea for him to continue in office into the new reign.[25] Leicester House was startled, but the idea was not to be forgotten.

A host of scholars have failed to remember it, most recently Professor Browning, whose biography of Newcastle is in some ways calamitous.[26] We need not rely merely on the word of the elder Pitt, a notorious liar. We can, if we like, examine a few test cases and see how they turned out. But we should always remember that the king's health was breaking and that as it failed, not only he but his entire generation lost power. Newcastle and Hardwicke might take very good care of Leicester House. They could never become companions of the young prince, for the gap in age was far too great. It was at best a relationship like that between Glubb Pasha and the young king of Jordan, bound to end unhappily. As for the king, there was one bout of fever in 1756 and there were three more of them in 1758. The illness of February 1759 was so bad that George II gave a packet of bank bills to Lady Yarmouth, a sign that they both thought he was dying.[27] Each of the king's illnesses weakened Newcastle. He might well continue to be first lord of the treasury into a new reign; but Bute would be minister, whatever office he might choose to accept.

Let us take a few specific examples to illustrate the position.

When Cumberland was ruined in the autumn of 1757, the voice of the nation demanded that he be replaced by Sir John Ligonier. Newcastle, the prince of Wales, and Pitt all agreed that Ligonier was the man. Then Newcastle went into the closet and secured the appointment. From then on Newcastle had an increasing share of military patronage, for Ligonier was not nearly so strong as Cumberland had been. Some of Newcastle's choices, such as that of Amherst for the American command, were distinctly superior to the candidates proposed by Pitt.[28] In the European theater, at least, Pitt could do very little. Thus, when the duke of Marlborough was going out as commander-in-chief of an expeditionary force to the continent and needed a secretary, he wrote both to Newcastle and to Pitt. It was Newcastle who got the right man appointed, and when Marlborough died it was, once again, Newcastle who named his replacement. By no means all the appointees had Leicester House support. Even fewer of them had Ligonier's support, and often he was informed about an appointment in his department twenty-four hours after the appointment had gone through.[29]

On political issues, the factions in the combined administration went their own way, but Newcastle's faction tended to win. Thus his party opposed the militia bill and held it up for a year. Pitt's attempt to expand the definition of habeas corpus was a much more serious affair. George II spoke out against the Habeas Corpus Bill in the Circle and Newcastle had it thrown out by the House of Lords, even though it seemed for a time that the government might fall. Pitt blustered and threatened and tried to bully Lady Yarmouth. That doughty soul had far more political courage than the king, and when Pitt tried blackmail — more money for Hesse in return for the bill — she became so angry that she refused even to pass the message on. The bill did not go through.[30] And on patronage matters, about which Pitt cared far more deeply than he would like us to think, he did badly. When the archbishop of Canterbury died, it was significant to both men, not only that Newcastle got Secker appointed but that he was able to do so without consulting Pitt. Bitterly, but with a fitting sense of humor, the secretary of state then asked Newcastle to get him a prebend's place at Windsor.[31]

In 1759 the mother country was stripped of men and equipment for the great assault on Canada. Usually large forces had to be kept at home in relative idleness, not so much to ward off a French attack as to sooth the nerves of the City. Throughout this administration, the king had continued to maintain his private intelligence operations and his private lines of communication; so had Newcastle, and so, apparently, had Devonshire. But the royal lines were the dangerous ones, for the king could use them at any time to make a separate peace. Both in 1758 and in 1759 he was negotiating on his own account with Vienna, as it happened, and meanwhile he was finding out much more news than Pitt could. The king's sources indicated the possibility of a combined Danish and Dutch attack on the British Isles.[32]

Pitt had always resented these royal channels of communication, but there were many of them of which he was unaware. And they were dangerous: George II did not agree with his English ministers about the purpose of the Seven Years War. He wanted to evict the French from the soil of North America, and on this topic Pitt came to agree with him while Hardwicke and Newcastle opposed him. They were much more afraid than the king and Pitt of the social consequences of wartime inflation.[33] The king's other war aim was a reparation for his German losses. An indemnity in money would be of frightening size, since it could be demonstrated that as elector, George's personal war losses exceeded two and a half million pounds sterling. A *dédommagement en terres et hommes,* which the king was trying to get from Vienna in 1759, would mean the acquisition of the bishoprics of Osnabrück, Paderborn, and Hildesheim, that is, a Greater Hanover somewhat resembling the one of 1815. Alternatively George II might be willing to accept East Friesland, whose inheritance had been taken from him by Frederick the Great in 1744.[34] Any territorial indemnity would change Hanover from a detestable electorate into a middling German, and indeed a middling European, power. It might well become a counter to the growing power of Prussia in the north, and Frederick was quick enough to recognize these ideas as a personal threat. He betrayed his uncle's plan to the English ministry in the hope of spoiling it. But it is quite possible that George II might have had his way had he lived to the end of the war. It is to this accident, that George II died just when he did, that England owed an outcome of the war so favorable to herself and so unfavorable to Hanover.

So far as the American theater was concerned, the king agreed with Pitt rather than with Newcastle and Hardwicke, and there is much evidence to indicate that Pitt's favor and influence in the Closet were increasing in 1759 and 1760 for just this reason. The third duke of Grafton thought that if the old king had lived, he *would have made* Pitt his minister.[35] But in 1759 Pitt did not believe in the possibility of a naval attack by Denmark and Sweden, because his own intelligence sources did not discuss anything other than the appalling economic collapse going on inside France and the low morale of her armies.[36] Thus, it became necessary to show Pitt the secret dispatches and intercepts, of whose existence he had never been told. Everyone was frightened to tell him, and at first there was an attempt to falsify the dates. In the end Pitt was told the whole story, and at first he kept his temper.[37] This was his way. Some months later there was a tremendous explosion about one particular link in the royal system, Joseph Yorke's secret work at The Hague. But Pitt seems never to have discovered all the channels of secret information, nor ever to have succeeded in stopping all of them.

Another very large area in which Pitt did not operate as master was that of money. It is a pity that students do not take Newcastle more seriously. He was not only efficient enough to run the Seven Years War on the basis of a four-day week, surely an administrative triumph in itself, but he was also able to pay for it at 4 percent, and in the early years of the war at $3\frac{1}{2}$. What other English prime minister ever did as well? Now, of course, the term *Newcastle* comprises not only the individual Thomas Pelham-Holles but also several different teams of experts without whose approval Thomas Pelham-Holles would not move. In diplomatic matters he had frequently used a small committee of resident foreign ambassadors against his own cabinet colleagues. At this time the committee was down to the single person of Count Viry, a remarkable intriguer who was the Sardinian envoy. On political matters Newcastle would consult not only Hardwicke but also a kitchen cabinet that usually included Sir Thomas Robinson, Andrew Stone, William Murray, and in later years the fourth duke of Devonshire. Apart from such consultations in committee, Newcastle was also careful to take soundings from a number of country gentlemen by mail. For a man who had never sat in the House of Commons it was particularly important to keep in close touch with public opinion; and on the whole it must be said that he knew a great deal about it, often more than his rivals. On financial matters he had no rivals. He consulted not only the gentlemen of the Bank of England, and such men as Sir John Barnard and Samson Gideon; he got much of his advice from Mr. West of the treasury. Newcastle did not take advice from Pitt, or from Pitt's friend Beckford, or from Henry Bilson Legge, the rather pathetic chancellor of the exchequer. Without advice from Pitt or from Legge, Newcastle turned in his best performance as a financier.

Pitt did not care for this at all and had tried to demand a majority of the treasury board in the ministry of 1757, three seats out of five. It was this demand that cause the "interregnum" to last for three months, from April until the middle of June. Pitt ended up with one seat, not three. What he retained was veto power, which he exercised to prevent the imposition of taxes on sugar. But Speaker Onslow also had veto power on tax questions and was also willing to use it. And if Pitt went beyond a veto and tried to attack Legge or Newcastle, which he did from time to time, he would be stopped by the disapproval of Leicester House. In time, Legge came to resent his humiliating situation, and in order to be tactful, Newcastle permitted him to present his own financial proposals in 1759. This happened to coincide with the one real period of financial stringency during the war years. Frederick the Great had troubled the money market by buying up gold, which he proposed to use to issue a debased coinage. Then the Dutch chose this moment to withdraw their investment in the English stocks, and the combination was too much for the bank. It had to buy gold bullion at a premium of 3 percent in order to have it minted, or else England would have to go off the gold standard. And no one can buy at 103 in order to sell at par for very long. It was soon clear to the financial world that, while Newcastle could save this country, no one else could, and Legge's reputation was blasted.

Ever since 1689 the moneyed interest had tried to influence the formation of policy. Crude attempts were made to blackmail William and Mary, some of them by Thomas Pelham of Laughton.[38] Whether Newcastle had learned the technique at his father's knee or no, he had certainly learned it somewhere. On the accession of George III, the new king kept his grandfather's ministers, but at first he talked of the changes he would be making after the first six months. Newcastle bowed his head and made no bargains for himself. His official attitude was that he was perfectly willing to run errands for Bute, without reward. Unfortunately, however, the financial community would not lend the money needed for the year 1761 unless assurance was given that the duke would remain in office for more than the year itself.[39] Clearly Newcastle had the votes, not only of the House of Commons but of the City counting houses as well. Administration could not do without him until he was betrayed by Mr. Martin of the treasury on a technical matter in May of 1762, and then he did resign.

One place where votes did not normally count was at meetings of the efficient cabinet. In 1747 and 1748, as I have pointed out on another occasion, Newcastle had been outvoted in the efficient cabinet by 3-1, and yet his policy had prevailed.[40] In the year after Henry Pelham's death, votes were infrequent, for at that time the efficient cabinet was really limited to Newcastle and Hardwicke. During the Devonshire-Pitt administration of 1756, there was a little more voting. Pitt seems to have believed in votes where Newcastle and the king were consensus politicians, but the administrative procedure of such a ministry would not set any precedents. A new situation arose, however, with the combined ministry of June 1757. Newcastle's people and Pitt's people disagreed on major issues, and how were conflicts to be reconciled if not by voting? On balance Newcastle won most of the battles and, in particular, he won on the issue of voting. He knew very well that his work in the closet could not be carried on unless most of the advice given to the king was the unanimous voice of the ministry. Nothing less powerful would sway the king's mind. Therefore, an informal bargain was struck. Newcastle spoke well of Pitt in the closet, as Lady Yarmouth did below stairs, and between them they made his court for him — no easy task at first. Pitt for his part had to give in on most of the issues, not only on the German issue, where he had to swallow everything he had been saying for twenty years, but also surrender on his liberal interpretation of the law, and on men. By now, establishment Whigs had become quite reactionary on legal issues, and among establishment Whigs Hardwicke and William Murray, Lord Mansfield, were far to the right of the pack. Even Lord Keeper Henley was considered suspect by Newcastle, though no one else has ever been able to find the liberal spark in that quarter.

In order to achieve harmony, Pitt and his friends were forced to postpone legal reform until after the end of the war. Indeed, Pitt went farther. When Newcastle complained of being alone in the efficient cabinet, and of the possibility of his being outvoted there, Pitt agreed to the addition of Hardwicke and in time of Mansfield and Halifax as ministers without portfolio.[41] This gave Newcastle such an overwhelming majority that votes were not heard of again until the new reign, and even then they did not matter much. Thus, on the famous occasion when Pitt and Temple resigned in 1761, they did so after the cabinet had voted unanimously against them. But this vote was taken just for the record, like a "tombstone" advertisement in the financial press recording a bond issue that has already been sold out. Pitt and Temple knew they were beaten, and that they were going to resign, well before the vote was taken. Later on, in the summer of 1762, Bute was once voted down by a unanimous cabinet. But at the next meeting, by which time it had been learned that Bute had the king's support, his measures went through. And if by chance they did not, as over the decision to return St. Lucia to the French, the cabinet might, if it pleased, insist on the retention of St. Lucia. Bute and Egremont simply let Viry assure the French that the island was theirs for the asking, and the negotiations proceeded on that basis.[42]

Votes did not matter, then, even during a combined administration. What did matter? Obviously, the mind of the king; and it is time for us to stop giggling about George II. Both in 1755 and in 1758 others wanted him to settle for less, but he insisted on the goal of evicting the French from the soil of North America. He won his point, and it is to George II as well as to Wolfe and Amherst that we owe the final victory. I would suggest, however, that this was one of the last meaningful survivals of the old system. For George III abandoned the German war in 1762, and with it any hope of securing a *dédommagement* there for himself. By doing so he ruined his finances. Later on in the century the military contribution of Hanover was limited to forces of some ten thousand men, and I know of no significant diplomatic activity by George III as elector.[43] In England he acted, as his grandfather had, as the operating head of the army and referred to it as his own department. He took over church patronage from his ministers. As a result, the church became far more aristocratic. But

George III took so little interest in Europe that he did not bother to have his two eldest sons taught German, and his German chancery in London was allowed to fall into decay. Then when it was wanted there was none, and the king himself had to translate German-language documents for his English ministers with his own hand.

A new age was dawning, an age of Indian and American empires, an age in which Europe was less important and so too were those who handled European matters—the secretaries of state and the sovereign himself. New men—home secretary, colonial secretary—would come into prominence as the older ones slowly faded into the background. George III did send his younger sons to Hanover for their education. But he sent his prize sheep to Australia and received from that continent a supply of kangaroos. His daughter longed for some to add to her private zoo; and so in the spring of 1800 a herd was sent off toward Württemberg with two couples of kangaroos. They arrived at much the same time as the French revolutionary armies and followed the duchess on her flight. Ultimately the duchess found a refuge for herself at Erlangen, where the beasts were put into a courtyard.[44]

Here were royal beasts just as insignificant as King Alexander's monkey. The kangaroos did not even bite the duchess of Württemberg. By 1800 the old system had been dead for a generation. Its survival even into the 1760s seem to have been an artifice of Bute, a device for achieving the Peace of Paris. George III's letters in that period give no indication of an independent mind: he wrote, verbatim, what Bute told him to. The Peace of Paris is the last whisper of an older, seventeenth-century monarchy.[45] In its death throes it had given England not only a new empire but also a series of new administrative devices. A relatively insignificant Europe did not deserve two secretaries of state, and after many years of complaint, a single foreign secretary emerged in 1782, together with a single home secretary. A third secretary, for the colonies, should have been appointed as early as 1757 and would have been but for the protests of Pitt.

Even more important was the establishment of the office of first lord of the treasury at the head of the government. I have been arguing for some years now, that as late as 1754 it was not clear whether or not the first lord of the treasury was the minister of the day. When Henry Pelham died on 6 March 1754, both the duke of Grafton and Henry Fox thought that Newcastle *continued* to be minister. He had, they thought, been minister as secretary and he continued to be minister after his move to the treasury.[46] Now, Fox and Grafton may have been wrong, but their evidence shows that the point was still in dispute in 1754. Eight years later, when Newcastle resigned, there could be no question. His work at the treasury had made that the first place. It was still possible for Bute to be in charge in 1760 without any office of business, and for him to be in charge in 1761 as secretary of state. But these were extraconstitutional anachronisms, with which the political world was most unhappy, and the situation did not become orderly until Bute followed Newcastle's example and took the treasury for himself. The long and, in domestic terms, successful ministry of Lord North consolidated the position; and so the process begun by Danby in the 1670s, and continued by Walpole, reached its conclusion.

Very likely the process would have been slower without the Seven Years War. As we all know, war tends to accelerate developments in many fields, to throw up ideas not all of which can be absorbed at once. Thus, not only the Stamp Act but union with Ireland and a progressive income tax were all proposed during the Seven Years War. That George II and Newcastle did not adopt them is to their credit. Their administrative work was of permanent value, while their successors were to find out the hard way that there were reasons for not imposing a Stamp Act or a progressive income tax or a union with Ireland. It is time to stop giggling about both of them.

NOTES

[Place of publication is London except where otherwise stated.]

1. John, Lord Hervey, *Some Materials towards Memoirs of the Reign of King George II,* ed. Romney Sedgwick, 3 vols. (1931); Horace Walpole, *Memoires of the last ten years of the reign of George the second,* ed. Henry Fox, Lord Holland, 2 vols. (1822); *The political journal of George Bubb Dodington,* ed. John Carswell and Lewis Arnold Dralle (1965); *The Yale edition of Horace Walpole's correspondence,* ed. Wilmarth Sheldon Lewis et al. (New Haven, 1937-); *The letters of Philip Dormer Stanhope, 4th earl of Chesterfield,* ed. Bonamy Dobrée, 6 vols. (1932); *Oeuvres de Frédéric Le Grand,* ed. J. D. E. Preuss, 31 vols. in 33 (Berlin, 1846-1857).

2. Perhaps the worst offender in this group was Basil Williams, whose *Chatham,* 2 vols. (1913), *Stanhope* (1932), and *The Whig Supremacy, 1714-1760* (1939) misled two generations of students. Not too many people read Morley or Rosebery today, but Julian Corbett's *England in the seven years war,* 2 vols. (1907) badly needs to be replaced.

3. The hostility of Sedgwick, at least, to the Hanoverians goes back to his 1931 edition of Hervey's *Memoirs.* It continued to distort his interpretations right down through the publication of his *The Commons 1715-1754* (1970).

4. Lewis B. Namier, *England in the Age of the American Revolution* (1930), p. 108.

5. During the first week of October, 1756, B.L. Add. MS 32868, passim.

6. Newcastle to General Wall, Newcastle House, April 28, 1755, Copy, B.L. Add. MS 32854, ff. 309-310.

7. Albemarle to Bedford, Paris, 28 March/8 April, 1750, B.L. Add. MS 33026, ff. 83-85.

8. Philip Chesney Yorke, *The life and correspondence of Philip Yorke, earl of Hardwicke, Lord High Chancellor of Great Britain,* 3 vols. (1913), II, 223.

9. See n. 46.

10. Colonel Joseph Yorke to Lord Hardwicke, Helvoetsluys, September 13, 1755, Yorke, *Hardwicke,* II, 284-285.

11. Sir Edward Wilmot to Newcastle, Kensington, June 3, 1758, B.L. Add. MS 32880, f. 309.

12. Memorandums, Claremont, December 10, 1758, B.L. Add. MS 32886, ff. 250-251. The secret channel kept open at the king's command between Newcastle and Joseph Yorke at The Hague was much friendlier to the Dutch viewpoint, e.g., Newcastle to Major-General Joseph Yorke, November 17, 1758, Private, Copy, B.L. 32885, ff. 365-370.

13. On the extraordinary situation in 1755, see Newcastle to Münchhausen, Claremont, May 23, 1755, Copy, B.L. Add. MS 32855, ff. 140-144; *Political Journal of George Bubb Dodington,* p. 319; Henry Fox to Hartington, July 1, 1755, Copy, B.L. Add. 51383 D, f. 17.

14. And of course he was right to feel that way; but his attitude means that the king was more important than modern scholars such as Plumb and Browning are willing to admit.

15. Newcastle to Harrington, Claremont, Entre nous, Copy, June 6, 1755, B.L. Add. MS 32855, ff. 365-366; Holdernesse to Newcastle [Hanover], July 6, 1755, P:S: Entre nous, B.L. Add. MS 32856, f. 553.

16. See, e.g., in 1754, B.L. Add. MS 32995, f. 307. In 1759 Onslow had exceptional influence because of the great political and economic disturbances of that spring: Henry Bilson Legge to Newcastle, Downing Street, March 8, 1759, B.L. Add. MS 32888, f. 414; and J. West to Newcastle [April 18, 1759], B.L. Add. MS 32890, ff. 162-163.

17. Legge was not dismissed for this until November, when he spoke

in the Commons against the treaty. It was thought at the time that Legge and Pitt acted as they did in expectation of a speedy demise of the crown. Hartington to Henry Fox, Dublin, November 8, 1755, B.L. Add. MS 51381, ff. 71-72.

18. A spy's report, dated Versailles January 26, 1756, and marked as received on February 7, is in the Newcastle Papers at B.L. Add. 32862, ff. 220-221. At Minorca the reports were so numerous that a general council of war sat from February 5. David Erskine, ed., *Augustus Hervey's Journal*, pp. 190-191.

19. Anson to Newcastle, Admiralty June 10, 1756, B.L. Add. MS 32865, ff. 251-252.

20. B.L. Add. MS 32869, ff. 305 and 320-326. For the crowd at Lady Yarmouth's, see Hardwicke to Newcastle, Powis House, January 7, 1757, At night, B.L. Add. MS 32870, ff. 58-62.

21. When angry enough at the king, Newcastle was prepared to deny such stories. "Papers laid before the king, by Lord Waldegrave, [10 June] and return'd June 11th 1757," B.L. Add. MS 32871, ff. 272-273.

22. See, e.g., "Paper read by my Lord Waldegrave to the King," March 9, 1757, B.L. Add. MS 32870, ff. 250-251. The difficulties are illustrated by Henry Fox to Cumberland May 20, 1757, B.L. Add. MS 51375, ff. 107-108. The documentation on what was called at the time the "Interregnum" is of course enormous.

23. Newcastle to Hardwicke, Newcastle House Monday at night [September 4, 1758], Copy, B.L. Add. MS 32883, ff. 273-275.

24. The negotiations began in the spring and went on for months. For the early discussions, see B.L. Add. MS 32996, ff. 403-404.

25. B.L. Add. MS 32886, ff. 384-386 and 411.

26. Reed Browning, *The Duke of Newcastle* (1975).

27. Royal Archives, Windsor, R.A. 52980, Note by George II of February 10, 1759, "Les billets de banque, que j'ai mis en dépôt entre les mains de M. la Comtesse de Yarmouth doivent lui appartenir aprés ma mort, comme un don que je lui en fais.

"GEORGE R."

I owe my dutiful thanks to Her Majesty the Queen for her gracious permission to work in these papers.

28. Pitt in 1757 preferred Lord Cornwallis and in 1758 was reluctant to abandon Abercrombie. Newcastle to Hardwicke, Claremont, September 3, 1757, Copy, B.L. Add. MS 32873, ff. 432-435; same to same, Claremont, September 17, 1758, B.L. Add. MS 32884, ff. 27-36.

29. See on this B.L. Add. MS 32885, ff. 148 and passim. Marlborough's successor was Lord George Sackville, and it was doubly important to Newcastle that he, not Pitt, made the recommendation, while Ligonier was not informed for another twenty-four hours.

30. Horace Walpole, *Memoires*, II, 295; Newcastle to Hardwicke, Claremont, May 16, 1758, Copy, B.L. Add. MS 32880, ff. 96-103; same to same, May 21, 1758, ibid., ff. 170-176.

31. William Pitt to Newcastle, Wednesday evening March 29th [1758], B.L. Add. MS 32878, f. 420.

32. Pitt of course turned out to be correct, but Steinberg's reports from Copenhagen were alarming. An amphibious attack on Scotland or alternatively on Ireland was the talk of London, entirely apart from the king's secret intelligence reports.

33. "Considerations on the present state of affairs at home, and abroad," Claremont, April 18 & 19, 1759, B.L. Add. MS 32890, ff. 130-151, especially ff. 138-142.

34. Newcastle to Hardwicke, Claremont, August 26, 1758, Copy, B.L. Add. MS 32883, ff. 114-119; same to same, October 5, 1758, printed in Yorke, *Hardwicke*, III, 230-231; same to same, October 31, ibid., pp. 241-242; Andrew Mitchell to Newcastle, Dresden, December 11, 1758, Private, B.L. Add. MS 32886, ff. 256-259. Taking all of French North America had been in the air in 1755: Newcastle to Hardwicke, Claremont, August 4, 1755, Copy, B.L. Add. MS 32857, ff. 568-569.

35. Sir William R. Anson, ed., *Autobiography and Political Correspondence of Augustus Henry Third Duke of Grafton* (1898), p. 12.

36. Compare Pitt's intelligence reports in P.R.O. 30/8/87 with those in the Newcastle Papers. They seem accurate, but they are confined to France. Hardwicke was contemptuous: "In truth the Southern Department seems to have no channel of intelligence at all." Hardwicke to Newcastle, Grosvenor Square May 18, 1759, Friday morning, B.L. Add. MS 32891, f. 171. The Dutch agent T. Palairet, like Newcastle and Hardwicke, expected a landing either in Scotland or in Ireland. T. Palairet to the Raadpensionaris Steyn, London, July 13, 1759, Algemeen Rijks-Archief, The Hague, Familie Archief Stein, 24.

37. B.L. Add. MS 32891, ff. 358-359.

38. Thomas Pelham was made a lord of the treasury for his loans, and was fired twice, in 1692 and in 1699. See S. B. Baxter, *The Development of the Treasury 1660-1702* (1957), p. 29.

39. "Points to be mentioned to Lord Bute," B.L. 32999, ff. 144-145, f. 145: "That the money'd men of the City had plainly told the Duke of Newcastle, that if he staid [on as First Lord of the Treasury], they would raise the money. But that, if he did continue, it must be with an appearance of duration; or otherwise they would not trust."

40. S. B. Baxter, "The Myth of the Grand Alliance in the Eighteenth Century," in Paul R. Sellin and Stephen B. Baxter, *Anglo-Dutch Cross Currents in the Seventeenth and Eighteenth Centuries* (Los Angeles, 1976).

41. Newcastle to Dupplin, Claremont, September 28, 1757, Copy, B.L. Add. MS 32874, ff. 353-358.

42. Romney Sedgwick, ed., *Letters from George III to Lord Bute, 1756-1766* (1939), pp. 118n and 124.

43. Professor Ian Christie tells me that he has put one of his students to work on the Fürstenbund episode of the 1780s. Professor Aspinall's splendid edition of *The Later Correspondence of George III* makes it clear that English ministers were neither consulted nor informed about that king's electoral activities.

44. Charlotte Augusta Matilda, princess royal of Great Britain, duchess and later queen of Württemberg. On the kangaroos see A. Aspinall, ed., *The Later Correspondence of George III*, 3, 346, 378. The animals did well and reproduced themselves in captivity.

45. Or very nearly the last whisper. The Regency Bill of 1765 is an exceptionally archaic document both in form and in content.

46. Archdeacon Coxe reported the attitude of Henry Fox in his *Memoirs of Horatio, Lord Walpole,* 3d ed. (1820), II, 346-347 but did not understand what he was reporting. Fortunately, Henry Fox's papers are now available in the British Library. As for Grafton, there is no room for misunderstanding. "From the late death of the respectable Mr. Pelham strong contentions had taken place between those statesmen who were entitled to have the lead.

"Notwithstanding this state of things the Duke of Newcastle was still the Minister: because he was supported by the body of the Whigs; and he secured this preference by the confidence they had in the sincerity of his principles, and the disinterestedness of his character." Anson, ed., *Autobiography and Political Correspondence of Augustus Henry Third Duke of Grafton,* pp. 4, 5.

X

THE NUMBER 45:
A WILKITE POLITICAL SYMBOL

John Brewer

Domestic political history of the Hanoverian era written in the
last generation has, in the main, been the history of ministries
and of party. Apart from electoral politics and the occasional
study of pamphleteering, political activity "out of doors" has
rarely been deemed worthy of serious scrutiny. Admittedly there
are exceptions to this rule—most notably George Rudé's discussions of the Georgian crowd[1]—but there are virtually no studies,
apart from the writings of J. H. Plumb, Lucy Sutherland, and
more recently of Paul Langford and Nicholas Rogers, which
tackle the question of the relationship between the political world
of St. James's and Westminster Hall, and the various forms of
demotic expression.[2]

The neglect of this problem seems to me to be largely explained
by certain assumptions customarily made by eighteenth-century
historians. It is, for example, a frequent supposition that Hanoverian political activity *properly defined* was limited to such
instrumental acts within the formal political structure as jockey-
ing for place and office, voting at the hustings and in Parliament,
and sending petitions and instructions to Westminster. This, it is
understood, is what politics were *really* about. Clearly all of these

activities were central to *la vie politique* and to the exercise of power—a matter that has fascinated political historians almost as much as it obsessed and repelled the Hanoverian Englishman. But do these actions adequately delineate or describe political activity in its entirety; were they the only means by which to exercise political power? It is one of the purposes of this essay to demonstrate that eighteenth-century Englishmen of all ranks and classes would not have accepted such a circumscribed definition of politics and of the exercise of authority and that, in consequence, historians' understanding of the term "political" when applied to Hanoverian Britain is, as often as not, both too narrow, and ahistorical and reductionist.

Such a constricted and anachronistic definition of politics and power is often accompanied in the literature by a reluctance to examine noninstitutional, and what are regarded as noninstrumental, forms of political expression because they do not conform to some preconceived notion of that ineluctable historical category, "public opinion." Just as those who have studied Georgian "party" have sometimes decided that there was no such animal in eighteenth-century England, because nothing resembling the monsters of modern Britain could be found in the Hanoverian political swamp,[3] so forms of political expression that were neither "modern" nor easily accommodated within current notions of representative politics have been overlooked or brushed aside.

The problem created by such sins of omission is not simply one of partiality; the incompleteness of the political picture prevents us from understanding the nature and meaning of politics as a whole for Hanoverian Englishmen. If we are to know what politics and the exercise of authority meant, we need to include considerations of the full range of actions which Georgian Englishmen would have regarded as "political." This may seem a severe injunction and a very bold one in view of the narrowness of my subject in this essay. But the example of the Wilkite political symbol, the number 45, does provide us with both the evidence and the opportunity to work toward a redefinition of the nature of Hanoverian political activity.

The number 45, of course, became notorious through association with John Wilkes. In April 1764, immediately after the resignation of the Scottish favorite John Stuart, Earl of Bute, Wilkes published the forty-fifth number of his acerbic, chauvinist, and insulting opposition paper, the *North Briton*. Number 45 was, in fact, a good deal more temperate and much less personally vindictive than early numbers of the journal, but it attacked the king's speech made at the opening of Parliament and thereby goaded the government (which had already contemplated legal action) into prosecuting the paper and its publishers.[4] This decision triggered a series of events, too well known to bear reiteration here, but which made Wilkes a popular hero and martyr, and the eponymous leader of a somewhat inchoate movement seeking parliamentary reform, accountable government, and the security of a free press.[5]

The number 45 was rapidly taken up as *the* symbol of this movement. It gradually became a metonymic sign for John Wilkes, for liberty, and for radicalism. This set of associations was made simply enough: the forty-fifth number of the *North Briton* had been written by Wilkes, and to think of the number 45 was therefore to think of its author as well as the cause that he came to personify. The fact that publication of the *North Briton* number 45 was the seed from which radicalism grew made "45" a portentous and propitious number: the birth of "45" was the genesis of reform. The symbol, therefore, not only represented reformist politics but acted as a reminder of the circumstances of their inception. At the same time, "45" had other associations. Though the prosecution of the forty-fifth number of the *North Briton* was largely fortuitous, it was singularly appropriate that an overtly anti-Scottish movement — Wilkes exploited anti-Caledonian feeling with extraordinary ruthlessness[6] — should have as its symbol a number that recalled the defeat and humiliation of the pretender in 1745.

The number 45 possessed several other advantages as a symbol: being a logogram, it was simple to execute and recognizable even to the illiterate. Above all it was a number, an abstract symbol rather than an object with symbolic import, and therefore definitely more flexible in its application or use. The creative possibilities of the number, indeed, were even greater than those of such ideograms as the Christian cross or the more modern peace sign. Apart from its use as a logogram — as a "sign" that could be attached to or drawn upon any object — the number was deployed as a unit of time, of space, and of mass, thereby converting an hour of the day (12:*45*),[7] a dwelling (45 feet in length),[8] or an object (such as the 45-lb. simnel cake presented to Wilkes),[9] into a component of Wilkite ritual. When 45 was used as a cardinal number, a comparable transformation occurred: 45 similar events or objects (like the 45 dumplings served at a Wandsworth christening)[10] were automatically Wilkite, just as the ordinal "forty-fifth" had radical associations: pro-Wilkite sermons, for instance, were usually taken from the forty-fifth verse of biblical chapters.[11] Finally, any object that could be broken down into forty-five equal parts also had a radical connotation: such as the special candlestick with 45 branches made for a Newcastle publican in 1770.[12]

Although the number 45 does not appear to have had very special associations before the Wilkite agitation, radicals could draw on the very long tradition of number symbolism to treat the number 45 in ways customarily reserved for such sacred, hallowed, or lucky numbers as seven, twenty-seven, or forty-nine.[13] The number 45, therefore, had tremendous potential as a symbol for those who wished to use it.

Not that Wilkes's supporters ever displayed much reluctance to demonstrate their allegiance to the number 45. Using provincial newspapers, legal records, and contemporary memoirs and letters, I have gathered data on incidents involving the number 45 from some sixty different provincial localities as far apart as Paisley in Scotland and Saltash in Cornwall, as well as over fifty episodes in London in such diverse *quartiers* as Islington, Chelsea, Seven Dials, Rotherhithe, Holborn, Clare Market, Southwark, and Westminster.[14] I have not included in my discussion similar occurrences in the North American colonies nor in Ireland, though several took place in both localities.[15]

Several characteristics of these events stand out. First and foremost, the number 45 was persistently associated with sociable and convivial activities—eating, drinking, and gift giving—which frequently took place as *public* celebrations and as acts of commemoration. Club meetings, lavish dinners, and extravagant celebrations were jampacked with Wilkite number symbolism. Take clubs: there were numerous societies established with forty-five members. The Minority Club in St. Paul's Churchyard; the "45" Society that met at the 45 Tavern in Gray's Inn Passage and was managed by Mr. Keys, a former cook of Alderman Beckford's; the "Free and Easy under the Rose" in Cursitor Street, and the

Liberty Beefsteak club, established by the more influential friends of Wilkes after his release from prison in April 1770: they all restricted their membership to the magical number.[16] Similar societies flourished in the provinces. Convivial gatherings of forty-five members occurred at such clubs as the "Templetonians" of Temple Street in Bristol and at the Patriotic Club in Newbury. Members sang songs to Wilkes and liberty and the number 45, drank toasts to the special number, and replenished their charging glasses from a punch bowl which, as likely as not, bore a radical motto and the inevitable number 45.[17]

If clubs were common enough, feasts and dinners arranged on the principle of "45" were even more frequent. It is difficult to convey the complexity and precision as well as the total effect of these events without recourse to contemporary description. Characteristic of these numerous dinners was one held at Poplar in April 1768:[18]

The company consisted of 45 gentlemen. At 45 minutes past one, there were drank 45 gills of wine, with 45 new laid eggs in them. Precisely at 45 minutes past two a very genteel dinner was served up, being five courses, nine dishes each, which made the number 45. In the middle of the table the figures of 45 were inlaid with mother of pearl, on which was placed a noble sirloin of beef weighing 45 lbs. The tablecloth and plates were marked 45. On the back of every chair these figures were carved, and exactly 25 gilt nails in a chair, which with the 20 on each chair 45.- The whole concluded with a ball in the evening, when 45 ladies entered the room; then the dances immediately began; and each lady was saluted at the end of every dance, which were nine minuets, with nine quadrils, and nine *cotillions,* and 18 country dances, being in the whole 45. After the ladies had been kissed round that number of times, and 45 couple of jellies were eaten, the company retired with great mirth and festivity, at 45 minutes past three o'clock.

This elaborate entertainment — naturally I have chosen one of the better examples — was uncharacteristic only in two respects. It was held privately, whereas most dinners were staged either in a large tavern or in the open; and second, in what, as we shall see, was an unusual move, the entertainment involved the segmentation of 45 into its divisors — in this case 9 and their multiples — rather than the constant use of the number in its entirety.

Feasts of this sort were often only one constituent element of Wilkite popular celebration in its most lavish forms. The *Cam-*

bridge Chronicle of June 1768 published the following description, sent in by a reader, of the celebration at King's Lynn that accompanied the news that the writ of outlawry against Wilkes had finally been reversed:[19]

There was a general display of colour in our streets, and on board ships in the harbour; the bells were set out, and rung for the greatest part of the day, and in the evening there was a bonfire on the Market Hill; the principal streets were illuminated, and made a very brilliant appearance. Several of the houses were lighted with 45 candles, several windows ornamented with 45 cut out of paper, and stuck on squares; and on one window was cut out in pasteboard Liberty Triumphant, no. 45, which from the lights in the room, had a very pretty effect.

All these celebrations involved veritable numerological orgies at which objects were inscribed with the special "ever memorable" number, or arranged in groups of 45. At dinners beef, ham, veal, pork, pigeons, salmon, turbot, whelks (used because of their punning similarity with Wilkes), oysters, turtle, dumplings, cabbages, potatoes, cucumbers, tarts, cake, and jellies, together with beer, porter, and wine were all served as 45 units — whether by numbers, pounds weight, or pints.[20] Most of these occasions involved either toasts to the number 45 or the drinking of 45 toasts, and frequently the smoking of 45 pipes of tobacco signaled the end of the feast.[21] At demonstrations crowds wore badges and blue ribbons or favors emblazoned with the number 45, though few went as far as Mr. Scott, the patriotic newscarrier, who was "remarkable for wearing at his breast a silver medal of Mr. Wilkes marked no. 45, as are likewise his sleeve buttons, breastbuckle etc."[22] The hats, coats, and coaches of passersby, especially if they were genteel, were chalked or inscribed by members of the crowd with the special number.[23] In May 1768, for instance,

as a Gentleman was going through the Mob in the Borough (of Southwark), a fellow observing that he had not got the no. 45 on his hat, insisted on his letting him put it on, to which the Gentleman readily agreed, in order to get through the crowd unmolested: He had no sooner got the Hat than he ran off with it, but being pursued and caught by some sailors, he was obliged to return it, and after a severe ducking was commanded to go about his business, with threats, that if he ever was seen among the Friends of Liberty again, they would tye a Stone about his Neck, and throw him into the Middle of the Thames.[24]

For the Wilkite crowd, marking the number 45 was a political act, a declaration of liberty; theft was not.

Such strokes for liberty help explain why Wilkes's enemies were the victims of marking. Justice Capel, a Surrey magistrate who was especially assiduous in his pursuit of Wilkites, had his coat chalked with the number 45 by John Perceval, a pewterer. When Perceval was sentenced to two years' imprisonment for this "crime," Wilkites "maliciously defaced" the "Front Door and Pilasters" of the justice's home by carving them with the number 45, as a more permanent and enduring reminder of the cause of liberty.[25]

Marking and labeling were not confined to the crowd nor to occasions of jubilation. Numerous artifacts, many of which survive, were embellished with the radical number. Coins and commemorative medals bore the legend. Many ceramic items including punch bowls, snuffboxes, mugs, and brooches had the number 45 as their motif,[26] as did many of the gifts that admirers presented to Wilkes during his confinement in the King's Bench prison.[27] Enterprising tradesmen produced Wilkite products based on the special number. Joseph Leech, a wigmaker of Romsey in Hampshire, advertised "my new-invented Cork Peruke of 45 curls," a sample of which was dispatched to Wilkes along with an excruciating verse praising the patriot's pate and its new covering.[28] A Worcester staymaker presented Polly, Wilkes's much loved daughter, who for a short while became a leader of fashion because of her father, with stays "of 45 pieces or quarters, 45 holes and the no. 45 beautifully marked on the stomacher."[29] In both these cases the sales of the produce seem to have been as important to their manufacturer as was the cause of Wilkes and liberty, but the ingenuity shown in producing these and many other artifacts provided good publicity both for their producer and for the radical cause.

The arrangement of Wilkite activities according to units of time and space based on the number 45 was one means of ordering conduct and regulating behavior at feasts and celebrations. Dinners at Newport, Isle of Wight, Bristol, Reading, Poplar, Alnwick, and Amford in Somerset all began or ended at precisely 45 minutes after or before a particular hour.[30] In Sunderland 45 skyrockets "representing the towering spirit and lustre of true patriotism" were fired off at 45-second intervals to celebrate Wilkes's release from prison; in London a 45-foot-long table was laid in the streets to commemorate the same occasion, while in Worcester the attempt of a local bell ringer to peal for 45 minutes led to an affray that produced litigation and a countersuit.[31] Probably the most notable instance of this sort of organization, however, was the assembly room erected, so it was claimed, by 45 patriots of Berkhamstead, and which was built as a square with walls 45 feet long.[32]

When did these extraordinary celebrations take place? Most, though not all, were held as acts of political commemoration, designed to impress the public with the importance of certain days sacred to the cause of Wilkes and liberty. Of these, undoubtedly the most important was 18 April, the date on which Wilkes was released from jail in 1770, and therefore the moment at which Wilkes and liberty were reunited. Radical groups throughout the country vied with one another, each trying to out-celebrate their allies in other towns and villages and to create a lasting local memory of one of the finest moments of the Wilkite cause.[33] Thereafter April 18 occupied an important annual place in the Wilkite calendar. Wilkes's birthday, October 28, was of almost equal consequence. Year after year this date was marked by dinners, treating, and numerological celebrations. Brewers sold beer at cut prices, street parties were held in the metropolis, and citizens illuminated their houses, either because they were supporters of the cause or because they feared that the mob would smash unlighted windows.[34] The Wilkite calendar also included the different dates of the Middlesex elections, when Wilkes had been returned by the county despite the opposition of the government. February 16 and 28, March 16 and 29, and April 18 were all remembered as the triumphs of the sturdy Middlesex electorate. On each of these occasions the voters had vanquished a venal Parliament and a corrupt adminstration by returning Wilkes to his rightful Commons seat. The jubilation of these days was contrasted with the somber atmosphere of the anniversary of the St. George's Field Massacre, held on May 10. The radical minister, Dr. Free, preached an annual sermon castigating the heinous murder of Wilkites by Scottish troops outside the King's Bench Prison in 1768.[35] This solemn commemoration was accompanied by parades of mourners, a visit to the grave of the massacre's most famous victim, William Allen, and by the tolling of muffled church bells. Each of these calendrical events, as well as the original incidents that gave rise to their commemoration, contained the full panoply of Wilkite symbolic regalia and were also the times at which the number 45 was most obtrusive.

The number also appeared on other, nonradical calendrical occasions such as May Day, Shrove Tuesday, and the annual feast days of such trades as flax dressers and wool breakers.[36] In Bristol in 1769, for example,

The 1st of May being annually a season for youths to erect Maypoles, decorated with garlands of flowers &c, one amongst others was set up at Limkiln Dock, Bristol. The pole was just 45 feet high and had 45 garlands on it, with this motto *No. 45 Wilkes and Liberty.* There was just 45 couples who danced around it, and drank 45 quarts of ale. —Just opposite the above pole was hung up the effigy of L—— B——, with a Scotch bonnet, white cockade and jack boots, which after a little season the enraged spectators cut down, quartered, and scattered over the face of the earth —The pole was raised 45 minutes after eight o'clock in the morning, and there was drunk 45 drams. —The children who ran about the streets playing at Thread the Needle, sung to their companions, Open the gate as high as the sky, to let FREE Wilkes, and I go by.[37]

This means of giving political import to a traditional popular festival paralleled the transformation of *rites de passage* into Wilkite occasions. Christenings—including one of a dog—weddings, and funerals were provided with a Wilkite connotation by the employment of the number 45.[38] In August 1768 a Rotherhithe gentleman "left 10s for every poor Widow in the parish, and 45 pots of beer for each hardworking man." At his funeral there were 45 old women, 45 young maids, and 45 bachelors, each of whom was given 10d., a peck load, and eight pounds of bacon.[39]

If most of this remarkable data is to be believed, then in the course of a few years the number 45 had become a ubiquitous and immediately recognizable political symbol, as much a part of the political vocabulary as the shibboleths of "liberty" and the "constitution." Just as the Hollywood "Roman" haircut has become a conventional indication or sign that a film or play is set in classical Rome, so the number 45 prompted recognition of the Wilkite context of any object or event.[40]

What exactly are we to make of the rich ethnographic information about the number 45? Can we raise its significance above that of the entertaining anecdote and trivial story? How was the number 45 used, and what did it mean? Indeed, how credible are the accounts of incidents involving the so-called Cabalistic number?[41]

It is difficult to envisage dinners and demonstrations of such precision and orderliness, especially when 45 gallons of ale were provided or 45 toasts drunk. The number itself is a large one: almost half a hundred; it is the equivalent of a full American football squad or three rugby teams. Groups of this size are not easy to control even today, and it is doubtful that a Hanoverian Englishman had a stronger internalized sense of discipline than does his modern counterpart. Such stories as the tale of the Irish chairman who wagered 45 shillings that he could drink 45 gills of wine in 45 minutes and who, having won his wager, fell into a deep sleep for 45 minutes excite the incredulity of even the most gullible reader.[42] Occasionally it is possible to corroborate some of the instances of the number 45; several of the gifts so marked are recorded both in the newspapers and in Wilkes's correspondence, Wilkite artifacts decorated with the number 45 still survive, and court proceedings enable us to check other reports of the way in which the crowd employed the number.[43] But the bulk of my evidence comes from newspaper reports, many of which cannot be substantiated by other evidence. The more orderly the occasion, of course, the less likely we are to have court material on the incident. All too often, the authors of memoirs seem to have relied on newspapers rather than on personal experience or recollection for their descriptions of Wilkite events.

This seems to present a major evidential problem. Eighteenth-century newspapers were, as both contemporaries and historians have noted, notoriously unreliable and inaccurate. Even the press itself recognized this: *Lloyd's Evening Post* and *St. James's Chronicle* both carried sections headed *Lyars Corners* in which they reprinted mendacious extracts from the papers of their rivals. This does not, however, invalidate the use of newspapers as the chief source of material for Wilkite symbolism. We should not automatically assume that accounts of Wilkite incidents were examples of factual reporting; certainly this would not have been the expectation of most eighteenth-century readers of the press. Newspapers were less purveyors of information that had been screened and tested for its veracity than a forum for accounts provided by readers and correspondents. A free press was one open to all, and a newspaper proprietor who declined to publish news items submitted by readers was likely to be castigated for an invasion of the liberty of the press.[44] Participants and observers sent in most of the descriptions of "45" festivities and dinners because they believed it the public duty of a newspaper to record these events. Such correspondents were fully aware of the value of such publicity—there were bitter complaints if journals omitted local celebrations and dinners[45]—and their accounts would doubtless err on the side of exaggeration.

In consequence, there were sometimes disputes over the character and significance of an event. The *Newcastle Journal,* for example, contained an acrimonious exchange about the celebrations held at Morpeth of Wilkes's release from prison. An anti-Wilkite contributed a mealymouthed account of the occasion, deprecating the participants; he was promptly refuted by a radical correspondent.[46]

It has to be conceded, therefore, that the most vivid and detailed descriptions of the number 45 were accounts written, *parti pris,* by Wilkites; they almost certainly exaggerated certain features of radical ceremonial and idealized the event. Paradoxically, however, this makes them more, rather than less, valuable as historical evidence. The way in which the accounts were written—what they emphasize and what they omit—is an important indication of what Wilkites themselves wished to stress and what they wanted to portray to the public. If Wilkite ritual and symbol is myth, then it is Wilkite myth, not the idealization of some "disinterested" reporter, and therefore extremely useful to us in understanding what number 45 meant and represented to those who used it with such creativity.

Symbols, of course, have many, sometimes ambiguous and even contradictory meanings, and the number 45 was no exception. Despite its orderly and regular numerical associations, it was also considered to be an important talisman or lucky number. Whether deliberately invoked or observed to be present coincidentally, its presence was seen as bringing good fortune. There were numerous reports of lotteries, raffles, and elections which explicitly linked the number 45 and an auspicious event. A Bristol clock raffle was won by the forty-fifth ticket, the clerk of the Durham turnpike and a Gravesend churchwarden were elected by 45 votes; the forty-fifth lottery ticket in 1768 won £1,000 and when another number 45 gained a similar though smaller prize, the event was construed as a favorable augury for Wilkes. Gamblers, a notoriously superstitious class, switched their betting habits to accommodate or include the number.[47]

The very frequent association of the number 45 with fortune and contingency, and its connection with the fragile and evanescent — the skyrocket, the spluttering candle, the toasting glass, confections designed for human consumption — suggest (and clearly I am speculating here) an acceptance of the transitory nature of the Wilkite phenomenon. It was as if Wilkes's followers recognized the peculiar circumstances that had led to his meteoric rise as a patriot hero, and knew that the wheel of fortune could easily and would probably turn to eclipse Wilkes and, by inference, what he stood for.

By linking the fortunes of Wilkes and the Wilkites with those of the number 45, political commentators were able to use it as an allegorical means of commenting on the fate of radical politics. The story of the Darlington clock that repeatedly struck 45 times during the Middlesex election, but which stopped totally when Wilkes became a London alderman, was clearly a metaphorical means of expressing the feat that Wilkes had sold out politically.[48] This type of report has a long history. During the Walpolean and Pelhamite eras, opposition papers such as the *London Evening Post* had used such devices as allegory, metaphor, and metonymy to convey their political attitudes, to provide sufficient concealment to hinder prosecution, to ridicule their opponents, and to entertain their audience. Humorous items on cockfights involving a bird called Wilkes, and numerological anecdotes about the eyes, arms, and legs of Wilkes's supporters were a part of this tradition.[49] They resembled the so-called Intelligence Extraordinary sections of earlier newspapers, which had attacked the 1753 Jew Bill with extravagant tales of national circumcision and mocked the Scots as scabious and ill tutored in the English tongue.[50]

The number 45, therefore, had not only a lucky but a humorous and playful aspect. Many of the coincidences mentioned — that Charles I was England's forty-fifth king; that Middlesex, according to Kitchen's map, was England's forty-fifth county[51] — were designed to amuse and entertain. Joke books such as *Wilkes's Jests* provided readers with "Bon Mots, Puns, Repartees, and other Witticisms, respecting *John Wilkes,* Esq; and the ever memorable Number Forty Five," by collecting the best anecdotes and tales from the newspapers and journals.[52] It was felt that the virtue and rightness of the Wilkite cause naturally generated good humor and high spirits. How could Wilkites not be joyous when celebrating the sacred cause of freedom and liberty? The oppressed, those who lived in tyrannical regimes or breathed the corrupt air of courts, were naturally devious, shifty, and sullen; Wilkites, *au contraire,* were bold, hale and hearty, ready and willing to laugh and *enjoy* their freedom. The creation of such a cheerful, jovial atmosphere was almost a political statement in its own right. This spirit pervaded Wilkite humor and celebration. William Penrice, the turnkey of the King's Bench prison, described the antics of the crowds that came to view Wilkes at his prison window as "humorous, montebank performances," "diversions and amusements . . . their fun as they termed it."[53] There was a festive, holidaylike atmosphere at Wilkite celebrations—a feeling of good humor that was reinforced by the puns and plays on the special Wilkite number.

To some extent, therefore, the number 45 was a constituent element in a festive and celebratory order which, as I have argued elsewhere,[54] resembled the misrule and license characteristic of such traditional holidays as May Day and Shrove Tuesday—occasions which, even though they contained disorder, license, and the violation of many social proprieties, were nevertheless affirmatory of the existing social order. Ridicule and tomfoolery, the inversion of the roles of ruler and ruled (as in the British army Christmas when officers serve the men) were tolerated occasions. Were Wilkite celebrations involving the number 45 any different?[55]

Few questions are more intractable or difficult to answer. It seems reasonably certain that many of the participants in Wilkite crowds regarded Wilkite celebrations as yet another occasion to enjoy themselves, poke fun at their superiors, and to eat, drink, and be merry. Some magistrates, as well as Penrice, the King's Bench turnkey, treated this ebullient conduct as little more than horseplay and, in consequence, adopted a tolerant attitude toward the crowd's conduct. Justice Capel, in contrast, was severely criticized for failing to humor the crowd, and for overreacting when his cape was chalked with the number 45.[56] Other, more congenial magistrates had entered into the spirit of the occasion by allowing demonstrators to mark them.

But we should beware of taking the number 45 too lightly. Though some "45" celebrations assumed a form similar to those of traditional holidays and calendrical festivities, they had a distinctive meaning for many of the participants. Above all, the dinners with 45 guests and the celebrations with 45 candles were more often than not commemorating or celebrating neither a traditional religious holiday nor an official public event. They were the feasts and bacchanalia of a group explicitly opposed to the government and whose leaders sought structural political reform. The rituals and the symbols of the radicals were not only a way of demonstrating the extent and enthusiasm of their support and of suborning others into apparently radical acts but were also—and this is crucial—a coherent and symbolic expression of what they regarded as the true political order. When we examine the structure of Wilkite events, we can observe a common pattern or matrix, an enacted scheme of political belief that explicitly defines the moral universe of radical politics. The cornerstone of this radical fabric was the number 45. If we are to understand this order and not be overwhelmed by the extravagance of my claim, we first have to make a brief but important excursus into the symbolism and rituals of authority, for it was these that the radicals sought to transmute and, ultimately, to replace.

Historians have paid far too little attention to the way in which the Hanoverian political calendar was used by the government and local magistrates to inculcate loyal values in the populace and to encourage the growth of a national political consensus. The anniversaries of events deemed to have been of national importance were celebrated in most county and market towns and were official public holidays, when the chief offices of government were closed.[57] Such occasions were recorded in nearly every almanac of the period, and they were frequently not distinguished from the older religious and pagan holidays such as May Day and Twelfth Night.

The political calendar included both fixed and movable feasts. Its main dates included the current monarch's birthday (May 28, October 30, and June 4 in the case of the first three Georges) and the dates of their accession and coronation, together with the birthdays of their most important children and relatives. January

30 — a fast-day observed in memory of the execution of Charles I — began the fixed annual calendar. In Newcastle, on that day in 1768, "being the anniversary of the martyrdom of King Charles I, the same was strictly observed here; the magistrates went in form to church; the bells were muzzled, and great solemnity observed."[58] May 29, however, was an altogether more festive occasion: as Charles II's birthday and the date of the Restoration it was celebrated by the wearing of a sprig of oak on "Oak Apple Day."[59] August 1, the anniversary of the Hanoverian succession, was a comparable holiday that coincided with the traditional Lammastide. There were First of August societies that met to toast and fete the Hanoverian monarchy, and other clubs of a political complexion such as the Bristol Union Club also held their annual feasts on this day.[60]

Between August and November there was a lull in the political calendar. The period traditionally devoted to gathering in the harvest was not punctuated by any official political festivals. November, however, was an active month. November 4 was celebrated as William III's birthday and the anniversary of his landing at Torbay. Even before the nationwide junketings in 1788, which celebrated the centenary of the Glorious Revolution, there were revolution societies that forgathered to hail England's delivery from popery and tyrannical power.[61] This, of course, was also the official reason for the holiday on the following day, November 5: it was intended to recall the happy escape of James I and his subjects from the heinous acts of Guido Fawkes and the Gunpowder Plot.[62] The final event in the political calendar was Queen Elizabeth's Day, which was celebrated — with admittedly diminishing frequency — on November 17.

In the early eighteenth century these political holidays were the occasion of considerable political violence. In 1715 warring factions of Jacobite apprentices and Hanoverian bullyboys, sponsored by the leading Whigs, fought in the streets of London and several deaths ensued.[63] Each side tried to celebrate its own holidays with special extravagance and to obstruct its rivals' efforts at commemoration. The calendar, like the nation, was divided between Hanoverian and Jacobite. However, by mid-century and with the triumph of Whig oligarchy, a more sedate, consensual calendar had emerged. Though Whig-Republicans still blasphemed January 30 by holding calves-head feasts and raising their glasses to "Old Noll" while the rest of the nation held their contrite fast, and though Jacobite drinking clubs persisted, most men, of whatever political persuasion, observed the official political holidays. The mid-Hanoverian calendar was a skilled amalgam of loyalism (January 30, May 29, November 5) and Whiggery (August 1, November 4); typifying the development of Whig politics in the period, it stressed allegiance to the Hanoverian regime, played down rights of resistance, and sought to circumscribe a Whig consensus.

These holidays, it is important to stress, were seen as didactic events and educational spectacles. The 1662 Book of Common Prayer contained special services for January 30, May 29, and November 5 that were intended to remind the public of their civic duties and to warn against disobedience, turbulence, and social presumption. As *Youth's Entertaining and Instructive Calendar* remarked of January 30, "Very justly, therefore, ought we annually to observe this day with the sincerest Sorrow and Contrition; since the murder of that Pious Prince is a Blot of so deep a Day in our *English* Annals, that the Tears of a whole Nation will never be able to wash it out."[64] It is not surprising that January 30 sermons have proved such a valuable source for historians who have sought to trace the continuance of ideas of passive obedience and nonresistance into the eighteenth century.

Not that attempts to enjoin loyalty and ardent patriotism were confined to January 30 and May 29. The duke of Northumberland had the Prince of Wales' birthday celebrated at Alnwick by collecting together local children born in the same year as the young prince. They were then examined on their catechism; the most proficient and, no doubt, the most precocious youth was rewarded with a crowned garland. The celebration concluded "with such innocent rejoicings as may strongly impress their little minds, and inspire them with sentiments of loyalty, as it were, from the very cradle." As the duke's agent remarked, "did all the nobility as strongly interest themselves in inspiring proper sentiments among their dependents as our good Duke and Duchess, we would see a very different spirit prevail amongst the lower orders, from what we do at present."[65]

Such events often involved vivid and dramatic spectacles designed to remind even the humblest members of society of the political order to which they belonged. The importance of political holidays and celebrations lay in their ability to transmit the great political heritage that was seen as both highly desirable and peculiarly English to all members of the community, even the illiterate. The annual jolting of the British collective political memory was therefore a vital task: an appreciation of the liberties and freedoms of the Hanoverian regime was doubly enforced by the celebration of those crucial historical moments that marked the triumph of freedom over liberty and of loyalty and good order over radical enthusiasm and political excess.[66] If this inheritance was to be transmitted to posterity and preserved from further attack, then the political calendar had to flourish. Participants were almost obliged to manifest their zeal with conspicuous and public enthusiasm, for this ensured a safe national political heritage. Thus, many feared that the gradual decline in political spectacle heralded a lack of concern with the body politic and a decline in patriotism.[67] Commemoration was an intrinsic part of political consciousness, hence Wilkes's annoyance when he visited the jetty where William III landed: "I was much provoked to find no pyramid, no obelisk, nor the least public memorial on such a spot."[68]

The official political calendar, was, of course, as much concerned with the present as with the past. Many of the political anniversaries had, in a Durkheimian sense, a "sacred" quality about them. They were special occasions set aside to create a symbolic and dramatic representation of the social order and its cardinal values, as construed by the leaders of the nation. The calendrical rituals were intended both to reinforce the social role of individuals and the unity of the society as a whole.[69] This is why many gentlemen, magistrates, and aristocrats sponsored and encouraged such events. They believed in the efficacy of such ceremonies, and were, on the whole, confident that they encouraged unanimity and social bonding. Admittedly, during the course of the eighteenth century, these occasions, like the more raucous traditional holidays, came under attack for their encouragement of drunkenness, sexual license, indolence, and social disorder.[70] But the political calendar was not abolished: it was tamed; its retention was deemed necessary as a means of securing loyalty and holding society together.

Moreover, it was felt that anniversaries bound men to one another in a *particular* way. The official political calendar was characterized by acts of largess, charity, and munificence—donating money, freeing debtors, providing food and drink—that helped to distinguish rich and poor even at the moment in which they were united.[71] The celebration demonstrated who the public's leaders and benefactors were, who held the whip hand, and just how magnanimous they could be. As many radicals complained, it was an essentially conservative force. Jean Paul Marat, an ardent Wilkite in his English days, singled out the calendar and public entertainments as one of the links in the "chain of slavery" with which the government sought to bind the British people. Such junketings, he and others complained, induced the people to "lose sight of liberty" and of their "independency."[72] Ministers and radicals, therefore, shared the belief that the calendar inculcated obedience, even when they differed violently over the desirability of such festivals. Because these occasions were generally regarded as symbolic and symptomatic of the political order, and because they involved an intensification and a compression of political feeling, they were both highly important and very dangerous to those in authority. We have already seen how the political divisions between Hanoverian and Jacobite manifested themselves with particular vehemence on calendrical holidays.[73] The existence of the anniversaries served to exacerbate rather than alleviate political tensions and exaggerate rather than heal political divisions. On the other hand, a lukewarm and desultory celebration was also threatening, because it indicated a dissatisfied populace. As one of the correspondents in the *North Briton* remarked:[74]

The custom of celebrating public anniversaries, I have always considered as a wise institution. Besides keeping up the memory of great events, it is one of the surest and most fallible methods of discovering the present humour and disposition of the people. If the people are in a good humour, they will naturally express it by those signs which custom has prescribed, or their own fantasy may suggest. If they are in a bad humour, they will either betray it by a sullen reserve, or such marks as are still less equivocal.

Thus one of the ways in which the government and local magistrates responded to the Wilkite threat was to increase the visibility of loyalist jubilation. It was remarked that in 1768 the royal birthday was celebrated more lavishly and more publicly than at any time during the previous twenty years.[75]

We are now in a better position to understand the meaning of Wilkite ritual and celebration. The Wilkite symbolic order, of which the number 45 was such an important part, was deliberately and self-consciously opposed to the ritual and spectacle of government. Thus, the Wilkites established their own political calendar to compete with the annual loyalist celebrations. This alternative focus of political expression was naturally very alarming: the more successful, the more ebullient and joyous the Wilkite dinners and demonstrations, the stronger political dissent and public dissatisfaction with government seemed and was seen to be. The ministry and local magistrates therefore sought to limit and constrain radical pageantry. They tried to forbid illuminations, they locked the belfries of churches to prevent bell ringing, and they stepped up street policing.[76] The threat posed by the Wilkite calendar was not simply one of public disorder and of the dislocation caused by an increase in the annual number of commemorative holidays; it was what these new celebrations *said* about the polity that was so alarming.

The number 45 played a central role in the creation of this Wilkite symbolic statement. It distinguished political friend from foe, defined Wilkite space, and ordered Wilkite time. This "party Mark,"[77] as the striking sailors of 1768 called it, was, as I have shown elsewhere, both a symbol of solidarity and identity and a means of symbolic appropriation.[78] The marking of individuals, of a coach or dwelling brought the person or piece of property *within* the Wilkite realm. This was regarded as no light matter. In 1768 two naval officers fought a duel after one of them had tried to force the other, a Scot, to accept a small cake of the type sold by street sellers which was marked "Wilkes and Liberty & no. 45."[79] Territory was also appropriated: Wilkites mapped out their processional routes by marking the way with the number 45, and created radical space by measuring it in 45 units.[80]

Displaying the number 45 conferred rights of access to this Wilkite realm upon its bearer. In March 1768 the crowd would not let men pass by Hyde Park on their way to the election at Brentford unless they sported the patriotic number.[81] In Southwark two months later the same principle was applied to those passing near the King's Bench prison, whether they were rich or poor.[82] Similarly, only those wearing a badge with the special number were admitted to a West Country tradesman's dinner held to celebrate Wilkes's release.[83] Entry and exit into Wilkite "sacred" time were similarly defined. Events began or finished (or both) at 45 minutes before or after the hour, the number 45 signaling the qualitative transitions that took place.[84]

The number 45, in other words, conferred order on Wilkite activity. It drew on the time-honored and traditional association of number with precision, with order, and with harmony.[85] Because it entailed the use of a number, Wilkite ceremony required extraordinary exactitude; as the gentlemen who arranged the dinner at Poplar remarked, it prevented men from being at "sixes and sevens."[86] Such mathematical discipline, such standardization, was not seen by most eighteenth-century Englishmen as intrinsically desirable. Indeed, the introduction of regimental numbers on the buttons of British soldiers had been greeted with considerable hostility: officers resented being numbered "like hackney carriages" and were publicly ridiculed for their new uniforms.[87] But Wilkite precision, discipline, and numerological order were self-imposed; their adoption was an act of choice, not one that had been forced upon the radicals by any outside body. Self-control, the demonstration of one's autonomy or independence, was indicative of the Wilkites' capacity to choose for themselves, of their power *to be free*. Paradoxically, the restraint and order of Wilkite ceremonial was symptomatic of the liberty that its participants enjoyed.

Of course, as we have seen, not all Wilkite celebrations conformed to these exacting standards and ideals. There were bitter complaints from the Wilkites themselves about the disorder of the crowd and about its coercive and bullying tactics. Before the Middlesex elections the radicals distributed "cards of caution," urging sober conduct on their supporters, and before Wilkes's release from prison in April 1770 there were several newspaper letters from Wilkites advocating restraint.[88] As one correspondent wrote:[89]

The friends of Mr. Wilkes are very desirous of being distinguished from his enemies, which wish of theirs, compelling everybody to put out lights, will entirely destroy. If we wish to be free ourselves, let us grant liberty to others. Let us cease to complain of tyranny, if we ourselves are tyrants. Liberty and property are too sacred to be sported with, and therefore compelling people to act contrary to their inclinations, must be considered an act of cruelty and injustice.

This attitude was epitomized by a Wilkite from Newcastle who remarked that, "every true friend to the glorious cause, was sensible that decency and harmony could alone contribute towards its support, and the establishment of freedom."[90] Self-imposed decorum, not coercive disorder, characterized the ideal Wilkite demonstration. Liberty was not license, the opportunity to act without restraint, but punctilious self-regulation.

Wilkites not only gained liberty through the pursuit of number 45 but also obtained equality. The internal structure and ordering of Wilkite events clearly created an egalitarian order. When the number 45 was employed as a cardinal number, the objects that comprised the number 45 were almost invariably *the same* — 45 loaves or 45 dishes — and it was almost unheard of to divide 45 into its denominators — nine fives, three fifteens — or to make up a total of 45 from different objects. Again, Wilkite artifacts consisted of 45 *equal* constituent elements: a wig with 45 curls, a barrel with 45 staves. And the units of measurement that feature so often in celebrations — units of mass (pounds), of space (feet), and of time (minutes) have, of course, to be standard and uniform. Each unit or object based on the number 45 usually bore a one-to-one correspondence, an equal relationship, with the other units and objects so designated. Forty-five guests drank 45 toasts, consumed 45 pints of beer, 45 pounds of beef, and so on. Each of the 45 men participated *equally* in the event; each had available to him the same amount of food and drink (at one Brentford dinner the beef was divided "in equal portions by compasses").[91] The entire symbolic order stressed the compatibility, the correspondence, the symmetry, and the equality of the occasion. The number 45 standardizes and makes uniform; precision of measurement is the guarantee of equality. Liberty and equality are united by the magical number.

Naturally, not all Wilkite celebrations were as precisely egalitarian. Some of the demonstrations involved the sort of munificence and treating that reinforced a hierarchical social order.[92] But in reports of Wilkite events this aspect of jubilation was often omitted or played down. The horizontal social bonds uniting men

Fig. 10.1.

Fig. 10.2.

Fig. 10.3.

Fig. 10.4.

who participated equally received far greater emphasis than the traditional vertical ties that bound rich and poor.

Wilkite ceremony, therefore, was an expression of freedom and equality; it was also an event that emphasized that those states could be achieved by precision, careful measurement, standardization, and the coordination of human activity. Some degree of order is, of course, essential to the staging of a major event involving at least 45 participants, but the exactitude of the Wilkites was truly obsessive. In fact, it is strongly redolent of those characteristics usually associated with what I shall call, for want of a better term, a bourgeois mentality. The features of Wilkite ceremony are also those of the market and modern industry. Let me repeat them: precision, careful measurement, standardization, and the coordination of human activity. Some radicals, like Robert Morris, the secretary of the Society of Supporters of the Bill of Rights, were eager advocates of a reform that would have produced standardized weights and measures.[93] Indeed, there is some evidence to show that Wilkites drawn from the middle ranks of society— and these men formed the hard core of the movement and were Wilkes's chief financial backers—were advocates of such values. They sought an economic and social order that was governed by the exact science and abstract, logical rules of political economy and the market rather than by personal, patrician discretion; in addition they wanted a penal system, modeled on the ideas of Beccaria, which would have ended judicial discretion and replaced it by fixed, finely graded, and constantly enforced pains and penalties.[94] The Wilkite use of number tended, therefore, not to look back to the traditions of medieval and renaissance numerology (despite number 45's value as a lucky number), but rather forward to the countinghouse, the shop, and the burgeoning world of commerce.

Let us take stock of the argument. I have tried to demonstrate that both Wilkite radicals and the Hanoverian government employed highly elaborate and symbolically sophisticated ceremonies and rituals as a means both of giving public expression to their political ideals and of attempting to ensure their reaffirmation and future security. In other words, all sides—not simply a fringe group of dissidents—saw such symbolic forms as a necessary and vital part of politics. Moreover, the deployment of these commemorations and the arrangement of these rituals were also seen as a means of exercising power and authority over eighteenth-century Englishmen. As Edward Thompson and Douglas Hay have both recently reminded us, the coercive physical strength, the brute force of the Hanoverian state was severely limited and circumscribed; legitimacy was at a premium.[95] The capacity to hold men's hearts and minds did and still does confer authority on those who have that power. Symbolic expressions of the political order therefore turn out to be far more instrumental than they appear at first sight. Indeed, the more closely one examines such events, the harder it is to distinguish instrumental and symbolic acts.

I am not, of course, claiming that the official political calendar was the sole means of integrating citizens into the Hanoverian state, nor am I arguing that the existence of such a calendar is presumptive evidence of successful "value integration" in the society as a whole. This would be as naive as to claim that the successful establishment of Wilkite ceremonial would have ensured the triumph of the radicals. It is easy to be carried away by a (very useful and illuminating) functionalist or neo-Durkheimian analysis of these occasions and to place more weight on them than they actually deserve.[96] Clearly, there were many other ways in which the Hanoverian government sought to unite political society, and other means by which the radicals tried to gain and establish power and influence. But the essential point is that, regardless of how effective such symbolic expression actually was, eighteenth-century Britons believed the functionalist argument and accepted the efficacy of political ritual. Commemoration and the symbols of politics were accepted as an important means of political expression and as a significant political forum: they were built into the eighteenth-century Englishman's understanding of the contentious business of politics.

As such, Hanoverian political symbolism is important to the political historian, not only as a means of elucidating the nature of authority and politics but as a means by which competing political ideals can be elucidated. The different *structures* of ceremony and celebration help reveal the *mentalité,* the presuppositions and attitudes of the participants. Again, political iconography is not the sole means by which such ideals can be recovered, but it is an important and useful one. The number 45, when placed in context, unveils a complex and, at times, ambiguous political order. Yet, in the final analysis, it shows the extent to which the Wilkites were beginning to equate liberty and equality and reveals how far they were moving away from the traditional assumptions of the Hanoverian polity.

NOTES

1. George Rudé, *Wilkes and Liberty: A Social Study of 1763 to 1774* (Oxford, 1962); *Paris and London in the Eighteenth Century: Studies in Popular Protest* (London, 1970).

2. J. H. Plumb, *Sir Robert Walpole*, 2 vols. (London, 1956-1960); *The Growth of Political Stability in England, 1675-1725* (London, 1967); "Political Man," *Man Versus Society in 18th Century Britain* (Cambridge, 1968), pp. 1-21; Lucy Sutherland, *The City of London and the Opposition to Government, 1768-1774: A Study in the Rise of Metropolitan Radicalism* (Creighton Lecture, London, 1959); "The City of London and the Devonshire-Pitt Administration 1756-7," *Proceedings of the British Academy* XLVI (1960), 147-187; Nicolas Rogers, "Aristocratic Clientage, Trade and Independency: Popular Politics in Pre-radical Westminster," *Past and Present* 61 (1973), 70-106; Paul Langford, "William Pitt and Public Opinion, 1757," *English Historical Review* CCXLVI (1973), *The Excise Crisis* (Oxford, 1975).

3. See John Brewer, *Party Ideology and Popular Politics at the Accession of George III* (Cambridge, 1976), pp. 39-40.

4. George Nobbe, *The North Briton: A Study in Political Propaganda* (New York, 1939), pp. 130-140, 202-224.

5. A good general survey is to be found in Ian R. Christie, *Wilkes, Wyvill and Reform: The Parliamentary Reform Movement in British Politics, 1760-1785* (London, 1962).

6. Brewer, "The Misfortunes of Lord Bute: A Case Study in Eighteenth-Century Political Argument and Public Opinion," *Historical Journal* XVI, 1 (1973), 20-22.

7. For the hour of day see *Pope's Bath Chronicle*, 7 April 1768; *Felix Farley's Bristol Journal*, 11 June 1768; *Farley's Bristol Journal*, 14 April 1770; *Western Flying Post*, 6 May, 11 December 1769; *Worcester Journal*, 14 June 1770.

8. *Salisbury Journal*, 8 January 1770.

9. *Worcester Journal*, 9 March 1769.

10. *Middlesex Journal*, 25 April 1769.

11. *Worcester Journal*, 26 May, 2 June, 4 August 1768, 12 January 1769. E.g., Genesis 18:28, "And He said if I find there Forty and Five I will not destroy it (Sodom)"; Psalm 119:45, "I will walk at Liberty."

12. John Sykes, *Local Records; or, Historical Register of Remarkable Events which have occurred in Northumberland and Durham, Newcastle-upon-Tyne, and Berwick-upon-Tweed, from the earliest period*

of authentic record to the present Times, 2 vols. (Newcastle, 1833), I, 271 seq.; *Newcastle Journal,* 7 April 1770.

13. Christopher Butler, *Number Symbolism* (London, 1970), pp. 3, 14.

14. See my map of Wilkite incidents in Brewer, *Party Ideology,* p. 175.

15. E.g., *Middlesex Journal,* 2 November 1769; Pauline Maier, *From Resistance to Revolution* (New York, 1972), pp. 170, 193, 205; *Felix Farley's Bristol Journal,* 25 June, 29 October 1768; *Newcastle Journal,* 28 April 1770; Thomas Gage to Barrington, 21 February 1770, Barrington Papers, HA 174/1026/6c, East Suffolk Record Office.

16. John Amies to John Wilkes, 30 June 1764, B[ritish] L[ibrary] Add. MSS 30868 f.89; Wilkes's Diary, 25 April 1770, B.L. Add. MSS 30866; *Middlesex Journal,* 20 April, 10 June, 26, 30 August, 9 September, 26 October 1769; *Cambridge Chronicle,* 14 April 1770.

17. *Felix Farley's Bristol Journal,* 8 July 1768; *Leeds Mercury,* 7 February 1769. For such artifacts see John Brewer, "Commercialisation and Politics" in J. Brewer, Neil McKendrick and J. H. Plumb, *The Birth of a Consumer Society: Commercialisation in Eighteenth-Century England* (forthcoming).

18. *Newcastle Journal,* 30 April 1768.

19. *Cambridge Chronicle,* 18 June 1768.

20. *General Evening Post,* 17 April 1770; *Middlesex Journal,* 25 April, 4 May, 18 May 1769; *Pope's Bath Chronicle,* 7, 21 April, 21 May 1768; *Felix Farley's Bristol Journal,* 14 April 1770; *Bristol Journal,* 24 June 1769; *Cambridge Chronicle,* 5 November 1769; *Gloucester Journal,* 16, 23 April 1770; *Newcastle Chronicle,* 2 December 1769, 21 April 1770; *Newcastle Courant,* 11 January 1766; *Newcastle Journal,* 30 April 1768, 17 March, 21 April 1770; *Western Flying Post,* 6 November, 11 December 1769, 16 April 1770; *Worcester Journal,* 21 July 1768.

21. *Oxford Magazine* (1768), p. 163; *Middlesex Journal,* 20 July 1769; *Felix Farley's Bristol Journal,* 30 July 1768; *Bristol Journal,* 21 April 1770; *Salisbury Journal,* 8 January 1770; *Worcester Journal* 5 May 1768, 17 May 1770.

22. *Middlesex Journal,* 13 May 1769; *Norwich Mercury,* 11 November 1769; *Worcester Journal,* 6 April, 16 November 1769.

23. *Felix Farley's Bristol Journal,* 14 May 1768; *Worcester Journal,* 19 May, 13 October 1768, 20 April 1769; *Gloucester Journal,* 16 April 1770.

24. *Worcester Journal,* 19 May 1768.

25. *London Gazette,* 2 December 1768, *Middlesex Journal,* 3 October 1769; *Worcester Journal,* 21 July, 18 August, 1 September 1768.

26. For all these artifacts see n. 17.

27. Brewer, *Party Ideology,* pp. 176-178.

28. *Salisbury Journal,* 8 January 1770.

29. *Worcester Journal,* 8 December 1768.

30. See n. 7.

31. *Newcastle Journal,* 21 April 1770; *Worcester Journal,* 14 June 1768, 16 March 1769; 19 April 1770; Recognisances for Benjamin Ward and Thomas Sabine, Worcestershire Quarter Sessions, Midsummer 1768, Worcester C.R.O.

32. *Salisbury Journal,* 8 January 1770.

33. Brewer, *Party Ideology,* pp. 178-179.

34. *Cambridge Chronicle,* 1 November 1768; *Western Flying Post,* 7 November 1768, 6 November 1769; *Worcester Journal,* 2 November 1769.

35. John Free, *England's Warning Piece* (London, 1769), passim; W. Rendle, *The Inns of Old Southwark* (London, 1888), p. 348.

36. *Newcastle Journal,* 17 March 1770; *Western Flying Post,* 14 May 1770.

37. *Western Flying Post,* 6 May 1769.

38. Note in KB.1.18.ii, Public Record Office; *Middlesex Journal,* 25 April, 13 May 1769; *Worcester Journal,* 21 July, 4 August 1768.

39. *Worcester Journal,* 4 August 1768.

40. Roland Barthes, *Mythologies,* trans. Anette Lavers (London, 1973), pp. 26-27.

41. *Gloucester Journal,* 23 April 1770.

42. *Newcastle Journal,* 16 July 1768.

43. Thomas Greaves to Wilkes, 5 July 1768, B.L. Add. MSS 30870 f. 56; Wilkes to Polly (Wilkes), 8 August 1768, Add. MSS 30879 f. 128; Worcester Quarter Sessions, Midsummer 1768, recognisances for Benjamin Ward and Thomas Sabine.

44. For these assumptions see Steve Botein, " 'Meer Mechanics' and an Open Press: Business and Political Strategies of the Colonial American Printers," *Perspectives in American History* IX (1975), 127-225.

45. *Newcastle Journal,* 28 March 1770.

46. *Newcastle Journal,* 28 March 1770.

47. For this paragraph see *Wilkes's Jest Book; or the Merry Patriot* (London, 1770), p. 9; *Pope's Bath Chronicle,* 4 February 1768; *Felix Farley's Bristol Journal,* 11 June 1768; *Gloucester Journal,* 30 November 1771; *Newcastle Journal,* 17 December 1763, 16 January, 19 March 1763; *Worcester Journal,* 21 January, 13 February, 21 April 1768, 6 April 1769.

48. *Newcastle Courant,* 14 January 1769. Cf. *Felix Farley's Bristol Journal,* 16 April 1768; *Gloucester Journal,* 24 September 1770, 30 November 1771; *Worcester Journal,* 26 May 1768.

49. *Worcester Journal,* 15 February, 5 May 1768; *Western Flying Post,* 13 March 1769.

50. Cranfield, "The *London Evening Post* and the Jew Bill of 1753," *Historical Journal* VIII (1965), 16-30; Brewer, "The Misfortunes of Lord Bute," *Historical Journal* XVI (1973), 21-22.

51. *Western Flying Post,* 4 April 1768; *Worcester Journal,* 10 August 1769. Cf. *Middlesex Journal,* 21 October 1769; *Gloucester Journal,* 23

April 1770; *Worcester Journal,* 16 June 1768; King ag. McLane, B.L. Add. MSS 30884 f. 74.

52. See the advertisement of *Wilkes's Jests,* appearing, inter alia, in *Felix Farley's Bristol Journal,* 20 January 1770; *Newcastle Journal,* 21 April 1770.

53. *The Extraordinary Case of Wm. Penrice late Deputy Marshall or Upper Turnkey of the King's Bench Prison* (London, 1768), p. 24.

54. Brewer, *Party Ideology,* pp. 190-191.

55. Robert W. Malcolmson, *Popular Recreations in English Society, 1700-1850* (Cambridge, 1973), chaps. 2, 4, 5.

56. *Worcester Journal,* 18 August 1768.

57. See the following notes and Brewer, "Commercialisation and Politics," in Brewer, McKendrick and Plumb, *The Birth of a Consumer Society.*

58. *Newcastle Journal,* 6 February 1768.

59. Edward Hughes, *North Country Life in the Eighteenth Century: The North-East 1700-1750* (London, 1952), p. 20; *Felix Farley's Bristol Journal,* 4 May 1768.

60. P. T. Underdown, "The Parliamentary History of the City of Bristol, 1750-1790," (M.A. thesis, Bristol University, 1948), p. 8; *Felix Farley's Bristol Journal,* 30 July 1768.

61. Wilkes Diary, 6 November 1770, B.L. Add. MSS 30866; *Protestant Packet* VIII (10 November 1780); *Newcastle Journal.* 9 November 1777.

62. *Farley's Bristol Journal,* 7 November 1772; *Gloucester Journal,* 16 November 1772.

63. I am grateful to Nick Rogers for showing me his unpublished paper, "Popular Protests in Early Hanoverian England," which is undoubtedly the best account of these incidents.

64. *Youth's Entertaining and Instructive Calendar for the Jubilee Year* (London, 1750).

65. Percy to Northumberland, 22 August 1768, Alnwick Castle, Northumberland MSS vol. 43/108.

66. *A Complete Collection of all the papers which have appeared from the different parties in the present contest for Members for the County of Northumberland* (Newcastle, 1774), pp. 73-78; Thicknesse to Wilkes (July 1769?), B.L. Add. MSS 30870 f. 92; Foley Scrapbook, vol. 3, Worcestershire R.O., 85.

67. E.g., *Northampton Mercury,* 12 November 1733.

68. Wilkes to Polly Wilkes, 14 August 1772, B.L. Add. MSS 30879 f. 194.

69. See Steven Lukes, "Political Ritual and Social Integration, in his *Essays in Social Theory* (London, 1977), pp. 55-62.

70. Malcolmson, *Popular Recreations,* chaps. 6, 7.

71. *Newcastle Journal,* 23 January 1768; *Worcester Journal,* 4 August 1768; *Northampton Mercury,* 9 August 1731, 16 October, 6, 13 November 1732; *Gloucester Journal,* 29 July 1771.

72. [J. P. Marat], *The Chains of Slavery: A Work wherein the clandestine and villanous attempts of Princes to ruin liberty are pointed out* (London, 1774), p. 32; *Hampshire Chronicle,* 6 June 1774; *Pope's Bath Chronicle,* 18 February 1768.

73. See n. 63.

74. *North Briton* CXXVIII (30 September 1769).

75. *Newcastle Journal,* 11 June 1768.

76. E.g., *Newcastle Journal,* 14 April 1770; The Ringers of St. Margaret's Westminster to Wilkes, n.d., B.L. Add. MSS 30876 f. 126.

77. *Worcester Journal,* 19 May 1768.

78. Brewer, *Party Ideology,* pp. 188-189.

79. *Worcester Journal,* 4 August 1768.

80. *Salisbury Journal,* 8 January 1770.

81. *Worcester Journal,* 31 March 1768.

82. *Felix Farley's Bristol Journal,* 14 May 1768.

83. *Western Flying Post,* 14 May 1770.

84. See n. 30.

85. Butler, *Number Symbolism,* chap. 1.

86. *Newcastle Journal,* 30 April 1768.

87. *Gloucester Journal,* 20 August 1770; *Worcester Journal,* 4 February 1768.

88. *Worcester Journal,* 21 April 1768.

89. *Salisbury Journal,* 16 April 1770.

90. *Newcastle Journal,* 14 April 1770.

91. *General Evening Post,* 17 April 1770.

92. *Middlesex Journal,* 22 April 1769; *Newcastle Journal,* 14 April 1770; *Worcester Journal,* 2 November 1769.

93. *Gloucester Journal,* 3 June 1771; *Worcester Journal,* 4 February 1768.

94. Brewer, "The Wilkites and the Law, A Study in Radical Notions of Governance," in *An Ungovernable People? Englishmen and Their Law in the Seventeenth and Eighteenth Centuries,* ed. John Brewer and John Styles (forthcoming).

95. Douglas Hay, "Property, Authority and the Criminal Law," in *Albion's Fatal Tree,* ed. Douglas Hay, Peter Lindebaugh, and E. P. Thompson (London, 1975), pp. 17-63; E. P. Thompson, "Patrician Society, Plebian Culture," *Journal of Social History* VII (1974), 382-405.

96. See the excellent critique of the neo-Durkheimian view in Steven Lukes, "Political Ritual and Social Integration," *Essays in Social Theory,* pp. 62-73.

Designer: University of California Press Staff
Compositor: Janet S. Brown
Printer: Braun-Brumfield, Inc.
Binder: Braun-Brumfield, Inc.
Text: 11/13 Baskerville
Display: Baskerville